Coming Out of the Woods

COMING OUT OF THE WOODS

the solitary life of a
maverick naturalist

WALLACE KAUFMAN

PERSEUS PUBLISHING
Cambridge, Massachusetts

Many of the designations used by manufacturers and sellers to distinguish their products are claimed as trademarks. Where those designations appear in this book and Perseus Publishing was aware of a trademark claim, the designations have been printed in initial capital letters.

A CIP catalogue record for this book is available from the Library of Congress.

ISBN: 0-7382-0258-4

Copyright © 2000 by Wallace Kaufman

Perseus Publishing is a member of the Perseus Books Group

Text design by Jeff Williams
Set in by 11-point Goudy by the Perseus Books Group

1 2 3 4 5 6 7 8 9 10—03 02 01 00 99
First printing, March 2000

Perseus Publishing books are available at special discounts for bulk purchases in the U.S. by corporations, institutions, and other organizations. For more information, please contact the Special Markets Department at HarperCollins Publishers, 10 East 53rd Street, New York, NY 10022, or call 1–212–207–7528.

Find us on the World Wide Web at http://www.perseuspublishing.com

*For Erika Salloch and Resi Lord
who have generously nourished
the mind, the body, and the heart*

Contents

part 3
Changes

Acknowledgments

WITH WARM THANKS TO

Marshall Atwater for his generous help in filling in details of the Bynum family and other Chatham history.

Wade Barber whose careful legal work and love of new ideas kept many back-to-the-land people out of hot water and even jail.

Gene Brooks who taught history and politics with enthusiasm and fairness and for whom Chatham County's humblest citizens are among the world's most important people.

Ed Duke, friend, hunter and an extra pair of eyes.

Louise and Frank Harris of Harris and Farrell General Store, farmers James and Margie Boone and Charlie Baldwin, Willa and George Austin—good neighbors all—who did not hesitate to welcome strange strangers.

Quinn Hawkesworth, actress and artist, who saw many things at Morgan Branch with the sensibility of Emily Dickinson, her best character.

Cindy Hogan, ornithologist, my tutor in the language and behavior of birds.

Ed Holmes, country lawyer and world class diplomat, who helped me bridge many divides and avoid legal disasters.

Sylvan Ramsey Kaufman, my daughter and Ph.D. in ecology, for her patience, her professional knowledge, and her presence for almost this entire story.

Elizabeth Frost Knappman, my friend and agent, who convinced me to write this book and who resolutely pointed me toward the right way of telling the story.

Parker Huber, Aina Niemala, and others who often welcomed me to their gathering of nature writers and who accepted my frequent dissent and even welcomed it.

Mamie Oldham who lived not far from Morgan Branch for most of a century and whose memories are a valuable library of information and intelligence.

Michael Paull for his constant encouragement over many years, who with his father Harry Paull helped me save several important pieces of forest.

Cathie Ryan, who writes and sings extraordinary songs of ordinary people and brought that talent to Morgan Branch.

Reba Thomas, Chatham County Register of Deeds and the finest example of a "public servant," for many years of help not only in finding history for this book but in other work.

Elizabeth Giovani Verville for her great patience and generosity in reading along as I wrote.

And with many thanks for my long time neighbors scattered through the woods at Saralyn who have lived uncomplaining with my mistakes and whose thoughts and lives inform these pages—especially Dave Smith, Susan Strozier, Steve Magers, Ernie Milloy, Joel Carlin, Peter Holzman, Susanna and Sandy Stuart, Jim Smith and Susan Kellerman, Lee and Edith Calhoun.

A note on people and places in this book: All of the places, events, and people in this book are real and recorded as accurately as possible from my records, from public records and other documents, and from the best of my memory and the memories of others. In a few cases I have changed the names and other details about certain people to protect their privacy or simply out of the sense that they might want to avoid the embarrassment of associating with other people and events in this book or with the author.

Coming Out of the Woods

—part one—

Songs of Innocence

– *chapter 1* –

Visitors

*Why people are afraid to stay at my house and how I
followed Thoreau into the woods and came out with
the opposite conclusion.*

My friend Bart stands as big as a bear, trained as an engineer, retired from
a life teaching and writing fiction. A few years ago he wanted to bring his
twelve-year-old son and stay at my house when spring was just stirring the
forest. I left him notes on where to spread the wood ashes, how to operate
the gas-on-demand water heater, and where I composted kitchen wastes. I
was glad to have a house sitter and left for a month's work in the Cuchu-
matanes Mountains of Guatemala. I particularly liked the idea of Bart and
his son being in my house and forest; it was the next best thing to a father-
and-son camping trip and a lot more isolated than a spot in a public camp-
ground. The house is heated with wood. The forest rubs the windows and
roof with its branches. My nearest neighbor lives a half mile south. In
every other direction stretch several thousand acres of uninhabited forest.
Bart and his son were gone when I returned home a month later. So had
the hatchet I use for splitting kindling and small pieces of firewood. After a
couple of days, satisfied I hadn't mislaid it, I called Bart.

Yes, he knew where it was. It was in the sleeping loft. The loft is warmer
than the unheated bedroom, so I understood why they might have slept
there despite the dangerous steep and narrow stairs and the low ceiling beneath which Bart would have had to dress and undress stooped over. But

nothing in the loft where a normal adult must walk stooped requires a hatchet. Bart said, "I couldn't figure out how to lock the door, so we slept in the loft and took the hatchet for protection."

I had made my foray out of the woods to spend most of the month with a young Mayan writer whose name had appeared on the death lists that circulated in those days. The lists were reasonably or perhaps unreasonably good substitutes for actuarial tables insurance companies use to figure the odds of death in more civilized places. We met in cafes and bars, sneaking from place to place as we worked on a translation of a harmless Mayan myth about the gods of lightning. That was a particularly dangerous time in Guatemala, but life there has been dangerous since at least 1,000 years ago, when a religious warrior priest called Quetzelcoatl descended from central Mexico and initiated endless wars, tyrannies, and human sacrifices among the Mayan tribes. In the panorama of history the Spanish conquistadors and the "death squads" are part of a larger drama of violence. I came back to the woods with a manuscript and a sense of having returned to the Peaceable Kingdom.

Few people who have come to house-sit for me feel the same way.

Of my five house sitters, four have left in fear. Each had come because he or she knew that staying here would be lovely. Of course, we don't always know what we know. Like Bart, some have feared intruders. One saw a copperhead. Another got bitten badly by chiggers, those almost unseeable bugs that crawl into your armpits and under your waistband and into your crotch and make big red lumps inside of which larvae develop and make you itch for a week. The fourth house sitter had retreated trembling to the quiet of the city after hearing too many noises—things banging on the roof (hickory nuts), crashing through the dark forest (deer), screaming like a violated woman at the creek (frogs), and calling out in the night like demons (owls and bobcats).

I have not laughed at any of them. Their mistake was believing they would be living in "the country," then finding themselves in a forest. The difference is that the country has lines and edges, defined spaces, a recognizable geometry. Le Corbusier, the architect, said that geometry is "protection against the arbitrary." Tracy Kidder, who quotes Le Corbusier in *House*, says, "You can say the same about the edge of a woods." At my house the forest comes up to the windows, rattles, scratches, and bangs on the roof. There is no protection here against the arbitrary.

We all get scared when the world does not act in familiar or controllable ways. Hansel and Gretl walked into a beautiful forest, but when night came the trees turned into a crowd of ghosts and ghouls. The woods most of us are familiar with are the woods of our imagination or of someone else's imagination. Look at Eliot Porter's pictures of cathedral groves of West Coast cedar and the woods are priceless treasures. Follow the blazes and signs on the Appalachian Trail and no day could be more peaceful and fulfilling. Get lost in the woods only once, however, and you understand that we take for granted the comforts of trail blazes.

An Audubon group came out to my forest to go birding one gray day when no sun shone to give directions. We had walked less than a mile from my house when the walkers began to ask, "Didn't we see that oak before? Isn't that the bent tree we passed earlier?" Whether or not President Reagan actually said, "Seen one tree, you've seen 'em all," sometimes it could almost be true. A thousand years ago, four hundred, or today—few people go alone into the wilderness. Almost no one lives there.

In any big bookstore you can buy several accounts of people who have lived alone in a wild place, but they are accounts of short periods. Usually the writer has taken one or more dogs, or a cat—another domesticated being. The most famous account of life in the woods, Thoreau's *Walden*, describes a stay of only twenty-six months. No one lives happily ever after alone in a wild place.

To say that human beings are social animals explains only why people *leave* wild places. Like my friend Bart, people came to live in my house alone for the same reasons they have always gone to wild places alone—because of who they thought they were or wanted to be. These thoughts have differed in detail, but in some way each person believed he or she loved nature. By leaving civilization behind, they believed they could do what every Zen master demands—not just believe you are part of the universe, but become one with it. When we are one with everything, clapping with joy would answer that troubling Zen riddle, "What is the sound of one hand clapping?" Maybe some people hear it, but for most the attempt is cut short by the sound of hickory nuts crashing on the roof, the sudden stigmata of chigger bites, or the unblinking stare of a snake.

It doesn't matter what ends it. Maybe we can't stand finding out that we are not who we think we are, or maybe we understand that wilderness is a nice place to visit and a difficult place to live. We venture into a wild place alone because of who we think we are or can be. We leave because, one way or another, we have had enough. We leave because we have changed our minds. Each person is changed, whether by one night with Outward Bound, one year in the Maine woods, or two years and two months at Walden Pond.

Venturing into the wilderness alone has always tested independence and courage. At the beginning of civilization, the great Gilgamesh goes into the forest in fear and emerges in triumph when he kills the forest god Humbaba. Jesus is said to have gone into the desert for forty days to be tested by hunger and the Devil (often one and the same in their ability to warp the mind). Some American Indian tribes sent boys out on solo survival trips to prove their manhood. Inuit shamen went off on the tundra to prove themselves. The climax of today's Outward Bound training is a night or two alone in the wilderness. The people who have fled my house and my forest share the feeling of the ages and the masses about dark forests. In all times and all places, being alone in the wilderness has been a special condition. A deliberate and brief experience is a useful test; an involuntary experience is an ordeal. Living alone in the wilderness is the choice of fools, misfits, eccentrics, and the unfortunate. I have been all of these.

When I began making notes about what I have learned in the forest, a friend said, "I'm sure you have had a lot of thrilling adventures and survived real dangers." I said I would think about that. Except for a few accidents I could have had in a New York City apartment or a Garden City backyard, I could not write about constant or even special perils. I have always felt safer here than in town. I was born in a city and have always been uneasy about life there. Before I could read, I had discovered that people are less predictable in their meanness than animals. Maybe the simple contrast with life in the city makes life in the forest look safe. My life seems normal, and maybe that's abnormal. I am reminded of what women in Alaska say about the abundance of men they are supposed to find there: "Alaska men: the odds are good, but the goods are odd."

For over twenty years I have not spent a frightened moment alone in these woods, but I have never lost the sense that I am also a visitor. Unlike the homeowner who lives in an ordered landscape, I control little here. The rights of ownership recorded in the local registry of deeds allow me to do what I will with this land—clear every tree, kill every creature, flood every valley. Or I can do what most people do— push back the forest until I surround myself with a comfortable geometry, a kingdom of my own. A house with a front yard and backyard or landscape of any design and size, however gently done, declares mastery and ownership. Yes, I master when necessary, and never having pledged my property as collateral for any mortgage, I own more surely than most. The landscape we master and the rights we grant ourselves are self-serving and happy reminders of how much security we have put between ourselves and nature. They help us forget that, despite all the favors of science and technology, the average person enjoys a visit of some seventy-five years. Maybe I have no fear of life here because I am daily reminded that every human being, past and present, has been no more than a visitor. Humankind, however it got here, is itself a visiting species, recently arrived and, some say, soon to leave.

I don't know where I will go when the visit is over, or where the rest of humankind has gone or will go. I came to the forest and made the least fuss possible in finding out who and what I am, where I came from, and maybe where I'm going. I have missed some comforts and happiness, but I have learned much. Yet I am not one of those people who hoists the banner of Thoreau's words, "In wildness is the preservation of the world." On behalf of the Wilderness Society, I did once lobby Congress for the Wilderness Act and for the power of wild places to refresh and preserve civilization. Our claims were greatly exaggerated. In the early 1970s, I believed our exaggerations. I had not yet gone to the woods to live alone. I am not emerging now, years later, to call in the bulldozers. I have lived in the woods ten times longer than Thoreau lived at Walden Pond. I am a slower writer than Thoreau, maybe a slower learner, but now I am coming out to give you my report. I tell you the story of how my life here has led to the opposite conclusion from Thoreau's, to the conclusion that the preservation of wildness is in civilization.

chapter 2

Turning Point

*Alternative culture is born in America and I face the
question of whether those who can, do; those who
cannot, teach. I propose my own answer to Tolstoy's
question, How much land does a man need?*

When I first began to talk about living in the woods, I did not intend to
live there alone. For one thing, I was married. My wife Sarah listened to
me talking about going into the woods to live with a quiet patience. "Well,
it could be nice, I suppose," she said. She liked the old farmhouse we had
just bought, sitting on a knoll under a single big spreading oak, surrounded
by old fields. She had grown up in a place like that on the outskirts of
Richmond, with chickens, dogs, and cats. Sometimes she would say, "I'm
pretty happy here." If it wasn't broken, why fix it? If I wanted to fix something, wouldn't that old farmhouse do for a long while?

My second problem was that I had no Ralph Waldo Emerson to lend me
his Walden Pond. At the same time I didn't intend to settle for less than
real solitude in unspoiled nature. How I developed this obsession with nature and solitude, and why I pursued it so passionately, comes later because,
like all epic stories, this one too has good reason for starting *en medias res*,
in midflight. This story is neither *Paradise Lost* nor *Paradise Regained*, but,
like Dante at the beginning of his *Divine Comedy*, "Midway upon the journey of our life, I found that I was in a dusky wood."

I do not deny that a person may have communion with nature on a quiet morning in the suburbs, on a winter walk through Central Park, or trying to understand the voices of birds around the feeder. A small investment in gasoline, hiking boots, tent, and sleeping bag gives you a few days or even a few weeks in the wild. You may go to secluded and spectacular places in national parks, forests, wilderness areas, and seashores. For me, however, neither brief communion nor short visits would do. From the moment I was liberated from life as a student, I was determined to run through civilized life as quickly as possible and go to live with nature.

In 1968, I walked deep into the woods of North Carolina. I had parked my three-quarter-ton Chevy pickup on the graveled public road. I followed what I thought was the rut and ditch of an old logging road into the forest, over a hill, and to a dark round and flat place where water seeped up through fallen leaves and gathered into the first trickle and trough of a stream. Except in a few deserts, waters that gather like this are usually going somewhere. When we find them, we have found a headwater. Headwaters have often been the beginning of great rivers and the goals of great adventures. The British spent vast fortunes and shed African and English blood searching for the headwaters of the Nile. Columbus thought the lost Garden of Eden lay at the source of the Orinoco. I did not know, that day my feet sunk into the muck in the woods, that I was about to start on a fine journey. Although my journey would take me only a few miles along creeks and over a few ridges and hills, it would also carry me through time, twenty-five years into the future and centuries into the past.

As I stood in that flat pan of land in the deep shade, I could not say where the stream began. I knew only that I was at a beginning. It was a place where the low round hills on three sides birthed the waters from their rock foundations. The clay my feet sank in had washed out from these rocks and would not let the water sink below it and hide. The water did not know it had to make a stream any more than I knew the time had come for me to make a life by that stream. Had I thought harder about why I was unhappy that day, about so much that had made me unhappy since I came tearing out of my mother as a dry birth, I might have realized what I should do for the next twenty years. Had I thought that hard, though, I might simply have joined all those people who spend their time thinking about their unhappiness or someone else's unhappiness but do nothing more.

I saw where the seeping land gave way to a ribbon of water no wider than my hand, but a ribbon that was an agreement between water and land, a ribbon with a direction. I followed it north and watched it duck underneath dams of tree roots and leaves and emerge as wide as both hands could spread. Where the land took a definite tilt downward, the hills folded in to make the crevice of a valley. Here, the ribbon of water swelled into a stream whose more powerful moments had cleared away all roots and carved a passage around large rocks.

I followed the gradually widening path. It ran due north. It grew to an arm's width and the land rose up on both sides in rocky slopes. In a half mile, I came to a place where my stream joined a slightly larger stream flowing from the west. Along both streams stood the thick, gray muscular trunks of beech trees that rose and spread skyward in confident branches. I walked up the valley of the stream from the west. Higher up the hills, oak and hickory filled the woods, but along the stream and over its slopes on both sides, the beech trees had wrested command. This was climax forest, old growth. I would not say virgin. Virgin is too romantic, too general to be true. Hunters had been here. Almost certainly Indians had camped by the streams. They may have burned the area from time to time to make hunting easier or to encourage the browse deer. This piece of forest, whether virgin, old growth, or mature, was rare.

I was tired and my shirt and pants were soaked with sweat. My feet were swimming inside my work boots. I stopped at a place along the stream about five hundred feet from where it joined the northern branch. On the south side, the hills backed away from the stream, leaving a flat disk-shaped grove of beeches. On the north side, the land rose steeply. Squarish rocks broke through the surface. A few hollies grew among the beech trees. At exactly this place, the stream dropped over the bedrock foundation of the hills and composed a little water music. I lay down and took a long drink from a rocky pool.

The high shade of the beech trees made this the darkest creek valley I had seen in this part of North Carolina. The water on this summer day was as cold as that of a mountain stream. I took off my clothes and eased myself into the water, almost filling the stream from side to side yet finding it deep enough to cover me. Minnows nibbled at the air bubbles clinging to the hairs on my calves. I got used to the water's chill and the summer sultriness washed out of me like silt from gravel. The woods were still and silent, as they often are on a hot summer afternoon. I rested my head on a rock and closed my eyes. I wondered how long this small creek had been flowing and for how long these blue-gray stones had ensured that it could be heard.

For a moment, I thought I was wasting time. I had a wife. Sarah and I had bought an old house in need of repairs. I had lessons to prepare for my students at the university. I had a novel to write. I had just joined the new Conservation Council of North Carolina, which needed help to defeat a proposed 48,000-acre reservoir. I felt like a soldier who had gone AWOL.

But what did all that mean if the goal, at least for me, was to come to a place like this and immerse myself in nature? I was almost thirty years old, in the middle of my life, it seemed. Sooner or later I would have to get up, put my clothes on, walk to the truck, and drive back into my life and into the battles of the day. I could not simply desert. Of course, I *could* have deserted, but in a way I had ridden the surfboard of my own life atop the great wave crashing onto American culture. America and I had reached a turning point at the same time.

At the end of the 1960s, America saw the birth of the environmental movement, the beginning of the sexual revolution, the rise of feminism, the end of segregation, the introduction of computers in business and education, and the first voyages into space. I became a professor of English. This does not compare with putting a man on the moon or with the Civil Rights Act, except in the limited world of my family. Becoming an English professor was no great step for humankind, or even for my students. Within my family, however, my journey to Duke University in North Carolina, then across the Atlantic to Oxford, and on to become a college professor, was more like landing a man on Mars. My mother and father had dropped out of high school as sophomores. My twin brothers, a year older, had finished high school with average grades and then enlisted in the Navy and the Air Force. Suddenly people started to call me "Doctor Kaufman," and I had a full year's salary for nine months' work. Sixty-three hundred a year was not much, but I measured it against what I knew. My friends and cousins who were construction laborers could make $4,000 a year, barring strikes and layoffs. I was earning almost 50 percent more than my father was earning when he had been crushed to death in a car crash on his way home from Grumman Aircraft during my senior year in high school.

In 1964, when novelist Reynolds Price recommended me for positions at Duke, where he taught, and at the University of North Carolina at Chapel Hill, he wrote that I had finished my academic wandering and was ready to settle down to steady work. I took the job at Chapel Hill, where I began to teach writing and American literature, and where I was allowed to teach a special course about nature in literature. I had written my thesis at Oxford University on William Wordsworth and his reverence for rural hermits, but my fellow citizens of academia did not consider me sufficiently wedded to that period in literature that I could be trusted to teach the Romantics. They were right about the commitment. I was not a specialist in the Romantics. I *was* a Romantic. Like Wordsworth and Coleridge, I peered through a microscope and a telescope and I was interested in everything in between and in writing poetry about all of it. I thought that cities eroded the soul and bred intellectual arrogance. With Wordsworth, I that thought simple people and children were "the best philosophers." In high school, I had sent Rosalie, the object of my desire, a note comparing her to Shelley's "sensitive plant." I knew nothing of the life of real prisoners and thought with Byron's Prisoner of Chillon that man needed only an indomitable soul to be free anywhere. My poetic ideal was to see the world as animals saw it.

Coming from a blue-collar family where most talk is about what people do, I have never been comfortable professing something I didn't intend to do. My father could explain simple math, but he preferred to teach us how to use a micrometer and calipers. When we began to talk about war, we made model planes, tried out wooden ships in puddles and rain-swollen gutters, and tied our toy soldiers to parachutes made from rags. Having to put every idea to a practical test is not always a blessed condition. From childish acts to tyrants' axes, we are better off talking than doing.

A number of toy soldiers who tested our parachutes were left hanging from the electric wires on our street. Often for months they taunted me with failure. Innumerable boats made of ice-cream sticks and scraps of vegetable crates rode torrents of oil-slicked rain water into storm drains. The world is full of bankrupt businesses and innocent corpses because people have put their words and ideas into action. The university, of course, hired me only to talk. Some in my department and in the administration thought doing an unscholarly diversion, but they mercifully refrained from doing anything final about it for eight years.

I was no sooner professing than my blue-collar conscience laid a worried hand on my shoulder. Speaking bluntly, it said, *Put up or shut up. What do you have to show for your talk?* I had to do something concrete. I wanted to make something with my hands, buy something with my earnings, transform something in the house or around it—paint, move a wall, wire new light fixtures. I wanted not only to teach what others had said about the rich lessons of nature, I wanted to go to nature and learn for myself. I was propelled inevitably toward that "dusky wood." I did not know how to go there directly, but headed in that direction, out of town.

Within six months, I had saved the $2,000 down payment on a $10,000 fix-up house and five acres ten miles south of the University of North Carolina at Chapel Hill. My colleagues considered it "out in the boondocks." It was tobacco land, a scrap of pasture, and a piece of orchard fast giving way to pine and gum trees. Farm people had lived in the house for a few generations, then abandoned it to move into town. It was a good enough first way station for my way out of town. With a dairy farm within mooing distance to the west, a paved road in full view of the front porch, and, a hundred yards away, neighbors with a yard full of junk cars and a green mercury vapor burglar light glowing all night, it was not solitude. The house was a hundred-year-old ruin that seduced me with deep honey-colored wide pine boards in the living room and five giant white oaks spreading their shade on the west side.

Whatever time I thought I'd have for writing a great novel and communing with nature corroded in efforts to rescue the house from a leaky roof, a plumbing system that froze and burst inside the walls, termites eating the sills, and clapboards warping off the walls. The greatest gift this house gave me was a catalog of mistakes that I determined I would not make again. I did not know it then, but I was already learning how hard it is to live in harmony with nature. Almost all serious problems that beset a house are conflicts with natural forces. Besides the time spent on the house, I often tutored math and English to five red-headed poor whites next door whose father was drinking himself to death.

I admit that I was not preparing myself well for a career in the English department, but I was learning a few things about myself and nature. I watched in dismay as thousands of carpenter bees appeared in early summer and hollowed out the otherwise invincible red cedar logs of an old barn. I learned that where poison ivy grows, sunlight is reaching the earth where a forest has been removed. It constantly sprouted everywhere but under the old oaks. I learned that certain plants welcome in suburbs become destructive invaders in the country, honeysuckle being the culprit here as it overwhelmed apple trees and fences and crawled under clapboards. I dug a cellar in red clay, and after the first rain, it remained an eight-foot-deep swimming pool for the next month. Southerners chose to live without cellars rather than have their homes sit half the year on top of dog-drowning, mosquito-breeding subterranean ponds.

Despite the hard lessons, I came to like the place. Out of respect for the floors and the great oaks, I had called the place Heartwood. Heartwood, however, was no Walden.

I found a more isolated house on another old farm, but this time with twenty acres, a small pond, and no one in sight. We sold the first house for a small profit and went into hock on the second house and its land. We moved there and soon I was seduced by the prospect of tilling the fields, restoring old apple trees, fixing old buildings. The mortgage, small as it was, stretched out ahead of me like railroad tracks for fifteen long years. I had made a mistake, but with luck we could sell this one for an even better profit and move farther out.

I knew that Walden, my Walden, lay farther down the road, and I was more fit now to find it. If one struggling young professor could buy this much of the countryside, several of us could buy enough for real communion with nature. I already had a very clear idea of how I meant to commune with nature and what my house would be like.

I had considered all this while lying submerged in the stream. I might have fallen asleep except for the gentle sucking of minnows at the air bubbles clinging to me. The water not only cooled me but eventually chilled me. I stood up and walked into a spot of sunlight to dry and get dressed. I climbed the hill on the north side in the late afternoon. I wanted to see a beech growing out of the purple and brown rocks, dominating the hillside with its height and spread, holding the hickory and oak at a long branch's length. I climbed a little higher and looked past the beech into the valley and across the creek at the silent grove in the disk of land. Nobody had lived here before. Nobody had plowed this ground, or grazed cows, or cut these trees. I sat on a rock above the beech tree. To live next to this tree and in this place where no one had ever grieved over a ruined life or a lost love or the failure of children or crops—this was the kind of place I had planned to live in ever since I knew there were choices.

chapter 3

Pieces of the Old South

I try to organize a company of scholar adventurers.
A battle for the minds of young southerners brings
me a partner.

The reason I had walked into those particular woods and found that creek was Michael Paull, a graduate student writing a thesis on Mahomet in medieval literature. In the dining hall over coffee or at an occasional party, Michael had listened to me talking with a few colleagues my age about pooling our funds, buying a large piece of land, agreeing on how we would use it and divide it among ourselves for our homes. The discussion went on every week for several months. My colleagues were excellent analysts and debaters but elusive business partners.

The new crop of English professors at the University of North Carolina at Chapel Hill were assigned two and three to an office on the top floor of an old brick building, apart from the senior professors. The crowded offices on the third floor of Murphy Hall concentrated people who considered themselves agents of change and new thinking. The three flights of stairs and the absence of air conditioning insulated our discussions from the ears of the associate and full professors who promoted and fired. I began a continuing conversation about where and how we should live.

Four of us formed the core of the discussion. I wish I had taken a picture because we were an odd group. Duncan Sutherland was a rotund and wild-eyed West Virginian whose father owned several small coal mines. Bud Roebuck had inherited from his Southern ancestors all the good manners of a Southern planter, but with all their brazenness filtered out through two generations of small-town schoolteachers. He taught Faulkner's hunting stories with a reverence for the Old South, but would never pull a trigger. Marion Ryerson, in his late twenties, already bore himself like a New England headmaster, stood six foot six, and played basketball politely and efficiently.

Others listened in, sometimes amused, sometimes tempted, like friends watching the formation of a team to find Noah's Ark. We weren't the only ones who wanted to live outside of town. Maybe it was because, in the 1960s, few people our age had ever lived in the country. We also wanted to be different from the older faculty, who lived in quiet old neighborhoods where nothing seemed to happen. Town was also the place where the entrenched powers lived, the people who lived in white-only neighborhoods and who had wished the civil rights movement had been more patient. Finally, despite the habit of calling Chapel Hill a village, it had already become a small city. The cost of buying into one of the old village neighborhoods was soaring. Bud and his wife lived in an apartment, Marion and his wife in graduate student housing, and Duncan, his wife, and infant daughter had the loan of a faculty cottage.

In an age where necessity and temptation were stronger, we might have become a company of scholar-adventurers, and we would certainly have needed exceptional good fortune to survive. In fact, we did think of ourselves as a company of adventurers, and we set about planning our finances and looking for a destination.

Pooling our purchasing powers would enable us to get close to nature without staying too close to each other. It would be community but not communalism. Together we would buy enough land to close out the sights and sounds of city and suburb, to remove those material things that come between us and nature. We intended to live what we taught, and we had a solid literary tradition to inspire us.

One of the odd facts about civilization is that the city is its incubator, bedroom, dining room, and living room, but most intellectuals find the source of civil behavior in the country. Decadent writers and artists live in the city. Government exercises its power from the city. It's been that way for two thousand years.

I thought of myself and my colleagues as passengers on a ship bound for the kind of island Shakespeare created in *The Tempest*, a play about the moral and spiritual renewal of Europeans who find themselves shipwrecked on a wilderness island of the New World. Old Prospero, like our parents or perhaps the older professors of our department, had been corrupted and jaded by life in the European city. Those of us who had been bored by growing up in the 1950s and cast spiritually adrift on the postwar flood of material things were not yet shipwrecked, but we were ready either to steer onto the rocks or to swim ashore.

The one close colleague who did not share our enthusiasm to return to the land was Jim Bryan, who had already begun his business career by creating Jungle Land Miniature Golf in Myrtle Beach, South Carolina. Jim dressed in the easy slacks and shirts of a golfer. His love in twentieth-century literature was J. D. Salinger, the creator of Holden Caufield, Franny, and Zooey, characters who never get beyond the suburbs and the beach. For Jim, life was a great comedy of soaring hopes and small successes, ideals as wondrously shiny and empty as soap bubbles. Jim, as a believer in the human desire for harmless oddity, looked on our talk of having land and living in the country as yet one more colorful soap bubble.

He could look at the older professors and see our fate some years ahead. Most lived in the old "village" part of town or in the countryside. We would do better, we said. We would not own estates or speculate in land. We would find a large tract and divide it among ourselves, each with enough privacy, all agreeing to keep our land natural and green and quiet. By guarding each other's flanks, on just a few acres we could achieve what required twenty or fifty acres for a single owner. We would live in confidence that our neighbor would not become a developer. We talked about hearing the birds sing in the morning, raising the kids in the country, and escaping the noise of cars and garbage cans and stereos. Our dreams of nature were straight out of literature and our sheltered childhoods. We would live in the shade of noble trees, sung to by birds and crickets, nourished by our own gardens. We would turn loose our pets and our children to enjoy the freedoms that would feed their bodies and souls.

I already knew that pursuing a dream tempts the dreamers to spend freely and others to bill heavily. To avoid having to work through brokers and pay large commissions, I took a night class, read a few books, and became

North Carolina Real Estate Broker number 1115. It was part of our plan to beat the system. Armed with my license, I set out to visit my fellow brokers; they would split commissions with me or cut them in half so that I could pass on the savings to our group.

Three miles south of the university, I found an eighty-acre "mountain" overlooking the town water supply with the imaginative name of University Lake. McCauley's Mountain rose in a gentle dome of deep green pines on the south side of the lake. The waters of the lake were almost always mirror-smooth. Near the shores, turtles lined up in rows on logs to take the sun. Boaters seldom disturbed them because the university restricted boats to those it rented and it rented nothing but rowboats, and most of those to fishermen who sat quietly at one spot in the early morning light or evening dusk. Where a country road crossed one end of the lake, occasionally someone from town would set up an easel. We could build a few houses among those tall pines without changing the scene. We would see out, but no one would see in.

The lake's seventy-five acres were just a few more than Walden Pond's, where Thoreau had lived in New England. The town's dependence on this clean water guaranteed to our mountain more peace on that side than Walden had given Thoreau. Quiet was guaranteed further by the half mile of woods between our tract and the public road. Finally, most of the adjoining land was in two large tracts, each owned by old university couples known for their lifelong devotion to humane causes. The five of us could not hope to have such large tracts, but by joining together we could divide this one large tract. Each of us, for $5,000 a head, could own four or five acres.

When I sat with Marion, Brad, and Duncan talking about the benefits of living in the country, Thoreau made frequent appearances. Jim, the creator of Jungle Land Miniature Golf, once broke into one of these conversations to warn us not to be too faithful to Thoreau. "The woods made him mean and arrogant," Jim said. "Don't you know, that business about not needing civilization was really an insult to Emerson and Alcott and the intellectuals who had big houses and money. If he had enjoyed Walden so much, he would have stayed there, but what he really enjoyed was telling people about it."

Jim's view has never damaged Thoreau's influence. Even for millions of Americans who love Jungle Land Miniature Golf and Disney Land, Thoreau is still the authoritative voice on the virtues of living with nature.

Few have read all of *Walden*, many more have read bits and pieces, and many times that number have read environmental writers or watched documentaries and even feature films thoroughly soaked with Thoreau's credo that nature knows best, that "In wildness is the preservation of the world." We believed Thoreau, but we agreed we did not have to live as simply as he had lived at Walden. We kidded Jim that we would have nice places in the woods and that one day he would probably build a Walden Miniature Golf Course.

"It would be too dull," he said.

In the end, Jim had spoken for Marion, Brad, and Duncan.

When we had the maps of McCauley's Mountain and a take-it-or-leave-it price, we did what academics like to do when solid reality begs a decision—we began to talk. We believed we were defining the pros and cons. We talked for several months about what we could do with this land. When time came to buy in or drop out, I learned we had really been talking about what we could *not* do with this land.

Duncan Sutherland, the coal mine heir, stood up to pronounce his greatest reservations. He was feisty and usually leaped to his feet to make important points, as if he were about to take action. His main action after such pronouncements, however, was to slump back into a chair and suffer rebuttal. More than likely he had learned by experience that short men get more attention standing up. Duncan had inherited from Scots ancestors his curly hair and blue eyes, and from a life of reading, his pear shape and perhaps his weak vision. He was a James Joyce scholar with ardent opinions on all hot issues, and this land, he said, was "too far out." He put his hand on his heart and said, "I will not become a slave to the automobile." He was a political radical who liked the idea of being in the country but not of being far from the civil rights, labor, and free speech action that was boiling on campus.

Bud Roebuck, who found models of courage in Faulkner's hunting stories, said places like this had copperheads and he wasn't going to risk his life. He spoke with a made-for-radio voice, but I recognized in him one of those kids who had never thrown a punch or even a ball. He was not skinny, but inside his rather normal and slightly tall body was a character from my childhood, Charles Atlas's ninety-seven-pound weakling who feared the sand-kicking bully would steal his girlfriend. Bud was a city Southerner with a beautiful northern wife with alabaster skin and flaxen hair. Country living, he said with slow and wise intonation, isn't as pleasant as it seems from a distance. He knew, having looked at it from a distance his entire life. He was not afraid for himself, he said, but he would worry about his wife's being out there alone.

Marion Ryerson, the biographer of Ford Maddox Ford with several Connecticut estates in the family, mused on McCauley's Mountain for a while. He already had a few gray hairs and a blue-eyed wife with farm-girl freckles and the social graces born of an upbringing among the families of business executives. Marion worried about the administration of our project. "Can we get a road in there? You know those little creeks are deceiving." He was talking about a creek his long legs could straddle.

I tried to force the issue. "We are all reasonable people and we're supposed to be smart enough to solve problems," I said. "Let's bet on ourselves and buy it while we can." I was outvoted three to one. Duncan said, "Now that we know what we don't want, you can find the right piece." In the end, they could not even abandon the project decisively.

I could have and I would have except for Michael Paull.

Michael Paull was a tall, soft-spoken Ph.D. student who looked gangly but moved gracefully, especially when shooting baskets, which he loved to do with a ball on a court or a wad of paper arched toward a wastebasket. He was the likable and unlikely offspring of short and modest Russian Jews. His grandfather was a carpenter from Pinsk who had taken his three-year-old son and fled to America to avoid being drafted into the Czar's army at the beginning of the First World War.

One night when plans for McCauley's Mountain were falling apart, Michael listened to me say that people could buy five or ten acres in the country for the price of a half-acre lot in town. It was a good business proposition, and it came with a noble purpose: Land could become affordable for people who never imagined they could afford owning land. To protect their new treasure, they would agree not to cut many trees, not to use persistent pesticides, and not to clear land next to streams.

Most real estate developers market exclusion, I explained. Even developers of trailer parks assume that most of the world doesn't want to be included.

"In a trailer park?" Michael said. "They don't. You don't."

"But I want to be included in nature. Everybody loves nature, and if everybody has five acres or more, no one bothers anyone else. We can include anyone who wants to build anything."

Maybe because Michael came from a long line of landless Russian peasants and still landless city merchants, my woodland fantasy stayed with him. When events moved him to abandon the South for a life of teaching in the Bronx, he left content that my dream and I were his Southern proxy. The events that put him on the road to the Bronx and me on the road to Morgan Branch began with the Elizabethan poet Andrew Marvell and his seventeenth-century poem, "To His Coy Mistress." With a little academic dissembling, older professors taught the poem without mentioning sex or seduction, but sometimes punctuating their lessons with a smirk or a wink. Michael taught the poem for what it was, and his students giggled when he asked them to write a similar argument of their own.

The first result of Michael's exercise was that word went forth from amazed student to surprised mother to mother's offended friend to outraged television commentator Jesse Helms, and thence to a million people in the eastern half of the state. The story had it that among the ever-increasing insults to traditional Southern values that were erupting on the university campus, an instructor from up north had ordered his students to write a paper intended to seduce a member of the opposite sex.

What followed has its own place in the annals of teaching, but what matters here are the results. Despite becoming the sympathetic subject of a story in *Life Magazine*, Michael was humiliated by removal from the classroom. He retreated into solitude and redoubled efforts to finish his thesis, "The Figure of Mahomet in Medieval Literature."

One wet, cold day in the winter of his discontent, Michael came into the dining hall and sat with me where I was nursing a cup of coffee and reading students' papers. The plans for McCauley's Mountain had died, but the concept had come back to life for Michael. "Tell me again, how you are going to find a piece of land and make a profit and keep your soul?" Michael, the lover of medieval morality tales, epics, and sagas, had started selling restaurant equipment with his father when he was five. He had also sold women's shoes, bagels, metal polish, and tickets to a pornographic movie. Like Wall Street analysts who buy stocks on their "story," Michael saw pots and pans, land, and ideas as something to be sold, and the sale was the conclusion of a story.

I told him the story again. He interrupted the way a kid interrupts a story—"What's a chlorinated hydrocarbon?" he asked when I told him we would ban these antitermite chemicals that contaminate groundwater. For

Michael, my dream of turning profits toward paradise, conquering these evil forces, and living in the woods was like the journey of a character in the medieval sagas he loved to teach.

To prepare me for the journey, we agreed to form a corporation to buy a piece of land. I would be president and treasurer. Michael would be vice president and secretary. Michael had absorbed from his immigrant father the understanding that the heroes of myths travel in the practical clothes of their day—for us, a corporation. It would be an alternative corporation for the newly rising alternative culture. We would subdivide, but in our subdivision, instead of lots we would have homesteads. Instead of rules requiring a certain number of square feet or a certain style, we would require only peace and quiet and the preservation of land for wildlife. We aimed to do for any good soul in the general public what my colleagues in the English department and I had wanted to do for ourselves—make home sites five acres or larger where one person's way of life wouldn't interfere with a neighbor's.

Late winter and spring of 1968, Michael's last months in the South, he and I had been crashing through forests and wading streams and slogging ankle-deep in red mud on and off for almost a year. His wife was happy he got out of the house. My wife, Sarah, was busy teaching English in a rural high school, exhausting herself over students' essays. We looked at tracts of land that were too small or too large. We looked at beautiful land deep in the woods with no legal access. We saw cheap land scalped by loggers. Other pieces were too flat or too swampy. I was beginning to think I was as afraid of making decisions as my colleagues were. Then I answered a classified ad in the state's free weekly agricultural bulletin: "330 acres of good timberland in Chatham County. Will sell all or part."

chapter 4

Saralyn

*A good ol' boy outwits two young Yankees and sells
them a piece of his heritage.*

I called the number. "Yes, that's a fine piece of land. Fine growing timber. Fine investment." The man's voice had a thick country accent, a slow and too-reassuring voice. "Fine investment" meant he knew right away I had moved in from up North. "Fine growing timber" usually meant small pines and scrub hardwood where fields had been abandoned or a forest had been clear-cut. We agreed to meet at a service station.

On the gravel beside the pumps outside Harris and Farrell's General Store "O.K." Pettigrew stood wiping the sweat off his brow, talking to three old men who sat on a wooden bench in the shade of the awning. You could have drawn O.K. with a series of circles—one for his balding head dotted by two round eyes and a round mouth, a squashed circle for his neck, two circles for his larded chest, and a huge circle for his mid-section. He watched me getting out of my Chevy pickup, his mouth forming a small round O. His hand had frozen at mid-swipe and he clutched the handkerchief mop above his brow. The old men on the bench said something to each other and turned their attention away from O.K. as if to let him get on with his show. "Dr. Kaufman?" he asked.

"Just Wallace Kaufman," I told him. He waddled over to me with his hand outstretched. His eyes were studying me hard. The men on the bench were watching both of us, but not hard. They had seen this play before.

O.K. said we should ride in his long blue Buick. The car sank as he low-ered himself into the driver's seat. Several rolled-up land maps lay on the back seat. We drove south over the Haw River toward the village of Pitts-boro, then west on a dirt road, trailing a rooster tail of red dust behind us. "This is the prettiest piece of land you'll ever see," O.K. assured me. "Real pretty. I hate to sell it."

We passed a small brick church with the sign in front, Russell's Chapel Church. A couple of old country houses stood on the opposite side of the road, and a "dollar down" Jim Walter prefab.

We rode on beyond the dollar-down houses, passed a few small fields and woods, and pulled off onto a rutted timber road that divided ten acres of head-high pines like Moses' road parting the Red Sea. O.K. wiped his fore-head, grabbed a rolled map from the back seat, and heaved himself out of the car. He stabbed a short and fat index finger on the road line. "We are here. There's about half a mile of frontage on this road. Then it goes on up almost two miles into the woods. Three hundred and thirty acres but I'll sell it to you one hundred, two hundred, or the whole three hundred acres. On terms. Five thousand down for each tract, and I'll give you fifteen years at 6 percent on the rest. Or I'll take $75,000 for the whole piece."

We walked down the timber road through the pines into the dark valley of a creek shaded by hardwoods. The water gurgled on the rocks, the only sound in the silence except O.K.'s hard breathing. The water was clear, not like the South's silty rivers and green farm ponds. When I stooped down and put my hand in, it was on the cold side of cool. Beyond the creek, the land rose up slowly, no small pines but a real oak and hickory forest. I wanted to follow the fading road into the woods. "It's just like that—good timber as far as you care to go. There's probably more than $75,000 worth of timber," O.K. said. "What do you say?"

I said I wanted the map and I wanted to come back and walk in it with my partner.

Michael and I could raise the down payment for two hundred acres. The payments would take almost a third of my salary and I was already paying a third on my house. Michael sold his old Nash sedan and cashed in his life insurance policy. He also told his father that he was investing in land and that we could buy the last hundred acres if we had another $5,000. His fa-ther knew that Michael would never run People's Restaurant Equipment. If his son wouldn't join him, he would join his son. This was the last and only chance he would have before Michael became a medievalist and professor. Michael's father and his Uncle Lefty agreed to put up $2,500 each. The corporation now had four stockholders. I signed an agreement to purchase from O.K. Pettigrew.

We were going to own 330 acres. We had just been pinhooked.

A pinhook is a fish hook made from a bent pin. Pinhookers went to property owners and suggested they had a buyer and established a price. With that price in mind, they went hunting buyers at double the money, hoping to pocket the difference. When my lawyer handed me the title report with the names of the real owners, I called O.K. Pettigrew. He didn't so much laugh as giggle, and I'm sure if he could have reached through the phone, he would have patted me on the head. If I could have reached through the phone, I would have torn out his Adam's apple. But I should have understood that he had a right to laugh: O.K. had never gone beyond grade school and I had a graduate degree from Oxford.

I wouldn't have had that piece of land but for O.K., and I might never have built my house in a wild place. The readers of *Walden* never ask where Emerson got the pond or the money to buy it. I came to my begrudging admiration for the impersonal justice of the market not while listening to O.K. Pettigrew laugh on the phone but many years later when I had a better appreciation of how funny life is if you don't take every surprise personally.

If I had not walked the land after O.K. showed me where it was, I might have hung up on him and started my search again. But I had walked the land several times. I had seen an otter slip out from the brush and slide into a swirl of water in the creek. I found a great outcrop of cabin-sized rocks at the top of a hill. I followed the groove of an old road far back over a ridge and down a steep slope to a small stream lined with smooth gray pillars of beech trees with roots looped under, over, and through rock outcrops. This is where I had immersed myself in the creek on a hot summer afternoon. High on a steep slope by that stream I sat on a big white boulder of quartz one warm afternoon and listened, and I heard silence.

There were other pieces of land to buy, but I had already found my place in this piece and I didn't think I would find another like it. I didn't hang up on O.K. for another reason, too. I had paid him $5,000 earnest money when I signed the contract. Whether the owners signed the deed to me or whether they signed it to him and he signed it to me made no difference to the law. The title was clear. I don't know how much O.K. made, but soon a piece of the Old South where sharecroppers and landlords and cotton farmers and saw millers had once lived and worked belonged to three Jews from Detroit and me.

Michael was nervous. His wife, Lynda, had an old car and didn't expect him to die soon, so she didn't worry about the cashed-in life insurance policy. She worried about the payments. So did I. I was happy, and I was scared. We were facing fifteen years of poverty, bearable poverty if Michael got a job and if I kept mine and if there were no emergencies. His father and uncle had not agreed to help make any payments. Michael was living on a Woodrow Wilson Fellowship. The first big quarterly payment was due in three months. My wife, Sarah, the daughter of two academic biologists, was stoical. Michael and I were like two guys who had just bet our families on the promise that a goose would lay golden eggs. With Michael's father from Minsk, his Uncle Lefty, we had become the stockholders of Saralyn, Inc. Michael and I named the land Saralyn.

–chapter 5–

American Dreamers

I become America's poorest corporation president, a reluctant salesman, and a humble student of human behavior.

Everyone loves to see someone else trying to fly on gossamer wings. Like a person about to jump from a tall building, it's news even before the results are known. My colleagues who had backed out of a joint land purchase asked regularly how the land project was going. Word got around. A big picture in the *Durham Morning Herald* shows me standing hands on hips and looking into the clear waters of Brooks Creek. The headline announces the unlikely event, "Poet Is Corporation President." My poetry had improved since my first poem in sixth grade, which celebrated a brook that flowed "from the mountain like a bubbling fountain." In the *Herald's* photograph, however, I was not conceiving a poem on crayfish or turtles; I was wondering how I was going to get a road across this creek without destroying both the creek and our budget.

The article faithfully reported my belief that I was doing something wonderfully new, that my experiment would allow average citizens to live in harmony with nature and turn capitalism away from destruction. About that time, Joni Mitchell was singing her famous line, "They paved paradise and put up a parking lot." I believed capitalism and development had powers that could also do good. I had been a capitalist since I was eight and my brother Art and I bought a pair of hamsters to breed for pets and science. I had sold newspaper subscriptions to build my own delivery route. I had mowed lawns and clipped hedges. In high school, I bought and sold used books by mail order. I believed in the ideal of a society in which each gave according to his means and received according to his needs, but I knew that money could buy land to build parking lots or to preserve paradise.

I was not put off by the mild skepticism of the *Durham Morning Herald's* final sentence, "And the land waits."

I believed both the land and the public were waiting for someone to do what I had in mind. The *Herald* had been attracted by the covenants (property restrictions) I had written and registered to protect Saralyn. Their provisions prevented people from cutting too many trees, polluting streams, and dumping junk in the woods—and from using chlorinated hydrocarbons to kill pests. I would keep costs low by by-passing the Realtors' commissions and paying for development from sales instead of from debt. And I would finance the lots so that anyone with a steady job in the local mill could afford to buy. Realtors assured me the idea was nice, but people wouldn't want to live in the woods thirteen miles away from town. One or two were blunt enough to say I was asking for trouble with a brochure that said, "There are no restrictions on who may buy. And on parcels of 5 acres or more we do not have to specify any particular size or style or cost of building." Even Chapel Hill's celebrated father of outdoor drama, socialist, and champion of civil rights, Paul Green, had put a "whites only" clause in the restrictions when he subdivided Chapel Hill land.

The sales brochure I wrote put the question bluntly: "Can a business corporation put the principles of ecology and natural balance above profit?" It also asked whether a person with modest income could really buy five acres. It went on, "Can rural land be developed without destroying its shade, quiet, wildlife, and clean water?" In large capital letters the answer followed: "YES, AT SARALYN."

I wanted the same people who sang along with Joni Mitchell to know that a developer also can prohibit parking lots. I wanted the people who Woody Guthrie championed to sing "this land is my land" and mean the acres they owned instead of coveted. "Land is not only for the rich," my brochure declared. The brochure, in fact, was more declaration than explanation. Most of the declarations were stated in noble naïveté.

Between signing the purchase contract in August and closing the deal in late September of 1968, Michael had moved to the South Bronx to teach Nordic sagas. In the sagas and in early Irish legends, before a character comes into his own he must possess land. He must put his mark on its boundaries and give it a sacred name. Michael, too, became part owner of the South's land. In the South Bronx he often worried less about the guns and knives on the streets than that his purchase of land was hubris and our endless debt a punishment from the gods. He sent his share of the mortgage payments, wrote encouraging notes, and told me how much he enjoyed explaining the terrible justice of Iceland's Snorri to slum kids.

For a year and a half, I guided prospective buyers down the rutted, red-mud logging road into the property. I was president of a company without money to build a road or survey lots. I tried to turn the situation to our advantage. I did as O.K. Pettigrew had done with me. I spread out the map of the 330 acres on the hood of my truck and stuck a finger on the point at which the logging road plunged through the small pines. "Anywhere in here you can have five acres or a hundred," I would say. I thought people would like the design-your-own-lot approach. They could choose how long and how wide the lot would be and what hills and trees it might have. But even trail-seasoned country lovers arrived expecting to see some hallmarks of development. They were not the heroes of Nordic sagas who could mark their own boundaries, name their own land.

If I had given prospective buyers directions and they had arrived before me, they would be standing by a little knee-high wooden sign saying SAR-ALYN, as if it were a necessary anchor in the wilderness. Some showed up in dresses and ties, some in sandals and shorts; some came with babies barely able to walk and too big to carry farther than the creek. The scant twenty-five acres that lay between the creek and the road was a field grown over by ten-year-old yellow pine too thick to walk through and just too tall to see over. No one wanted short-and-dense pine brush. Once visitors got beyond the pines and over the creek, they were disoriented. They saw only woods. No roads, no lines, no painted or ribboned surveys led the eye or the imagination. As I led them through the forest I barely knew myself, they asked, "Where are we now?" or "You do know where you're going, don't you?" I said yes when I knew and kept silent when I didn't. They went back to town and talked about their crazy afternoon in the wilds with an English professor. They didn't buy.

I was puzzled because I was trying not to be a developer. Yet I was learning lessons two and three in my new career.

The first lesson I had learned when my colleagues at the University had worried our joint land purchase to death: *No development in the world can pass all the safety tests that concern even a small number of people.*

The next two lessons followed with textbook logic.

Lesson Two: *People buy a sense of place.* They want a recognizable order, a road that leads somewhere, driveways that tell where a house might go. They want electric lines and phone lines. Maybe they have their ideas of an ideal lot and home, but most people want developers to go ahead and give them something about which they can say yea or nay. This lesson followed from something an English department colleague had thrown at me during one of my odes to nature and wilderness.

"Wilderness areas don't exist," Tom Stumpf declared.

Nonsense, I said, and I named a dozen great wilderness areas in America. What could Tom know? He was a Shakespearean. A Falstaffian lover of huge feasts who saved up for a long weekend in Paris solely to eat fine meals. But he was right.

"How can it be wild and have boundaries?" he asked. "Once we have drawn lines around it, it is inside a fence and it's not wild."

Think hard about all that literature of wilderness and you realize that it is not about the love of wilderness or even understanding it. It is about mastering it at best and at other times about surviving it and respecting it. The heroes of Michael's beloved sagas were the forerunners of civilization; they tamed the wilderness with boundaries and names. And even as I brought people to find a home in a wild place, they insisted that I tame it.

Lesson Three: *Satisfying this desire for a sense of place and security means investing a lot of money before answering the first inquiry.* Front money means more risk. More risk means that investors expect more profit. It also means more interest expense. In sum, it means more expensive development.

I didn't come to pity the poor developer, but I did come to understand the cookie-cutter approach. Development requires a lot of money before the first sale is made, and that in itself calls for a big risk. By imitating what has already succeeded, by doing what masses of customers have already voted for with their money, developers avoid additional risk. I had despised that caution as timidity. But timidity is no crime. The people who came to me looking for land were also timid when it came to their own money. Developers often risk their own money and the money of family and friends. If they are risking money put up by partners, stockholders, or banks, then the law, not to mention a bunch of nervous strangers, is always looking over their shoulders. Michael was looking over my shoulder from the Bronx. His father and Uncle Lefty were looking over his shoulder from Detroit. They believed in Michael. Michael believed in me. He once wrote to me, "I think of you as a character in a Russian novel." I was supposed to change the world while retaining my virtue, enriching my partners, and retreating into my own solitude.

chapter 6

Walden,
Where Are You Now?

America's first Earth Day sends thousands seeking the Walden Pond experience waiting at Saralyn. We begin with two women pioneers, and I lose my environmental virginity.

For six months I tried to make people imagine the wonderful life they could have in this forest. I began to feel like a man trying to sell bottles labeled The Elixir of Happiness. I told people about the piece of land I was aiming for. I told them how I could put the boundaries of their homestead wherever it suited them. I showed them beautiful southern slopes where they could build solar houses with winter sun streaming through the windows and summer shade keeping them cool. I showed them where I had seen a river otter. I showed them rare putty-root orchids and big walnut trees and glades carpeted with running cedar, a rare creeping ground cover with bright green leaves like flattened cedar foliage. I wanted them to understand that, instead of watching nature on television, they would live the action; they would pay little to possess great treasures. Everyone in Chapel Hill could go to a Tar Heels basketball game, but how many had ever seen a river otter?

The response to the sale of my dreams was a lot of serious head nodding, then departures, often punctuated with words that I have often thought about for my own tombstone's comment on life, "It's an interesting idea. We'll think about it."

I thought I was trying to sell land, but in fact I was trying to sell poetry. Even well-known poets know that's impossible. I should have kept W. H. Auden's line in mind: "Poetry makes nothing happen." But even the poorest salesman scores eventually, and I did.

An unpoetic couple, as it turned out, bought the first home site. They were not visionaries from the exploding alternative culture movement. They did not even communicate great enthusiasm about Saralyn, but they lifted my spirits as surely as if they had made the sound of a key turning in solitary confinement. They were about ready to retire from Kodak in Rochester, New York. In the spring of 1969, they took a quick look and chose an area near Brooks Branch where they thought they could build a retirement home. And if they didn't, they were sure the land was a good investment.

I promised that I would have a road to the property within a year. They left their deposit, went back to Rochester, and a month later their check for $3,000 arrived. The money was not nearly enough for a road, but I was convinced I would sell more land. With that confidence, I sold stock in the company to two friends who were environmentalists. What sold the stock, however, was that $3,000 was twice the price we were paying for the land. Gross profit margins like this sound big to people who do not know land development. It sounded big to me, until I began to learn the costs of building roads and crossing streams.

I looked in the yellow pages and called a couple of contractors. That particular spring, 1969, grading contractors needed work and I found one who had enough machinery for the road and either a bridge or a culvert to cross the creek. Jared Jernigan was a foul-mouthed, cigar-chewing, I-can-do-anything Pennsylvanian who had married into the South. He wore cowboy boots with high heels to lift himself just over his average height. He told me about a job he had done around a new house where the master bathroom had both a toilet and "one of them European things that squirts up your butt." He said he didn't understand it because "that man's wife was just plain ugly."

He said, "My D-8 can knock down anything out there and pile 'em up ten times faster than you can cut 'em."

I knew I could not tell this man the deeper reasons for wanting to cut the trees myself. I had seen bulldozers in forests, all noise and brute strength, trees splintering as they fall, not a moment wasted contemplating what the grandest tree or the most exotic form had to say about its past or its place. Using a bulldozer seemed like gobbling a church dinner without saying grace. I rented a little chain saw from Rent All. The saw was little because I wanted to do only a little damage. I rented it because I'd get the job done, give it back, and wash my hands of killing trees. This would be a merciful job with the least possible waste. I wasn't going to have a bulldozer pushing over my trees and piling them up. I intended to select a road line that avoided big trees. In the end, if I cut carefully, maybe someone would come in and take away the best logs.

Because I couldn't tell Jernigan these things, I told him I wanted to save some of the logs and might try to salvage a few for sale. I already knew that no one was buying hardwood timber. I spoke to a couple of old black men who hauled pulpwood by the truckload. Two dollars a cord, they said, but without some kind of road to it they didn't want to bother.

First minilesson: Big trees don't grow in rows and they seldom grow more than twenty feet apart. No matter which way I tried to run the road, big trees stood in my way. As soon as I got past the small pines and into the flood plain of the creek, I had to bend the line to avoid a black walnut. Then I found myself headed straight at an old sycamore lifting its branches in bone-white bark into the sky as if praying for deliverance not only of itself but of the entire valley. Trying to avoid the big trees was like trying to shovel a blizzard with a teaspoon. And trying to cut the first big oak with the little saw and its dull blade was like bludgeoning an elephant with chopsticks. The saw roared. The chain smoked. After half an hour, the blade had gone six inches. I was exhausted. The tree stood immovable with the saw resting in it.

The next day, I took a company check and went to town. I was looking for power, just like everyone who has tried to make nature bend to his will. I told the owner of the farm supply and tractor shop, "I need a saw to cut a lot of trees." He showed me several small saws on the concrete floor. "I need something bigger, for big trees," I told him.

He went behind the counter and hoisted onto it a Stihl 041 saw with a twenty-one-inch bar. "This is what all the loggers are using," he said. "It will cut all day long. It will cut your leg off." The chain was slick with oil. Each black tooth had a bright and sharp tip. I wrote a check, grabbed the handle of the saw, and turned toward the door feeling like an assassin who had just bought an Uzi or Kalashnikov. As I walked out of the store, the owner shouted after me, "Be careful."

I was not worried about myself but about trees. I had marked the road line across the creek and a thousand feet beyond. Like the hunter eating his kill, I intended to execute every oak and hickory, every holly and loblolly pine myself. If I was going to build a road, I was going to take the emotional responsibility as well as the legal.

I managed to curve the road around a few special trees—a tall, straight walnut by the creek, an ancient pine with an S-curved trunk, a white oak cradling a resurrection fern in the crotch of its first limb. But I cut dozens that had been standing in place for 150 or 200 years. I rubbed my nose in the damage. I counted rings and learned the marks left by weather and animals and the fall of other trees. I severed grape vines as thick as my arms, and returning the next day saw their rubbery sap still bleeding from the stubs. I learned the licorice smell of a pine stump, the acid urine smell of red oak, and the musky tannin of white oak. I watched the chips of holly fly out on the saw chain as white as Ivory soap and I felt the hard white wood with barely visible grain. Holly has been used in place of ivory on piano keys.

Within a week, I had cleared the first half mile. Not too bad, I told myself as I walked back through the stumps and trunks and limbs. I remembered every tree. I had cut a narrow road and the canopy would soon grow over it and make a shady country lane. When I was still a kid sharing a double bed with a cheap sheet metal headboard with my brother Art, we had lain awake nights talking of finding this kind of road. In those days we were reading Kipling's *Jungle Book* and *Bomba the Jungle Boy* and watching Tarzan movies, and we planned to head for real jungle and have a farm with panthers and monkeys. Art's dream, or a version of it, came true for a few years when he managed a dairy and apple farm by Lake Erie. For a brief day or two, I imagined I was creating the path to my part of that dream.

Buddy Jourdain, Jernigan's bulldozer operator, was a big man who wore loose coveralls over a round belly. His hair had thinned to a monk's fringe below a bald pate. With no audience to primp for, he nevertheless came to work every day clean shaven. He chewed his tobacco slowly. He backed his Caterpillar D–8 off the lowboy trailer, pivoted on the steel tracks, pointed it down my road, lowered the blade to the ground, and turned off the engine. "Let's walk in and you tell me what you want," he said. He was not a walking kind of man. He had grown into his machine. What I wanted was clear enough in the lane I had opened through the forest. All he had to do was clean it up and smooth the ground. I also wanted him to be surprised that an English professor had cut so many trees. When we got to where my lane dead-ended against a wall of oaks and hickory, we turned around and looked back. Buddy laughed.

His laugh was not mean. It was amused, and his comment was a summary of the facts. "Hell, I can't even turn the dozer around in that space." He then gave me a crash course in road building.

I already knew that for people to get mortgages I had to build my roadway to state specifications. A road fit for service according to the state of North Carolina had to have the following characteristics:

—the roadbed must be twenty feet wide.
—beside the road must be shoulders. These may be soft, but add four feet on each side.
—the shoulders must not be soggy, however, so they are accompanied by ditches. And the ditches must be rounded to take seeding, so add six feet more on each side.
—if the land beyond the ditch slopes up or down from the road, that embankment must be gradual and grassed. Add five or ten more feet.

Accommodating all this kindness to man and nature requires cutting a swath through the forest that is from fifty to sixty feet wide. That was no job for one man, even with a Stihl 041.

In three or four places I had left an especially large tree near the edge of what I wanted to be the country lane. These trees stood in front of the dozer something like Frost's "tuft of flowers" left by the mower in haying. In the poem Frost is turning cut hay to dry when he notices the mower has deliberately avoided cutting a bunch of butterfly weed. He imagines the mower has left them as a message. I had left my roadside trees as a message, hoping they would say to people who would walk and drive along the lane what Frost said to the mower:

"Men work together," I told him from the heart,
"Whether they work together or apart."

Real life, however, is different from life in poems. In one day, Buddy and the D–8 Caterpillar had pushed all the trees I had cut, and a lot more besides, into three mounds that looked as though a giant beaver expected someone to turn a river down that roadway. Buddy was a big-hearted man but a heartless editor of landscapes. Most of my trees had to go or have their roots cut. You can't run a road ditch around a tree. The dozer simply lifted its blade eight or ten feet up the trunk of a two-foot thick oak and pushed until the tree's own whiplashing top helped break the roots' hold in the earth.

One weekend, while the piles were drying, I climbed over them looking for good logs and crotches to salvage for woodworking. Everything was pinned at some point under something else. I did find a large hollow gum tree that I sectioned and split, intending to use the curved pieces for benches. When I scraped and pried the rot from inside the log, thousands of carpenter ants, beetles, and millipedes fell out and scattered in chaos on the ground. In that insignificant and dying tree an entire community of life had been carrying on confidently through years of darkness. I had destroyed it in a few minutes. But ignorant people, including passionate environmentalists, wipe out entire habitats every day. Even the Jains and Hindu holy men cannot avoid stepping on the habitats and ecosystems they can't see.

The words "habitat" and "ecosystem" are popular with people who want to sound scientific in their pleas for preservation, but most people have only a faint idea of what they mean. Habitats and ecosystems are like planets, solar systems, and galaxies in the universe. They can be too small for the eye to see or as big as an ocean cruised by a blue whale. They exist inside one another. As a man with a chain saw and a hired bulldozer, I had stood somewhere in that continuum and destroyed worlds within worlds of life. And I had moved rocks and soils that had rested for a million years or more.

On Monday, Buddy arrived with a dump truck load of old tires. We threw them on the piles. He clambered up and down the piles with a ten-gallon can of gasoline, soaking the tires, allowing little pools of gasoline to settle inside. The first pile lit with a great whoosh of flame. Soon a thick column of black smoke was rising high into the still air, a huge insult to the country sky. Saralyn's first flag was air pollution.

I had often ridiculed people who burned leaves instead of composting them. I was embarrassed. I had called a couple of loggers and sawmills about selling the logs, but the answer was always the same. Nobody wanted oak and hickory from this part of the country. It didn't make good furniture; loggers couldn't sell it. For paper pulp it might bring $10 a truckload, but I didn't have enough to bother with. So I burned it, contributing to the oncoming global disaster that environmentalists such as Carl Sagan and the Ehrlichs then believed would be global cooling. I didn't know a better way to build a road.

I sat in the shade of the forest along the road and I watched. The smoke rose into the sky in black and gray pillars that could be seen miles away. I remembered the times when I was a kid and sneaked up to the attic to smoke the butt-ends of cigarettes I had taken from ash trays. When I heard steps on the stairs, I would squash the butt and drop it into the wall cavity, which opened into the attic. Now I had finally caused a terrible fire and everyone could see the smoke.

In the late afternoon, Buddy cranked up the dozer and stirred the shrinking piles to bring buried stumps to the surface. By evening, the charred piles smoldered, not a tree or stump recognizable as oak, hickory, gum, or anything else. Except for the blackened piles of stumps, dirt, and rock, the road was clear—a red avenue of clay with walls of big trees standing at numb attention on both sides. The South has a sad old iron-rich soil. I wish it were black or brown or yellow or white. Clearing a forest and cutting a road in the South's red clay is like peeling the skin off a muscle live with blood.

During the few days before the next phase of the work, I tortured myself by walking up and down that red boulevard with the trees standing at attention alongside. Near the creek I found three or four arrowheads. We had bulldozed our road through a settlement of five hundred or a thousand years ago. One more act of destruction. But the discovery also consoled me because I was not the first to disturb this place.

As a fifteen-year old, I had worked on an archeological salvage crew in South Dakota, excavating a Mandan village by the Missouri. That cured me of sentimentality about Indians. They had lived with their garbage of stinking buffalo bone piled three and four feet deep around their earth lodges. The Indians executed the last of the mammoths, American horses, giant bears, camels, and tigers. They denuded fragile arid ecosystems in the Southwest to plant corn and they carved their crowded and dirty apartment buildings into the face of pristine rock cliffs. In the East, they stripped great old-growth hardwood trees of bark for their long houses and wigwams. In the eastern forests, Indians had burned the undergrowth or the forest itself to make hunting easier and to encourage the grass and brush that deer feed on. In their callousness toward "useless" small animals and plants and the interdependence of all species, they were as materialistic as any modern developer.

We are all limited by our ignorance, temptations, and the choices we make to please our gods, our societies, our families, and ourselves. After the Indian came the loggers and farmers. Their wagon roads remain as deep ditches in the woods. The young pines at the beginning of Saralyn and older pine stands scattered throughout the woods were healing their exhausted fields and filling the gullies that eroded in the bared soils. From the point of view of trees, maybe men really are all alike and "seen one human tribe, you've seen 'em all."

My road was only the most recent development on this land, the latest way in which human beings have tried to take from nature what they needed at a certain place and time. I put the arrowheads in my pocket and hoped I was no worse than the people who had come before me.

–chapter 7–

Armageddon

With trees gone the destruction must begin in earnest. I realize the way to one's home should be the way of one's life.

One morning in late July at the first show of light, while the air was still cool and a gentle mist rose from the creek and birds were calling to each other in the trees, I was at Saralyn an hour before I was supposed to meet "Jar" Jared Jernigan at the beginning of the new road. I had walked down the new road to the creek and up the creek to where I could see no raw earth. I sat on the trunk of a fallen tree and I listened to the calls of birds I couldn't identify. I watched minnows and crayfish in the clear water. The crayfish browsed on things I couldn't see among the stones. The minnows nosed into the almost invisible current, waiting to eat or be eaten. The attack might come from a kingfisher, a water snake, or a raccoon. Or the world they all lived in might be ruined by me. The first time I had walked into these woods alone, I thought I had come as an admirer and a friend. I still wanted to be that, but I knew I wasn't to be trusted.

I heard the rumble of gravel in the distance, then the skidding stop of Jar's pickup on the public road. I walked out to meet him. He was standing by the big red truck and lighting a cigar. He kept his truck waxed to a shine. Filling half the bed of the truck behind the cab was a tank of oil for his earthmovers, and even that he had wiped clean down to its aluminum paint. I looked up and down the road and wished we had never met. Jar had helped me lose my innocence. I had lost my environmental virginity. It was as dead as the black and gray piles of burned stumps, as gone as the trees that had grown from those stumps. He had appeared like Faust to carry on with the bargain, his road for my soul.

Jar was enjoying himself. He chewed on the cigar and said, "Oh lawdy, what a fine morning." A minute later, his caravan of earthmovers arrived on four yellow lowboy trailers. They came thundering down the road as if part of a celebration he was staging. There were two bulldozers, a road grader, and an earth-scooping "pan" as long as an eighteen-wheel trailer truck.

Jar had not been to Saralyn since Buddy had piled and burned the trees. "Let's you and I walk in and take a look," he said. His men were unloading the machines and drinking coffee and eating donuts. They threw the papers in the road ditch.

Jar moved at an easy pace as if we were walking in a park after supper. He stopped at the creek. "What do you want to do here?" he asked. "Have you decided?"

I didn't want to do anything to the creek. When I first thought about putting a road across it, I thought about laying down three or four runs of concrete pipe, covering them with crushed rock, and pouring over the rock a concrete cap for a driving surface. In a big rain, the water would run over the top. It would be a simple, small, and cheap creek crossing that could be built by a few men with a cement mixer. On those few days when the creek rose in heavy rains, the water would flow over the crossing. Even bridges were once made this way on back roads. The State of North Carolina still had a few low-water bridges in the country. They were heavy creosoted timbers on steel beams with no railings. They were cheap and quick, but when the water flowed over the top, driving was tricky, and sometimes impossible. The state maintained them, but would not let a developer build one. Jar had told me to go talk to the State Highway Department and find out what they would let me build. I did.

They were matter-of-fact. They examined the U.S. Coast and Geodetic Survey maps that showed the Brooks Branch valley and every ten-foot rise in the land beside it. They roughly calculated how much water might run off the surrounding slopes in wet weather when the woods and fields were too saturated to absorb the rain. One of them scaled the valley of Brooks Branch and its several tributaries with the side of his triangular ruler, which was suited to the scale of the map. I had looked at this map many times. I had followed the tributaries to Brooks Branch, but only to determine whether any of them might originate in a populated area. I had not added their lengths or calculated the drainage area or thought about the volume of runoff. The engineer started punching numbers into a pre-electronic calculator that had a long metal carriage and whirred and clanked like an old cash register. He might as well have been adding money. The more it whirred and clanked, the more runoff area entered his calculations, the more water he added to the maximum flood. I listened helplessly while the noise of wheels and levers added new numbers to my naive estimate.

After a few minutes, he looked up at me. "I figure you will need something with an opening about ten feet high and twelve feet wide," he said. "That's a minimum." It was the minimum because state regulations said that for a subdivision (to them that's what Saralyn was) a water crossing had to be ready to stand above as much water as might run off the drainage basin during the heaviest rain in the next hundred years. They assumed the forested basin had been cleared for housing and roads and fields. Engineers speak of "the hundred-year flood" as if it were a single event, predictable in size but not in time. It could happen tomorrow or a hundred years from tomorrow. There is also one chance in a hundred of such a flood happening in each year of a century. I had walked Brooks Branch a mile in each direction from the road. Its banks were no more than three feet deep and often no more than one foot. Its widest channel was ten or twelve feet. The deepest pools were barely swimmable, and for most of its course the water ran less than a foot deep.

I asked the engineers if it could really rise ten feet high.

"Higher," the engineer at the map said. "Where your road is, this creek is draining almost five square miles of land. Look at how wide the flood plain is upstream." He held his ruler across the creek and showed me that between the first contour lines on each side of the blue line of the creek there lay almost five hundred feet of land. "The creek made this flood plain," he said. "It can fill it, and some day it will. Your roadbed crosses that flood plain like a dam, so you are going to squeeze all that water under your bridge or through your culvert."

With an afternoon's help of highway planners, I learned to see beyond my immediate experience. Often abstractions such as numbers and maps help sharpen the eye. The way the engineers read two-dimensional maps taught me how to read three-dimensional nature.

The next day, I went back to Brooks Branch to see whether I could see and understand on the ground what the engineer had seen on his map.

I stood on the banks of the creek and surveyed the flat land on both sides. When I knew what I was looking at, the story became clear. It was not just flat land covered with trees. The creek, rising and falling and whipping from side to side through thousands of years, had leveled this land. The creek with its small floods, hundred-year floods, and five-hundred-year floods had picked up and heaved hundreds of thousands of tons of soil and gravel a hundred miles and more toward the ocean. The creek was its own earthmover but one without purpose or deadline. It had taken the land that was easiest to take and moved it in the only direction gravity permits—downhill or downstream.

I walked through the trees in the flood plain and I saw the evidence of habitation by water. Clumps of twigs and grasses caught in brush and briars told of the last time the water had flowed over this land. Where a tree had fallen over, I saw that the earth in its roots was not the red clay of the uplands, but dense gray clay, the fine silt of weathered stones washed into these lands by floodwaters. The flood plain was immense compared to the normal size of the creek. It used space as extravagantly as any millionaire who allows a ballroom to sit unused for months on end. No wonder entire cities grew in the vast flood plains of the Missouri and Mississippi.

I understood how badly I had underestimated nature's variability. The men at the Highway Department were no Sherlock Holmeses, but I had been the dumbest Dr. Watson who could have investigated Brooks Branch. The human psyche did not evolve to comprehend such a wide variation in size or think so far into the future.

Say what you want about developers and paving paradise, long before there were government regulations, the best of them planned far beyond the usual human horizons. They could read the land and anticipate their expenses. Planners came along later to assure that the worst also looked farther ahead.

The loggers and vanished farmers whose old road I chose to follow across the creek had found a place where the land on both sides of the creek was relatively high, where it contained too much stone or heavy clay for the creek to carve a wide plain. We are not talking about the Yangtze River Gorge or Hell's Canyon, of course, but a place where the creek ran through a relatively narrow valley with the land rising from its banks on both sides. This was also a place where the creek in big storms, unable to spread out, would have to rise up.

If I laid in a few pipes and topped them with a concrete cap, my crossing would be several feet underwater, maybe for two or three days at a time. I had two choices: I could demand that future landowners live like scattered farmers had once lived in these woods, subject to confinement by unpredictable rains; or I could build a bridge or culvert at least ten feet high and twelve feet wide. To raise the road to the top of the bridge or two feet over the culvert, I would need tons of fill dirt. I was looking at a project that would cost four or five times my annual salary.

I visited dealers who sold prestressed bridge decking and others who sold big metal or concrete culverts. I didn't tell anyone I was an assistant professor of English. I listened hard, trying to bury my ignorance before they smelled its vulnerable odor. I wanted to build a bridge, a wooden bridge laid over steel beams, one that rumbled when you drove across it. At the Highway Department they said they would approve bridges with creosoted timbers, but prestressed ready-made concrete beams had already replaced wood for durability and price. Bridges were almost twice as expensive as metal culverts.

I told Jar I could not afford anything but a culvert. Jar started scribbling calculations. Calculating almost always meant disappointment and money. An eighteen-foot-wide roadbed on top of a culvert had to have shoulders, and beyond the shoulders it could slope only so steeply to the flood plain. Road plus shoulders, plus slopes on both sides, required digging up seventy feet of creek and putting it inside the corrugated metal tunnel covered with dirt. Jar said he would have the materials and his crane on the site by the end of the week. I felt I had just ordered a coffin for Brooks Branch.

"It will last for twenty or thirty years," Jar said. He turned his back on the creek and began to walk out of the bottom.

We walked to the first pile of charred stumps. The fires had consumed all the limbs and most of the trunks, but the heavy wood of the stumps and the roots mixed with dirt and rock remained in the middle of the road and were piled higher than my head. Jar stared at them for a moment and then made a gesture I recognized as dangerous—he took his cigar out of his mouth and spat. "Where do you want us to put these?" he asked.

I had not thought about putting them anywhere, but I did not admit it. I did not have to. Jar looked up the swathe of red dirt to the two other blackened piles. "We could haul them off to a landfill but it's fifteen miles. It'll be a lot cheaper to pile 'em up out here somewhere."

I asked if we could bury them. He looked around for no more than a few seconds. "You ain't got no place to bury them unless you want us to clear some spaces and dig holes. That'll cost you and we'll only have more stuff to bury," he said. "We can push 'em off into the woods. In a few years they'll rot away to almost nothing."

I could hear his machines revving up on the state road. The four big diesels together sounded like distant thunder. They were his machines, and he was the field general, but I was the commander-in-chief. The buck both started and stopped with me. I had already run the figures for the culvert and this first two thousand feet of road. It would cost twice as much as the money from the sale of the first two tracts. I was caught between my ideals and survival. More than thirty years later, I still look through the trees beside the road and see those piles of rotting stumps whenever I leave the woods. Maybe no one else notices them. The edges have softened and grass and moss grow on the dirt left in them. To me they are like small grave markers, like the crosses people put up along the road where a friend or relative perished. These piles, however, are the thing that perished, several acres of old forest diminished to rubble. Each pile was also a lumpish grave for my lost innocence.

Fortunately, money worries gave me no time to grieve. I had made the most common mistake in all new businesses: I had underestimated the costs of making a profit. I took small comfort in knowing that I was in good company. George Washington invested in land and wrote to a friend, "I have found distant property in land more pregnant of perplexities than profit." Washington was followed by thousands of speculators, developers, and community organizers who lost their fortunes even when adhering to the principle of conformity; that is, success is most certain when doing what has already succeeded. Real estate appraisers learn another principle, however: the principle of competition. It begins with the sentence "Success breeds competition." I thought of it as "Success breeds imitation." If I succeeded, I expected to be imitated. Others would spread the idea of environmentally sound development and I would retire to my own Walden and live happily ever after.

When I had settled with Jar on places to push the stumps where they would be least noticeable, he looked at several big trees I had protected from the bulldozer. My "tuft of flowers." I had decided we could bend the road around them, or narrow it just a few feet in passing to leave the roots intact. Several great oaks spread powerful arms over the roadbed, and one huge pine curved into a tall and slender skyward S.

"Those trees have to go," Jar said. Or else I had to realign the entire road. I could not keep the trees and fulfill the mandate for a state road that said a car traveling fifty miles per hour must be able to see two hundred feet ahead. True, the trees were outside the part of the road that would be graveled, but they were not beyond the part where we would need to cut drainage ditches. Jar said he could lay in a pipe just before each tree to carry the drainage to the other side of the road, but I'd have to add at least a thousand dollars for each pipe.

If a few months earlier I had heard about a developer who cut down trees instead of paying the extra money, I would have been the angry environmentalist talking about greed. Now I was a developer in spite of myself, and other people had entrusted their money to me. Someone has said that if it came to a choice between betraying his country or betraying his friends, he hoped he would be faithful to his friends. I could choose between the trees and my investors. I told Jar, "I'll cut the trees."

He turned around and went back across the creek to give his crew final instructions.

Before noon, the dozer with the hinged maw started picking up the piles of stumps and carrying them into the woods where I had flagged a path free of larger trees. The second dozer with the wide blade got to the pine tree with the S-curve before I could get my saw and return. The operator lifted the blade ten feet up the trunk, pushed, backed off, pushed, backed off, and pushed. The top of the tree whipsawed across the sky in wider and wider arcs. Each time the crown came back in the direction of the dozer's push it put more strain on the roots. I heard roots rip out of the earth. The tree crashed into the road. The dozer pivoted the root end and drove the pine out of the road and into the woods.

With the trees down, the dozer began shaping the road, cutting through the small rises and sloping back the sides. The small ups and downs of the land were averaging into two steady and gradual slopes toward Brooks Branch. In a few places, the dozers had sliced through veins of fractured quartz; in others, they had gouged out rocks and boulders that had no more than trembled for hundreds of thousands of years, slowly rising or sinking through the clays, some decaying slowly in the mildly acid earth. Most of the land we had to flatten was almost pure red clay. The red clay that begins in Virginia and extends through the Southeast into Alabama is an ancient soil rich in iron oxides and poor in most other things needed to grow crops.

When the road had its shape and proper slopes, the taming of the creek proceeded according to formulas and standards calculated to counter nature's attacks—erosion, corrosion, compression, gravity, abrasion, thrust, and backwash. At the end of the week, Jar returned with a newly renovated crane that crawled on steel tracks like a dozer's. When dozers had cleared the big rocks from the stream bed and dump trucks had filled it with a smooth bed of heavy clay, the crane began lifting the eight-foot sections of culvert from the supplier's trailer. They were bolted together with bolts as thick as my wrist and nuts as big as my fists. In two days the culvert was finished. The dozers loaded the dump trucks with more red clay and dumped it off the road on both sides of the pipe. Every time they added a foot of dirt, men with pneumatic tampers went down along the pipe compressing the clay to make sure it was packed solid and that water wouldn't work its way around the sides of the pipe. All this meticulous fortification was worthy of an army preparing for a dimly imagined war. As the tampers thudded on the clay, they were packing underground money I could have spent on surveys or on making the lots cheaper. Defense spending has never been popular.

I stood inside the pipe one morning when they were dumping dirt over it. The temporary dam had been removed and the creek was running through the culvert, a thin sheet of water bumping its way over the corrugated bottom. I could not hear the wheels and steel tracks overhead through two feet of clay. Their sounds came in through the ends of the pipe, but well muffled. The sound of my own feet was magnified. I said hello and my voice boomed off the steel walls. When my own echo died, I heard the heightened sound of the water pushing a few pebbles. I heard Robert Frost reading his lines from "A Brook in the City."

> The brook was thrown
> deep in a sewer dungeon under stone
> In fetid darkness still to live and run—
> And all for nothing it had ever done
> Except forget to go in fear perhaps.

After the massive moving of earth by dozers, pans, backhoe, and crane, the spidery road grader looked graceful. The driver sat high above four large wheels set far apart at either end of a long beam. Beneath him a long narrow blade shaved a channel in the roadbed for gravel. For two days the grader evened load after load of gravel into a gently crowned surface whose edges were even with the shoulders.

After two weeks and a few days work, a car could turn off the paved road and drive at fifty miles per hour into the woods. Everything was slick and smooth. The half mile of road stopped suddenly and absurdly at a wall of oak and hickory. I stood in that roadway, looked up and down, and thought, "God help me, did I do this?" I was like a man returning time and again to the scene of a hit-and-run. But there was no one to report to and not even a corpse to bury.

About that time, Carolina Power and Light came along. They could not put their poles in the road right-of-way, so they cleared another fifteen feet alongside the road, felling trees, hacking brush, and planting their poles. When they left, I was alone with my road, a highway into the forest. I cut up the trees the power company had felled and tried to hide the debris in the woods. I drove my pickup in and out of the road. I spread grass seed on the shoulders. The rain that came to make it sprout also washed clay out of the gravel and cut through the soft clays of the roadside ditches. I stood on top of the culvert and watched my road turn the creek bright red with silt.

–chapter 8–

Whose Woods These Were

In the woods next to Saralyn I meet a family who isn't there. I am glad they were not going as I was coming.

I was depressed and humiliated. I was also thankful that I had not had the money to build a longer road. This first two thousand feet would be the last road in Saralyn that conformed to the specifications of the Highway Department. It also ended more than a mile from the place where I aimed to live my own life beyond the sound of cars and in cooperation with nature. The kind of road I had built could never lead to the place I wanted to live.

Where I stopped the first two thousand feet of road, the old woods road emerged again and continued on its faint way north toward my land. Another wagon road forked to the west. It was fresher and the invading brush shorter. I followed it on foot across the Saralyn boundary line, up a hill and into a brushy clearing. Just beyond the west boundary of Saralyn stood a fine two-story farmhouse and several barns. The next day when I asked the Register of Deeds, Lemuel Johnson, whose house that had been, he spread out a map of the county, ran his finger up the road from Pittsboro, west along the road to our land, then north into the blank space where I was

49

building the new road. "That's the Carney Bynum place," he said. Then he added, as if it were a forgotten legal necessity, "A Negro family." When they moved, the Bynums had sold their seventy-three acres and everything on it to local white chicken farmers who had no interest in the house. They were parking a little extra money and waiting for the pines to become timber.

When I walked through the hushed clearing toward the house, I felt fully uninvited. Nature and the house were melting into each other. Trees pushed from under the high front porch. Thick creeper vines clutched the second-story windows. The roofs of two sheds had collapsed when termites or dry rot ate the posts. Half the farmhouse windows had been broken out, but its hand-hewn heart pine clapboards, its wide board floors, its stone fireplaces, and the piping and fixtures for its acetylene gas lighting system were untouched.

The house sat on thick straight columns of stone and carefully carved and notched red cedar posts. Inside one barn, the departing owners had left their two horse-drawn, upholstered carriages. Mice had nested in the stuffing of the seats, but otherwise the carriages stood ready for hitching. Inside the house, clothes and 1954 newspapers lay where the departing Bynum family had left them. Behind the house, pine seeds blowing in from timber company land to the west had colonized almost seventy acres of worn-out fields. They had grown taller than I had and too thick to walk into. No one knows in what proportions sorrow and joy mingled in this house. No one knows if Carney Bynum grew as tired of his land as the land grew of his plowing and planting. The Bynum house and land, like the lands and cabins near Morgan Branch, had been a stopover in an important American journey. Pieces of the story were easy enough to find. I would later learn that these pieces were also pieces of Saralyn's story and my own.

In 1860, Charles and Nellie Bynum worked as slaves for a white Bynum family, the owners of a profitable mill on the Haw River and the descendants of Luke Bynum, who received the mill site and 520 acres of land from the Earl of Granville in 1761. The Bynum family held forty slaves on the eve of the Civil War. In less than half a century, one child of the slaves Charles and Nellie Bynum had earned enough money to become a landowner. By 1913, forty-eight years after the Civil War, Carney Bynum, bearing the same first and last name as two past and one future white

Bynum, had earned enough to pay $509.25 cash for the seventy-three acres. He bought it from the white Millikens, whose family had held it since the 1760s. Carney and his sons cut, sawed, and planed the pine and oak from which they built one of the most modern homes in Chatham County.

On the road from slavery, the Bynums had paused long enough on their own lands to get their bearings, to earn as many comforts as their white neighbors, and then to move on to be part of America's towns and cities. Like the small landowners who held the lands in and around Saralyn, Bynum's big crop had been cotton. Mamie Oldham, who ran a store nearby, says Bynum also made a good living from selling baskets of scuppernong grapes and eggs at the cotton gin. "He never carried a bad egg over there in his life," she says. When one of his sons was convicted of robbing a store, Carney told Mamie, "Well, it's good enough for him. He wouldn't listen to anybody no ways." Carney and his family prospered by expecting as much from themselves as from their poor land.

About half of the lands in these hills west of the Haw River had come to be owned by former slaves and their descendants. Almost all the former slaves used their farms and woodlands as stepping stones. The business of making a living from the land enslaved them almost as firmly as slavery itself. White farmers were also moving out. The white chicken farmer who had bought the Bynum place could not imagine a time when anyone would ever want to live on a narrow dirt road in an old house. Local brick pits and kilns had popularized brick veneer. Cheap plasterboard had become much easier to install and more prestigious than wood. A room enclosed by boards spoke of the old rural poverty.

Not one person lived on the 3,000-acre strip almost a mile wide and seven miles long on the west side of the Haw River until people started moving into Saralyn. When Michael Paull and I started Saralyn, and when I moved to Morgan Branch, the forest had seemed pristine with only a few old logging and wagon roads in the dark shade. If the ghosts were watching, they would have laughed. They would have seen us the way I see people with money in their pockets and remodeling romance, moving into termite-eaten old farmhouses and mill-village cottages with tiny rooms and sagging roofs and floors made from the cheapest pine boards. Moving onto the lands of their defeat, in many ways we were like scavengers or squatters moving into an old abandoned house, into someone else's leavings.

Looking at the once-fine house, every board, beam, and post made and placed by hand, I was embarrassed by my confidence that I had come with bulldozers and road graders and ten-ton gravel trucks to make something out of other people's honorable defeat. The Carney Bynum place was not part of Saralyn, but the world that made it extended over Saralyn and beyond. My road was a road through the cemetery of their dreams.

-chapter 9-

Busting the Budget

*Sarah forces me to consider two things I had no plans
for and every reason to put out of my mind.*

Wouldn't you like to have a baby?" Sarah had asked me at breakfast one
morning that spring as I was getting ready to go to Saralyn and supervise
more road clearing.

I looked at her hard to see whether this was really a question, or whether
it was an announcement. "Now?" I asked.

"Not right now, but we could begin thinking about it."

"I thought you were talking about going somewhere exotic on a vacation," I said. Several times during the spring she had said how nice it would
be to get away from the farm and Saralyn and instead of visiting parents or
my brother or her sister we could go somewhere by ourselves.

I had never been on a vacation in my life. I had worked every summer
since I was twelve. Since Sarah and I had married in 1965, we had spent
summers working on the house or trying to grow and sell vegetables. To
make extra money, I had bought a Sears Roebuck walking tractor and
plowed an acre of the cleared land by the house, fertilized it with chicken
manure, and planted it with fancy vegetables: kohlrabi, herbs, stringless
beans, golden beets, snow peas, black radishes, Chinese cabbage, and Bibb
lettuce. I pruned and renovated half an acre of raspberry canes. Sarah and I
tore up our arms picking wild blackberries.

To prove a point about organic farming, I guaranteed never to price my produce higher than that of the local supermarket. With the naïveté of economics and market ethics that is possible only to English majors or the rich, I thought principle, not costs, should determine prices. Word spread. Soon, people were coming to the house to buy cheap and healthy produce. No one ever inquired whether the prices they were paying would give us a minimum wage. No one wondered if eating salad grown on chicken and horse manure was safer than chemically fertilized greens. Buyers then as now followed fashion and expected producers to do all the ethical thinking.

Sarah and I also bought six Muscovy ducks and a dozen pheasant chicks. Her parents had raised Muscovies, and she said they were good breeders and could fly from danger. She didn't remember that hand-plucking a duck clean enough to sell is a few hours labor. The pheasants fit my policy of high-priced specialty products. What would be more expensive than pheasant under glass? A blacksnake ate six of the pheasants in one night, two more another night. A snapping turtle in the farm pond fed regularly on ducklings or took a leg off one of the adults. A one-legged duck isn't good for much besides eating. We also ate one pheasant (not under glass), and we let the others loose, hoping they would multiply in the neighborhood.

After the summer's expenses, we had earned a few hundred dollars. We were making less per hour than I had made pushing a lawn mower as a kid. Some days after wrestling with the tractor and tiller in ninety-five-degree sun, I would collapse on the porch and drink a quart of lemonade Sarah would bring. Then I would go in and mix another quart and drink it.

The truth is, I didn't know how to take a vacation. I didn't know what a vacation would cost, and I already knew how we could invest any money we could save. I believed Saralyn would make a difference in the world and I was in a hurry to prove it. Money would help.

"We could take a vacation *and* have a baby," Sarah said, and she laughed as if it were the most natural and obvious revelation.

I gave her all the reasons why we should wait at least another year for either a vacation or a baby. Saralyn was about to take off, I felt. With Saralyn, we could make a real difference in the world. We needed to invest just a little more money. We had plenty of time to think about a baby.

"Don't you want a little Wallace running around?" She laughed, and added, "Well, I suppose it could be a little Sarah. It wouldn't eat much."

I loved kids. She knew I loved kids. We talked. We decided we would go on a vacation and think more about children. She wanted to go someplace warm. I wanted to go someplace wild. We bought two tickets to Ecuador on Ecuatoriana Airlines. In the first week of August we were on board an old prop plane watching the stewardess demonstrate the life jackets. The backs of the life jackets carried the stenciled name of the plane's former owner, Air Cathay; the name had been used by the Chinese nationalists after World War II. Lightning flashed in the black sky outside the windows as we crossed the Caribbean.

Quito was cold and the jungle was three days away on buses that looked as though they had already suffered a few falls in the mountains that lay between Quito and the Amazon basin. The only warm thing in the mountains was the thick sulfur baths at Baños. As we descended toward warmer lands and wilder places, we rode through land that looked worse than any cut-over forest in North Carolina. The "jungles," cut long ago, had grown again in dense thickets and scrub as far as the eye could see. The storekeepers in the provincial center at Puno had draped their facades in the ten- and twelve-foot-long skins of pythons and the crudely cured pelts of tropical cats and deer.

When we came to the Napo River on the east slope of the Andes, we rode an open pallet on a cable across the quarter-mile-wide river to the jungle town of Tena. That was the end of our trip toward the jungle. We stayed in a second-floor room of a small hotel nailed together from rough boards and painted a dark blue. A single bulb hung from the ceiling and burned at various magnitudes depending on the load other residents put on the town's diesel generator. The walls were a single board thick. The holes cut for windows had screens stapled across them. The weather was warm, but the town was not wild. Tena was a tame little village, a gateway to the wild Amazon basin downstream. We didn't have the time or the money to take a dugout downstream and fly out.

Sarah enjoyed the weather but not the food. I was unhappy. I could not leave her alone, and I had no place to go except to sit in the town park and read. We had spent our savings to come to the edge of the wilderness I had dreamed of with my brother when we were kids, and I would not see it. I would see only people getting into the long dugouts and disappearing around the river's bend beyond Tena. I wanted to be back in North Carolina in the forest at Saralyn.

Ten days later, Sarah and I were back in Chatham County. She was sick. In my journal for August 30 I wrote one line: "Sarah is pregnant." We had had our vacation and the doctor said that in early March we would have a family. Sarah said that, yes, on looking back, she had noticed some signs of pregnancy, but she had assigned them to the adjustments of going off birth control pills. We had agreed she would do that as a safety measure, to relieve her body of four years of drugs that had not yet established their long-term effects.

A family, that is to say a child, and the long growing up we would have to oversee, seemed to me a thousand times less predictable than buying 330 acres, building roads, surveying and selling land. To begin with, we still had six months in which we could do almost nothing and know very little that could matter. Sarah's father had actually met the announcement of our intention to marry with a reminder of the cruelties of biology. Her mother and father were Dr. Robert Ramsey and Dr. Sybil Street, well-known among America's physiologists for their rigorous work on muscles. To them, Sarah was still their well-sheltered daughter "Sally." When I had come into the kitchen in their Virginia farmhouse the morning of our revelation, her father's first sentence had been, "Sally has told me and I disapprove." His second sentence was, "At least when you two have children they might not be nearsighted." Sarah was mildly nearsighted. Her father did not know I was wearing contact lenses to correct my 20–400 vision.

Probably our child would be born when I would not be home. During that spring semester, I had already been chosen to travel to small American towns presenting shows for the experimental National Humanities Series. I would write and present one show on "The Outsider" and a second show on environmental ethics, called "The Good Life." I would have two or three professional actors and singers to help me bring the value of the humanities to life for people who lived near no university or college, people like our Chatham County neighbors. The organizers said they could open a three-week pause in my schedule for the baby.

The third week of February 1970, we played Whitesburg, Kentucky in the heart of the poorest coal country where the almost sunless mountain hollows still cradled cabins without electricity or plumbing. Wrecked cars and trucks studded the creeks and rivers and floods had hung trees and bushes along their banks with rags, papers, and plastic. Giant coal trucks churned up and down the main roads and out of the mountain's hollowed width mineshafts. By comparison, the forest at Saralyn and the little community seeded in it was paradise. One evening, we had supper with Harry Caudill, the crusading local lawyer, arch foe of the coal companies, and author of *Night Comes to the Cumberlands*. He was Letcher County's outsider. I saw little left around Whitesburg that insider or outsider could save.

From Whitesburg we went on to Toccoa, Georgia, where blacks and whites were just beginning to call each other's cards in the earliest efforts at integration. Their great natural attraction was Toccoa Falls, a thundering cataract that the Flying Wallendas, high-wire walkers, had conquered in midair. Their own outsider was musician James Brown. I talked to Sarah by phone and she said the baby was moving around a lot. My leave began on the morning of February 25. I came home from the airport and Sarah made me a sandwich at noon. At two she said, "Take me to the hospital." In a few hours her water broke suddenly and the nurses rushed her to the delivery room, threw a gown at me, and ordered me to put it on and come along.

We had never chosen a name for a boy. At 7:30 P.M. our daughter was born. I told the doctor what to write on the card: Sylvan.

chapter 10

The Road to Everyone's Walden

The new road brings the followers of Thoreau, each seeking a Walden Pond. They teach me Lesson Four about development.

In the spring of 1970, we possessed an infant daughter, six Muscovy ducks, three chickens, a donkey, a dog, and a three-legged cat that had pounced on the rattling teeth of my sickle bar mower. Every dollar I could save from my salary I targeted for the next mortgage payment on Saralyn. The road construction work had swallowed the $3,000 from the unpoetic Kodak couple as well as almost every penny I had raised by selling additional stock in Saralyn. A lot of people looked. Ads placed in a few new alternative publications such as *Vocations for Social Change*, *Workforce*, and *People's Yellow Pages* brought dozens of letters. While I was on the road with the National Humanities Series, Sarah read them to me over the phone.

Many people wanted a lake or a stream. Some people wanted to "commune with nature," and others asked if Saralyn was an "intentional community." A young lecturer at Brown University intended to start a "cooperative organic farm" as an "alternative to the American death machine." From Denver a woman wrote, "I would like to know if you would be willing to lease land to people to live in tipis and if North Carolina codes allow tipi-dwellers."

Anything that might help us pay for the land I would consider, but from dozens of such letters and my encouraging replies nothing worked out. The couple from Rochester remained the only buyers who had enough imagination to envision a home in the woods at Saralyn. Sarah had earned a little extra money sewing boutique pants and dresses for a shop in Chapel Hill, and she had taken her real estate license test so that she could also show and sell property. I hired a former student to plow and plant while I was traveling, but I didn't expect much more money from farming than I had made the year before. The ledger book in which I kept a running balance of our funds was below a hundred dollars as summer approached. A mortgage payment was coming.

Michael wrote from the Bronx, "I'm still in the process of digesting the possibility that I might have to shell out $2,000 in February. Are you sure??? It seems like an awful lot for a 20-year mortgage. I can get the money together (and besides, I hear that sleeping on benches is sort of comfortable once you get used to it)."

He also had an idea about saving money on land clearing. "How would it be if a few New York City kids (my students) were to come to North Carolina for the express purpose of clearing our land for roads or whatever? It might be an interesting experience for them and a profitable one for us. Several of them who know about the land have approached me and expressed a desire to see it or work on it (I guess to satisfy primitive needs, which can't be satisfied in the Bronx)."

I had visions of street kids slashing away with bush axes and machetes, satisfying their primitive needs on vines and trees instead of on each other, but unable and uninterested when it came to distinguishing walnut from scrub pine. I needed sales, not more labor, not even cheap labor.

Free publicity saved me. In April, the Woodrow Wilson Foundation, which was managing my work with the National Humanities Series, asked me if I would give a lecture in Princeton, New Jersey, where they were located. The occasion was the local celebration of a national event its organizers had decided to call Earth Day. It was just another lecture and I quickly forgot what I said and the audience did too, but the publicity given to the hundreds of lectures like mine across America was the real beginning of the environmental movement. It was like a birth. Since Rachel Carson's 1962 *Silent Spring* predicted the end of birdsong in the world, everyone had known America was pregnant with a new social movement, but the baby was officially delivered only on the first Earth Day in 1970.

Organizers modeled the meetings across America on the teach-ins of the Vietnam era when teachers-for-a-day and tenured professors leaped from the classroom into the political arena. That first Earth Day gathered discontented Americans under a revival tent. Like all revivals, that Earth Day preaching offered Hell fire and salvation. To carry the message beyond the teach-ins, several popular books appeared. Friends of the Earth collaborated with Ballantine Books (which had also been a premier publisher of science fiction) to put out *The Environmental Handbook* especially for country-wide teach-ins. The Sierra Club issued ecotactics as instructions for activists. Consumer activist Ralph Nader had already expanded his own Nader's Raiders and declared that all American commerce was now as dangerous as the Chevrolet Corvettes that had made him a national celebrity. Charles Reich wrote his best seller, *The Greening of America*. He declared that as a "matter of biological necessity" Americans would create a new revolution and a new vision of the world, which he called Consciousness II. The first issue of *Mother Earth News* appeared and promised monthly instructions that would help readers become "the first members of a civilized society since the early Neolithic to wish to look clearly into the eyes of the wild and see our own selfhood, our family, there." The message of Earth Day was clear: Polluted cities would kill the body and suburbs would kill the soul. If the movement had a bible, it was Thoreau's *Walden*.

A small but determined part of the new environmental movement decided to leave the cities and the suburbs and seek the shelter and spiritual inspiration of nature. America still had its Walden Ponds. In North Carolina, a couple of newspapers located a new Walden in Chatham County.

The covenants I had written, my brochure, and a newspaper feature about the subdivision created by a poet-developer promised that we would discriminate against no one. The same covenants also guaranteed that we would become victims of discrimination—our own discrimination. I even boasted to a critic that we had no need to discriminate because people who couldn't live with our covenants, who weren't willing to promise this minimal respect for nature and their neighbors, wouldn't buy. They didn't.

At Walden Pond, Thoreau had been plagued by hunters, fishermen, tramps, and neighbors who cut off their timber and conducted commercial ice-sawing operations in winter. Through his solitude, only two hundred feet from his house, ran the well-used Fitchburg Railroad. Like any other developer, I had written covenants to select a community. From Moses on down to hippie communes and guard-house country club subdivisions, covenants have always meant to exclude certain people or certain behavior. If the wild community is formed through natural selection, developers have learned how to form human communities through legal selection.

My covenants brought in a lot of mail and a few phone calls. People who read about them knew right away that they were intended to select people who would be fit neighbors for Walden Pond. My file of responses to notices and ads in the alternative culture publications grew thick with mail from across the country, Canada, and even Venezuela. The sales that saved us from poverty, however, came from local calls, and they brought despair and delight.

Theresa Riggsbee said, "I am coming home to North Carolina, but I want to be a country girl." She was moving back to North Carolina after a few years of performing street theater in California. She had grown up in the rows of flimsy wooden shacks in the Edgemont section of Durham with a mother who worked on the line at American Tobacco. Theresa had talked her way into special student status at Duke, tasted culture, dropped out, hitched to California, and married the heir to a used-farm-machinery fortune who was intent on revolutionizing America through street theater. He had introduced her to alternative culture, then killed himself.

Theresa returned to North Carolina with two kids and a pony-tailed boyfriend who proclaimed himself a socialist and a song writer. They had arrived pulling a painted-over U-Haul trailer and she wanted her land yesterday. Teresa was short and plain, but she made something special out of the ordinary, the way kids used to customize Fords and Chevys. She inspected the land in hotpants, a halter, and Birkenstocks. She had overcome her poor-white heritage to the extent that she did not dress so tightly that she seemed painted in, but with a looseness that suggested she was about to pour out. Her blue eyes looked at everything with a wry humor and birdlike intensity. She had let her silky blond hair grow down her back to her belt. She liked the idea that she could clear some of the small pines on the land along the public road and have a garden. We made a deal for five acres on the road so that she could move onto the land immediately.

A second urgent call also came from a woman: Susan Ahearn, who said, "Call me Sam." She taught physical education. She was wiry and quick of eye like a tennis player. She wore her hair short and simple, and, despite the name, she walked, talked, and looked like a woman. She had two teenaged daughters who got mad if you called them Harriet and Louise instead of Harry and Lou. Her son, Thomas, was content to be Tom. Her seventy-three-year-old mother, who had been a homesteader's wife in New Mexico, was called Granny Violet. Sam wanted her kids to grow up in the country, in unspoiled nature. Sam told me she had just bought two redwood prefabs. If she could find a place to put up one for themselves as a model, she could become a dealer and pay off the land by selling the second package. I needed buyers, so I stifled all comments about the environmental symbolism of buying redwood homes.

Need also forced me to grant her an exception from my intent to keep people out of each other's hair and out of wildlife's prime habitat. I had intended to keep a strip of land about a hundred feet wide along both sides of the creek as the common property of the community, a protection for the richest wildlife habitat and the rarest plants. Sam wanted to buy ten acres on the public road, with a good portion of the small pine stand and a strip of hardwoods along Brooks Branch. She planned to put her house where she could see the water. The land she chose was at the far western end of Saralyn where the creek entered from the lands of a timber company. Letting her buy to the creek's banks would shorten the commons area but not cause an interruption. I gave in. She signed, and I paid off my overdue road construction bills.

In *Little House on the Prairie*, Pa and the neighbor men do all the heavy work, but at Sam's the women worked while Tom looked on and fetched what they called for. The redwood A-frame went up closer to the creek than it should have; I had permitted one more insult to the harmony I had dreamed of. Within a month, Granny Violet had a chicken ranch. She populated it with birds that were forever escaping from cages piled ten high on the chicken trucks that scattered feathers up and down the main roads of Chatham County. She would splint their legs or wings, dope them with aspirin, and soon have them laying eggs. She gave each one a name. A female name.

Theresa and her boyfriend, Wayne, moved onto their land in the early summer. They wanted privacy, and I was glad my covenants gave it to them. I also gave thanks that the covenants hid them from view with the requirement that no more than half a homestead could be cleared and that each owner must keep a fifty-foot border in its natural condition. Another covenant required that all dwellings sit at least seventy-five feet behind the boundaries. I had written the two rules to create continuous corridors of forest cover for wildlife and to prevent one neighbor from looking into another's life.

Wayne and Theresa lived in their private hobo jungle. Along the old field line where the new pines met the hardwoods that grew down into the floodplain of Brooks Branch, they bushwhacked a narrow lane into the middle of their land. They cleared a space for a salvaged U-Haul trailer, the kids' room, and a stand-up army surplus tent, the master bedroom. The creek and the adjoining woods was their master bathroom. They cleared a garden plot in the young pines. They hauled buckets of water from the creek to water the garden.

Wayne spent his days in Chapel Hill at the university library. Theresa stayed home to cook on an open fire and to tend the garden. She declared that she had found the freedom she had always wanted; she could walk in the woods or work in the garden without wearing clothes, the way nature made her.

That was almost the way civilization found her one day after she had called the local phone company to install a telephone. She heard the service van stop on the Saralyn road. She wrapped herself in a towel. The installer, a thirtyish local boy, tried to look everywhere but at the towel cinched just above Theresa's breasts, barely touching her stomach, ending four inches below her pelvis, and parting on the front of her thigh every time she moved.

"Excuse me," she said, "I don't wear any clothes when I garden." Theresa had a laugh that was half shy, half worldly.

The service man tried to distract himself with business. "You ordered a phone?"

"Yes, I did," Theresa said.

"Where is your house?" he asked.

"We're not going to have one for a while," she told him. "We are clearing."

He said he could put in a line but he would have to come back with the phone when the house was built.

"If you can put in a line," Theresa said, "you can put a phone on it, can't you?"

"No, Ma'am," he said. "I can't put a phone in a tent or a trailer. It's got to be someplace permanent."

"Then put it on this tree," she said, pointing to a large gnarled cedar at the edge of the field that was now pines. "It's been there longer than most houses."

He took a while to look around and asked about where the house would go. Then he told her she could call again when she at least had some kind of building. "I could fix you up in a garage or shed," he told her.

"I'm sure you could, Sweetie," she answered, laughing such a worldly laugh that he blushed hard. He was still a country boy, and Theresa had been around the country and returned a widow with two wild children.

The next day when I was in Pittsboro, a lawyer I used there asked me if it was true that I had sold a home site to a naked woman who wanted her phone on a tree. At the agriculture building, I couldn't talk to Arch Pilkington about a rumor that the town planned to dam Brooks Branch for a reservoir until he had talked to me about Theresa. Arch was a gruff skeptic about to retire, disappointed from years of trying to persuade farmers to try new crops alongside tobacco. He was big on catfish farming and pick-them-yourself strawberries. He liked my covenants, but said we would always get silt running into the creek from our gravel roads. Nothing was good enough for Arch, but he was always eager to help you improve by pointing out your sins and suggesting you try something new. In that spirit he told me that when he had gone into McCrimmon's Drugstore for his morning coffee, he found the clatch of men who usually gathered there had taken to calling Saralyn "Hippie Town."

Theresa and Wayne reinforced the new label with their every appearance in Pittsboro. The county seat of seventeen hundred people sheltered enough Southern eccentricities to support its own *National Enquirer* or to populate the stage of a Tennessee Williams play. The county had absorbed its native eccentrics as children of its history, strange weeds and sensitive plants now as familiar as any tree or weed in the backyard. They threatened no one because they were individuals and not a movement moving in. But no man in Pittsboro wore his hair in a ponytail or walked around in sandals and tie-dyed shirts. No woman walked down Main Street in hotpants and a halter. And because whites didn't talk like black jazz musicians, the local bank's lending officer had both financial and language problems when Theresa sent Wayne looking for a loan so they could start building.

"What kind of work do you do, Mr. Farcas?" the loan officer asked.

"You can put down song writer," Wayne said.

"And your income?"

"No income," Wayne said. "I'm not one of those kind of song writers, if you know what I mean. I write for myself."

"Well," the officer asked, "do you have income from an inheritance, or a disability pension, or something like that?"

"Hey, my father worked in the steel mills in Birmingham and he croaked when I was sixteen. And I'm not disabled, am I?"

"Sorry," the loan officer said, "I didn't mean to imply that."

"Hey, it's okay, relax, man," Wayne said.

"Do you have anything you can put up as collateral for a loan? Like a car, jewelry, bonds, or anything else that has value?"

"All's I have is a 1953 Nash," Wayne said, "and it's beat to shit. I'm putting in a new clutch. American cars are pieces of shit and they lose their value like ice cream in sunshine. The unions have sold out to the bosses." He launched into the story of how American capitalists had worked his father nearly to death, paid him almost nothing when he cut off two fingers on an assembly line, and then his father found himself with lung cancer and no help from the union or the company.

"Well, Mr. Farcas," the loan officer said, "I'm afraid since we don't know you and you have no income or collateral, there is not really any way we can offer you a loan. You're welcome to come in again if your circumstances change. I hope you understand."

"Yeah, man," Wayne said, "Don't blame me. This wasn't my idea. My chick just sent me down here and said ask the bank for a loan."

The name Hippie Town caught on in Pittsboro. Stories about Theresa gardening in the nude, Wayne's request for a loan, and the family of women who insisted on men's names and nursed escaped chickens made the rounds. They made the rounds like snowballs, growing as they traveled. Theresa didn't just garden. She turned into a statuesque beauty who ran through the woods with her naked lover and children. Sam, Harry, Lou, and Granny Violet were suspected of witchcraft and maybe they used Tom for a slave. Maybe their A-frame house, a design meant for Scandinavian or Alpine snows, was no more out of place than the Greek revivals or brick ranches, but local people had never seen an A-frame house; to them it was all roof and no walls. It looked more like a tent or a church than a house.

The Ahearns and Theresa were the only residents at Saralyn in the spring of 1970, but Pittsboro was already talking about a woods full of hippies.

Late one night when Sam Ahearn and her kids had gone to bed and left Granny Violet sitting up with a book, there was a knock on the door. Granny Violet opened it and greeted a fifteen-year-old girl with a gym bag. As if it were the middle of the day, Granny said, "Come in, dearie. What can I do for you?"

The girl looked around the neat living room of the redwood A-frame. "I'm not sure," she said. "I'm leaving home and I'm looking for the place where the hippies live."

"Well, dearie," Granny Violet replied, "there are no hippies here but you're welcome to come in."

The girl came in and told Granny Violet how much she wanted to be free from school and her mother and father so that she could write songs.

Granny Violet gave her a cup of chocolate and talked to her about her parents. "It's very interesting that you want to write songs," Granny Violet said. "What do you want to write songs about?"

"About freedom and about love," the girl said. "I want to write about love."

"It's a wonderful thing," Granny Violet said. "Oh, yes, it is a great subject. You know, I came all the way here from New Mexico because I love my grandchildren and my daughter. And I think your parents love you."

The girl drank her chocolate and said nothing.

"Don't you think so?" Granny Violet asked.

"Yes. I suppose so," the girl said.

"Oh, I can tell they do," said Granny Violet. "Let's call them. I'll tell them you got lost and came for a visit."

When Granny told me the story later that week, she said, "Oh, they were so glad to see her. They were nice people too." What the parents said about Granny Violet I don't know. Nothing changed in Pittsboro.

If I happened into McCrimmon's Drugstore between eight and nine in the morning, when the old-timers took their coffee, Baxter Riggsbee the insurance agent would greet me loudly: "Well, here's the mayor of Hippie Town. Come have a cup of coffee." He always got up and shook my hand. It was a congratulatory handshake.

But I didn't want to be mayor of any town.

chapter 11

Thoreau's Delinquent Children

Business is a success and a community forms.
Thoreau would have disapproved.

I was not aiming to build a town or to found a community. My intention was still fixed on the meeting of two creeks at the northern-most end of Saralyn, and on its refuge from the sounds and sights and demands of even the simplest society. If getting there meant that I had to build a road, install electricity, sell most of the land to other people, and create a landowners' association to bind them together, these things were the price of fulfilling my dream. In the summer of 1970, however, Hippie Town was a community of two families and an absentee couple. Saralyn, Inc. was still deeply in debt, and if I had to continue using my salary for my share of the mortgage payments, I would be twenty years older before I owned the land I wanted or built anything there.

I had to admit that I had gone into business unprepared and navigating by instinct. I had bought land with only a vague business plan; I had done no research on the costs of developing that land, and even less on the market. I had assumed that what I wanted, lots of others would want. I mistook the strength of my own passion for a popular movement. Two colleagues at the English department who had once planned to buy land with me had already bought houses in new Chapel Hill subdivisions.

I wrote to Michael apologizing for my failure and mused on whether I would finish and sell the novel I was writing, or become a good teacher, or succeed as a husband and father, or save the world from pollution. He said again that I reminded him of a character in a Russian novel. Did he mean Tolstoy's Levin, tormented by his love for the unobtainable? Maybe Dostoevsky's gloomy killer, Raskolnikov, or the epileptic and idealistic Prince Myshkin of *The Idiot* who eventually plunges into insanity. At least Michael had written "hero." I didn't ask him to explain.

At that moment of doubt, my market blossomed as unexpectedly as Jack's beanstalk. The message of April's first Earth Day moved the imaginative, the adventurous, and the gullible to action. Thoreau's *Walden* was again a best-seller. Thoreau was quoted at meetings, teach-ins, seminars, and classrooms. He became a prophet of a new back-to-the-land movement. The forest became the place where nature could exert its most healing powers.

Earth Day reaffirmed the intuition that out in the country was a good place to live. A book written in 1965 suddenly gained a wide audience: Supreme Court Justice William O. Douglas asked legal consideration for nature in *A Wilderness Bill of Rights*. The preamble sounded like my sales brochure. I said we would emphasize man-in-nature and Douglas said that people had the right to understand "their place in nature's community." He believed that nature spoke a universal language and could heal the psychic wounds of a society. These wounds would eventually convince one of the back-to-the-landers, Albert Gore, that America is a dysfunctional family.

Even back-to-the-land revolutionaries were typical consumers. They had waited to see what other people did and where the trend was heading. Two families living on the land and the growing publicity for Earth Day's messages kept the phone ringing. The mailbox brought new prospects almost every day. Two more sales, together with the money from selling stock, took us through the year.

Dan Brown, who had left the Marines Corps a few years earlier to be a technical writer at the university, chose six acres and hacked a bicycle-wide path into the back of them, where he began to clear ground. He and his wife, Martha, carried bags of cement, tools, concrete block, bricks, glass, and lumber in on their backs and in a wheelbarrow. From my cutting on the Saralyn road they carried in enough logs for their first room. If the

Viet Cong could hold their own against the U.S. Marines, Army, Navy, and Air Force supplied by bicycle caravans on the Ho Chi Minh Trail, Dan and Martha could leave America the same way. They intended to build a two-room log cabin and wanted no cars within sight, no uninvited visitors.

Earth Day's inspiration brought the total number of buyers at Saralyn to five people owning thirty-one acres. Selling 10 percent of the property in two years should have been discouraging, but Earth Day and its consequences convinced me that we were about to catch a ride on a wave of social change. The variety of the five buyers also demonstrated that my covenants were working. My covenants and the brochure that translated them into everyday English invited buyers to Saralyn to include themselves as they pleased. "There are no restrictions on who may buy. And on parcels of 5 acres or more we do not have to specify any particular style, size or cost of building. Saralyn has information on new building techniques and encourages experiments in new and less wasteful building practices."

Covenants state values, and I thought my values were right, at least for that time and place. So did the people who bought land, at least until they began to build and to live on it.

By the third Earth Day, April 1972, I had sold all but the thirty acres at the northern end of Saralyn. This was the first business success for Michael and Lynda and Sarah and me. Michael's father had hoped his son would not be a hopeless academic. Michael wrote: "The news of the land sounds better than great. It's a little beyond my comprehension why Saralyn should all of a sudden catch on—it almost argues that man is a rational creature and knows what's best for himself. As for the profit, do what you want with it." He was ready for another investment.

Sarah and I were talking about building a house on the land at the north end, or maybe I was talking and she was listening. She didn't understand why we would want to go into a forest when we already owned a good house, a pond, cleared land, and a couple of old barns. We were almost ten miles closer to Chapel Hill and its culture. Sarah had also started law school in Chapel Hill. Sylvan was too young to have an opinion, but she was always ready to go to Saralyn with me, something I did often because I could grade papers or meet students in the evenings and take care of Sylvan during the day if Sarah had to be at school. I don't know whether it was what I showed her in the forest or the ice cream we bought at Harris and Farrell's General Store on the way home that made Sylvan so agreeable to our outings.

The people who had begun to settle at Saralyn are the casts of two or three sitcoms. Three Irish bricklaying brothers moved down from New York to do artful brickwork. A shy young Quaker not long out of Haverford College and learning stone masonry wrote from California that he and his "woman" were looking for a place "where we can live in piece and harmony with the world around us." A saxophone-playing dentist started a forest fire when he threw out his wood ashes. An Episcopal minister built a log house, then soaked it with toxic preservatives. A cigar-chewing retired drill sergeant defined the perimeter of his five acres with a string that no one should cross. A newly retired lieutenant colonel, the great-grandson of John C. Calhoun, and his wife, who had grown up among tobacco farms north of Durham, built a Japanese solar house and started an orchard in which 350 heirloom apple trees stand at espaliered attention. An Irish-American registered nurse from Boston became a stonemason and carpenter. A recent Duke graduate newly married to a former high school football-star-turned-sculptor gathered a milk-goat herd that roamed the woods and ate both common and rare plants. Two married pediatricians convinced the entire county that Saralyn was full of communists when the wife marched around the courthouse carrying a sign exhorting WORKERS OF THE WORLD, UNITE. (Her husband was later shot to death in a gun battle between Klansmen and Communist Worker Party members in Greensboro, North Carolina.)

Theresa continued to expand the diversity of residents by booting Wayne, building a cabin, and moving in with the younger brother of a famous black civil rights activist.

In Pittsboro, when I talked about Saralyn at the drugstore, in the diner, or at the courthouse, I would casually mention the dentist, our two retired military families, or the unpoetic couple from Kodak, but still I remained the mayor of Hippie Town. I would describe the elegance and size of Colonel Calhoun's Japanese-inspired house. They would ask about the fifteen-foot-high tipi owned by the long-haired son of a radical New York teacher, or about the foam geodesic dome, the inspiration of two refugees from North Carolina State University's engineering program.

I built another mile of roads, but not with Jar Jernigan. I decided that building to state standards was too destructive of the forest and my self-respect. The new roadbeds and their shoulders were narrower, their slopes steeper. Eventually, the trees on both sides would almost meet overhead. Everyone signed a document creating a landowners' association and recording their promise to contribute to the maintenance of a private road system.

While I built roads, our buyers built houses. Except for two or three families, everyone started as owner-builders. They were impatient and romantic and experimental. A boatbuilder moved a home in from a tobacco farm soon to be flooded by a new government lake. A recently discharged soldier who had been stationed in Alaska asked an old man down the road to bring his mule to move pine logs for a cabin. Jason and Kathleen and cartoonist Sandy Huffaker bought old log tobacco barns from farmers, moved them a log at a time, and resurrected them as cabins, to the amusement of local people, whose minds maintained strict separation of barns and houses. A painter bought a small house started by a sculptor friend and added on towers, turrets, gables, porches, and curving overhangs until he had a three-story fantasia, a kind of Japanese-Victorian dream.

The unusual became the expected. The familiar became eccentric. Everyone was surprised and a little dismayed one month when a contractor's building crew showed up and began building a conventional two-story house for an English professor and his dancer wife. It might have been built in any subdivision of America with its asphalt shingles on the roof, masonite siding, central heat and air, and two bathrooms. This couple became genuinely odd when they built a swimming pool surrounded by a grass lawn. In their way, they were also rebels. Both had been born and bred Boston Brahmins; they rebelled by settling for a middle-class house in Saralyn.

Saralyn even acquired its own church when Kathleen, the Irish nurse-turned-carpenter-and-stonemason, divorced Ralph. She married Nicholas, a Zen monk from a wealthy California family, and they built a Zendo, a meditation hall, large enough for thirty or forty people to sit on two rows of cushions while trying to empty their minds. I occasionally attended "sittings," but it became odd to me that I would be in a building trying to become one with the universe when just outside in the forest there was nothing between me and the rest of the universe.

Long before the locals would get used to athletes who shaved their heads, Nicholas puzzled them with his unfailing politeness, his easy laugh, his talents as a carpenter, and his immaculately shaved head. For people at Saralyn and others like us, Nicholas also became the alternative to getting married by the local magistrate or an ordinary minister or priest. I attended the wedding of two former Roman Catholics. We stood on the banks of Brooks Branch, upstream from the culvert, with twenty or thirty people in jeans, tie-dye dresses, sandals, and T-shirts. The parents of the couple wore coats and ties and dresses. Nicholas gave a short talk about becoming one with each other and nature and the universe, then chanted the syllables of a Buddhist *sutra*. When he pronounced the couple man and wife, their friends cheered and their parents looked as if they had just survived an exorcism.

Most of the buyers were paying Saralyn, Inc. on time. Even had I known how to do a credit check, the idea repelled me. Saralyn was a new life and I didn't want to look into past lives. I believed in contracts, however. They were written in the clumsy but unforgiving language of law. A legal document is like a collection of clamps and vices, each holding a single proposition in place. The language of literature flirts and suggests. It invites abuse and even rape. Even in those days, when I still wanted to be a poet, I understood that clear contracts full of details could fix responsibility in a way circumstance or convenience could not change. Although Saralyn was paying all its bills, most of its profits still existed in the promissory notes that financed the homesteads. O.K. Pettigrew's clients could foreclose on the company and on the people who owed the company if we missed a payment. Our buyers had to trust us to make those payments. Saralyn had to trust the buyer's regular payment. The contract, among other things, said we understood this situation. It also said that if Saralyn defaulted, the buyer could pay off O.K.'s clients and be free and clear. If the buyer defaulted, he or she agreed that Saralyn could take back the home site.

I was practicing what is now a fashionable cure for underdeveloped countries—microfinance lending, small short-term loans to people whom commercial lenders don't trust. The money they sent in each month began paying off Saralyn's own debt and soon we were ahead of the company's own mortgage payments and paying dividends to shareholders. I used my dividend to buy the thirty acres of Tract 30.

Once or twice I tried to think how I might spread the word in Pittsboro that real hippies didn't sign contracts and buy land. I had enough sense to know that people in Pittsboro would make up their own minds on what they saw in the next few years, not on what a newcomer told them. I was right about hippies, nevertheless. The real hippies of America were not buying land. The hippies who were not dependent on their city clans and neighborhoods were following the footsteps of Thoreau, wandering in nature as they pleased or living in communes. Many of Thoreau's friends joined the brief-lived communes of Brook Farm or Fruitlands, but Thoreau at twenty-four turned down the invitation to join Brook Farm. "As for these communities," he wrote, "I think I had rather keep bachelor's hall in hell than go to board in heaven."

Thoreau scorned attachment to a piece of property with equal disdain. Property was only the rope that bound a person to society and all the obedience of mind and body it demanded from its members. Ownership was a creation of government and commerce that imprisoned the owner in taxes and labor and debt. Thoreau heaped scorn on farmers who struggled to make a living from their land and on homeowners who had to dust and clean and make repairs. Like the monk in his cell, or the Indian fakir, Thoreau wanted to be free from all obligations. Maybe this was why he never married. He was the embodiment of a man committed to his own self-interest, his own education, his own pleasures. Perhaps he really wanted to be free from his own temptations. He was, after all, a Harvard graduate, son of a middle-class pencil manufacturer; he never lacked funds for trekking and canoeing, and surrounded himself with wealthy friends. In *Walden*, he never mentions that to build his cabin he borrowed the land owned by his rich friend, Ralph Waldo Emerson. As a rebel against the society that made him and sustained him, Thoreau was the first hippie.

Thoreau was fortunate to have lived when a great part of the New England he never left was uninhabited and when private landowners seldom worried about occasional travelers crossing their forests or farms. Thoreau never intended or wanted to live in the wilderness. If he had, I like to think he would have quickly recognized the necessity of owning it.

I started my own building four years after Theresa became the first resident and two years after people had reached the ends of the road that went east and the road that went north from my first road. The fork of two creeks that formed Morgan Branch was still half a mile from the end of the north road and from the nearest neighbor, Susan and her herd of goats.

The land I bought was a long north-south rectangle on the surveyor's map, but two small streams met within it, tumbling through the dark shade of beech trees. When I had risen out of that stream, shivering near the end of a hot summer day, the place had taken more than the heat of my body. Whatever it had kept, I was now buying back.

—*part two*—

Settling In

–chapter 12–

Orientation: Life

I make an informal list of the life around the site of my house. The inventory tells me that the most important part of my environment will be my own ignorance.

In the first week of my freshman year at Duke University, history professor Harold Parker began our seminar by asking each of us to put a penny on the table. Parker's thin mouth always smiled slightly and kindly when he asked us to think about something whose significance only he knew. His eyes searched the table, reading our reactions. He was a slightly stooped little man with a faint halo of gray hair around a bare scalp. Among intellects, his was the unchallenged giant. We put our pennies on the seminar table. "Imagine you are a traveler from Mars," he said, "and you have arrived at a deserted place on earth. You have heard nothing about human beings. You don't even know there is life on earth. You find this penny. List all the things this penny might tell you about its origin, the planet, and any possible inhabitants."

I remembered this exercise one early spring morning in 1973 as I stood by the beech tree on the slope above Morgan Branch, the spot I had chosen for my house. In Parker's story, we assumed the Martians would find out how accurately they had inferred a society of humans from a single artifact. As I stood near the beech tree, I contemplated the silent land around me and realized that I would never find the forces that had created this valley, nurtured the ferns along the creek, or the tree. I paused a half-hour, maybe an hour, to look at everything, to consider the evidence of events long passed. What I was about to do would destroy that evidence forever.

An hour earlier, I had driven my pickup to the end of the north road and up a rough drive to the broad flat top of a hill where Susan the goatherd and Jason the electrician camped on their building site. This point was the highest land in the northern sector of Saralyn, and I thought I could find a route from here that was downhill all the way to Morgan Branch.

I unloaded the wheelbarrow I used for hauling dirt and mixing cement. I loaded the barrow with tools for clearing brush and trees, for planting and digging. I also had a dozen fruit trees I had bought from the farm store—a few apples, two plums, two walnuts, and two peaches.

A week earlier, I had set out from the same spot, armed with a bush ax and a roll of red surveyor's ribbon, I had followed the gentlest slope of the land north toward Morgan Branch. I saw myself as a small creature moving through deepest shade, yet I knew I could summon forces far mightier than these trees if I chose. But I chose instead to use as little force as possible in finding the path to my future house. As well as making a statement about how I intended to live in this forest, I was doing penance for the havoc I had created in building the first section of road.

I moved a few large rocks, cut brush here and there, and picked a path around several fallen trees. I could have cut them out of the way with a chain saw, but those trees were not garbage or corpses. They still worked and produced, their actions beyond human notice. The reunion of a dead oak with the soil its seed sprang from is a thirty- or forty-year act of fusion. What I did not have to disturb, I didn't disturb.

Toward Morgan Branch, the slope broke into several broad tongues with sharp creases between them. With a couple of exploratory forays I found the tongue of land that halted abruptly across the creek from the large beech tree.

Making the path was easier than pushing the loaded wheelbarrow half a mile through the forest. A wheelbarrow is the most maneuverable of all rolling tools, but it demands that the user carry half the weight. The barrow bumped over roots and small rocks, tools clattering in the metal pan. I held the barrow back on the final descent to the creek; from there I carried the tools up the other side. I cleared the leaves and brush from a small spot so that I could set down the tools without losing them. I stood there, a stake in one hand and a sledgehammer in the other, and remembered Dr. Parker's seminar exercise.

The hillside I stood on was like the penny I had put on the seminar table. What could it tell me about the forces that had created it? What should I know before I disturbed the evidence? The longer I looked the more I saw. Even the small rectangle I intended to clear and excavate for my foundations was a living museum.

To most human beings, a good forest means big trees. If people look for anything, it is an animal in flight. The human eye responds to big patterns, bright colors, motion. I have often gone walking with friends who can spot deer or birds but stride across box turtles, step on mushrooms, and saunter by copperheads. Now and then a visitor plunges knee-deep into the hole left by a rotted stump. The cultures of cities, laboratories, rain forests, or ice age plains teach the eye to alert the brain to other data the way we can teach a dog to take an interest in marijuana or a truffle. I love wild mushrooms, and I occasionally walk in the woods with a young friend who is an ornithologist. I spot all the interesting things she walks over. She spots all the interesting things I walk under.

My natural inclinations are the same as humanity's in general. I notice first the big, the bright, and the moving. The big beech with its pale gray bark and spreading crown drew me to the hillside I was about to dig into. This tree had claimed and held its place with the other dominants, the tall trees—red oak, white oak, hickory. I saw no stumps. If the hillside had ever been cut before, the last time was more than a century past. When I noted the four varieties of big trees around me, I was suddenly aware that I was standing in one of the world's great food factories. All four were nut trees: red and white oaks producing acorns, hickories with their leather-jacketed nuts, and beeches raining small three-sided nuts.

Setting a house near a beech tree evoked a certain irony and maybe a degree of protection. The irony arises from "beech," which derives from the Old English word for a written document, *boc*. In Dutch, it is *boek*; and in Russian, the word for beech is pronounced *book*. Ancient Saxons and Germans carved runic characters in the smooth fine-grained wood. The smooth bark heals its wounds by growing a raised corky scar tissue. Around the world, beech bark bears names, dates, and history, sometimes across centuries. In *As You Like It*, Shakespeare's Orlando wanders through the Forest of Arden and says to his beloved:

O Rosalind! These trees shall be my books,
and in their barks my thoughts I'll character.

On the Presidents' Tree in Takoma Park, Maryland a Union soldier named Samuel Fenton carved the names of the presidents from George Washington to Andrew Johnson, and signed his work. One of the most famous American inscriptions lasted 156 years on a beech tree by the stage road from Blountsville to Jonesboro, Tennessee: "D. Boone Cilled A Bar On Tree In Year 1760." When the tree fell in 1916, the Forest Service estimated that the seventy-foot-high and twenty-eight-foot-diameter tree was 365 years old.

I was glad that the beech I stood by, and every other beech on the land around me, presented a blank book. I might write about them, but I would prefer to read their bark, their roots, and their branches for the history of the land and their own lives.

I felt about these old beech trees the way a friend's father had felt in the 1920s after working with the Russian dramatist Bulgakov. As much as he admired Bulgakov's willingness to stand up to Stalin, it was the discovery of the dramatist's love affair with the poet Anna Akhmatova that touched him; he had cried when he realized he knew a man who had loved this beautiful and unbreakable woman. The beech by my house site, with others along the creek, had once sustained the most awesome population of birds in America. The forest I was about to live in sheltered other admirable ghosts, too.

When the beech trees were roosts, they had provided the favorite food of the extinct passenger pigeon. The passenger pigeons arrived in flocks so large that they darkened the skies. In 1810, Alexander Wilson, a Philadelphia naturalist making observations for a book on American birds, carefully estimated a flock in Kentucky at over two billion strong. The last pigeon, named Martha, died in 1914 in the Cincinnati Zoo. The pigeon's death is cited endlessly as evidence of human stupidity. Extinctions are irretrievable losses, and humanity made an unnecessary choice, but there is another side to this story.

The forest of oak and beech I had come to live in had to be different from a forest favored by passenger pigeons. In the early 1700s, John Lawson saw them near here and wrote:

I saw such prodigious Flocks of these Pigeons in January or February, 1701–2, . . . that they had broke down the Limbs of a great many large Trees all over those Woods. . . . they clear all before them, scarce leaving one Acorn upon the Ground, which would, doubtless, be a great Prejudice to the Planters that should seat there, because their Swine would be thereby deprived of their Mast.

Alert Indians could protect their usually small fields from the pigeons, but colonists, whose croplands stretched farther than Indian fields, tried to fatten their pigs on the forest nuts. I do not justify the extinction of any animal, but in a way the settlers' battle with pigeons represented species competing against species: Each fought for its own urgent needs.

When I lived in England as a graduate student, I was surprised by the many people whose most intimate companion was a "budgie," or budgerigar (parakeet). The English who sailed to the seventeenth-century Carolinas detested parakeets. The Carolina parakeet, with its bright red-and-yellow head, had evolved to harvest seeds from the bottomland sycamores. This bird also loved fruit. John Lawson wrote in his merciless record of competition: "They visit us first when Mulberries are ripe, which Fruit they love extremely. They peck the Apples to eat the Kernels, so that the Fruit rots and perishes. They are mischievous to Orchards."

Piedmont farmers have never been rich, and in the last century, only home-grown crops stood between poor farm families and malnutrition, crippling diseases, and even starvation. Farmers killed passenger pigeons and parakeets as mercilessly as Indians had hunted out the last mammoths and camels, or as wolves will tear apart the last deer or moose in their region. I am grieved that I will never see a passenger pigeon or a Carolina parakeet, but as sorry as I am, I cannot condemn humanity for acting out of necessity, even though later generations have seen those actions as a mistake.

Many afternoons, when I took a break from my digging and building, I would walk up Morgan Branch and admire the beeches and think about passenger pigeons roosting in these trees. The imagined presence of the birds sufficed. Pigeons would not break the branches of my beeches, or steal nuts from turkeys and deer, or surround my house with an inch-deep snow of dung. I was happy to settle for the mourning dove, the pigeon's cousin, who cooed sadly and scratched in the dry leaves for beechnuts. Mourning doves live at Morgan Branch, one, two, or three pairs at a time.

The surviving beech by my house site may have protected my life if there is any truth to the old belief that beeches are lightning trees. Do they actually keep away lightning as some country people claimed? I have never seen a lightning-stricken beech. I can walk through these woods and see pine, poplar, oak, and hickory with tops blasted apart, their trunks reduced to splinters or scarred with narrow wounds ten to thirty feet long where lightning has split them open and their sap has boiled out.

If beeches do not attract lightning, the reason may be the oils beneath their bark. These are the same oils that were once used as a soothing syrup for the cough of tuberculosis. The oil in the nuts gave Beech-Nut Gum and Beechnut Coffee their distinctive flavors.

Every time I came to Morgan Branch, I took a short walk in a new direction. Sylvan was a good walker and a good learner. From the day she came home from the hospital with Sarah, I had spoken Spanish with her. I wanted her to be bilingual like my friends among the immigrant kids on Long Island. I was turning the remnants of my high school Spanish into a usable language, and together we learned the Spanish names for trees and plants, insects and birds. Sylvan developed an especially good eye for mushrooms. In the spring after her third birthday, she found the first morel I had seen in North Carolina, a small cone-shaped, crinkled brown mushroom nesting in brown leaves.

On every walk I came to know my neighborhood better. I had seldom seen woods in this part of the state with larger red and white oaks and hickories. With the exception of two or three beech stands on Morgan Branch, this was not virgin forest, or even true old growth, but it was close.

Sometimes I would lie on my back for a few minutes and look up to the interlacing top branches of the big trees. I looked through a dark shade. Had I been flying above the forest, I would have looked down upon a sun-bathed green sea. Because the sun supplies almost all energy that supports life on land, the difference between the light above the canopy and the light below roughly equals the amount of energy the big trees grab for themselves. Above my head, hundreds of thousands of leaves were trapping solar energy for photosynthesis. The dim light that struggles through is what's left for every other plant and animal in the forest. A second level of trees reaches up to trap this remaining light; because these trees reach for the light where it is brightest, they do not grow in straight columns. The trees of the understory fight with each other for scraps of light. I saw myself becoming part of that understory. The life I would lead beneath the big trees would be a short story compared to the lives behind them and ahead of them. I would live about as long as a dogwood, a black birch, or a sourwood. I was a typical understory tree.

On the hills around Morgan Branch, skinny dogwood ruled the understory. Dogwood grows in shade with a slow perseverance. Every spring in the old forest by Morgan Branch, the white petals of dogwood float like a blizzard of great flakes arrested in motion ten to twenty feet from the ground. In earlier times, the dogwood's flowering signaled planting season to Indians. Sourwoods with their deeply checkered bark and elbowed limbs grew at sharp angles as if they had been broken and redirected in their search for light. Black birch or cherry birch grows straighter but smaller. When I finished lunch at Morgan Branch, I often picked a twig of black birch and chewed its end into a stiff frayed toothbrush, the bitter flavor better than any after-dinner mint.

The dim light that filtered through canopy and undergrowth at Morgan Branch glowed green. In this light I have often felt that I was living on the bottom of a green ocean. In the forest as in the ocean, the great engines of life work near the sunny surface. Life at the bottom of the ocean and the forest must survive on what is passed down. Nevertheless, the soft, slightly tinted light below great trees has moved many writers and visitors to see old-growth forests as sacred places, like cathedrals.

My first task at Morgan Branch was to plant those fruit trees. I walked up and down Morgan Branch. I crisscrossed the hills on both sides, but I could not find any spot where sunlight came in for more than an hour or two each day. I planted the walnut trees in the rich soil by the creek, next to a flat area where I had planned a garden. I found a few soft mounds of soil on a hill across from the house site and planted a tree in each mound. That would do for winter. In the spring, I would have to move them or cut big trees to make a hole in the roof of the forest. It seemed everything a human being wanted meant cutting big trees.

Fortunately for wild animals, the forest's dominant trees share what they produce from sunlight, and they can be made to share. High in the trees where bees and other insects gather pollen, nectar, and each other, I might have heard a black-throated warbler or golden-crowned kinglet. I couldn't mistake the loud *Figaro, Figaro, Figaro* cry of the Carolina wren. Under the beech trees lay a matting of the pea-sized spiny three-petalled husks from which squirrels, mice, and chipmunks had harvested the nuts. Among the leaves, scatterings of hickory nuts and acorns fed mice, squirrels, turkey, and deer, all dependent upon the rise and fall of the forest's nut crops. As animal populations themselves rise and fall, so do the numbers of ticks, along with the possibility that a human passing through will contract Lyme disease or Rocky Mountain spotted fever.

The leaves, twigs, and dead limbs around me were also food. They fed insects, worms, and other orders of small animals, as well as fungi and bacteria. I rolled a fallen limb and watched the inevitable legions of soft white termites as they recycled large and small trees, the cellulose, in turn, feeding the organisms deep in their guts that aided digestion. I peeled the bark from a rotting limb and uncovered a jet-black carpenter beetle as long as my thumb carving a gallery in the pulpy wood. I turned over a large rock. Red ants panicked and picked up their oval sacks of ant bread to hide again. Had I turned over a few more rocks, I might have found a black widow and probably a six-inch-long ring-neck snake.

Yet the leaves that fall at the end of summer's shade always rise again for another summer. In the first wet days of fall or under the snow, they lie plastered against the earth. New life pushes them aside or grows through them. As fungi, bacteria, and invertebrates break down the leaves and twigs and transform them into their component chemicals, the leaves start their journey through the soil. Most of them percolate down through the darkness, past new life rising. When roots find them, perhaps their own, they rise again. The leaves that shaded me as I prepared the land beneath them for my house gave me recycled shade. I didn't know who had enjoyed their shade in the past or whether I would live beneath them the next time they rose.

Every time I went into the woods at Morgan Branch, I was aware of this great rising and falling, the circling of life. When Sylvan went with me, I sometimes watched as she played with rocks or studied an ants' nest or drew pictures on scrap paper. At thirty-four, I was already declining; but Sylvan was rising. I knew that when she was my age she would remember almost nothing from these days. What did I remember? My grandmother singing the Tom Thumb nursery rhyme about the little man who killed the little duck. I remembered the green park across the street from her house and in it the live ducks. I told Sylvan as much about the forest and its life as I thought would interest her. We sat together and watched birds and frogs and snakes and crayfish and examined flowers and smelled the root beer smell of wild ginger. I knew she would not remember the days, the events, or any single animal or plant, but I also knew that almost everything we are capable of loving deeply, everything that is most comfortable and familiar, is something we cannot remember meeting the for first time.

Among the things I showed Sylvan was death. She found a dead fox lying by the creek one day, the white bone just beginning to emerge through the rotting pelt. I explained to her what was happening. I showed her the beetles and maggots that were making their living from the fox. We poked through the life in rotting logs. I pried apart the pellets of owls and showed her the pieces of bone and the hairs of animals that had kept the owls and their chicks alive.

The education I started for Sylvan was as important as the education Sarah was then getting. Sarah had decided to have a professional career, and she was in the second year of law school. Sylvan was in her first year of natural law school. She could study unchangeable laws at Morgan Branch. Neither Sarah nor I went to church, and I knew that Sylvan would grow up without the comfortable sense that beyond death lay Heaven. The best I could do was to be sure that she understood that life leads on to life.

I have never thought about this cycle without reconfirming the logic of my wish to be buried in an easily rotted cardboard box and above me, ready to send its roots downward, a black walnut or the acorn of a white oak. It's the closest I'll come to resurrection.

chapter 13

Orientation: The Land

I lose my job at the university, my marriage ends,
I discover lost continents, and start my house.

The beech trees and the rocks pushing out of the hillside could have told me something important about my house site, but I didn't have the experience to read their signs. I had made a few plans for the house above the ground but none for anything below ground. The beech tree stood on the south-facing slope about twenty feet above Morgan Branch and I decided to drive the stakes for the first two corners about ten feet farther up where the slope became more gradual. This downhill foundation wall would be eight feet high above the ground. The uphill or north foundation wall would be about four feet high. In the downhill area, I planned to level the ground behind the wall for a long and narrow shop.

I gave the first stake a few taps with the sledgehammer to steady it. The first hard whack drove it against hidden rock. I moved it a foot. It struck another rock. With a little work, I drove in the three stakes that defined this first corner. I nailed horizontal batter boards between them to form an L. One board faced uphill, the other across the hill. I tapped a small nail in one board, looped the end of my tape measure over it, and measured across the face of the hillside to the west corner. The beech tree would stand before the center of the house. The floor of the house would be eight feet above the ground and almost ten feet higher than the base of the beech tree. I would be elevating myself into the understory.

I hit rock again and again staking out the southwest corner of the house. The two uphill corners offered no rock. Now each corner had three stakes joined by batter boards making an L. I tied taut strings from the batter boards in each corner across the hill and up and down. I would lay the real corners of the foundation below the points where the east-west strings crossed the north-south strings.

In this part of the South, *foundation* does not mean digging as deep as northern climate requires. In the bitterest winters our soil freezes no deeper than one foot. At that level, foundations are safe from the possibility that thawing earth will turn to mush and sink under the weight of the house or that ice will move the foundations. In New England or Montana, the bottom of a foundation, or the footing, may have to go eight or ten feet underground. I was planning on eighteen inches deep and eighteen inches wide.

When someone comes to the southern piedmont for the first time, the redness of the soil shocks the eye. The soil is not the red of the flag or any rose, but closer to the red of freshly rusted iron. It is iron that makes the earth red.

The beech tree should have warned me that below the soil I would not find red clay but massive rock and hard digging. The rocks beneath this hillside were just what a beech tree needs. Beeches have high and spreading crowns heavy with leaves and nuts in summertime, and heavy with water. A strong wind has a lot of beech tree to push on. The surface area that wind pushes on is much greater than that of a racing yacht's sails. People and animals have jointed bodies so they can bend. Trees have no joints because their survival depends upon standing up to support the huge weight of their solar power–gathering crowns. Above all, trees like this must stay firmly anchored. The rock on hillsides and along streams are among the best anchors a tree can find, and beech-tree roots have adapted better than most others to growing around jutting rocks and sending finer roots deep into cracks and crevices. Years later, I would find out how important that difference among trees and roots can be to both the trees and anyone who lives in them, under them, or beside them.

I had dug only a few minutes and a few inches when my shovel struck the top of something its blows did not even shiver. I took the heavy pick and stabbed down through the dirt. I shoveled away around the object. The reddish brown rock had a squarish top but its sloped sides disappeared into the earth. It was either a boulder or bedrock. I could see a fine crack running into it. I moved up to the most powerful tool in my barrow, a six-foot-long steel pry bar made from the unbending metal of a truck axle. It weighed forty pounds and had a sharpened broad point at one end. I started slamming this weapon at the crack in the rock. After a while, it bit in and the crack started to widen. I pried and felt a large section of rock break free. When I lifted the slab out of the ground, its freshly split face was not brown but a blue-green. The rock was pitted, grainy, and dark gray lumps pressed into the lighter blue. This was tufa, ash from a volcano that had been cemented together under great pressure for millions of years. I had discovered a lost continent.

The closest volcanoes to North Carolina are in the Caribbean, Mexico, and the Pacific Northwest. When I had dug out a few angular blocks of this gray-blue rock, and as I wrestled with it day after day, I sensed my real address. It was not an address the post office would recognize; it had no importance to anyone but me. Most addresses serve the limited but useful purpose of getting mail to our homes or of guiding visitors, delivery trucks, and good people who are always ready to rescue us from fire or heart attack. As useful as these addresses are, they say nothing about our place in the universe or eternity.

To say that I had chosen to build my house at Morgan Branch, Chatham County, North Carolina, is to give only the smallest end of a long address. My real address was created long ago on a continent at the bottom of the earth.

Over a billion years ago, the longest-lived continent on earth encompassed the South Pole when it began to break up. The rest of the earth was then truly "without form and void." Life on the continent of Rodinia, if it had any, would have consisted of soft one-celled organisms. With a certain unconscious arrogance we think of that time as the youth of the earth. The three or four billion years before the breakup of Rodinia represent most of Earth's history. Another billion years would pass before today's continents took their present places on the Earth's face. The history of human beings in North America starts mere seconds ago in geological time. My wheelbarrow and tools arrived at Morgan Creek only a nanosecond ago in this scale of things. The event was important only to me, a dust mite in the fabric of the universe.

What forces cracked Rodinia into smaller continents geologists don't know, but it happened more or less in Biblical fashion: "Let there be a firmament in the midst of the waters, and let it separate the waters from the waters." Great chunks of Rodinia started their drift north. Over the next

500 million years, a chunk called Laurentia moved north to the equator while other pieces of Rodinia moving north crashed into each other and fused into the new giant continent of Gondwanaland. In that giant were today's Africa, Australia, South America, India, and Antarctica. The land I had attacked with my pick and bar and sledge rose above the primeval waters of earth as a ridge of volcanoes blasting poisonous gases, ash, and lava into the ancient atmosphere. This was the island continent, Taconia, which moved north through the Iapetus Ocean in the wake of Laurentia. Soon Taconia had fused itself to Laurentia. A few hundred million years later the fused mass would be renamed for an Italian mapmaker, Amerigo Vespucci.

I had made a mental calculation that digging the trenches for the footings would take five days of labor, one for each of four walls, another for a footing along the center, which would support the back wall of the basement shop. I planned to level the floor area inside the shop later. After wrestling that first slab of rock out of the earth, I decided to rake the leaves away from the entire footing and probe for rock. The lowest footing and the two running up the hill had rocks everywhere. The top footing had few. I could move the site uphill, to more level ground and deeper soils, but I would have to dig a place for the shop. I would also be that much farther from my beech and the sound of creek water falling across the ribs of Taconia.

I went back to the first corner and resumed digging. It was a typical late-twentieth century housing decision. I chose a location for the beauty of the place, not from practical reasons. I had seen the foundation stones and chimneys of hundreds of houses built in this region before the middle of this century. Not one of them is built on the side of a hill. I approached building with the attitude, inspired by Thoreau, that infected my generation:

> Practically, the old have no very important advice to give the young, their own experience has been so partial, and their lives have been such miserable failures . . . I have lived some thirty years on this planet, and I have yet to hear the first syllable of valuable or even earnest advice from my seniors. They have told me nothing, and probably cannot tell me anything, to the purpose. Here is life, an experiment to a great extent untried by me; but it does not avail me that they have tried it.

There it is, a big strand of the genetic code of 1970s counterculture—life as an experiment to remedy the failures of an older generation corrupted by tradition and greed. Yippie leader Jerry Rubin wrote: "The pre–1950s gen-eration has *nothing* to teach the *post*–1950s."

In the spring of 1974 when I started digging, my students at the univer-sity and activists across America were repeating a slogan that came from the Free Speech Movement in Berkeley: "Don't trust anyone over thirty."

I knew my insistence on digging those footings into the ancient rock of Taconia was a sentence to weeks of hard labor. I felt about hard labor the way Br'er Rabbit felt about being thrown into the briar patch: It was my es-cape. In February of 1974 I knew I would lose two dreams; only hard labor could convince me that I was building a new one.

In January, I had begun my last semester as an English professor. The de-partment had denied me tenure. I had published more work than many of my older colleagues had, including scholarly articles, poems and short sto-ries in respected magazines, and dozens of newspaper articles. I had no spe-cialty. I had published two English texts for freshmen, but texts don't count as scholarship. I was actively working with the high school English teach-ers' association to improve the teaching of writing, but I was also encourag-ing them to demand a lighter workload so they would have time to read students' papers. On a committee of three, I rewrote the freshman writing curriculum, but a distinguished full professor called it anarchic and social-istic because it recommended a "happening" in class to illustrate how the writer makes order from chaos.

Maybe I had attracted too much of the wrong publicity. When the *Durham Herald* wrote its article on the poet developer, it quoted me, "If you do nothing but academic work, you're dead. I couldn't write or teach if I did nothing else." Michael would have called that "sticking it in their faces."

Students protested when they heard that the full professors had denied me tenure. The department chairman, a soft-spoken civil libertarian whom I have always liked, met with them and told them the official reason. The department, he said, had no position for a generalist. I did not argue with that decision. I had given them this petard on which to hoist me in the routine letter young professors send to the chair of the tenure committee. I said I had deliberately established a record as a generalist instead of a spe-cialist: "I consider the role of the true generalist to be legitimate. . . I feel there is great value in it for me as a teacher. . . I would have it no other way." They decided on that basis not to have me.

I believed then and I believe now that part of academic freedom is the right of established faculty to pass judgment on the quality of would-be professors and to determine whose abilities best serve the institution. As long as their criteria do not include race, sex, age, and other destructive prejudices, they should enjoy the same privileges as churches, charities, and corporate boards. That is what I told some of my best students, who wanted to take the issue to the administration. Except for a few occasions when my bank account bumped along for months with less than a hundred dollars, I have never coveted tenure in civil service or academia. The only tenure I have needed is a clear mind, good health, and sound title to my land.

The second dream I lost in the new year cut much deeper. My marriage ended. Sarah of Saralyn was finishing her last semester in law school. We had no fights, no other lovers, no great moral differences. In a different time or place maybe we would have stayed together. In the 1970s, people like us, who often condemned greed and selfishness in other parts of society, were quick to discount the consequences to family or community of breaking up marriages to follow personal passions. It was the time of "I'm Okay, You're Okay," and "do your own thing." Divorce seemed orderly and conservative compared to the highly publicized (but relatively rare) practices of communal living, open marriages, and live-in partners. None of that made our separation and divorce less painful. Marriage begins with a promise and can only end with the breaking of a promise. Yes, the promise is between two people, and perhaps it is dissolved if both agree, but it is a promise created by a society. The two people speak it in the presence of family and friends. Marriage is a promise shared with other people. It is an institution created not only for those who speak the vows but for the larger community.

In my personal life, as a writer, and in business, I had always thought the ability to keep a promise was an essential measure of human quality. The best rationalization I could offer was that with my academic career ending and my writing little more than unconnected pieces, I faced an impossible choice. I was caught between what I thought I must be and what I was.

What I was and what I possessed should have sufficed for most of the world. To anyone who cared to look, I had an intelligent and attractive wife, a fine four-year-old daughter, an interesting old farmhouse, and a few acres of land. I had all that, but what I didn't have taunted me: I could no longer teach. A novel I had written brought nice words but no contracts.

A promising young producer named Tony Bill had asked my agent for the chance to read my novel for his division of Warner Brothers. Then he almost killed himself in a motorcycle accident and we heard no more.

The old farmhouse demanded endless attention to its decay. The land itself demanded even more time—to cut brush from around the pond, prune the apples, spray the peaches, cut the pasture, weed the crops, thin the old raspberry canes, mow the big lawn.

I saw myself as Thoreau saw his neighbors:

The twelve labors of Hercules were trifling in comparison with those which my neighbors have undertaken; for they were only twelve and had an end; but I could never see that these men slew or captured any monster or finished any labor. . . . I see young men, my townsmen, whose misfortune it is to have inherited farms, houses, barns, cattle and farming tools; for these are more easily acquired than got rid of.

Perhaps because I came from a family that never had much and because I wasn't faring much better, I was ready to believe Thoreau's famous prescription, "None can be an impartial or wise observer of human life but from the vantage ground of what *we* should call voluntary poverty."

Life-changing decisions have no end of ifs and buts to be thought about. Most of us think about them too little before and too much after making decisions. Other things contributed to the end of our family, but a well-known piece of advice from a modern Polonius is a reasonable summary: "Follow your bliss," anthropologist Joseph Campbell told Bill Moyers on national television, and Moyers dwelt on it over and over with great reverence. It's not much more mature than Jerry Rubin's radical egotism, "Do it," or "Do your own thing." I was sure some experience essential to healing old wounds, correcting old deformities of character, and producing lasting happiness was slipping away. I had to do my own thing, just do it, or I would never be able to follow my own bliss.

If I abandoned my own bliss, I would not be worth being married to, but maybe that was a selfish rationalization. I had good reason to expect the worst. I had watched my own parents' marriage disintegrate into alternate shouting matches and stone cold silences. My mother overdosed on pills. When she came out of the asylum after electric-shock therapy, her marriage was doomed to nine years of bickering. My two brothers and I fought hard not to get sucked in by becoming the confidants of one against the other.

I had good hiding places. A gruff old waiter who ran a used bookstore in the afternoons and evenings hired me to build shelves and type file cards and learn his business. He talked to me like another man, and he gave me any book I looked at for more than ten minutes. One was Schopenhauer's *Studies in Pessimism*. I also hid in the Eighteen Trails, a wooded bluff above the harbor. Sea Cliff had only a few hundred yards of sandy bathing beach and a mile where the bluffs came down to the water behind old timber bulkheads and rows of boulders. Before sunrise and after sunset, I could hide on this stretch of beach. I cracked open red hematite stones to find fossil willow leaves and dug in the black mud for fishing worms and soft shell or long neck clams. (We called them piss clams.) As soon as I could take out a boat on my own, I escaped onto the water, and into the water whenever it was warm enough to swim, spear fish, or dive for clams.

A friend on Long Island who had come to visit Sarah and me saw part of the problem and warned me in a letter:

You seem driven—not by time, but by your own demands on yourself, your work. I wished you could relax, knowing quite well that one side of your nature makes that very hard for you, but also knowing that you can very well do it. In fact that another side of you is longing to do so. Why don't you try? I'm afraid that you don't give yourself any time for joy. This faculty (being able to enjoy) is after all the best gift given to us. You have yourself, your family, friends, your land, your work, but you don't give yourself a chance to enjoy it really. Try it once in a while. It's the best source of strength.

I replied that this was the right advice at the wrong time. I would relax when my work bore fruit. I don't know if my trips to the woods along Morgan Branch grew more frequent before or after I recognized that Sarah did not want my work to drive her, too. A dangerous silence grew in our marriage. I think it was the week in February 1974 when Sarah left with our daughter that I drove the stakes in the ground by Morgan Branch.

Sarah and I did not easily divide our lives, but we easily divided our property. That demonstrated the different bliss we wanted from life. For seven years we had been living in the old farmhouse surrounded by lawn and gardens and pastures, with a couple of barns and an acre of pond. The twenty acres was only six miles from Chapel Hill and its value had begun to soar. We had no argument at all—she kept that house and land and the farm equipment, and she let me have the woods at Saralyn. Because she had already rented a small house in Chapel Hill, she agreed that I could stay at the farmhouse until November.

Our friends, those who went beyond saying they were sorry, said they were glad we had handled it well. That was true, but I felt as though I had suffered an amputation and they were remarking on the color in my cheeks. I ached with the phantom pain an amputee feels in the missing limb for the pictures, the furniture, even the ducks. Sylvan spent days with me, days with Sarah. She passed back and forth, an unconscious emissary. No one could deny that our four-year-old would look like her mother. I promised myself I would not let her down.

I lived at the farmhouse as if it were a base camp for an expedition. Every weekend, every spare afternoon, and all spring I took a canteen of water and a couple of sandwiches and went to Morgan Branch. Each time I loaded tools into my wheelbarrow and made my way deep into the woods, I had the same feeling I had when I was a kid taking refuge from my parents in one of my hiding places. The house I was aiming at was like the elusive ideas in books or like fish at the bottom of the harbor; the rocks I uncovered were as important as new words I had learned or small strains or tugs on my fishing line. To build a house, I first had to wrestle with the remains of a 500-million-year-old continent.

Maybe I should have called the scene of this wrestling match Peni'el. This was the name that the Bible says was given to the place where Jacob wrestled all night with an angel. Jacob had sent his wives and children across the river Jabbock and was alone in the hill country of Gilead at night. In high school and college, I had been a wrestler, dogged but only half successful. In the two matches that I still remember, I conquered boys two or three weight classes heavier than I. This mass of rock was like one of those opponents.

I had expected rocks on this hillside, but I had not expected that almost every foot of the lower trench would be a contest. The first thing every wrestler needs is a handhold, and next, a point of leverage. I learned to uncover the rock and find its weaknesses. Where the rock seemed solid, often a few minutes work with the sledge or the forty-pound axle pry bar opened a hairline crack. Day after day I hammered, rammed, pried, and drove wedges. I pushed and lifted small chunks and great slabs of stone. My sweat and the soil covering the stone mixed and coated me in mud. At the end of the day, I would take off my clothes and lie in Morgan Branch where its cold water passed through a rock channel. I would lie there until the cold water chilled me. Then I got up and walked through the woods to my truck. I wished I did not have to come back, but I knew I would. I no longer had a wife waiting for me on the other side of the river, only an empty house, and that was on loan.

When the stranger in the Gilead hills could not defeat Jacob, he demanded to be released. Jacob said, "I will not let you go, unless you bless me." The rock rising from deep in the earth where I wanted my house could not defeat me, yet I knew I could never carve or hammer a trench eighteen inches deep in the rock. The angel touched Jacob on the inside of the thigh and made him lame. The tons of rock I moved for the house and later raised in a chimney and walls have done their damage to me. From my struggle with the rock of the earth I expected, and I have received, something like a Jacob's blessing at Peni'el. The name means "he struggles with God."

Sylvan often came with me. She wanted to work, too. She had a plastic shovel and a pail. She learned the names of tools, held boards, and acted as general gofer. When I rested after wrestling a particularly large piece of rock, we drank water sharpened with lemon juice or went to the creek to look for crayfish and salamanders hiding underneath rocks. As I worked, I made up stories about the forest and its animals. I told Sylvan what I knew about the birds we saw and heard, about the flowers she gathered, about the anole lizards that darted up trees or waited on limbs for insects. We sang in time to the digging, and Sylvan picked up chips of rock and threw them downhill. She was too young to understand volcanoes, plate tectonics, the metamorphosis of rock, or that she, one of the newest members of earth's newest species, was blithely throwing something through the air that had moved no more than inches in millions of years.

If we think of the 5-billion-year history of this rock as a single year, the human species appeared on earth only on December 30 of that year. On this scale, one hour is 36,000 years, a minute is 602 years, and Sylvan's life was less than half a second. My life was three seconds old. Sarah and I had lived together for just more than one second. Compared to the rock in my foundation, humans have the life span of a mosquito. Yet newcomers such as Sylvan and I, along with every other human gnat who has ever lived, have had the arrogance to rearrange the earth's own scheme. This is why environmentalists weep and why others praise the human spirit.

After a month of work with shovel, sledge, wedges, pick, and pry bar, I had separated tons of rock from the old continent below. My footing was not eighteen inches deep everywhere, but where it was shallower, the walls would rest on solid rock. As I worked, I sometimes humored myself by grunting a line of song:

House built on a rock foundation will not move, oh no!

Well, not in my little lifetime.

chapter 14

Dynamite

*After a month's labor with pick, pry bar, and rock
chisels, I turn to the poor man's bulldozer—dynamite. I learn this is not an art you should teach yourself and that the more power we have the more we
must learn to focus it on good results.*

Jacob wrestled with the angel only once. I would never again dig by hand
in the bedrock of Taconia. For chimney, walls, and planters I would dig
out, split, and carry many more stones, but at my own pace and without
deadline and in places I chose. If I had cleared a drive to the site, I could
have had a machine dig the footings. I could have driven my own truck to
Morgan Branch.

I would have preferred to do everything at Saralyn from main road to
house footings with hand tools. It seems fairer. One natural force against
another. Maybe it is just more macho. We are not stirred to praise bulldozers and backhoes but we cheer and swell with pride when we see a man
wrestle with angels. The heroes of American individualism and optimism
are figures like Paul Bunyan and John Henry. They are larger than humans,
but not supernatural. They use only hand tools. They were born like you
and me and received no special favors from divine powers. They are monu-
ments to real human effort.

I had another reason for the way I chose to work. Breaking ground and
laying a foundation by hand was the right way to appreciate the ground on

which my house would sit. Every day I loaded the wheelbarrow and started into the woods was like entering a church to say confession. I worked sometimes until I was desperate for water and barely had the will to walk out, but I always finished in a better mood than when I had I started. When the trenches were done and connected in the rectangle of the house, I knew I did not need to wrestle the angel again.

It was also clear to me that another match of this kind would end in my defeat.

The number three is to blame if three cubic yards of concrete sounds small. That is how much I calculated to fill my footings. Think of it another way. Each cubic yard is twenty-seven cubic feet. One cubic foot of water fills seven one-gallon jars. Carrying one cubic meter of water, sand, or concrete is the same as carrying 189 one-gallon jars. Three cubic meters would be 567 one-gallon jars. Concrete is made of cement, sand, and gravel. Each weighs more than water. When John Henry died driving more railroad spikes than a steam engine, witnesses chronicled his story. I did not intend to die anonymously trying to John Henry a dump truck. Time had come to clear the way for the internal combustion engine to reach Morgan Branch.

When Jason and Susan and their neighbors on the hilltop had opened a drive to their sites, for the first two hundred yards they had cleared brush and small trees from the trace of a wagon road. I could see that trace heading north, roughly parallel to the spring-fed trickle that first led me to Morgan Branch. It was a faint ribbon of flattish land between big trees. It had been worn or cut into the east flank of the long ridge that had served as the track for my wheelbarrow. Here and there a boulder bulged up into the trace. In a couple of places, the gathering creek had cut its channel within a few feet. The big trees on either side had shaded the trace for over a hundred years, and only dogwoods and sourwood understory and brush had taken hold to block the way. And in two places, the bedrock of the hillside protruded too far into the path or up from the ground to let even a truck pass.

I hired a small dozer to clear the brush, but the operator said he could do nothing with the big stone. I should get someone to blast it, he said. This wasn't mining territory and I could find no one who would come to Saralyn to blast two small outcroppings, not for money I could afford.

On the south side of the hilltop where Susan and Jason had set up camp, a registered nurse and her husband had reconstructed a log tobacco barn and added a kitchen on one side. In his late twenties, Ralph had already shed a few personas and was earning as much money as he needed as a plumber, but he aimed at earning his necessities from ferro-cement sculpture. He had spent his first two years as an undergraduate at Colorado's School of Mines in Golden. "Get yourself some dynamite and I'll show you how to use it," he said. Whether it was the benefits and safety of smoking pot, the future of ferro-cement, or the uses of dynamite, when Ralph was positive, he was absolutely positive.

I had to go to Southeastern Hardware some fifty miles away in Greensboro to buy dynamite. Southeastern serviced the farm and construction trades. Buying a few sticks or enough to blow up a pass through a mountain was simple. The salesman didn't ask if I knew what I was doing. He stuck a carbon sheet between two forms and asked my full name, height, and weight, and checked the box for white race. Where will it be used? What will it be used for? Where will it be stored? Finally, Have you ever been arrested? Used drugs or marijuana?

He disappeared into the back of the store and returned fifteen minutes later with a five-pound paper sack and some smaller bags—twenty sticks of dynamite, a bag full of caps, and a reel of tough orange fuse cord. The salesman suggested that I buy a few extra caps in case I lost some or had misfires. I said thirty ought to do for twenty sticks. He put the inch-long copper caps in one of the small bags. The foot-long sticks of dynamite wrapped in oily brown paper he laid in a box. "How much fuse do you want?" he asked. Ralph had told me fuse burned at two minutes per yard. I bought four minutes a stick, or sixty yards, an hour and twenty minutes' worth of fuse.

The salesman's only advice was to keep the caps separate from the dynamite. I put the caps in the glove compartment and the box of dynamite on the floor and drove home imagining the results of a crash. I was sure I was piloting a bomb.

I was also the beneficiary of a great labor-saving device, a synthesis of prehistoric fossils and modern chemistry. A century earlier, Alfred Nobel of Sweden had gathered the courage to continue experiments with the highly sensitive nitroglycerine that earlier researchers had abandoned. Nobel mixed the dangerous liquid with the microscopic skeletons of algae deposited in ancient sea floors millions of years ago to be transformed into diatomaceous earth. The combination made an easily handled solid explosive, dynamite. Within five years, Americans were using dynamite to blast the mile long Musconnetcong railroad tunnel in eastern Pennsylvania. Where New York City's East River joins Long Island Sound in the well-known Hell's Gate, most of the hell was removed on October 10, 1885, when a single blast of 289,000 tons of dynamite obliterated Flood Rock and other hazards.

The dynamite in my truck weighed no more than twenty pounds, and its safety had improved considerably since Nobel's invention. The technology performed flawlessly, but I did not.

I was in a hurry. I had promised to be out of the farmhouse by November. It was mid-May and I had done no more than dig a few trenches in the woods. At Harris and Farrell's General Store, where Sylvan and I bought ice cream and picked up the mail, I asked a few of the old men on the porch about the best way to blast out rock. One had seen this, another had heard that, but no one had actually used dynamite. Tuck Snipes said, "Throw a stick down a dry well and she'll blast open the seams in the rock."

One Saturday afternoon, Sylvan and I brought the dynamite to Ralph's house. Jason had dropped the transmission out of an old truck near the house and rolled out from under to say hello. Ralph had told me he would be home, but he might have been on marijuana time wherever he was. His wife, Kathleen, was working the day shift at the emergency room. As a calling card, I decided to blow out a big oak stump he had left on the far side of the one-acre field he and Kathleen had cleared. I also didn't want to set off my first blast with no one to help me out of trouble except Sylvan. She was perfectly happy and confident. She did not know what I did not know.

We took a stick of dynamite, a cap, and the roll of fuse cord to the stump. The weather had been hot and dry. I used a pick and a pry bar to dig a twelve-inch-wide hole slantwise down under the center of the stump; the hole was about two feet long. A friend who had demolitions training for Vietnam had told me that if I crimped the cap to the fuse with my teeth, macho fashion, I might lose my jaw. "Hold it behind your ass where you have the most padding." I carefully sliced the fuse cord nice and square for maximum contact inside the cap and slid it in tight against the powder. I held it behind me and squeezed gradually until I felt the cylinder give and bite on the fuse. I poked a small hole midway down the stick of dynamite, slid the fuse in, and taped the cord to the upper part of the stick. I now had the fuse fixed firmly in the explosive and a charge ready to go off. I slid the charge into the hole and carefully began to push dirt around it. When it was covered, I selected rocks to provide enough mass to keep the explosive force in the hole under the stump and filled the hole with them.

For my first ever explosion, I had cut six feet of fuse cord to make extra sure I had time to take cover. I told Sylvan to run across the field and tell Jason I was about to blow the charge and that they must both hide behind a big tree. When I saw Jason stand up and disappear with her behind a big oak, I set a match to the fuse. The sparks flew and smoke rose in a little ribbon. I ran to join Jason and Sylvan.

We stood behind the tree waiting. Minutes passed. Nothing happened.

"Damn," I said, "it didn't go off and I sure don't want to go dig it out."

Jason chuckled and shook his head. "I wouldn't either," he said.

The day erupted in a great noise. I heard gravel and rocks falling. I waited a few seconds and looked out. A cloud of dirt obscured the stump. Then I heard a loud crash of something on metal. Then silence. I looked at the chicken shed to one side of the garden; the roof was fine. I looked for other metal objects. A wheelbarrow and a wood shed near the house were fine. I looked at the roof of the house two stories up. Next to the chimney in the metal roof was a black hole the size of my head.

When I had dug the slanted hole under the stump, I had stood with my back to the house. The hard dry red clay hole two feet long, topped by more dirt and the heavy stump, was a fine barrel for a short cannon pointed at the house. The rocks I had loaded into the hole were the cannon balls. I had scored a direct hit on Ralph and Kathleen's roof. At the other end of the field the stump stood unmoved, unscarred.

Jason looked up at the roof and shrugged. Jason has shrugged off years of unexpected events. "I guess you have to do something different," he said. He looked up at the roof and laughed. I laughed. Sylvan laughed. The roof tin could be replaced.

We decided not to explode any more dynamite that day. I went to several used bookstores and found two useful and encouraging books from the DuPont company. The books described how to use the dynamite they sold under the ironic brand name, Red Cross Dynamite. The thin 1912 edition of *The Farmers' Handbook: How to Use Red Cross Dynamite* was a mix of instructions and testimonials that today might be called *Dynamite for Dummies*. The cover had a drawing of a red-roofed farmhouse sitting beside the curve of a country road amid deep green pastures. The lower third of the back cover could be torn off at the dotted line and sent to DuPont as a one-penny postcard: "If you want to take up agricultural blasting—cut out, fill in, and mail this card." The sender's message was already filled in: "Gentlemen—please explain how I may become an agricultural blaster and how you will help me secure work at blasting from farmers in my neighborhood."

This is the kind of booklet that helps someone in my situation feel the force of a noble tradition. Inside, dozens of letters testified that "French Prunes Do Well in Blasted Holes, Plant Six Hundred Acres for $6 an Acre, Dynamite Cheaper than Donkey Engine, and Dynamiting Highly Endorsed by Chief Moore of U.S. Weather Bureau." There were also headlines to whet the curiosity and imagination: "A Controversy Settled," and "Found That Dynamite Kills Fungus."

The back cover testimonial from Mr. Thomas H. Benton of Tennessee started with a passage I identified with: "My attention was first called to the agricultural uses of dynamite by a friend and neighbor. . . . I had no one to instruct me. . . ." Mr. Benton went on to put the Handbook's instructions into practice: "I am glad to say that Agricultural Blasting puts a man in touch with the very best people in the country."

The fifteenth edition of DuPont's *Blaster's Handbook* for 1958 reassured me that the stories of 1912 were no fluke. Most of this book was for people whose ambitions ran to major mining and tunneling projects, or maybe a new Panama Canal, but in the back I found just the set of instructions I should have read. Here I learned how to place charges for trees with spreading roots, and how to tamp the earth back in over the charge. (Always use a wooden tamper because a metal bar might strike a spark from a rock in the ground.) The safety instructions don't mention houses but do warn the reader to "make sure that all persons, animals, and vehicles are beyond the range of flying fragments." It adds, "Do not investigate a misfired shot for at least one hour." Also useful if you have curious pets or livestock is the advice, "Never leave dynamite or the paper from dynamite boxes where livestock can get at them—they may eat them with fatal results."

I found the method that would work best for me on page 445, the Mudcapping Method. I could lay one or more sticks of dynamite right on top of the exposed boulders in my drive covered with "a three- or four-inch layer of mud." In parentheses the writer added what I now knew from experience, "free from rocks and other material which might constitute a missile hazard."

Armed with the miracles of modern chemistry, I was ready to return to do battle with Taconia. So was Sylvan.

One afternoon, we wheelbarrowed my pick, pry bar, sledge, shovel, dynamite, and blasting caps through the brush that had grown up in the old wagon trace I wanted to clear. I took the tools first, the blasting materials on a second trip.

I chose a large boulder whose top protruded from the ground like a giant broad skull. Following the instructions from the books, I slit open two sticks of dynamite and reshaped the explosive in a mound over the top of the rock. I used the wrapping paper from the sticks as gloves to "prevent absorption of nitroglycerine by the pores." I was not sure whether the danger was toxic poisoning or exploding hands. I fitted a cap with a yard of fuse, inserted it into the mound of dynamite, and covered it with the wrapping paper. If one of Susan's goats happened to wander this way, it would find no paper to eat and she would be in no danger of a milking-time surprise.

At the creek below the boulder, Sylvan and I dug clay from the banks. I dug out two buckets that made a good eight-inch cover for the dynamite. If two sticks of dynamite had launched a head-sized rock thirty or forty feet in the air, I did not understand how a mere six inches of mud would direct the force of two sticks down into solid rock. DuPont was sure enough that it had been using the formula continuously from 1912 to 1958. I knew that Rachel Carson had accused the giant chemical companies of callous disregard for human health, but mistakes with dynamite would have been more noticeable than mistakes with DDT and other insecticides.

For shelter, I chose a beech tree a hundred yards away. Its trunk was wide enough to completely hide a human body from flying debris. I put Sylvan behind it and went down to the boulder and lit the fuse. I went back to the beech and put her between the trunk and me. The charge exploded. Stones whistled by the beech tree. We were safe from direct hit, but I had forgotten about ricochets. I scrunched Sylvan beneath me, my head over hers, her body inside the cage of my arms and knees. The stones crashed against other trees and fell into the dry leaves. Nothing hit us. Another lesson learned. "Can we go see?" Sylvan asked. I liked her attitude.

The boulder smelled of explosive. The blast had not destroyed it, but the force had broken off a few large pieces and cracked the top of the rock. I went to work on the cracks with my long pry bar and the sledge and soon wrestled the rock level with the ground. We loaded the tools in the wheel-barrow and headed for the next lump of Taconia.

Another week's work cleared the brush and small trees and revealed a relatively flat dirt ribbon between the small creek on the east and the foot of the low ridge that ran from Susan and Jason's to Morgan Branch. Farmers with horses and wagons had flattened this road in the last century. In one place, I could see an earlier route where the traffic had cut four feet into the soft earth before moving a few yards east to more solid ground. Eventually they found the most solid route, including that part where I had blasted rock. Having no gravel, they must have sunk in during heavy rains and in the winters, when freezing and thawing often turns dirt roads into muck a foot or two deep. Only the most pretentious towns had paved roads, and those plank roads were paved with rough-sawn and slow-rotting boards of white oak. The plank roads were the first great exploitation of the old-growth forests, the first cutting of paradise to build a parking lot.

While I was clearing brush, Sylvan often played in the small branch that first emerged in the shallow bowl of land below Susan and Jason's. She later counted the springs that fed the branch and named it Seven Spring Branch. Where Seven Spring Branch joined Morgan Branch flowing in from a ridge west of my land, the two continued north for two miles and joined the broad flow of the Haw River. The old road followed Morgan Branch to the river. I wanted to follow myself, but where Morgan Branch assimilated Seven Spring Branch, I left the old road and cut a new route onto the slope just above my freshly dug footings.

I hired a tractor with a long blade to scrape out the roots of the brush and small trees and spent a month's wages on a thin coat of gravel. Once again the old wagon road led somewhere. I ordered sand and gravel and trucked in bags of Portland cement. Before I started mixing and pouring, I decided to use three of the last four sticks of dynamite to blast the highest rock out of the footings. I could have used another case. In several places, the rock would allow no more than four or five inches of concrete. Enough, I told myself. The old continent may not meet building code, but we had no building code then in this county. Taconia had not moved for tens of millions of years, and I was content to have my house rest on its back.

I took the last stick of dynamite up the river to a friend's land where he had drilled an expensive four-hundred-foot dry well. I tied the end of a ball

of string onto the stick of dynamite, inserted a cap crimped onto four minutes of fuse. I let the string slide through my hands quickly as the dynamite
and lit fuse descended hissing into the darkness. I stopped it just short of
the bottom and capped the well casing with a rock. The dynamite down
there deep in the rock made a hollow popping sound. Two days later, water
had flowed into the well shaft. Taconia could be coaxed.

– chapter 15 –

The Owner-Built Home

*In the honorable frontier tradition, I intended to de-
sign and build my own home. With the arrogance of
the 1970s, I thought I could do it with almost no experience. There was a guru for that, too.*

Like many Americans, I have always lived with two houses—the one
whose walls surround me at a given time, and the house in my head. Maybe
these are proxies for the person we are and the person we want to be. The
house in my head when I came to Morgan Branch had a lot in common
with the first house that built itself between my ears when I was in high
school. One night when I was fifteen, I described my house to Judy Brown
and Betty Sprague, who were working behind the counter that night at the
soda fountain in Dobkins' drugstore. I had a crush on both of them, and
though they were both going out with other boys, they liked me well
enough to give me free seltzer water.

My house, I said, would have only one normal room. In this room, guests
could talk and eat. The rest of the house, my spaces, would be bare wood,
no paint or plaster, no varnish or cabinets or fancy light fixtures. Who
needed the expensive finished surfaces and built-ins, the labor of cleaning
and painting? That house was allegory, not architecture. The finished
room was my agreement not to close all the doors to people around me.
The bare living spaces I proposed for my own life declared that I wanted no
distractions between me and what I then thought was the pursuit of Truth.

Truth would come from books, hard thought, and debate with people whose only interest was ideas. I would put it all down on paper in poems and stories. I wanted a house where nothing would get in my way.

That first house-in-the-head had no shape, no architecture, no floor plan. It was a declaration of intent. To put it less grandly, it was all talk, mainly at Dobkins' soda fountain.

Judy and Betty said I had to have more than one ordinary room. Suppose someone wanted to stay overnight? I answered that this guest would have to live the way I lived.

The house in the head is like a caterpillar that moves from cocoon to cocoon, from dream to dream, but turns into a butterfly only once. In each reincarnation, certain elements of that first house appeared, but by the time I was ready to build, the house in my head had acquired shapes and surfaces and purposes. I hoped these would combine the simplicity of my first house, the elegance of traditional Japanese architectural style, the experimentalism of the 1970s hippie builders, and the environmental thrift that was supposed to save scarce resources for future generations.

My final guideline came from my repulsion for installment payments and debt. Making a new, ongoing, or final payment on something—stove, washing machine, refrigerator, car—had been a constant of my childhood. About such debt Thoreau noted that most people lived and died as economic slaves, survived by their children and their mortgages. Activists in the 1970s agreed that money is the root of all evil. Postwar economic expansion liberated us from the Great Depression our parents had suffered through and we did not want to look back. I had hated the small but festering economic wounds in my family. I feared debt the way city people fear chainsaws or guns, especially after they have seen a wound or two or have watched *The Texas Chainsaw Massacre*.

We were more ready to accept Thoreau's bachelor naïveté than the plain lessons from our own families. The washing machine that had taken us three years to pay off liberated my mother from long hours of rubbing clothes and bed linen for five people up and down a rippled metal washboard. For most Americans, a degree of bondage to debt still buys freedom from slavery.

Although I was untainted by debt, I was handicapped by near poverty. In that state, I began my house plans. This house, as much as the first, declared a set of principles and prejudices, but its form was more necessity than choice. My only alternative to becoming a simple-living owner-builder was to rent; but renting an apartment or a house represented as much bondage as renting money in the form of a loan.

Chatham County offered another vital freedom for the alternative home builder. The county had no building inspector and therefore no building-permit requirement. It had no department demanding to inspect detailed plans. A house could spill right out of the head and onto the ground. Except for this legal vacuum, my environmental ideals, economic virginity, and financial necessity might have forced me into the agonizing kind of choice St. Thomas Becket had to make between principles and martyrdom on the one hand and the king and the Pope's favor on the other.

The plans for my house took up two sheets of notebook-size graph paper. One was a floor plan, the second a side view. The concept was as simple as the house was small. In the center of a single living area a stone chimney divided the kitchen and entry from the living space and heated the living space. Sylvan's small bedroom and space that might become a bathroom was on one side of the house, and my own small bedroom on the other. Bedrooms did not have to be heated, I decided, because you can do everything necessary under warm blankets. If and when I had an indoor bathroom, there, too, the only activity requiring more than a few minutes would be a hot shower.

Until I had money for a pump, I would continue hauling water from Morgan Branch. An outhouse had been good enough for my mother's family of twelve and for most Americans until the twentieth century. The forest provided enough dead wood to heat the house. The central chimney would have four flues. A woodstove would heat the main living area and a fireplace would face a built-in bench-bed for reading on cold nights. A flue on the kitchen side of the chimney could serve as a small wood-burning cookstove or water heater. On the fourth side, I would build an oven-sized recess with a flue for a charcoal hibachi. The chimney would be a trapezoid—a rectangle pulled out at two corners. This did not change the basic five-foot by seven-foot dimensions, but created a wider divider between the cooking area and the rest of the living space.

The north-facing roof would rise higher than the south roof to make a sleeping loft with a few sun-gathering windows in the gap between the two roofs.

Those were all the details I had put on paper. For this simple small house I was confident I could work out windows, doors, partitions, shelves, and eaves as I built them. My excuse for such minimal planning was that the house would be organic. As it grew from the ground, it would demand decisions, one feature leading to another. Building this way is like taking off in a small plane without a weather report or a flight plan. The shorter the trip or the simpler the house, the less the risk. Simple houses can be built this way. It's not smart, but building without a plan is less dangerous than flying without one and is usually more forgiving.

Some of my neighbors had built this way. Our self-confidence had famous supporters: Thoreau said the that past offered little guidance and that life in general should be spontaneous. Frank Lloyd Wright said that when he discovered organic architecture, the past was irrelevant: "The old architecture, always dead for me so far as its grammar went, began literally to disappear. As if by magic new effects came to life, as though by themselves, and I could draw inspiration from Nature herself. I was beholden to no man for the look of anything. Textbook for me? The book of creation."

Seeing is believing in home building. The year I began building, a small but important picture book celebrated the marriage of Wright and Thoreau. A middle-aged carpenter and a counterculture photographer published a beautiful book about owner-built homes: *Handmade Houses: A Guide to the Woodbutcher's Art.* Here was a portfolio of wonderfully small and personal statements in wood, glass, and adobe. Art Boericke, the carpenter-author, said the new owner-built homes "tumbled everything we'd slowly and painfully learnt—thrown among the skittering enthusiasms and youthful glee that bobbed up everywhere we went."

I thought my house should flow from my heart into my hands; they would coax and shape my house, make it rise up from the ground the way a potter fashions a jug from formless clay. From within me came a house that was simple and practical and durable. I began to build what I had read; I did not know then that I would spend the next twenty years tearing down and rebuilding. That's organic.

Those of us building organic homes for ourselves were not so much original as primitive. We had texts and models, almost all of them from preindustrial times. Popular starting points included log cabins, adobe, rammed earth, tipis, and sod houses. We made concessions for glass, electricity, and metal roofing. If you really wanted to make fun of America's materialistic and commercial culture, you created a house from garbage. Alternative culture magazines showed pictures of houses made from beer cans, bottles, stacks of old tires, cardboard, and the hoods and roofs of junk cars. Logs were the favorite at Saralyn, usually from old tobacco barns, but builders also used scrap lumber, fiberglass, old trailers, foam, and, of course, Theresa's U-Haul trailer.

Some owner-builders had more money than others, but like all forms of alternative culture, we were out to beat the system. For housing the *system* meant mortgages, the high costs of materials, and building codes. Once again, we would multiply Thoreau's example:

> If it is asserted that civilization is a real advance in the condition of man . . .
> it must be shown that it has produced better dwellings without making them
> more costly; and the cost of a thing is the amount of what I will call life
> which is required to be exchanged for it, immediately or in the long run.

I knew we were defying one of the honored rules of real estate—conformity. When I was teaching myself real-estate appraisal, I learned conformity as one of the ten principles that create value: Maximum value is realized when a reasonable degree of sociological and economic homogeneity is present. The few Realtors who had ventured to show clients a home site in Saralyn had warned me that our freedom to build turned off their customers.

Few people today who love Thoreau and make the pilgrimage to Walden Pond and add a rock to the piled homage where his cabin stood would permit such a cabin-home in their own neighborhoods, no matter how philosophical the inhabitant. They would not favor exempting rural philosophers from the county building codes that now prohibit anyone from building those "humble log huts and cottages" that Thoreau said were the most beautiful architectural subjects and that were the beginning of the community south of me in Saralyn.

We may celebrate Thoreau in our literature, but to live as he did is to live in malnutrition, in violation of the law, and in generally substandard conditions. People who live much more comfortably than Thoreau can still be considered poor and given food and money from government programs as well as fuel and labor and materials to rehabilitate houses that Thoreau found to be the most habitable for the soul.

The owner-builders of the 1970s had a guru just like the mystics and the political activists. Meditators had Raj Neesh. Antiwar protestors had Phil Berrigan. Political radicals had Jerry Rubin. Environmentalists had Dave Brower and Edward Abbey.

My first contact with the guru of owner-builders had come in a letter from one of his followers four years before I started building. In the summer of 1970, shortly after I had written a paragraph about Saralyn for a newsletter called *Vocations for Social Change*, a letter arrived from California. It was two sheets of cheap tan wrapping paper, folded to a quarter of full size, taped shut. The address was printed in bold square letters. Inside, the letters were bigger but hooked and curved playfully. Some of the language was familiar. The writer and his woman friend were looking for cheap rural land. "We are quite eager to find a place where we can live simply and in harmony with the world around us. Are you interested in working something out?"

What interested me was that the writer had moved from the Bhoodan Center of Inquiry into an apprenticeship with Ken Kern, the author of *The Owner-Built Home*. Ken called himself "a designer-builder of contemporary homes—a self-appointed specialist in the low-cost field." His growing popularity had preceded his apprentice's letter. He struck the right chord for people who wanted to give form to the loud counterculture of the 1960s and 1970s. You could demonstrate on the streets and shout at rallies and sing along at concerts, but that was the easy stuff, the stuff of a momentary event. A home, Ken said, "should be expressive of its owner's life." He knew what we wanted to say.

"I have yet to find one critic who comprehends entirely why our houses are so poorly constructed," Ken wrote, "why they look so abominable, why they cost so much for building and upkeep, and why they are so uncomfortable." We, his readers, were too eager for the message and too ignorant of the world to ask which houses was he talking about. The fine old houses on farms? Neat split-levels and ranches? Victorian and Edwardian houses in small towns? American housing was as cheap, as functional, and as easy to maintain as anything in the world of equal quality.

From the point of view of hundreds of millions of people around the earth who lived in huts, yurts, shacks, lean-tos, tenements, workers barracks, and the grim concrete cubicles of Soviet apartments, the American building that Ken derided was revolutionary. After World War II, the wood frame house, adapted to mass production by specialized building crews, had housed hundreds of thousands of young veterans. Those historical facts, however, were not admitted to discussions among people who felt America had betrayed its revolutionary mission to the poor and oppressed. Ken Kern promised to deliver "a how-to-think as well as a how-to-do-it book."

Before I ordered the book, I ordered the apprentice. Steve Magers had gone from Haverford College to California to join a commune and translate his art major into artful building. With Ken Kern he had studied stone masonry. In a rapid exchange of letters, he agreed that if we put him up for a while, he would pay his room and board with stonework. I had invited inspiration for the building I would begin several years later.

Before Steve came to live with Sarah, Sylvan, and me for six months, he had lost his friend Sally but not his enthusiasm for stones and masonry. I was expecting my version of a stonemason—someone as solid as a boulder, someone decisive and rough. Steve was thin, boyish, and gangly. He was the kind of kid you would probably choose among the last for any game. Stripped to his waist, he looked like the famous ninety-seven-pound weakling in the old Charles Atlas ads. My mother-in-law, a brilliant little embryologist, visited from Virginia and whispered to us that this young man would run himself down if he continued life as both vegetarian and stonemason. Steve's salvation as a mason was that he gripped every move with his mind before he employed his hands. He didn't move things unnecessarily; he tackled heavy things from the best point of leverage or with smallest incremental moves.

Steve had come from Ken Kern's certain that he could start a new relationship between people and nature's materials. Ken said to use materials at hand, build with natural materials. A couple of years after Steve had started working in our area, he was overjoyed when a black logger down the road from Saralyn asked him to build a small retaining wall along the driveway to his modest house. The logger was a John Henry of the chain saw and a thrifty man who saved his money. Steve believed he could bring his building art to working-class America. He was pleased to be a white man working for a black neighbor. As Bob Dylan sang those days, "the times they are a-changing."

The logger brought in a dump-truck-load of fieldstone. Steve set to work on a beautiful knee-high wall that was mortared from the back and so tightly fitted in front that the stones seemed locked to each other like a jigsaw puzzle. When he was half done, the logger looked at the wall carefully. No, it was not what he wanted, that pile of stones with no mortar. He wanted a real wall, with thick mortar joints. Thank you, he said to Steve, but he would take it apart and redo it himself. The times were a-changing but human nature was not.

Within weeks after he arrived in North Carolina, Steve had picked out a fifteen-acre tract on a gentle slope near the beginning of Saralyn, and he began drawing plans and writing to Ken Kern for advice. I looked at a pencil sketch and a paragraph of text Kern sent on the back of a blueprint paper. The house was a stone triangle with a revolving metal fireplace in the center. The fireplace could be turned to any one of the three living areas—kitchen-functional, sleeping-privacy, or living-social. Each area had its own windows onto the outside world. On a single sheet of paper, Kern had drawn and described a practical and beautiful small house.

I respected Steve. Steve respected Ken Kern. So I sent Kern a check for $8 and a couple of weeks later I had his four "volumes," about 250 small pages held together by three cheap loose-leaf clips. He promised readers that they could buy and clip in future volumes, or additions and changes to existing volumes.

The Owner-Built Home was the building permit for people who despised permits. It began with the owner-builder's seven axioms.

1. *Build According to Your Own Best Judgment.* Get away from building codes and the judgment of inspectors, into the country.
2. *In Building Your Home, Pay as You Go.* Building loans were "legalized robbery" where interest rates made homes unaffordable thirty-year burdens.
3. *Assume Responsibility for Your Building.* Cut out the general contractor, "an expensive and nonessential luxury" who adds 10 percent for his services and rakes in an additional cut on the materials.
4. *Use Native Materials Whenever Possible.* Didn't common sense tell you that materials you get free on your own land are the cheapest? Kern warned that timber and earth had to be "properly used," but cheap was what we wanted to hear.
5. *Supply Your Own Labor.* "So long as the master-and-slave type of employer-employee relationship continues to exist in our society, one can expect only the worst performance from his hired 'help.'" The hired help included overpaid and under worked union labor, according to Kern.

6. *Design and Plan Your Own Home.* Don't let someone else do your thinking. "Most contemporary architects design houses for themselves, not their clients."

7. *Use Minimum but Quality-Grade Hand Tools.* Plan and organize to avoid the expense of power tools that will only break and burn out. "Whatever way you look at it a certain amount of labor must go into building a home."

The introduction to the book ended with Thoreau:

What of architectural beauty I now see, I know has gradually grown from within outward, out of the necessities and character of the indweller, *who is the only builder*—out of some unconscious truthfulness, and nobleness, without ever a thought for the appearance, and whatever additional beauty of this kind is destined to be produced will be preceded by a like unconscious beauty of life.

So it was that Ken Kern translated Thoreau's idea into ideas for concrete, timber, earth, tin, glass, stone, and brick. So it was that I set out to design and build my own house, to be its only builder. The house in my head had been remodeled and reshaped by many hands, but Ken Kern put the tools in my hand.

chapter 16

Materials and Methods

I begin building with the idea that an owner-built
home is the pinnacle of self-reliance. I find myself
building alone but relying on people whom I'll
never see.

I had finished digging the footings in the middle of May 1974. The balmy moist weather was the kind that inspires lines such as "Nothing could be finer than to be in Carolina." Overhead, spring's lacy shade had turned almost solid green but the leaves were still young, and the sun made them glow with green translucence.

I calculated the amount of stone, sand, and cement I would need to make the concrete. Three yards sounds small, but they are cubic yards. Imagine a block of cement three feet on each side and three feet high. Then imagine two more on top of it—a nine-foot-high, three-foot-square pillar of concrete. Half would be stone. A third would be sand. One sixth, Portland cement.

To buy these materials you went to Pittsboro Fuel and Ice to see Mr. Arthur Thomas. Mr. Thomas was always glad to see me. This may be because he was one of the first Pittsboro businessmen to make money from Hippie Town, or maybe he enjoyed meeting people. Pittsboro Fuel and Ice was a long dark building that had inside walls but no outside walls. That is to say, it was an old wooden warehouse with the boards placed on the inside of the posts and no siding had ever been put on the outside; it sat next to railroad tracks that had not been visited by a train for more than ten years, maybe since the close of the mill that stood there and had once turned cottonseed into chicken feed and cattle fodder. A kerosene pump still stood on the wooden porch, but over the years the business had evolved from fuel and ice to building materials.

Mr. Thomas sat at an old desk in a small room. On his desktop sat a concrete block painted with waterproof cement and on the wall hung a calendar with Jesus looking down over the days. No one hurried at Pittsboro Fuel and Ice, least of all Arthur Thomas. His relaxed and friendly reception made standing up to speak your order almost bad manners. Most people sat down on the metal chair on the customer side of the desk and said a few words about the weather, business, or another common bond.

I had to give directions to the driver. He was another graying man, as easygoing as Arthur Thomas, a square man in his late fifties, with white eyebrows and a soft voice. If he had heard of Hippie Town, he didn't say. When I had drawn a map of the Saralyn road and my new drive, he had said, "You live up past the old Carney Bynum place. You and I are almost neighbors."

The driver took my pencil and extended my map to the Old Graham Road west of Saralyn. He came to his land off the Old Graham Road from a mile-long drive. He lived in the house his parents had lived in when he was born. "We had neighbors then," he said of his childhood. "Now I'm the only one out there. Except you." In fact, he was only there on weekends and an occasional holiday. "Daddy's fields are all growed up," he told me. "The trees have come right up almost to the house." I calculated his house was a mile west of mine through the woods. His name was Clarence Dean and he owned 175 acres of his family's land. We would not be neighbors much longer.

For a week I hauled buckets of water from the creek and mixed sand, gravel, and cement in the wheelbarrow. I dumped each load farther down the footing than the one before. I was depressed by how much sweat I put into each barrow of concrete and how short a section of trench it filled. The tops of the footings were level except where bedrock rose through. In the trenches that ran up the hill, I poured the concrete in eight-inch steps, the height of a concrete block. I explained to Sylvan why leveling the footings was important, then I gave her a trowel. She started smoothing rough places. It was unnecessary but it was something she could do; it would not harm the foundation or the girl. I wanted her mark to be on the house. Somewhere in the footings, I engraved her initials, SRK. The R was for Ramsey, her mother's maiden name. There was no need for the family to be separate in everything.

Now came the precise part that I would trust to neither Sylvan nor myself—getting the corners of the foundation exactly square and level. The footings didn't have to be exactly square. They were twelve inches wide, four inches wider than the block they would support. The block foundation walls, however, had to be exactly the same length and they had to have precise ninety-degree corners or everything framed on top of them would be cockeyed. I did not want this part of the house to be an expression of the character or talents of the indweller.

I ordered seven hundred concrete blocks and called Steve Magers to set the corners. In one day, he had four corners rising from the ends of the trenches. They were perfect, not a half a degree off vertical or horizontal; plumb and level, as masons say. Steve had the unusual gift of perfection with brick and block and stone. This is uncommon. The machined regularity of brick and block demands the same mechanical precision from the mason. Laying to the line, laying in square and rectangular patterns becomes a habit. Sometimes it becomes an art that produces elaborate patterns and shapes. The more a mason can do with brick and block, the less likely he can adapt to stone. The uniqueness of every stone—color, shape, cleavage, weight, and texture—often drives a brick-and-block mason crazy.

Steve built each corner four or five blocks high. From the highest block, he stepped the corner down one block at a time in each direction. He had created perfect beginnings for me to follow. Between the top of the lowest blocks in each corner he stretched strings to mark the top of the first row of blocks. Steve left me a paint-by-the-numbers site. All I had to do was lay another six hundred or more blocks and lift the guide string for each row.

A small "alternative" business I helped organize came to my aid. For several months, Steve had been working with a student who had taken my sophomore literature survey and with two other university-educated carpenters who said they got more pleasure out of making houses than from learning facts and taking exams. They called themselves Heartwood Builders. After two or three houses for university professors, they had won a reputation for craftsmanship, imagination, and low prices. They accomplished the low prices by paying themselves what they considered an ethically low wage to match the simple lives they were trying to lead.

They did not consider at first the irony of working for low wages to build houses the owners would fill with luxuries, including new luxuries they could buy with the money they saved by using Heartwood Builders. Maybe it is true that those who live by the sword die by the sword, but businesses that do not live by economics usually die by economics.

Heartwood Builders stayed with me for another week after the foundations were finished. We brought in a generator to run saws, and within a week we had framed the exterior of the house, covered the floor with plywood, and covered the plywood roof sheathing with tarpaper. The outside of the house we covered with four-by-eight-foot sheets of blackboard, a light fibrous half-inch-thick panel tarred on one side. Blackboard had replaced the wooden sheathing that was common until the 1950s; it lasted into the 1970s, to be replaced in turn by blue and pink panels of polyurethane foam. It's easy to scoff at blackboard as a flimsy and artificial substitute for wood, but the wood replaced by blackboard and foam in American housing would have come from hundreds of thousands of acres of leveled forest. Wood sheathing is also a much greater fire hazard.

The drying in of the house went so fast that I remember clearly only two parts; one was the dull repetition of hammering nails into the plywood sheathing of the floor and roof. One nail every six inches on the edges, every eight inches where the plywood lay over a floor joist or roof rafter. The average small house requires over 50,000 nails. If the average nail takes five seconds to be placed and hammered in, a builder using a hammer spends seventy hours, or a week and a half, banging nails. (The pneumatic nail gun would soon do for house building what the sewing machine gun had done for sewing.) Whenever I regret that I have not personally changed the world or the nation or even my state, I think of nails in a house. No single nail does anything very important, but they must all be there. The vast masses of human beings contribute to the building of civilization as the pounders of nails contribute to the building of a house. We are necessary but unnoticed. A few people are noticed because, instead of building, they destroy. Only the very rare person changes the world with individual acts.

The other part that I remember about framing the house is the happiest task of all construction—framing the windows. When we had nailed down the floor sheathing, and before we had framed the walls, I could stand on a broad open platform some ten feet off the ground on the south side, the downhill side. I could now walk around the spaces where I would cook and sit and sleep. I walked to the various edges and looked out of imaginary windows. I stood in the center and imagined a wall and a window.

In the 1950s, Frank Lloyd Wright had popularized houses built with entire walls of glass. A decade later, as oil prices rose and the first oil embargo made heating costs skyrocket, Americans realized these glass walls burned up huge amounts of coal or gas or oil. The large single glass panes could not be fitted with storm windows. In the winter they frosted at night and thawed in the mornings. The melted frost ran down to the windowsills and eventually rotted the wood.

My idea of windows came from a house I had never seen in life or in pictures. When I studied in England, I was madly in love with a Norwegian nursing student named Sissel. Her most durable gift to me was her description of an uncle's home in Norway. Instead of big windows, he had many different sized windows placed irregularly in his walls—high and low, isolated and in groups. They created numerous pictures and mosaics of the world outside.

I intended to build each of my windows in a place and in a size that would create a frame for a special view of the forest. I spent hours standing on the floor platform looking into the trees. The first thing I realized was that in any large view, it would be difficult to see the trees for the forest.

In my bedroom on the west side of the house, a long tall narrow window would allow me to see the moon in the night sky and in the mornings long sections of a few big tree trunks. Sylvan's room would have a window in the east wall so that she could awake and see the rising sun's rays reaching through the crowns of fine oak and beech trees. In the north wall, which was low and looked out onto the parking area, I planned only one small window long enough to provide light for washing dishes and to identify arriving guests.

The most important tree to see was the beech whose presence first brought me to the site where I decided to build. My floor level was only a foot or two beneath the first forking of the trunk into four powerful gray limbs. I decided to make a tall window wide enough to take in the trunk and its branches. The window would be opposite the front door; the first thing to greet visitors would be the central point of this tree, the point at which it began to lift its crown above the house. It would be the view of a fine torso.

Robert Frost had written about the tree at his window,

> let there never be curtain drawn
> between you and me.

Like me, he had a window between himself and nature, and every window on nature is an instrument of domestication. It frames and tames the
wild. My careful placement of windows continued a tradition started by
the painter Claude Lorraine, who after his death became the most popular
landscape painter of the late seventeenth century. In Europe and America,
ladies and their gentlemen walked out into the countryside with framed
pieces of glass to create instant pictures. The glass was tinted to give the
pictures the golden hue of a Claude painting.

In my house no curtain has been drawn or even hung. Except for the
kitchen window, every other window is too high for a human being.
Should a forest creature look in, I hope it is as entertained as I am when I
look out on finches, owls, snakes, raccoons, lizards, squirrels, and deer.
Turnabout is fair play. I am happy to have two-way frames for my windows.
The truth is that I have rarely seen an animal pause to look in, and I've
never seen one look in twice. They are not curious about anything that is
not danger, food, or sex. Unless it threatens them, human life bores them.
Their only interest in windows is when they see their own reflections. Year
after year a male cardinal batters his head against the bathroom and
Sylvan's window.

When Heartwood Builders left for good, my house looked like any new
house frame in suburbia. Skeletons are much alike in housing and humans:
Few people could distinguish Arnold Schwarzenneger's skeleton from Bill
Clinton's or John Cleese's. The skeleton of my house did have one distinction. A house with a peaked roof must have something to support the peak.
Because the interior of my house was a large open room with no partitions,
we cut four trees, measured posts out of them, and hauled the trunks inside.
I had chosen one cedar, one white oak, one red oak and one poplar. With
one at each end of the living area and two in the middle, they were the forest's delegates and witnesses to all deliberations that went on inside. They
have been constant reminders that this is a house built from a forest.

Framing is the easiest and most satisfying part of building a house. In a
few days it claims its place in space, establishes the shape of the house,
fixes its entries and exits, and frames its views of the outside world. Its rela-

tion to a house, however, is something like the relation of a skeleton to Frankenstein's monster: Everything that will bring the house to life—everything that will allow it to function like a home—has yet to be done. It must have insulation, inside and outside skins, roofing, wiring, plumbing, floors, stairs, doors, a chimney, storage spaces. I was not qualified to do these things, but I would and I knew why.

The first time I had seen a man build his own house, I was nine or ten. My friend Franky Thorn invited me to go with him and his family to see the house his father had almost finished in what was then a rural area fifteen miles north of New York City called Yonkers. I didn't believe that one man could build an entire house.

My own father, and the father of everyone I knew, worked with his hands, but only to repair something already built—the plumbing, a light fixture, porch stairs, a car. They worked in garages repairing things or in factories making a piece of something. My father had made fuses for bombs during World War II, and after the war he had chrome-plated the pieces that went onto the black bodies of DeJur movie cameras.

For a boy from a laborer's family, surrounded by other kids from laboring families, a man who could build and assemble an entire house was the culmination and convergence of intelligence and skill. Despite all I did not know about the uses and reaches of intelligence, seeing that this man had built a home by his own wits and hands was like seeing that someone had climbed Mt. Everest.

When Franky and his family moved, I kept their address and wrote until Franky died of cancer several years later. The address was engraved in my mind. Thirty years later when I was visiting New York, I borrowed a friend's car and drove to 1092 Midland Avenue in Yonkers to see the house that one man had built alone. The house was a simple and very small square bungalow on a corner lot. It was dwarfed by modern brick apartments extending along Midland Avenue like the Great Wall of China. In its world it was just one more aging and obsolete house occupying a lot suited to a much larger house, an office, or a few apartments. I was sure it soon would be sold and demolished. In my world, however, it would always stand like a monument.

Franky Thorn's father, of course, did not begin his labor by wresting from nature's raw materials all that he needed. A factory made the drywall and glass, a sawmill cut and sized the lumber, a foundry cast the furnace. Franky Thorn's father assembled work others had done. And I suspect it has always been so in home building. The Indian who made the wigwam did not himself or herself strip the bark from the tree or cut the brush for the frame. Not long after homes began to require more than one form or source of material the division of labor began. The sheepherders of Central Asia trade meat for the lattice of lathe that forms the circle of their yurts. Women sheer the sheep and pound the hair into felt mats. Men do no more than erect the pieces.

No one method of building a house possesses superior virtue. I admired and learned in the accomplishment of Frank Thorn's father that in a house as in a family, a government, or the theory of a universe, one human mind can bring together, understand, and make a comfortable order out of whatever wealth the world offers.

House building was no different for Thoreau at Walden Pond. The boards Thoreau bought for his cabin had been sawed by a mill, or by two men pushing and pulling a long pit saw, in work more destructive of health and mind than any factory ever invented. The pit saw itself was rolled and cut from the best metal of the times. The plaster Thoreau paid contractors to spread on his interior walls was the product of chemistry and engineering developed over centuries. Such things are not created by simple minds in simple rural environments. The technologies of housing usually have been developed by the narrow minds and studies that Thoreau merrily disparaged—men and women peering through microscopes, reading micrometers and digital displays, reading the results of a chemical reaction in a gas chromatograph.

Where is the civilized man or woman who has ever set out over the desert, into the forest, or across the ocean in the manner of our primitive ancestors? We have not lacked the courage to return to the wilderness, but try as we might to disguise our modern advantages, we depend on them for our very lives. The sailor in a small boat who circumnavigates the globe is safer in thirty or forty feet of modern technology than Magellan or Columbus were in their well-manned 150-ton carracks. Even the improved iron of Thoreau's ax, the forge that shaped it, and the grindstone that sharpened it, were not developed by a savage or even by the wisest frontiersman. Only ignorance refuses to acknowledge that broad accomplishments are made possible by many narrow minds devoted to long and esoteric study.

Building my home would occupy my free time and be my entertainment and agony for another year after Heartwood Builders left. No part of the work was happier than those first weeks alone in June. I had a roof over my head and a floor under my feet. I had holes in the walls that even without moldings and glass were like picture frames. As much as any person loves being out in the landscape, I believe he or she loves a picture of nature more, or at least nature in a frame. Human beings crave composition. A forest or a prairie is a random and ever-changing collection of forms and events. It has no frame to say where it begins and ends. It has no order that we can fully understand. Not one of us remembers nature in its full complexity. Whether we capture an image from nature with the mind or with a camera, we are selecting and framing. Why else has no culture on earth looked at the stars in the sky without finding and naming animals, humans, gods, and kitchen utensils?

chapter 17

Simple-Minded Simplicity

I finish my simple house, but not without considerable damage to body and soul.

Before winter I had insulated the walls, hung the front door, put glass in the windows, and covered the roof with sheets of galvanized metal. At a local sawmill that cut railroad ties, I bought rough oak boards to cover the outside walls with boards and battens. I nailed them in place within a week. A nail goes through freshly cut and wet oak easily enough, but let oak dry and it bends nine of ten nails. As soon as I had covered the house in this natural oak, I was embarrassed. It looked raw and wounded. These were boards that had been cut with little care, a by-product in the process of squaring a tree trunk into a railroad cross-tie.

It has become fashionable in our country to have naked wood both inside and outside a home. It's the "natural look." What is natural about a tree that has been sliced and placed with its insides to the weather? Except for the poorest shacks in times past, rural people clothed cut wood with a "coat" of paint. This was not to protect the wood. The old slow-growth cedar, white oak, and heart pine with its crowded growth rings made dense wood whose natural chemicals resisted bugs, bacteria, and weather. Unpainted boards could have protected themselves a century or more, but they were painted anyway. On the inside or outside walls of a house, and often on the floor, naked wood was considered too rustic, even crude. Barns and packing crates, not a civilized home, were made of natural wood. Certainly common pine and oak were seldom allowed to stand naked in cultured company.

I did not worry about that kind of company. I considered it shameful that the hastily cut oak boards would stand facing fully clothed trees in the forest. It was like the skinned carcass of a cow hanging in dairy barn, but I knew that in a few years the boards would clothe themselves in a patina of gray weathering, the color of stone or the bark of maples and beech. I have never understood the popularity of cleaners and restorers whose chemicals make weathered wood look as though it was cut only yesterday. To have a tabletop or a fine box made from a select piece of wood is very different. The artist or craftsman selects, shapes, oils, and polishes to let us to see inside a tree. This art is entirely different from nailing hundreds of naked boards to a wall.

In a few years, the rough oak board siding I had nailed up would weather unevenly. The house would become mottled grays, blacks, and browns. I would pull off and replace the oak with cypress, which would quickly begin to weather into an even gray. I didn't foresee any of this as I drove thick screw-shank nails through the oak into my framing. Removing them from dry oak as hard as rock would be tough penance for what I had done.

The wood I chose for my floors, shelves, and ceiling beams could stand naked with no embarrassment. It had been sawn from "original pine" in the nineteenth century and sawn and hand-planed into boards by a family of Baldwins in the sandy tobacco lands in the eastern part of the county. When the Corps of Engineers bought those lands to build B. Everett Jordan Lake, I bought the rights to salvage the house for $50.

The Baldwin house stood at the pyramid of old-time quality. Whoever built it was one of those fabled proud craftsmen of old, and he had the blessing of local materials that are among today's greatest building rarities. The house had endured because builders had selected the very best yellow pine and white oak. They had used only slow growth heartwood that is heavy with crowded annual growth rings. Before cutting finished lumber, they had quartered the logs. In boards and timber cut from quartered logs, the growth rings (or grain) run perpendicular to the wide surfaces; this makes lumber with great strength and weather resistance. The heart of a white oak is full of natural tannins that insects despise. Wood-eating bacteria and fungi need the softening-up help of water and a dry piece of white oak will last centuries. Heart pine lasts even longer, wet or dry.

I once rode through cut-over pine lands with Billy Belote, the owner of a logging empire in Florida and Central America. He braked to a sudden stop to ogle the thousands of stumps poking up in the grass and briars. "I will have to buy these," he said. I asked him why. "Those stumps are 95 percent chemicals. I'll truck them to Reichold Chemical in Georgia and get a good price." The chemicals in heart pine are as persistent as many dreaded pesticides. Few life forms have learned how to survive the ingestion of the chemicals in heart pine. A homeowner with a heart pine floor or table walks or eats on a veritable platform of pesticides.

The greatest danger I know of from heart pine's chemicals are their readiness to burst into flame. Small sticks of heart pine are often sold in little bundles as fire starters. In the South, heart pine was always used for that purpose and called "lighter wood" or "fat wood." Indians used knots and stubs of heart pine as torches. They also used them as torture. The Englishman John Lawson, famous for his *History of North Carolina*, probably met his death by heart pine. The Tuscarora Indians captured him as he and Baron DeGraffenreid explored the upper reaches of the Neuse River. His colleague Christopher Gale, who later became Chief Justice of the territory, said he believed the Tuscarora subjected Lawson to a well-known death ritual. Many little splinters of heart pine were stuck into him, then fired.

By the time I began taking apart the Baldwin house, I had looked closely at a lot of old houses other people wanted to buy, and Sarah and I had lived in two of them. I had seen how unpainted quarter-sawn heart pine clapboards stay flat against a wall unpainted for a hundred years, while modern boards cut from young pine, painted or not, will warp in the sun and pull an ordinary nail right out of an ordinary two-by-four in three or four years. I had seen dozens of houses built six or twelve inches off the ground eaten to the roof eaves by termites. I had seen powder-post beetles emerge in a living-room floor, climbing out of the tops of little pyramids of dust. I remember a friend who thought all oak was mighty. At a local "old time" sawmill, he bought thick boards of red oak and laid them on his new porch floor.

About the time I began digging my footings, he was building a porch onto the tobacco barn he had rebuilt at Saralyn. "Those red oak boards will rot," I warned him.

He had grown up in Brooklyn and had developed a way of hugging you as he tried to put you in your place. He put his arm around my shoulder and said, "I am touched by your concern for my oak. Doesn't it look beautiful there?"

Three years later, the boards had turned black and mushrooms began to grow out of them. The people who cut their own logs and built homes found that after two or three years, beetles were drilling holes everywhere and turning the growth rings to powder. They had to drench them with preservatives. Even before I began framing my house, I had learned that only the wood with built-in pesticide endures. I had also learned that every house is a fortress against nature. From the moment a house is built nature lays seige to it.

Frank Lloyd Wright designed what he described as the "natural house," but his houses are notorious for falling apart. Houses that have endured only pretend to be natural by color and form and surface textures. The best of either primitive or modern architecture can only coax and beguile a little cooperation from nature in keeping us warm or cool or in providing us light. Even this is not so much harmony with nature as domestication of natural forces. The great achievement of architecture is the conquest of natural forces. Just as we fight some forest fires by getting ahead of them and setting backfires to consume fuel in their path, so we can make some conquest of nature by using its strongest pesticides against its pests.

Nature never volunteers to help us. Rain and the air itself corrode a metal roof. Slate cracks and flies off in storms. The earth moves imperceptibly, but eventually cracks most foundations. Nature will triumph over us eventually. The purpose of housing is to delay that triumph and the expense of repair and rebuilding.

By the end of October when I had to move out of the old farm house, I could heat my new house well enough with a woodstove, but I was far from finished. I had built the partitions that created small rooms for Sylvan and me on opposite sides of the living area. The rest of the house reminded me of two lines from a song by The Band:

> Old Uncle Jed he built him a house
> Roof was a window and the floor was a dream

I had left a large hole in the floor through which the chimney would rise into the living space. On its shoulders it would support the rafters of the loft. Above the loft floor and out through the roof it would be a narrower brick chimney. Until I could finish the chimney, I covered the hole in the roof with a loose sheet of metal roofing. I had a woodstove next to the hole in the floor and its stovepipe ran up and through the loose sheet of roofing.

That first winter, cold air came in through the roof and up through the hole in the floor. Winters in central North Carolina seesaw ten or fifteen degrees above and below freezing, the daytime almost always above freezing. The damp cold filters through clothing that is warm enough in a dry ten degrees below freezing. The drafts crawled around my house that first winter like fat cold ghost snakes. If I stayed near the wood heater to read or eat, the drafts crawled up my back; if I sat farther away, they wrapped around my feet.

Fortunately, I had little time to sit. When I wanted warmth, I could work on the chimney. I could mix mortar and lift one big rock after another to find the right fit. The fit was especially important once the chimney rose above floor level where it would be in view forever. Maybe long after the house had disappeared, it would stand there, my most permanent work. The woods of the piedmont are sprinkled liberally with old chimneys still standing when not a trace of the wooden house remains. And these are chimneys built with cheap sandy lime mortar.

I wanted six things from this chimney—support for the loft's floor joists, a divider between cooking and the rest of the space, a fireplace, a safe conduit for a wood-burning water heater, a cookstove, and a room heater. For heating, it would be the utility core of the house.

Fireplaces are environmental crimes, but I built one anyway. I knew that 10 percent of the heat produced in a fireplace warms the air in front of it. Ninety percent goes up the chimney as greenhouse gases, particulate pollution, and carcinogenic chemicals. Any environmentalist with a fireplace should be ashamed to speak about air pollution or global warming. Benjamin Franklin never gets proper credit for the environmental salvation brought to America by his "Franklin stove." As the seventeenth century turned into the eighteenth, Americans were cutting down vast forests of hardwood trees every winter for that 10 percent of the calories that might emanate from a fireplace. A Franklin stove was 500 percent more efficient.

Even dead trees would be better left on the forest floor to nourish mushrooms and arthropods and replenish soils. I limit my own fires on the hearth to four or five special occasions each year. The most active of the four flues in my chimney is the flue that carries the exhaust from a cast-iron wood heater. The circuitous route of the burning gases passing through this stove delivers 60 percent of the heat to the room. On warmer days, however, I have to close down the air intakes and burn a slow fire. This makes a smoky fire and more air pollution.

My choice when I designed the house came down to this—my economic freedom versus air pollution. I could spend $100 a month on gas or oil. They deliver 90 percent of their energy to the user and make negligible pollution. I could have spent a lot more on the house for insulation and so-lar water heaters. I could have cut the beech and other trees on the south side, installed insulated glass, and increased my solar heating. That would have required enslavement to a mortgage. Thoreau, with his hatred of eco-nomic bondage, would have approved of my choice.

Like most back-to-the-land environmentalists at the time, I chose air pollution over economic bondage and association with the fossil-fuel in-dustry. To lessen the burden on my conscience, I wrote articles and white papers for the Conservation Council documenting the evils of oil and gas and begging for more industry attention to solar and wind energy. I was president of the council when we won the right from the Nuclear Regula-tory Commission to challenge the licensing for a nuclear plant. We knew what we didn't want from the behavior of public companies: We didn't want them to behave the way we behaved. Maybe it is a high compliment to capitalism that individuals believe corporations may behave with greater morality and civility than individuals.

Besides, my polluting chimney was going to be beautiful as well as func-tional. Nothing in the building of the house took more time, damaged my body more, or gave me more satisfaction than building the chimney. Be-cause I had skewed the basic five-by-seven-foot rectangle into a trapezoid to make it a wider divider, I had no right angles. For reasons of geology and physics, nature seems to produce a fair number of stones with right angles. Two of my corners demanded 120-degree angles, the other two were a sharp 60 degrees. I quickly exhausted the few choice pieces in the piles of stone wedged out of my foundation trenches. I found a few more lying among the trees. The rest I had to find in and around Morgan Branch.

Often I found myself with a tub of mortar already mixed and the urgent need to find a stone of a certain angle for the corner or a certain shape for the face of the chimney. After Steve Magers's tutorials, I could not simply pile stone upon stone and use great spaces of mortar to make them sit on one another. In fact, I had determined to fit the outward surfaces of the stones so closely to each other that mortar would be all but invisible in this chimney. This choice forced me into hours and hours of sloshing along Morgan Creek examining and measuring stones. I was a man assembling a jigsaw puzzle without a picture and a puzzle whose pieces were hidden throughout the forest like Easter eggs.

The choice taught me a lot about the stones on my land and about its geology. The volcanic tuffs were streaked with veins of white quartz. I decided my chimney would represent that geology and I built a quartz vein into one face of it. I also built in several shelves and alcoves, large and small.

When I had finished in the spring, I was relieved and disappointed. The stones did not fit as closely as Steve fit his stones. I had already seen that the cracks between the stones and the shelves were in need of constant cleaning. Nevertheless, this was a deliberate chimney and the effort required to lift and then level the larger stones gave each a special place not only in the chimney but in my memory. Lifting and fitting a stone made as permanent an impression on the soft gray matter of my brain as it did on the soft gray mortar.

A few that weighed near a hundred pounds sat comfortably in the chimney, though I would find out soon that they had added quick years to my back and shoulders. I remember particularly the largest shelf, a blue slab of stone seven inches thick and nearly a yard square. I found it by Morgan Branch angling out of the earth. I pulled it free and debated whether I could possibly carry it the fifty yards through the woods to my truck. It was too fine a stone not to try. I inched my way over fallen wood and lumps of earth. I thought that at any moment the vertebra in my spine would turn to mush. When I set the stone in the back of the truck, I lay down next to it, my heart pounding hard against my ribs. I had had this same feeling in high school when I had wrestled and beaten a boy thirty pounds heavier than I.

Twice I lifted my blue stone into its proposed place shoulder high on a corner of the chimney before laying a bed of mortar and stone and placing it for the final time where it sits. If I had slipped with it in my arms at shoulder height, it would have crushed my chest or hips.

Whatever my disappointments with the chimney as art or architecture, my satisfaction is that I achieved a small reorganization of the earth itself, a small monument, a gathering of stone into the air in the honor of stone itself.

By summer, the house was finished, at least until my regret for my mistakes and craftsmanship would drive me to begin the still unfinished process of tearing down and rebuilding. My house was not as simple as Thoreau's, but if we compare both to the average house of their day, mine was simpler than Thoreau's. I had the benefit of technology and science that Thoreau could not use. I filled my walls and ceiling with fiberglass insulation. Although my house was twice the size of Thoreau's cabin, on a day of weather as cold as New England's, I would burn half the wood and have a warmer house. I would produce half the air pollution that Thoreau's fireplace had produced. My house was also somewhat more Spartan. A stove and chimney heated Thoreau's one room. I heated my main living space, but the two small bedrooms were unheated. The activities that belong can be done quickly or under the warmth of a quilt or two.

The cost of my house was many times the cost of Thoreau's, which he says he built for $28.12. That was something of a lie since he said he paid for no labor. That first winter he went to live with his family for a month while professional plasterers finished his interior walls. Let's assume that Thoreau's total investment was $35. What he had when finished was a wooden box and a rough stone chimney. Wages were about a dollar a day and his house was 150 square feet (the size of a modern medium bedroom.) He paid $.35 per square foot. Since an average wage might be $1 per day, a square foot cost him 2.8 hours of labor or, as he would put it, *of life.* The same simple framing, roofing, and interior walls set on stone or block piers and joined to a simple one-story chimney would cost about $10 a square foot. This is one hour's wage for any beginning carpenter or mason. Mexicans who sign up at the local chicken slaughterhouse get paid $8 an hour plus health insurance and with an hour's work could buy twice as much of Thoreau's cabin as Thoreau himself. If we want twice as much for the same money, we are not enslaving ourselves to luxury. We can be thankful that a century and a half of economic development has given us more comfort, freedom, and safety for less labor.

The $15,000 or so that I spent on my materials is in fact not so monstrous compared to Thoreau's $28.12. Let us consider that he might have put that money in an account bearing 5 percent interest. By the time I began my house 130 years later, the money in the account would have been $18,452.90. Put it another way: If we allow for inflation between Thoreau's time and the time I began to build, our costs were similar. And for this I built a better house that was kinder to the forest around it.

-chapter 18-

Survival and Luxury

*Curiosity, a commitment to simplicity, and need lead
me to find out how much of necessity and comfort I
can get from the forest itself.*

Spring of 1975 began as spring always does here, with a teasing and luxurious slowness, promising, promising, promising. For me spring that year was the promise that I would no longer have to keep cutting firewood. My feet would no longer freeze as I sat reading. I would not have to sleep under layers of old blankets that lay on me like a fallen roof. I would not have to come home after a day away to a cold and empty house, the worst of homecomings. I was watching for the first sign of spring.

Winter in this part of North Carolina has almost nothing to recommend it. I far prefer the scrubbing cold of winter on the tundra, or the white snows of New England. I like the music of dry snow squeaking and crunching underfoot much better than the swish and sloosh of wet snow. Winter here brings no skiing, no ice-skating, no sledding, no white Christmas. Friends who grow apples pray it will be cold enough long enough to discourage some of the pests and to prepare the trees to set fruit. Then they pray the bursts of warm weather in February and March do not last long enough to call forth doomed buds.

The first irrevocable sign of spring is the reddening of twigs on the twisted southern maples scattered around the woods. Maples usually die before they get to be sturdy trees, but they are the first trees with a visible response to spring. When I saw that happening toward the end of February, I stopped cutting firewood. During a late February warm spell, I awoke to a great noise in the woods, hundreds of small voices competing in a big chirping chorus. The acorn-sized frogs in the creek are called spring peepers. Along the creeks and in low areas, scattered tufts of blue-eyed grass began to flower. Sylvan picked a small bouquet one weekend. In early March, the tips of the maple twigs broke out in feathery maroon flowers. The third week in March, without regard to the weather, the first redbuds appeared, sprays of magenta flowers on their twisted trees along roadsides and edges of fields. The last week in March, slivers of green appeared at the tips of dogwood twigs. Spring was like an extended performance of Beethoven's "Eroica." When it reached its last triumphant measures with the first dogwood blossoms, I knew Morgan Branch was where I wanted to be.

In the spring of 1975, my house had two small bedrooms, electricity, no bath or toilet, an outhouse, and water hauled from Morgan Branch. My life had become as simple as it would ever be, and after a little finishing I would have a home comfortable enough for a full life.

Fifteen or more home sites now had houses. They were all simple and owner-built. Few, if any, had yet installed a flush toilet. Everyone heated with wood. We all lived in some form of Thoreau's voluntary poverty, and we intended to win from it a new understanding of our planet and of ourselves. Thoreau's true philosopher was no cloistered scholar or gentleman of letters, but someone willing to live "a life of simplicity, independence, magnanimity, and trust" and to "solve some of the problems of life, not only theoretically, but practically."

In the fall, just before I moved off the farm and out to Morgan Branch, my mother wrote worrying about how I would support myself without a job and spending most of my time in the woods writing. I had already done my accounting, just as Thoreau had. I wrote back in detail:

By growing my own food and not eating junk stuff like sodas, canned foods, precooked foods, etc., I eat for about $25 a month. My house is being built with cash as I get it. When I move in, I'll have no debts, only miscellaneous gas and entertainment expenses. Electricity will run about $15 a month, heat by woodstove, water free from the creek. I am hoping that a cash income of some $200 a month will be all I need. Add to it anything I can make by writing and woodwork.

Those were my figures for a simple life, and I thought my neighbors probably expected to get by in the same way. A half mile separated me from my neighbors to the south in Saralyn, but soon I was aware that a minor war had broken out.

The first complication to the lives of simplicity everyone intended to live were the animals they brought as coadventurers. Animals were everyone's alter egos. Even goats and chickens were pets. Pets are emissaries from nature, at least in their owners' minds, but they usually make bad emissaries between neighbors.

Lou and Tammy, a couple in their early twenties who loved their seventeen hound dogs no less than each other (and they were inseparable), moved into a trailer on land next to Dan and Martha Brown, the ex-Marine and his wife who had loved their privacy so much that they had carried every log, board, nail keg, and cement sack into the seclusion of their six acres. When the hounds got to howling at night Dan would step outside his house, load his shotgun, and fire several volleys at the stars. That would quiet the dogs. Their owners were also quiet, despite Dan's reputation with other nearby residents who let their dogs roam. When one of their dogs returned from a night of carousing with a nasty slice across its back, those residents said they were sure it was caused by that crazy man who lived next to Lou and Tammy.

At the other end of Saralyn, Ralph and his first wife Kathleen, the nurse who later became a stonemason then an acupuncturist, owned a beloved Siberian husky. Upon moving to Saralyn, Ralph and Kathleen gave it the gift of running wild as its wolf ancestors had done in arctic forests. It found no ptarmigan, moose, or hare, but it found their neighbor Susan's chickens. Susan and her husband, Jason, had not yet moved onto the property, so their chickens at times escaped their pen and also enjoyed the gift of freedom, churning the forest floor for several hundred yards around home base. After one slaughter, Ralph drew on his Brooklyn Jewish heritage. He cleaned and plucked the chicken, rendered the breast fat for soup, and served the bird to Jason and Susan as a supper of atonement. Susan was surprised by her first look inside one of her chickens. There she saw the assembly line that produced the eggs she sold, starting with an egg the size of a pea and ending with one that, but for Ralph's husky, would have been delivered that day. A while later, one of the few Saralyn residents who had grown up in North Carolina taught Susan how to kill and clean a chicken. That was the only chicken Susan ever killed.

Susan's goats were also intended to be among the friendly and willing workers. Sylvan and I bought their milk for our breakfast cereal. I was happy enough to have Susan occasionally take them for a walk down my drive, letting them chew back the brush on their way. Like the chickens, they also staged frequent escapes, and then their foraging included whatever weeds, flowers, or rare plants suited them. I doubt the goats destroyed anything of great value on my property or in the woods nearby, but I rankled at the idea that they had the choice. Usually they had no sooner broken free than they headed for Ralph and Kathleen's garden. Kathleen would hear their hooves clatter on the oak boards of the porch and find them standing outside her windows, chewing her spinach and broccoli. In an inevitable but unintended quid pro quo, Susan was at her chores one afternoon when the Siberian husky exploded into an attack on one of her goats, throwing it to the ground and tearing at its neck. The goat was rescued when the hay delivery she expected arrived and the driver helped her separate the animals. They then took the goat to the vet, who sewed its gaping neck wound shut.

These were the major skirmishes in what I called the Animal Wars. Minor events occurred regularly: Dogs frightened children and barked late at night, stray cats haunted bird feeders, dogs raided a neighboring chicken farm, and a cat destroyed a cherished pair of turtledoves.

People were not immune from attack, either. Ray Reiback, who had returned from divinity school in Pennsylvania to become a travel agent, gave his St. Bernard freedom suited to its size. The huge dog had a nose for company, a mouth in constant slather, and long strings of spittle dangling from its jaw. More than once, Sam Ahearn or her mother, Granny Violet, who lived almost a half mile from Ray's, were surprised by the dog breaking its way through their screen door with a single blow of its paw and walking in to beg for food or to steal it if no one was in the room. The dog was ecstatic one day to find Kathleen's eighty-seven-year-old elfin-sized mother-in-law walking on the Saralyn road. He jumped up to lick her face in greeting. She was fortunate the dog's full weight did not crush her when she fell. That incident at least ended Ray's denial that his St. Bernard would cause anyone trouble.

I had become used to the occasional lost hunting dog turning up at the old farmhouse Sarah and I had lived in and would not have been surprised if one turned up at Morgan Branch. They inevitably wore thick leather collars with the owner's name and phone number. A telephone call always brought a humble apology, and within the hour the owner and his pickup retrieved the dog. I saw one hunter who loved his dogs so much that he sat down on the ground and cried as they licked his face. Hunters, however, expect their dogs to stick to their jobs and their homes. The dogs that came to Morgan Branch were not hunting dogs but two distinct packs of Saralyn dogs. In the middle of a quiet afternoon or summer evening they would burst into my solitude, howling after the scent of fox or coon and in hot pursuit of the prize. Cats also showed up. I don't know why they strayed so far, but when they were here, chipmunks were not. One friend who came to visit and brought her cats was shocked when I pointed to one of them playing by a pile of stones. She went to take a close look and found the cat tearing apart a lizard.

"I've never seen her do that," she said.

I replied with the simple fact of feline ethology: "She's a hunter."

Half an hour later, the cat brought another lizard to where we were sitting. The evidence that most people invent nature rather than observe it is the almost universal belief among pet owners that their dogs or their cats are not bloodthirsty. The journal of the American Birding Association once estimated that cats kill 4.4 million songbirds a day.

During the Animal Wars at Saralyn, most owners reacted like the friend who brought her cats to visit. In retrospect, I see this was an omen, a warning. Susan wanted to build a better goat pen and apologized many times for the damage her goats did to Ralph and Kathleen's garden and orchard. Her husband, Jason, laughed at the way the goats stood on his neighbor's porch and chewed their vegetables. Why don't they take some responsibility, he argued with Susan. Bring them back to the pen and close them in instead of calling us all the time. What are neighbors for? Two years later Jason and Susan were divorced.

Everybody knew what he or she wanted from the simple life, but few knew how they were going to get it or what the problems would be. Animal Wars were only the visible sign of quiet conflicts. The women at Saralyn had already begun weekly meetings that modeled on the popular women's consciousness raising sessions that had started to flow from a variety of activist issues. They started out by telling the stories of their lives, Susan said, "but we usually ended up talking about our men and what was wrong with them." The simple life had plunged everyone into a life demanding more work and harder work than they had been used to in the middle-class lives they came from. The women generally agreed their men were not pulling their weight. On my list of nineteen couples who were living at Saralyn by 1975, only two were together ten years later. It is interesting that one of the two couples, still together in their late fifties, came from rural North Carolina. The wife, who taught Susan to kill chickens, dropped out of the women's group early; she wanted the women to *do* something, even something as traditionally female as quilting.

Sarah had never stood back from work in the house or with our animals and crops, but the year Sylvan was born, she began to chide me for working to the exclusion of our marriage. I believed my work was necessary, but I didn't know it was also fatal to our family. In the spring of 1975, as I welcomed spring and settled into voluntary poverty, I knew this was a life we could not have led together. Sarah already had a good job in the university counsel's office and was about to begin remodeling our old house.

Sylvan was at home in both worlds and had her own reasons to object to my unending work, but she never did. I seldom asked her to help with anything except picking up or bringing her dish to the kitchen, but she always preferred working together to playing alone. The year before I moved to Morgan Branch and Sylvan was three years and seven months, she came with me to Saralyn, where I had to spread seed and straw on the sides of the roads. As soon as I broke open a bale of straw, Sylvan picked up an armful of it and carried it to where I would spread it. I described her in a letter to my mother:

> Sylvan works with me on the tables and other stuff. She'll go for a half hour or more contentedly rubbing a little piece of sand paper over one end of a log. She has 2 or 3 she plays with incessantly, but when she's alone she's usually doing some small chore she sets herself in the garden—picking kale, flowers or mustard greens are her present favorites. She also likes to water the pony because it means getting to play with the hose.

I ended with the note, "Be interesting to see how long she likes working." To my continuing surprise, the next year and the next and on without stop when she was with me at Morgan Branch, not once did she hesitate to join my work whether it was cooking, gardening, carpentry, or mixing cement.

The easiest part of the simple life was building a simple house. None of us built quite as simply as Thoreau, but Thoreau never intended to live more than a year or two in his cabin, and he spent many days and nights visiting the more spacious and comfortable houses of his affluent literary friends. None of us who went back to the land in the 1970s left all civilization behind and went naked into the woods, even if the occasional naked gardener became the focus of gossip in town. We were, however, different enough for the media to take an interest in us.

Local papers had featured Saralyn several times. A television station sent a crew to interview me. The Associated Press came for a look and used Saralyn as an upbeat ending to a series on environmental pollution. The *Greensboro Daily News* covered the entire front page of a Sunday feature section with three stories about Saralyn. The first, "A Dream of Open Sky, Green Fields Come True," was about how I had become both an environmentalist and a developer. The second article was titled "Saralyn, A New Way In Housing." I told the reporter, "Our whole thing was that we wouldn't discriminate against anybody. You know, they could build anything they wanted—anything from a split level to a one-room log cabin."

Saralyn was one of many places across America where owner-builders could create a home without exchanging a large portion of life for it. We weren't going to exchange our time studying the building trades, either. We were the last people in America who didn't have to. Anywhere in Saralyn or all of Chatham County in the 1970s, Thoreau could have built his ten foot by fifteen foot cabin sided with cheap untreated slabs, his brick fireplace with sand and mud mortar and no flue liner, and his unscreened outdoor toilet from which the flies might commute to his dinner plate. Saralyn enjoyed the same freedom.

Saralyn built a reputation as a place to go to see strange houses. A few Pittsboro people came to see what hippie houses looked like. Most of the lookers were fresh out of college, with and without diplomas. Some picked up hammers and saws and contributed a few hours or a few days of labor. Saralyn was a small living museum of daring and nostalgia: Two dropouts from North Carolina Sate University had framed a geodesic dome on a plywood platform and covered it with polyurethane foam. Two or three people had torn down log tobacco-drying barns and resurrected them as cabins. The itinerant son of a radical school teacher had erected a sixteen-foot-high tipi. A former student of mine returned from a tour with the Army in Alaska in love with log cabins. He cut forty or fifty big pines and hired an old black neighbor to bring his mule and skid the logs to the house site. Another builder begged unused logs from a neighbor's log pile. His only machine was his Volkswagon Beetle. He tied a rope to the door post of his car and dragged the foot-thick, ten- and twelve-foot-long logs to his home site.

The final article in the Greensboro paper featured this builder with the Volkswagon mule. Bill Newnam, a twenty-eight-year-old owner-builder, spoke for most of Saralyn's new residents. Newnam had dropped out of graduate school in English at Syracuse University and had decided to "live like Thoreau and sit in the woods and read books." Newnam told the reporter, "The aim of technological society is to make people dependent on it. That's what keeps it going. In the technological society, people are not equipped with the knowledge for living, and it's best for society if they are kept ignorant and know just how to do their jobs. That lifestyle is not for me."

Every Saralyn house declared both its owner's message to the world and his or her personal desire. For me, the Japanese tradition offered what seemed directions for simple design and cheap furnishing. I posted a sign on my door, PLEASE DO NOT WEAR SHOES INSIDE. In my living space I had no chairs. From two fourteen-inch-wide pine boards I had found in a small building behind Frank Baldwin's house, I made low Japanese tables. Four people could sit on cushions at one table.

These tables had two problems. Sitting cross-legged on cushions takes almost twice as much space as sitting upright in a chair. Elbows can be pulled in, but not knees. People who grow up eating or sitting in this position can grow old in the position. Try hunkering, for instance. All over Russia and Central Asia, people can hunker with both feet flat on the floor because they have hunkered in squat toilets at home and in office buildings. In Russia, men who have spent a good part of their younger years in prison are comfortable hunkering. Kazakhs and Uzbeks hunker in the shade and talk, play cards, or eat. Most Americans cannot balance with the balls and heels of their feet on the ground at the same time and fall over or become painfully uncomfortable in a few minutes. The few guests who came to my house to eat often looked pained as they sat at the table. Before the meal was over, they would stretch backwards or sideways or take their plates and sit on a stool or a bucket.

When my mother came to visit that spring, I had to borrow a chair and I bought a folding television table for her to eat at next to the Japanese table where Sylvan and I ate. She wrote to me later and said she felt very sorry that Sylvan did not have a toilet or a tub or a shower. I reminded her that she had grown up using an outhouse and a tin tub. "It's different, now," she wrote back. "People need more things." That last statement was exactly what everyone at Saralyn and back-to-the-land people across America had set out to disprove.

I was already having a hard time, even with things like the table. I fought the pain of sitting cross-legged. I had friends who could sit for hours cross-legged in Zen meditation or yoga. I was sure I could get comfortable; sooner or later, my cartilage would adjust. I sat at the table and played my recorder (blockflute). The music eased the pain. Sometimes I played the Shaker song, "'Tis a Gift to Be Simple":

> 'Tis a gift to be simple,
> 'tis a gift to be free,
> 'tis a gift to come round,
> where we ought to be.

My legs would never come round. My knee joints threatened to burst apart. Like everyone who set out to live the simple life, I was learning my limits. The table was a good height for Sylvan, though. It was also light enough that she could move it out of the way when she and a friend wanted to run around the room and slide on the polished floor boards.

After seven or eight years, the table's second problem gave me an excuse to build Western-style furniture. The two boards had come from a smoke-house where, for years, the Baldwins had salted and smoked their hams in that shed. The salt had saturated the boards. On warm moist days, the salty boards absorbed water from the air, become damp, then sopping wet. They burned with a black and green smoke. I replaced the simple Japanese table with a simple trellis table I built to Western height.

Nothing in home furnishings seemed more over-done, more unnecessary, and more extravagantly expensive than the modern bed. All over the world people slept on straw mats, thick quilts, hammocks, and futons. I never fully appreciated how two people could sleep, no less make love comfortably, in a string hammock, but Americans with their box springs and form-fitting mattresses seemed like a nation of princesses afraid of finding a pea. I made a box from four wide gum boards, screwed in supports for a bed of plywood, and carpeted it with wool blankets. Lying on the floor to sleep has the same sense of humility as lying on the ground.

The ground or the floor is also the coldest place to sleep. Cold air is heavier than warm air and winter drafts crawl over a sleeper on the floor. I had always wondered why people of the eighteenth century and earlier thought sleeping with the window open was dangerous, but it may have been because they slept on or close to the floor. In the coldest nights of winter I sometimes slept in the loft on a single-bed mattress I put there for guests. The heat from the woodstove rose into the loft. One night, I rolled over on the mattress up there and felt twigs or leaves under me. I reached down to grab them and they grabbed me. The brown wasps that live under the siding and in cracks of country houses are always ready to respond to an unusually warm sun. They had come out into the loft during the day and the heater had kept them limber in the evening.

I knew when I moved to the woods that I would not undertake the labor to live off the land. If I had wanted to, I could have done it better than the Indians whose arrowheads, scrapers, and adzes I had had found when I built the Saralyn road. I had binoculars, microscope, chain saw, steel knives, shovel and pick, and a .22 rifle. (With apologies to vegetarians, I have to note that a single human being with a rifle or shotgun is a much kinder hunter than prefirearm natives who, like wolves, most successfully hunted in packs. Using uncontrolled fire, driving herds over cliffs, or poisoning fishing waters, they often killed much more than they could eat or preserve.) With few exceptions, hunter-gatherers the world around must be constantly on the move. The early tribes in these parts had corn and a few vegetables as well as game, but to support their small clans, they had to move as they exhausted local game and soils. Without domestic meat or dairy animals to provide manure, they cleared and re-cleared forest to plant crops. A few dozen people will exhaust local game animals very quickly.

At the same time that Rachel Carson had published *Silent Spring* in 1962, her prediction of worldwide environmental doom, a much more useful book had made a much quieter appearance. A one-time cowboy, hobo, carpenter, boatbuilder, and teacher, Euell Gibbons, said of the great offerings in supermarkets:

The devitalized and days-old produce usually found on your grocer's shelves has been raised in ordinary dirt, manured with God-knows-what, and sprayed with poisons a list of which would read like a textbook on toxicology. They were harvested by migrant workers who could be suffering from any number of obnoxious diseases, handled by processors and salespeople and picked over by hordes of customers before you bought them.

Along with the high cost of supermarket food, Gibbons said, "people are beginning to suspect that we have paid a high spiritual price for our plenty." Gathering food in the wild would reconnect us with nature, Gibbons promised.

I did not go to Morgan Branch intending to practice what Euell Gibbons preached about wild foods, but I was a booster and a part-time follower. A few years earlier, I did not endear myself to the university's maintenance people when I wrote a wild foods article for a local alternative newspaper. I declared that no member of the staff or student body should ever complain about the cost of eating because the very green campus offered an abundance of free food along its paths, in its gardens, on its lawns, its wooded spots, and in its cemetery. The nuts included walnuts, pecans, hickories, and acorns. Berries started early in the spring with wild strawberries and went on into the summer with blackberries and mulberries. For greens, the fringes of lawn and wilder spots offered dandelions, dock, purslane, and poke *salat*. Here and there where the grounds crews did not mow or weed, Queen Anne's lace could be plucked for its carrot-like roots. The planted flowerbeds offered the buds of daylilies. Fruits included cherries, persimmons, quince, grapes, and crab apples. Occasionally the base of an aging oak offered a huge bouquet of chicken-of-the-woods mushrooms. Mushrooms also grew on the lawns and in leaf mold. The campus even offered a citrus, the ornamental orange that grows with those two-inch green thorns on low shrubs. It is a very bitter orange, but with enough sugar makes a fine tart marmalade. I never saw anybody gather any of these free eats. Only two obstacles prevented people in the university community from living off the campus: labor and laziness.

When the back-to-the-land movement started in the late 1960s, we made Euell Gibbons' *Stalking the Wild Asparagus* a best-seller. It was the kind of practical advice we needed. In eating, some people were as likely to skim the expert advice as they were in building. One couple had almost killed themselves for lack of such advice. A down-and-out folk singer and his wife had seen the term pokeweed *salat* somewhere and were pleased that ordinary pokeweed could substitute for store-bought lettuce. Maybe they had read the first paragraph in Gibbons's chapter on poke calling it "the most widely used wild vegetable in America." As soon as they finished their salads, they became deathly ill. Had they read two more pages in Gibbons, they would have learned that the leaves must be boiled and the water thrown away with the poisons it dissolves.

The saddest call I ever got from someone living on Saralyn property was from this couple. Ethan called me one afternoon and in a voice that sounded like a sleepy old man's said, "Wallace, can I bury our daughter on your land?" Ethan and his wife let their infant daughter crawl around as free and naked as their hound dog. That morning they had forgotten about her in another room and she had quenched her thirst and her life from an open can of kerosene. The law in North Carolina allowed home burial in a cardboard box. Ethan built a rough wooden box and they buried her under an old pear tree and marked the grave with a circle of stone.

The moral of this story is that the same search for quick easy answers that got us in trouble with building houses spells trouble with nutrition, too. One or more of three guides had better protect anyone who is going to bet a fortune or a life on dealing with nature. The scientific approach of careful observation and experiment requires the patience and tedious record keeping that few of us are willing to undertake. The alternative is reading reports by people who have experience. The only other defense is an inherited tradition, the wisdom and folklore of ancestors. Few of us had inherited any strong tradition of dealing with the natural world. Instead, we had grown up on the romantic vision of nature as a peaceable kingdom.

chapter 19

Meat

Meat is the easy way to live off the land, but I become a vegetarian for the wrong reason.

The first spring at Saralyn, when Sylvan came to stay, she and I began to take stock of what we could gather from the forest. For kids, foraging for wild foods becomes an exotic Easter egg hunt, and the finds are more useful. I showed her everything that I knew was edible—nuts, ferns, buds, flowers, roots, and berries. If we had gathered and processed most of the possibilities, we could have lived off the land. We couldn't have done much else.

The sad fact is that most of the wild foods in my woods or any really wild area require hard work or tedious preparation. Most require both. This is especially true if you want to keep anything for more than a few days, not to mention into the winter months. Hickory nuts are among the finest nutmeats in the world, but getting at the meat requires a smashing blow that mashes the meat and sometimes your fingers into the shrapnel of the shell. Indians and colonists gave up and boiled smashed shell and meat together to skim off the fat that rose.

Some of the acorns of oaks provide good food and drink, but they contain enough tannin to turn your stomach into a leather bag. They, too, require several boilings, after which the tannins are gone; so are most of the nutrients. Beechnuts are fine right out of the shell, but the shell is too small for a nutcracker. The work requires sharp strong fingernails. Or the beak of a bird.

Nature's interest is not served in most cases by making food easily available to human animals. The work required for humans to consume wild foods says once again why humans set out to conquer nature with technology, the two first forms being tools for hunting and gathering.

Before agriculture transformed the face of the earth, humankind found hunting much easier than gathering. A good fire will burn the hair off any corpse and render everything from the skin to bone marrow edible. Gathering and preparing an equivalent amount of vegetable nutrition from nuts, roots, berries, or hanging fruit requires much more work. The plant world has evolved a wonderful variety of ways to protect itself against unwanted animal attackers, poisoning being the most common. The power of beans to inflate the mammalian gut with painful gasses is a common example and only partly overcome by the technology of cooking. The most efficient way for the human animal to feed itself is to allow other animals to take the chances and do the hard work of gathering, then to eat these animals. Let the squirrel gather the good nuts and pick the meats. Let turkeys and deer take the tannin out of acorns and detoxify the mushrooms. Let the bears gather berries and roots. Let the birds eat the insects and thistle seeds. Let the minnows browse the algae and the big fish eat the little fish. Indians in the Carolina piedmont forests ate songbirds as well as turkeys and pigeons. They ate raccoons, bears, deer, possums, and beavers. They considered the beaver's tail a delicacy.

I brought my .22 rifle and an old single-shot 12-gauge shotgun to Morgan Branch with me. I have always shot quickly and accurately. I could have survived quite nicely as a single carnivore in these woods, especially after the deer came back. This should have been deer country, but farmers and hunters had crowded them out. Between 1698 and 1715, Carolina colonists, the Indians eagerly helping them, were shipping to England, Germany, and Europe over 50,000 deer hides each year. In Virginia in just three years, from 1699 to 1701, traders exported 130,000 hides. A deer population of from twenty to forty on each square mile made this huge trade possible.

When I first moved to Morgan Creek, I had gone to the woods of Saralyn every week for several years, and I had never seen a deer. I wouldn't see the first deer for another year. Not far away, the federal government had been buying land for a new reservoir. The state had begun to stock abandoned farms with deer. One cold November afternoon as I stood on the porch, I heard something walking on the dry leaves. A large doe was making her way up the hill from Morgan Branch, nibbling the bud ends of bushes here and there. How could she know that forty or fifty years ago on this same land chances are good that she would have been run down by farm dogs or shot by one of the Burnette boys? She was the beneficiary now of a government reservoir project and of the towns and cities that had lured the local farmers away.

The forest along Morgan Branch was not the best deer habitat, and I didn't expect to see deer when I began to live at Morgan Branch. True, deer were already stocked only eight miles away, but deer are not adventurous, sometimes suicidally so. Where food is plentiful, they seldom wander more than a mile. Deer have been known to starve to death rather than leave their home range. Exceptions exist in every crowd: Bucks are more likely to leave a range than does. They are not more aggressive eaters or explorers; they would rather leave town than fight stronger bucks.

In my second winter, deer that had no place else to go as their population exploded came to browse. Within two years, they appeared regularly around every house clearing in Saralyn and along the roadsides where grass and brush had begun to grow. I used to see six or seven together. Susan had moved onto her land next to her goat pen, but now deer instead of goats ate Ralph and Kathleen's garden—with no warning clatter of hooves on the porch. They left behind total destruction. Had I chosen to hunt, from two mature deer I could have put away a hundred pounds of meat if I used livers, hearts, and tongues. Five ounces a day of high-quality protein is a good start on living off the land. Deer might also have been a rescue of last resort if I had decided to live off the land and found myself starving. Indians rescued people from severe starvation by feeding them a broth made from the partially digested contents of the deer's compound stomachs and its intestines. They said this mustard-colored mash was the only food that would not make a starving person vomit.

Even if deer had never appeared, I could have made do on squirrel, possum, and raccoon. I can think of good reasons not to eat any of them, but none involves friendship. Squirrels are simply too much trouble for too little; they are also too much trouble alive if you happen to have apple or nut trees whose fruit you want to harvest. Possums are too fat, though William Faulkner reported that Mississippi hunters gave him their best prehunt breakfast—possum and chocolate.

A friend who is a great cook once prepared a raccoon that a hunter gave him. The body looked too much like the body of a headless child, but then the raccoon belongs to the bear branch of mammals, and like bears and humans it is a plantigrade: It plants its foot—sole and heel—flat on the ground as it walks. The high-energy meat is dark, sweet, and oily. Southerners have often hunted raccoons for reasons that have changed with the economy and culture. I had already decided not to plant corn because it draws raccoons like flies. The raccoon harvests corn a few days before it is ripe enough for humans and adds to the insult by shucking many ears and eating none entirely. Like any animal, they take whatever they can get even if it belongs to or is meant for another citizen of the forest. Animals have never been restrained by the commandment *Thou shall not steal.*

Sylvan and I had no sooner set up a bird feeder hanging by a long wire from a limb of the beech tree than a raccoon found it. I opened the door to the porch and shined a light on the animal as it perched on a limb and pulled the feeder up to where it could help itself to seed. I hung the hummingbird feeder in the same way, but from an even higher limb and on a longer wire. The coon reached out from an adjacent limb, grabbed the wire, hauled in the globular feeder full of 30-percent sugar water, held it upside down with two hands, and drank it dry.

From the start I had set out to learn the habits and behavior of all the animals in the forest, especially the benefits they bestow on human endeavors. The only good use I have found for raccoons is cleaning up table scraps. On cold nights when I didn't want to walk to the compost bin, I started setting scraps on the porch. Raccoons are also good for disposing of dead bodies. When I trapped mice in the house, I didn't have to bury them or throw them off in the woods; a corpse on the porch was always gone in the morning.

I don't find much in nature worth imitating. Recycling, however, nature does very well and with little smell. A dead body in a healthy forest does not last long. A dead deer or raccoon may lie by the side of the highway bloating and sustaining flies for several weeks. In this forest, the smelliest parts are gone in a day or two. Foxes, coons, vultures, and possums get the easiest meat cleaned off the bones in a week; the smaller bones disappear into a den somewhere. Bone disposal is a slower process, but the forest is not a jumble of wildlife bones; this testifies to a certain balance of life and recycled death.

The average squirrel lives one year. (They can live twelve years in protective custody of humans, but in a forest they are under constant attack by hawks, foxes, and snakes.) Of the dozens of squirrels that live on my land, I rarely find their bones in the forest. A bird skeleton is even rarer yet. Large predators and scavengers eat most small bones. If the reader will pardon a scatological digression, it's worth noting how efficient an owl is as a corpse recycling machine. An owl pellet (in common language we have to call it a turd) has little smell because the owl has digested and absorbed almost everything except this small, dry, whitish oblong of hair and tiny bone fragments.

I take some exception to the idea that nature recycles efficiently. If we truly imitated nature in this business, we could take a lot of our trash and simply strew it all over the ground to let it decay. When nature gets done with her leaves, she drops them all over the forest floor. The trillions of tons of vegetation nature forgot to recycle for some 30 million years in the Cretaceous Period is stored underground in vast toxic pools of pollution we call petroleum. We think nature is a good recycler partly because it's true and partly because most of her garbage is either out of sight, or as useful to us as petroleum, or, like leaves, pleasant to look at and walk on.

This brings me back to the raccoons, where my digression started. Their Latin scientific name promotes the myth that raccoons are wonderfully clean animals. *Procyon lotor* means procyon the washer. Germans call raccoons *waschbar* or washbear. But Raccoons are happy eating unwashed garbage. If their food is near water, they may dunk it to soften it. Because they don't see very well, they may also be softening their paws so they can verify what they are eating with the sense of touch.

Possum is the only other common mammal here large enough for a decent human meal, and it is the one animal I haven't tried. Looks make a difference, but I don't know why. I don't like eating an animal with a naked tail like a rat. I also have an inhibition against eating vicious animals. So-called nature stores sell cuddly stuffed possums that help a lot of people think of wildlife as cute and cuddly and nature as a nursery school. These toys have been a great boon to the psychological underpinnings of wildlife conservation. It's called doing the right thing for the wrong reason. Nothing is less cuddly than a possum. As my neighbor Susan learned very quickly, a possum will slit the throats of the entire population of a chicken house and eat one, and only the preferred parts at that.

Among the edible mammals, I finally have to mention the bat, although I have never been tempted. One of my first pleasures at Saralyn was sitting outside on a balmy spring night watching the bats cruise up and down the cleared lane above my drive and the adjoining row of fruit trees. This is one animal that is all blessing as it sweeps the skies on any warm night, killing insects as efficiently and with considerably more grace than the electronic bug sizzlers people put in their back yards. Bats, however, were eaten in connection with an unusual habit among this region's poor people. Around 1710, John Lawson saw that "the Indian Children are much addicted to eat Dirt, and so are some of the Christians." South Carolinians earned the nickname "sandlappers" from eating clay. To this day throughout the Carolinas, clay eating ("geophagy") continues among the poorest people. Most are women, often pregnant women. In some places, two or more generations have eaten enough clay to create large pits in the clay soils. Clay eating was once common in Africa as well. Ancient healers prescribed clay for several ailments. A common medicine for diarrhea contains kaolin, a form of clay.

Lawson also noted a cure for the practice: "But put a Bat on a Skewer, then pull the Skin off, and make the child that eats Dirt eat the roasted Rearmouse [the English name for bat] and he will never eat Dirt again." He did not offer his opinion on whether roast bat was a physiological cure or an effective punishment.

Now that I have listed the mammals, I am down to the smaller animals. Among these the only ones that would not take too much preparation are snakes and fish. The fish in Morgan Branch occupy every little pool among the rocks, but they are minnows, and here and there a darter as long as six inches. I never swallowed goldfish as an undergraduate, and preparing something like anchovies or the other little fishes eaten head and all takes curing, salt, and oil.

Snakes are much easier to eat and as mild as chicken. Two or three feet of snake is enough for an intimate supper. Snake skins peel off easily enough, the meat slides neatly off the fine bones and resembles chicken. Black snake is a catchall phrase for king snakes, coachwhips, and racers. Even the small racer can be five feet long, and kings and whips reach eight feet. I see more five- and six-footers than three-footers. When Sarah and I kept chickens and ducks and pheasants, I occasionally acted on behalf of my birds and killed black snakes. Many mornings I would look in on a chicken sitting her eggs only to find her paralyzed with fear and a black snake next to her. The front half of its body would be five or six big lumps. The black snake is a constrictor; it crushes live victims like a boa, but it seems incapable of cracking an egg it has swallowed. Here in the forest, black snakes have no interest in my vegetables, nuts, or fruits, and they reduce the mouse and squirrel population that does eat these things. They also climb well and eat plenty of birds, but I will not quarrel with them even if they are invading a birdhouse.

I could also eat the common water snakes and copperheads, but I prefer to leave them in their special niches. The water snake suffers enough from being mistaken for a copperhead. It is often brown and about the same size. Canoeists and fishermen on the nearby Haw River often kill water snakes and believe they have saved someone from being poisoned. The curator of the Philadelphia Zoo's reptile collection told me once that 90 percent of the "copperheads" brought in (usually dead) were water snakes or harmless hog-nosed snakes. The senseless killing is the uncontrolled elaboration of a hard-wired human fear. Even experienced snake handlers feel what Emily Dickinson called "zero at the bone" in that first instant when they unexpectedly come upon a snake within striking distance.

In Southern culture, fear of snakes has been translated into a habitual reaction that novelist and former carnival snake handler Tim McLaurin described to me: "If you run over a snake, what you do is back up and run over it again." Tim loves snakes and was not recommending, only describing. I solidified my reputation as one of the weird people of Hippie Town one afternoon when I was riding along the woods road that would be my driveway. I was with a grading contractor who was also a local farmer. I saw a three-foot copperhead lying across the wheel ruts ahead of us and said loudly, "Stop."

If he hadn't stopped before he saw the snake, he probably would have run over it and backed up and run over it again. I got out, slipped a stick under the middle of the snake, and looped it off into the woods. "My God," the farmer exclaimed, "you oughta killed it."

I told him it was a long way from anyone's house and dropped the subject. He didn't. Every year someone tells me that he has told this story again. If I had had a little more courage and guile, I should have picked it up by hand and tossed it and quoted the Bible passage that says a man with faith can handle serpents and not be bitten. That was the foundation text for a cult of snake handlers that continues to practice in scattered churches of the South.

Among the edible animals on my land, I have left out several. These include many insects. I have eaten and enjoyed fried ants with Mayan friends in Mexico and Guatemala, but when I tried the local black carpenter ants, they were too acidic. Most of us eat unseen grubs and insects cooked with our rice, grains, and mushrooms, but out of sight is, well, down the hatch. Sylvan once put a container of mushroom soup in the freezer with a note, "Don't serve to anyone squeamish. There may be some worms or grubs."

The only wild animals in America to be successfully domesticated for food are the bison and the turkey. I have only turkeys, and they are so rare that I leave them alone. In New England and New York, wild turkeys appear in fields as often as deer. They are an American conservation success story that has much more to do with the sentiments of suburbia about wildlife and hunting than about laws and regulations. Unlike the small farms and gardens of New England, my forest demands that a turkey work hard for its living, especially in the years the oaks do not drop a large crop of acorns. Turkeys have a hard enough life without me shooting at them.

The other bird I could put on the table is the mourning dove, a cousin of the extinct passenger pigeon, but smaller. Summer and winter they pick up seeds under my feeder and prowl the rows in my garden. Unlike the pigeons, they are not interested in vegetables or fruits. Because I have only one or two pairs each year, I would be doing away with a year-round display of bird behavior for one small meal of dove breast and thigh.

I have left out several edibles from this catalog of walking, flying, swimming, and crawling protein, but the truth is that once I became my own cook, I also became a vegetarian. I did not become a vegan (pronounced "VEEgun"). New Age people launched that word to distinguish themselves from ordinary vegetarians. The organization Vegan Action tells us that "veganism, the natural extension of vegetarianism, is an integral component of a cruelty-free lifestyle." Vegan Action is making a statement about the treatment of captive animals. They are culinary pacifists. They are abolitionists who want to abolish animal slavery (although some keep dogs, cats, and goldfish). They want to make a moral statement. In the service of their ideal they have enlisted all the information available about the bad health effects of animal fat, eggs, milk, cheese, and butter. Sturdy but impoverished Eskimos, Siberian reindeer herders, Berbers, Mongolians, and Kazakhs would find this a bit odd because they pass from birth to death eating little but meat, milk, butter, and cheese.

I think the term "vegan" deliberately sounds like the name for a space alien because these people would prefer to live on another planet where evolution has not created such murderous ways of feeding critters at the top of the food chain.

I am not a culinary pacifist. I am a competitive vegetarian, and I don't mind spilling blood when necessary. As soon as I became a vegetarian, I also started to kill squirrels to save my apples and filbert bushes, and I felt no guilt; yet I have never found pleasure in killing any animal even in self-defense. Most good hunters live by the rule of eat what you kill. For me, the reverse holds: Kill what you eat. To this, Dr. Larison Cudmore, a cell biologist, suggests a version of the golden rule: If respect for life motivates vegetarians, she says, they should eat animals. This would show their respect for the pacifism of plants, which eat neither animals nor each other. Her suggestion might be summed up as kill what kills.

My vegetarian habit is not respect for animal rights and it is not an attempt to include them in the rules of civil behavior. Just the opposite. An animal that is going to eat another animal must either kill it or eat carrion. If I were to shape my behavior by the animal examples around me, I would be a hunter. That I do not kill other animals to satisfy my own appetite does not express my kinship or fellow feeling for other animals; it reminds me that as a human being I have the intelligence and choice to exempt myself from the rules hardwired into their brains.

I practice my vegetarianism faithfully enough that I feel no guilt when I eat with friends and enjoy a rack of lamb at Easter or the turkey of Thanksgiving dinner. I have spared more than enough life to occasionally enjoy my place among carnivores and omnivores with no more guilt than the lion feels when eating a zebra brought down by another member of the pride. Humans are the only meat eaters who practice mercy.

When I moved to Morgan Branch, I made one exception to my vegetarian regime. I brought with me from the old house a pair of goats. Sarah had given me my first goat, a large old white nanny, the summer after Sylvan was born. A pack of dogs killed her one night, and I replaced her with another nanny with a somewhat unpredictable nature. Sylvan named her in Spanish, *No-Sí*. No-Sí had two kids, both males. Sarah did not want to look after them, and I had work for them to do. Their job was to clean up a few small patches of honeysuckle and poison ivy and cat briar that had established themselves in patches where the falling of old trees had opened the canopy and let in sunlight. I did not eat these goats; but goats being goats, they had babies, two babies each year. For three years toward the end of fall when the grass and weeds and vines and briars stopped growing, I killed the young goats because they were always males. (In the animal world, in the wild and on the farm, it's usually the males who are killed or driven out.) A female goat I might have given to someone for milking.

Farm children do not grow up more callous or violent than other kids do, and most farm kids see animals killed from the time they can walk in the farmyard. Sylvan already knew nature was a bloody place. She wrote to her grandmother in December about a stone turtle, a dress, and matter-of-factly about a dog attack on one of the young goats: "My turtle has a bed made out of paper. My thing that is made out of rock is the turtle and his pillow is made out of cotton. One of my goats died and my father said a dog ate the goat's skin and a dog did it. My mother gave me a dress for Christmas."

I told myself that I did not want Sylvan to see an animal die before she was old enough to understand, but in retrospect I think I was embarrassed for her to see me kill. It was my problem, not hers. When I brought the dead goats to the house and hung them up to be dressed, she stood by to hand me knives and pans. We had seen dead animals in the woods and she had watched her mother and me clean ducks and chickens. This was her first full view inside a large animal.

Evolution may have hardwired into us some responses to nature, like the fear of snakes or the habit of sleeping at night, but squeamishness in the presence of blood and guts is learned, not wired. Children are not naturally squeamish or saddened by the death of an animal. From this beginning, two directions are equally possible. An old task of civilization is to be sure that children move from this beginning toward respect for life instead of toward callousness and brutality. With the spate of publicity about violence and murder by children at the close of the twentieth century, we have also received a list of signs that warn us when a child has turned in the wrong direction. Teasing, torture, and wantonly killing animals are the clearest signs.

Many hunters say civilization has overdone respect for life and turned it into revulsion toward natural processes and an ignorance of how food gets on the table. Everyone knows that rib roast might come from a cute little lamb, and the steak was a round-eyed steer or cow, but no one wants to admit personal responsibility for their deaths and dismemberment.

Sylvan at age five watched so intently as I cut the goat's skin open from neck to hind legs that I might have been opening a jewel box or sliding back the door to a mysterious cave. The complexity of living organisms, even a single-celled plant, makes black holes and galaxies seem merely mathematical and mechanical. I was no anatomist and had struggled through freshman zoology, but even I could tell Sylvan more about this goat than the greatest scientists of the Renaissance or an Indian hunter could have. I removed the skin carefully, showing her how the spidery white tissue attached it to muscle and bone, and how a jerk of the thin layers of muscle under the skin had caused the twitches she knew from petting. I gently opened the thin sheath of the abdomen to reveal the team of organs that refine everything from briars to nuts into heat, energy and materials for repair and maintenance of every working part. I opened the chest to show her the bright pink lungs. I took out the heart and opened its chambers.

I remember the cleaning as a long and careful lesson. Sylvan doesn't remember. When I asked her about this not long ago, she said she remembered waiting at the house and hearing the rifle shots. And she remembers eating goat meat. She still eats meat and I'm satisfied that she has always known how it gets to the table.

What I might have hunted at Morgan Branch is a purely theoretical discussion, not only because I chose to be a vegetarian, but because I had prohibited hunting anywhere at Saralyn. When I wrote the covenants for Saralyn, I put in ARTICLE XI: "No hunting, capture, or killing of any forms or species of wildlife shall take place within the confines of this subdivision, except that poisonous snakes and insects which endanger human health and comfort may be controlled or exterminated." I had once gone to upstate New York, 150 miles northwest of New York City, at the opening of deer-hunting season. At dawn and dusk the woods and fields sounded like a shooting gallery. Deer were rare but increasing in Chatham County, but hunters pursued dove, quail, rabbit, fox, coons, turkey, squirrel, and possum. My first fall and winter in the woods were blissfully quiet. I heard a few muffled shots from fields far away.

A coon hunter one night followed his baying beagles from lands west of Saralyn over the ridge and down Morgan Branch, waking me up at two in the morning. Coon hunters bay to their dogs almost as loudly as the dogs bay after their prey. An intrusion like this into my woods and my sleep in those first few years here seemed as outrageous as a buffalo hunt in Yellowstone Park. This was my park. I took my old shotgun and stuffed a shell in it. I stepped onto the porch; the hounds were passing below the house. I saw the hunter's flashlight two hundred yards behind. I heard him baying to his dogs. I saw two flashlights. I was doubly outraged. I pointed the gun at the stars and pulled the trigger.

The flashlights searched wildly all over the forest. A man called, "Don't shoot. Who is that?"

I let them search for a few seconds before answering. "Who are you?" I shouted back.

His flashlight found the house but I stood back on the porch where it couldn't reach me. "I'm out here with my boy coon hunting," the man shouted back. "I didn't know there was anyone out here. Can I talk to you?"

The dogs were down the creek, their baying getting fainter. The man howled to them several times and they stopped barking. I stepped to the edge of the porch and told him to come on up. We talked outside by my truck. The coon hunter was a few years older than I was. His son was twelve or thirteen. When I introduced myself, he introduced himself, Billy Allen, and his son, Tommy. The boy said, "Glad to meet you, sir," and he also shook my hand.

"I wanted to take my boy out in the woods and teach him something about coon hunting," Billy said. "I'm sorry if we disturbed you, but you didn't have to shoot at us."

"I shot up in the air," I explained.

"Sure surprised us. I liked ta died," he laughed.

I apologized and said I probably should have yelled to him but I was a little ticked off.

"I understand," he said, and apologized again. "Do you mind if I call for my dogs 'fore they get too far off?"

I told him I didn't mind. He called them and in a few minutes I could hear them coming our way. Billy apologized again, and he and his son headed back up Morgan Branch the way they had come. I liked them, and I have liked most hunters I have met. I have never met a hunter who enjoyed making an animal suffer. I don't pretend to know what moves any person to hunt. I've heard different explanations, but none of them hinted at sadism. Plenty of animals hunt for play, sport, or at least practice. Few animals eat all of a big kill. I suspect that in humans some primeval need remains that wants to test the power to dominate, to hunt, and to be the arbiter of life and death.

Hunters have preserved and restored more wildlife and wildlife habitat than environmentalists, and they often do it with their own money. Environmentalists put out bird feeders; hunters plant thousands of acres in wildlife crops. Environmentalists specialize in nearly extinct species;

hunters have paid their license fees and have supported habitat protection with hundreds of millions of dollars. Long before the environmental movement began, hunters in Ducks Unlimited were doing work that would save over 6 million acres of wetlands. The game departments of western states have earned more than $20 million from hunters to restore wild sheep habitat.

I could get annoyed with hunters who came into Saralyn, but by the time I met Billy Allen and his son, I knew that my antikilling covenant was a mistake. The coons and possums that came to our porch and the deer that would soon be taking over gardens and landscaping had no natural predators. Only the human animal could keep their numbers in check, and in my sentimentality I had condemned Saralyn to a fate that had already overtaken a few places in New York and New Jersey.

–chapter 20–

Water

*A biological necessity leads me from living water to
fossil water and also to a new profession.*

In listing the goods of the forest, one above all others was most important
to my comfort and survival. From the deserts of Arizona to the ocean islands of Maine, so many people now live in cities with public water supplies that few think or understand how water determines where and how
they live. A biologist once said that human beings are walking bags of sea
water. The point is valid: Take away our water, minerals, and salts and the
body shrivels to a small pile of bone and fiber. The saline content of our
blood equals the salinity of some sea waters. We can live for weeks without
food, three days without water. Water is the most critical element of life on
earth.

Many visitors to Morgan Branch surprise me the way children amuse
their parents when they find out that milk does not come from a supermarket bottle but from a cow. Grownup visitors to Morgan Branch ask if it is
expensive to get water put in "all the way out here." Nature put in the water supply long before I or anyone else came here, but using it is not simple.

Visitors are used to ponds made opaque and green by algae and our warm
Carolina weather. They are used to rivers that are almost always brown
with silt washed from their banks or from road ditches. They look into the
cold clear waters in Morgan Branch and say, "It's so clean you can drink it."
This is yet another case of inventing nature rather than knowing it or even

using common sense. A friend once found out the truth in a wilderness area when he took a pause from his hike and took long and wonderful mouthfuls of water from a crystalline stream. When he stood up again and looked around, refreshed, he saw a dead deer lying twenty-five yards upstream. No one should need that kind of knock with a psychological two-by-four. A stream running brown or black or devoid of life may seem quite polluted. A stream with any life in it is sure to be polluted. Every creature with a mouth, from a single-celled paramecium to a deer, also has a second hole—ingest here, excrete there. Streams like Morgan Branch are also popular toilets for the animals that walk along the banks, wade in the water, or fly and perch over them. How many people would pour a cool drink from a goldfish bowl or from a pitcher through which I had just run a three-foot water snake?

When I was digging my foundations, I sometimes ran out of reliable water or juice when I was exhausted and desperately thirsty. I did drink from the clear cold waters of Morgan Branch, and I have done so on a few occasions since. Streams like this seduce because they have a real taste, but that very taste tells you that in between the tasteless molecules of H_2O are molecules of something else. Probably many other things—rock, clay, soil, dead leaves . . . I will stop before I get to the excreta of living things or the larvae and cells of life itself.

My excuse for not hiring a well driller was money. My excuse for not digging a well by hand was time. The deciding truth was that I didn't want to be at the bottom of a narrow thirty-foot hole looking up at a tiny ring of sky. I also remembered a local man telling me how the farmer who hired him had hit hard rock far down a well hole and tried to dynamite it. The dynamite didn't go off and the hired man was lowered into the hole to retrieve the dynamite. That was good enough reason not to dig a well—or to be a black farmhand in the old South.

I simply walked down to Morgan Branch and filled two buckets of water at a time. I filled a barrel at the house for wash and cooking water; I left buckets under the eaves for rain. A gallon of boiled water would last two or three days. I bathed from a bucket inside, or from a tub of hot water outside. From June through September, when the days are hotter than blood, I would save myself from heatstroke by lying in a deep wide pool of Morgan Branch whose waters are cold year round. Even on the hottest day I had to lower myself in slowly. Once in, I could lie there with my head on the pillow of a stone and soon the minnows would come nibbling. In fifteen minutes or half an hour, the fatigue of the day's labor had bled into the slow current and on downstream over the rocks and through the woods to lose itself in the broad fast back of the Haw River a few miles away.

The second year, when I had enough money for a pump, a friend helped me dig a hole in the thick clay next to Morgan Branch. I sank in a two-foot-diameter section of clay pipe. In the creek I set a plastic pipe with a screen filter on its end and buried the ten feet that ran from the creek into my clay pipe. Another line ran from inside the clay pipe up the hill to the pump under the house. I now had Morgan Creek running out of my kitchen faucets. In the space reserved for a bathroom, I built a tiled enclosure for a shower. I still boiled my drinking water.

The system worked well enough but had two or three quirks. Whenever a heavy rain fell, the sediments it stirred and washed into the creek got through my intake screen and gradually filled my reservoir. The faucets ran dry. I would have to go down to the pipe with small saucepans and scoop out the gray sediments. In dry spells when the creek shriveled, the sources of the water's wild taste concentrated unpleasantly and the smell lingered in the dishwater and shower.

One morning, my shower smelled particularly bad. It smelled like death, wet death. I went to the reservoir and lifted back the sheet of metal covering it; a foot-long bullfrog lay belly-up on the surface of the water in an advanced stage of decay. I decided to put more effort into saving money for a drilled well.

I knew by the end of the first summer that I would have to follow Thoreau's example and earn enough money for such luxuries as a drilled well. The government's reservoir-building project had already qualified me for a new part of the real estate business and had paid for some of the materials in the house. Two years earlier, my friend Wade Barber, who had come home to Pittsboro to join his father's venerable country law firm, called me one morning. He was to the point as few Southerners are, and he prefaced his business with a laugh, so I knew he was about to announce a surprise. "Can you do a real estate appraisal?" he asked me.

"No. I haven't a clue," I told him. I still had my broker's license and I was even the nominal owner of a little firm called Heartwood Realty.

"Well, nobody else in Chatham County can, either," he told me, "but I am sure you can." He made it sound simple. "I need an expert witness on land value in this part of Chatham County and I think you're an expert. You've sold a lot of land, right?"

Thoreau had earned his cash surveying, and I would earn mine appraising. I bought a few books and read about appraising real estate. I looked at
the seventy-three acres of pines that belonged to a retired farmer and made
a list of similar property and what it had sold for. I concluded that if the
other properties had sold for X dollars an acre, my client's might have sold
for Y dollars. The government was offering $300 an acre and I thought the
property could have sold for $750 an acre. (The last lots in Saralyn had
sold for that much.) I have lost that appraisal and I'm glad of it. If Wade
knew more about appraisals than I did, he had the good sense not to unset-
tle his key witness.

For my day on the witness stand I got a haircut, shaved, and put on a suit
I had not worn for a few years. I put my appraisal in a respectable-looking
leather briefcase that a craftsman friend had made for me. A panel of three
retired judges and lawyers sat behind the bench; two were robust and well
fed, the third gaunt and sallow. All three seemed slightly impatient from
the start. After Wade's opening remarks promising that his expert witness
would show how wrong the government's professional appraisers were, he
sat me in a witness box before the panel and said, "Your Honors, I tender
Mr. Kaufman as an expert appraiser of land values."

The United States District Attorney objected. "Mr. Kaufman, have you
studied appraisal?"

No.

"Are you a member of any appraisal institute?"

No.

"Have you ever appraised a piece of property?"

No.

"Do you subscribe to any appraisal magazines?"

No.

He paused and mulled something in his head. I was afraid the next question was going to be, "Are you the developer of Hippie Town?"

"Your Honor," the U.S. District Attorney said, "the government objects
to Mr. Kaufman's testimony."

The three old men conferred briefly in whispers. The chairman said,
"Well, we'll admit him as an expert on land values in Chatham County.
Overruled."

I was far from an expert appraiser, but I was not a bad teacher. Expert testimony is largely the process of teaching, of filling a void in the minds of
your audience. The expert's effectiveness depends on his ability to explain

how a member of the jury or the commission might do what he did, and how to arrive at the same conclusion and feel it is correct. An appraisal is also a story: It is the story of how a piece of property has taken its place in a particular real estate market and how the forces in that market have changed its value for better or worse. Those market forces are mainly the desires and judgments of people. I did know how people looked at rural property and how much they would spend, and I wanted the commissioners to understand the characters in my story, the people who bought and sold land. We waited several weeks while the commissioners considered our case and several others, and I wondered if they had understood my story.

They understood. As I recall, they awarded the landowner over $600 per acre. I was soon getting more calls to appraise farms and woodlands the government was taking to make what would become Jordan Lake. The cross-examination questions got harder and my appraisals got better. Three years after I moved to Morgan Branch, I called a well driller.

The foundation rock of the old continent of Taconia lay only inches below the soil in which I dug the footings for my house. The rock near the surface defeated me, but the real rock, the blue-gray tufa, begins deeper. On an eroded hillside, it may be ten feet below the surface, thirty or forty feet down in flatter areas. A man with hand tools can only chip at it. Even this rock, hundreds of feet thick, has cracks and flaws and lenses of silts and sands. Rain that falls on the land here slowly works its way down through the red clays, moving inches in a day. Sooner or later, it reaches the foundation rocks; there it finds the cracks and flaws, few thicker than a sheet of cardboard. In some places, the rock is merely wet. In others, water runs as freely as a small stream or collects in pools and puddles.

To find the water in the flaws of the rock, many of my friends hired water witchers, or dowsers. Dowsers are men and women who say they can find a vein of water by walking over the land with the two branches of a forked stick held in their hands. Some use hickory, some willow, others peach. I have seen them zigzag across a piece of land, plodding slowly and carefully, the forked stick held out before their waists. Suddenly the point just beyond the union of the two legs dips toward the ground. Many dowsers announce their finds: "One hundred feet below this point you will get five to ten gallons a minute."

Most of our local dowsers were good church-going country people who refused to get paid for what they called their gift. They willingly took a donation. The owner-builders I know believed in dowsers for several reasons: First, finding a good vein of water in the unseen rock is largely chance, so a dowser could do no harm and might do good. More important, I think, was that the dowser, if you believed in him, was a human being solving your problem by tuning in to nature. We wanted to believe that the old country people could tune in even if they never turned on. I wanted to believe, but I didn't.

Yes, I had seen Walker Farrell plodding in his coveralls over a friend's hilltop until the tip of the black birch fork in his hand suddenly dived toward the ground. "There is good water under here," Walker said. "You will get it in a hundred and fifty feet." My friend said no, that was not a convenient spot and would he please do another. Walker said he only did one spot on a property and that was that. My friend ordered the driller to drill in a more convenient spot; he drilled for two days through blue-gray tufa until they capped a dry hole at 455 feet. At $6 a foot, it was an expensive hole. He drilled the second hole on Walker's spot and got two gallons a minute, not much, but enough for a small family.

Incidents like these become local history and proof, at least to the would-be believer. But in fact they prove as little as Aunt Jenny, who smoked for seventy years and never got lung cancer. People believe in dowsers because drilling a well in old Taconia is expensive and uncertain and we would like to believe that someone knows what he is doing. Life itself is like a well—costly and uncertain. For that reason alone some people believe in God.

I have watched wells drilled all over this region, dowsed and undowsed. I've made an informal tally and here's the score: People who know little about geology and water and choose convenient spots do worse than dowsers. Dowsers know from experience where the best guesses can be made; their experience tells them what hydrogeologists have confirmed— underground water tends to collect in the same places you might expect to find it on the surface. It runs off hilltops onto hillsides and into ravines and pools in low spots. The bedrock of Taconia generally follows the contours of the surface. People who follow the advice of hydrogeologists have the best record of finding good water.

A well-drilling truck is forty feet long and not very agile. Michael Manness, the young driller who had taken over his father's business, had a hard time following the old woods road to my house. He had few choices when he got to the house and none of them were first rate in geological terms.

He couldn't drive into a ravine, and I didn't want to cut the old trees along Morgan Branch. We settled for a spot on the hillside west of the house, far enough below the top of the land that it might not be dry. Even here, the rear end of the truck, the business end, had to be jacked five feet above the ground to stay level with the front end.

Each drill section is a twenty-foot-long, six-inch-diameter tube of hardened steel. As the first section with its grinding teeth inches down, new sections are threaded on above it. A pump forces water down the hole to flush it and cool the drill tip. When the water flowing out of the hole exceeds the volume being pumped in, your luck has begun. The diesel that powers the drill cranked up and drowned all conversation. It became the only voice in the forest. The first section sank quickly and red mud flowed from the hole. Just before it was about to disappear, the red turned to blue and the descent of the drill slowed. We had hit Taconia. Michael pulled the drill out and forced iron casing into the hole to keep the red clay soils from contaminating the water I hoped he would soon find in the rock.

From that point on, I watched hour after hour as one drilling section after another disappeared into the earth. Each section cost me $120. We quickly passed a depth equal to the distance of Morgan Branch below the site. No water. One hundred feet, no water. Two hundred. All the time the flushing water was bringing out ground-up blue-gray rock; it began to flow away from the well shaft into the woods, a stream of cold lava. At 255 feet Michael said, "We are getting about two gallons a minute."

I said stop. Pressure forced the water out of the cracked rocks into the path of least resistance, the well shaft. It rose quickly to within twenty-five feet of the surface. If it had risen above the surface, I would have had an artesian well. I had never seen one here, and I was content that my reservoir stood 225 feet high; in a six-inch pipe, that's about an equal number of gallons. Michael fastened the three-foot-long stainless steel cylinder of a submersible pump to two hundred feet of black plastic pipe and a couple of thick electric wires and lowered it into the hole. He trenched another length of pipe two feet deep from the well into the cellar space below the house. I connected it to the pipes fed by the pump that had brought water from Morgan Branch.

That was the last time I would shower or brush my teeth with the funeral waters of a dead bullfrog. I had regrets about abandoning Morgan Branch despite its difficulties; suddenly I was little different from my friends whose water was delivered by the city. My water was out of sight and would easily stay out of mind. I would have liked my house to be like the famous tea-room built by the tea master Rikyu in the early seventeenth century. His house was on a hillside overlooking the sea; when a few invited friends arrived with great expectation of the view, they found he had planted a screen of evergreens between his garden and the view. When they were invited to prepare for tea, they followed the garden stepping-stones to the water basin where they performed the ritual rinsing of mouths and washing of hands outside the tearoom. When each guest bent to the basin to dip water, he discovered he could see through a break in the evergreens the bright and distant sea. At that moment, says Dr. Jiro Harada in *Japanese House and Garden*, the guest realized "the relationship between the dipperful of water in his hand and the great ocean beyond" and also his own humble place in the universe.

−chapter 21−

The Bean Patch and the Corporate Farm

My commitment to the simple life requires a garden.
The garden requires protection. I become legislator,
enforcer, judge, and executioner.

When people dropped out of universities and jobs to start living off the land they imagined growing their own food would put them in humble and happy collaboration with nature. We subscribed to Robert Rodale's *Organic Gardening*, which promised that moral and physical health and giant vegetables would be won by abandoning chemical fertilizers and pesticides. I had become a confirmed organic gardener by the time I came to Morgan Branch, but I also knew that laying down straw as mulch meant sewing its seeds in your own garden. I knew that digging manure into the clay was a lot harder than throwing around granules of fertilizer. Our second Bible of rural living was *The Foxfire Book* from a rural high school in Georgia. It was a collection of oral testimony of old mountain people about farming and rural crafts and the good old ways of splitting shingles, making baskets, planting, and preserving food. Nothing in it told why their lives had left them looking so beat up and toothless.

The first garden I ever planted a seed in was a failure of farming and patriotism, but the hope of putting a bare seed in bare soil and reaping a tomato or basket of beans promised a miracle worth pursuing. That was the summer of 1943 and my parents and neighbors seemed consumed by a single purpose—win the war. I had seen a picture in the newspaper of a Japanese soldier poised to cut off the head of an American captive. That was all the reason I needed to understand why winning was important. Everyone must help win the war. While soldiers, sailors, and airmen were fighting "overseas," the President Roosevelt told people in America how to help. Plant a Victory Garden.

We had just moved from a small apartment in Queens, where dangerous kids lived on our block, to the Long Island suburb of Roslyn Heights. We rented a cheap and narrow row house on a street with a nice name, Geraldine Place. The house had a narrow back yard and a front yard big enough for one Norway maple. This was the first place I had been happy to live and my happiness came from having our own land. Of course we should plant a garden for the president.

My two brothers and I followed my father into the backyard where he hacked at the ground with the coal shovel from the cellar. Under the dirt we found coal ashes that had been hauled out of the furnace in earlier years. When he had made several rows, he handed us seeds and told us where to put them. He covered the seeds and spread water on them from a kitchen pot. We waited, one week, two weeks, three. Nothing appeared. Nothing ever rose from that dead soil. The coal ashes had defeated the Victory Garden but the defeat only confirmed the sense that raising food from the ground was a miracle.

When Thoreau called the twelve labors of Hercules "trifling" compared to the labor of his farming neighbors, he had already grown his bean patch. In his two years at Walden, he tilled his bean patch only the first year. His profit for the entire endeavor was $8.71 and some $4.50 worth of food for himself. In other words, he had done worse than I had. For the work of an entire spring, summer, and fall he pocketed the equivalent of a week and a half's wages. His second year at Walden he turned over less than one third of an acre with a shovel. I intended to turn over much less at Morgan Branch.

Growing beans, or any other crop to eat, is the most fulfilling and the most enslaving of all labors, with the exception of raising children. It is also more often heartbreaking. The intensity of reward in growing food begins to fall on a steep slope after one has fed oneself and put up enough for the off season. When I went to live at Morgan Branch, I knew enough of farming than to try to make money from it. I wanted only my own vegetables, and then only with the least demand on my time. Morgan Branch fortunately offered a good piece of soil to turn over and plant.

I was not the first person to choose the small piece of flat land along Morgan Branch to grow a crop. As soon as I began turning over soil in that first spring, I discovered pottery, stone knives, scrapers, and arrowheads. I had found the right spot, but so had others. They had come and gone. It wasn't chance that led me to choose this site. In our forests, finding any patch of land with topsoil more than a few inches deep is almost as hard as finding gold. Where Morgan Branch joined the little run that followed my drive, the branch Sylvan named Seven Spring Branch, their occasional floodwaters and runoff from the surrounding hills had covered the piedmont clays with a foot-and-a-half-deep layer of dark brown loam. A long forgotten act of commerce also rewarded me: A small rectangular pit in this area told me that loggers had once built a saw mill here. These steam-powered portable mills were never more than a half mile from the trees being cut, so I could judge from the age of my trees and the few remaining stumps when this mill might have operated. It had been gone seventy years or more. The millers would have left all over this ground sawdust, bark, and whatever slabs they didn't burn to make steam. Thanks to the endless work of termites, fungus, and beetles, their waste had become my soil.

The trees had also grown back, but not on this little triangle of loam. The nearby trees were the greatest problem. When you have sixty- and eighty-foot trees around a small garden, even the summer sun does not shine in until ten or ten-thirty in the morning and shade reclaims the place at three or four in the afternoon. Look at the southern edge of any field that borders a forest and you will see the corn or soybeans are stunted there.

Every garden and farm is a battle between its creator and creation. The first necessity is sunlight so that photosynthesis can take place and plants can create the energy to produce beans or potatoes or ears of corn. Few vegetables in the human diet enjoy shade. Thoreau was lucky to have his bean patch in a scrubby tract of woods where pines and hickories were just beginning the long march from logged land to climax forest. The huge expanses of old-growth forest that early settlers discovered demanded something like heroic effort to clear a garden plot and enough trees on the east, west, and south to gather good light. The choicest sights were on gentle south slopes or floodplains of rivers and creeks or along the shores of lakes and bays. The Indians had already occupied most of these sites and often fought with each other for their possession.

Rather than cut huge hardwoods with hand axes and two-man saws, the colonists joined the fight for open land. Fields the Indians cultivated were not little garden plots. They often occupied ten, twenty, or even a hundred acres of burned-over forest. In 1614, when Captain John Smith cruised the coast of New England, he noted by Boston Harbor, "Many Iles all planted with corne." Two years later, European diseases swept through New England's Indian population, and by the time the Puritans arrived, these same islands were thick with young trees. When Thoreau ploughed his garden at Walden, he, too, discovered arrowheads and stone tools and concluded "that an extinct nation had anciently dwelt here and planted corn and beans." He blamed that long-gone agriculture with partly exhausting his soils. Historians estimate that from the Berkshires in western Massachusetts east to the coast almost every acre of land was at one time cleared and planted by Indians. It is probably fair to say that Indian agricultural technology had eliminated most of the virgin forests of the eastern coastal plains three or four hundred years before Europeans arrived.

Given the hard labor required for even a small garden or orchard, I cannot blame Indians for resorting to the greatest power they had, fire, and I well understand why in the late nineteenth century clearing land and loosening the subsoil for orchards made dynamite popular.

"Let there be light" is the first great commandment for the gardener who would subdue creation to create a garden in a forest. I did not have enough light in my garden, but I could grow beets, cabbage, lettuce, and other vegetables that tolerate some shade and do not thrive in the middle of a southern summer.

The second great commandment of gardening is "Let there not be life." At least not weeds or animal life. One of the few joys of creating a garden in a forest is that for a year or two the winds and animals have not brought enough weed seeds to require the hoeing that plagued Thoreau. Indians who practiced-slash-and-burn agriculture abandoned their plots in part because they drained the soil's nutrients and in part because the weeds began to take over. I have always agreed with Indian planters that a good offense is the best defense against weeds. Plant your crops thick and mix them so that the low-growing squashes shade the ground with their big leaves. Let the beans climb the stalks of corn or okra.

English settlers on the East Coast often made fun of the wild-looking Indian gardens the way some of my visitors make fun of my wild-looking garden. The Indians avoided all the hoeing the English garden and its sense of order required. I had learned another valuable lesson about weeds in my first garden: Eat them. One day when I was selling corn, a Korean woman came to the farm and after setting aside some beans and tomatoes, she said, "Would you mind if I pulled some weeds in your corn?"

I try not to be surprised by unusual human charity and I said I would be very grateful. She came back with a big basket full of green leaves, a weed I had methodically pulled up in the corn rows. I knew it was amaranth. I didn't know how good the tender top leaves taste when cooked like spinach or mixed with sautéed onions, a little garlic, and a dash of soy sauce. I had also read a pamphlet put out by North Carolina State University on what chemicals could eliminate amaranth in your fields, but, being a small organic farmer, I pulled some by hand and let the rest grow.

The first year of my garden by Morgan Branch, I had almost no weeds. What a great pleasure that was after farming on fields that had been open for a century. The second-year weeds appeared from seeds that had blown in or that had been dropped from the front or back end of an animal passing through. The new weeds included Jerusalem artichokes, and I have come to welcome them even more than amaranth. This is not the green artichoke of laminated petals, tender hearts, and the gourmet vegetable bin. This is not a native of the Holy Land, either. This is what southerners call "sunchokes." The flowers on top of five-to-eight-foot-high stalks look like miniature sunflowers when they come out in mid-September. Because they look like sunflowers, which the French explorers would have called *girasole*, the English who followed heard "Jerusalem." Artichoke may be the corruption of an Indian word, the same word that was applied to the Artichoke River.

One scientist claimed that the artichoke and the sunflower were the only crops whose cultivation was initiated by North American Indians. No one has to cultivate this artichoke. It comes uninvited and aggressive into any open space where another vegetable might grow. The challenge is not cultivation but control. Jerusalem artichokes are a true weed, an opportunist that takes control of ground where other plants have only weak claims. A freshly turned garden is precisely that kind of weakly claimed land. It invites weeds. No one has to weed a mature forest. Once established, it stays that way for centuries. An untended garden won't survive more than a few weeks. It is the ultimate affront to natural processes. It is as much the commandeering and domineering of nature as making a better world through chemistry.

As soon as you have cleared land and turned over the soils, you have created a wrestling mat for nature's combatants and your vegetables. The artichoke will win the entire space in one season. While they are putting up those nice stalks and flowers and while the leaves are turning brilliant yellow in the late autumn, underground their roots have swollen into tubers that will be sweet and crisp after the first frosts. These tubers have also begun to stake claims underneath the other vegetables.

The first year that I dug them up from the edge of my garden, I was more than happy with the crisp, slightly sweet roots. They are fine pickled, eaten raw, sliced and dried for chips, or cooked any way you might cook a potato. The second year of my garden, however, I discovered that in digging up these roots I had spread their invasion. My shovel had cut many of the tubers, and I unknowingly scattered small pieces beyond the place where I had dug them out. In the spring they sent up hundreds of pencil-thick ravenous shoots.

If Europeans had not been so lazy, they might have taken the Jerusalem artichoke back home along with the potato as a commoner's food. The artichoke would have done much better in Ireland's cold and wet soils. With perfect hindsight I can say that with the artichoke, the wet cool summers of 1845–1850 that blighted Ireland's potatoes would not have been disasters. The Irish would not have suffered the famine that killed a million people and drove another million onto boats for America. But then America's population stew would not have been so rich.

I had no sooner put in my garden than nature reinforced a lesson I had not learned well enough in my farming days in more settled areas. The most dangerous and costly invaders of the garden in the forest are not weeds but animals. Thoreau said that woodchucks had eaten a quarter acre of his beans but that he would gladly share a third of what he grew with his wild neighbors. With rich friends in town he could afford the luxury, though I suspect his generosity was more talk than fact. He writes that he spent seven hours a day hoeing. Was he really willing to lose two of the seven for the sake of feeding wildlife? I certainly wasn't. Even Thoreau admits that in the second year at Walden, when his garden was smaller, "Once I went so far as to slaughter a woodchuck which ravaged my bean-field—effect his transmigration, as a Tartar say—and devour him, partly for experiment's sake."

I didn't come to Morgan Branch to work for squirrels and raccoons or to have them work for me. This was an honorable but unilateral treaty—one they could never understand or agree to. By their limited understanding, whatever grows in their territory is their food. At least it is theirs if they can win it. I began to learn this as soon as I dug up and fertilized the first year's garden.

As an organic gardener, I decided to fertilize according to my principles. I had tried horse and cow manure, but that's an excellent way to bring into a garden the tragedy of Johnson grass and Bermuda grass. Farmers here joke you can stake your tomatoes on Johnson grass. I once tried to smother a patch of creeping Bermuda grass by putting bales of hay on it, two bales high. Within a few weeks the grass had sent runners up through the hay and into the sunlight. I decided on fish. Didn't Squanto teach the Puritans to put fish in their hills of corn? (The answer to that is probably no. The facts are that Europeans used to fertilize their fields with fish and probably brought the practice to America. The Indians, who had not invented the wheel and had no carts or horses to haul heavy loads of fish, may have used them near rivers or the coast. Women did most of the Indian gardening, and maybe they stopped short of hauling fish. In any case, the practice was not widespread.)

I had a friend in Chapel Hill who smoked bluefish and bass. He often had batches that didn't turn out well. Sure, he said, go out in back of the shop and help yourself to the boxes of rejects. I filled the back of my pickup. When I opened the boxes I was tempted to eat, but if my friend Andy said they were spoiled, I wasn't going to risk it. They were beautiful two-foot-long bluefish. They deserved a proper burial. I dug a long trench where I planned to put each row of seeds. I buried the fish a foot deep and mounded the soil over them. I had done this with fresh chicken manure once and had wonderful crops as the vegetables slowly sank their roots into the nutrients.

Two days after preparing my rows and planting seeds, I came to inspect the garden. It looked as though someone had decided to turn over the soil during the night, but only in spots. The carcasses of ocean fish lay all over the ground and the odor of dead fish hung like plague in the still spring air. I found some of the carcasses in Morgan Branch along with the tracks of raccoons. During the night they must have engaged in something like the frenzy of a White House Easter Egg hunt, only the prizes were better.

The attack on my fertilizer was only a warning. Put anything in this garden that tastes good to a citizen of the forest and it's first come, first serve. The situation reminds me of everyday life in the old Soviet Union, where I have often visited. Under law, almost everything belonged to the people. Leave anything of value more than a few inches from your front door and the first person to pass by would carry it away. So it was and ever shall be in the wilderness, from the nectar in flowers to nuts on the trees to vegetables in my garden. Harvard biologist E. O. Wilson, who has spent a lifetime marveling at the social structure of beehives and ant colonies, says these societies are wonderful models. As far as the model's use for human society, Wilson has said, right model, wrong species. "Ants are the most hostile warriors of the animal kingdom," Wilson told an interviewer for *Forbes* magazine. "If ants had nuclear weapons, the world would end in a week!" Reminders like this make one wonder all over again about the Sierra Club's hasty adoption of Thoreau's declaration, "In wildness is the preservation of civilization."

Compared to the plants of my garden, the plants that grow naturally in a wilderness have developed a variety of devices that protect them from being so generally eaten that they are entirely erased from their habitat. Since the beginning of agriculture, successful crop development has depended on breeding out defense systems in fruits, nuts, and vegetables, at least those defenses that discourage mammals. Defenses include spines, poisons, hard shells, very small fruits or grains, unpleasant tastes, irregular ripening patterns, and camouflage. The black walnut and the hickory nut are a hundred times thicker than their cousins the pecans and English walnuts. If humans had not learned to tame fire, we would never have enjoyed Boston baked beans, and some of us wish others would not. Until cooked, most beans contain a chemical that causes the guts of mammals to produce painful amounts of gas. (Maybe one day we will find a way to pass raw beans through the gastric juices of mammals and produce commercial quantities of clean-burning methane gas.)

Some plants, of course, have evolved to attract animals. The plant wants a partner to carry its seeds and disperse them and it is not fastidious about where the animal deposits them. The leaves and stalks of tomatoes keep mammals away with two nasty poisons, tomatine and tomatidine, because it needs those green parts to produce seed. If the fruit (really the ovaries of the tomato's sex organs) also held these poisons, it would never find a carrier for its seeds. The seeds of tomatoes and other seeds that are too heavy to blow in the wind have developed a coating that allows them to pass through the guts of a bird or mammal, usually emerging prepackaged in organic fertilizer ready to root in new territory.

Because our ancestors bred plants so defenseless against mammals and cultivated the edible parts to grow so large and attractive, guarding a garden in a wilderness becomes an act of endless defense. I soon learned what animal ate which plants and when. Deer strip the leaves from almost anything except basil. They have picked my bean poles clean, leaving only naked vines. They also have little taste for peppers, but denude the plants. Raccoons love watermelons and corn but ignore Brussels sprouts and tomatoes.

In my first year of farming, I had already learned one of the best reasons for staking tomatoes. Being a gardener who believes in growing the most produce for the least labor, I once followed a neighbor's example and let my tomatoes hang low near the ground; I came to the garden to find the bottoms had been chewed off the ripe ones. Good thing box turtles can't stand on their hind legs.

Squirrels seem close to believing in the formula of an apple a day, but not a whole apple. My Twenty-Ounce apple tree bore a few fruit my second summer at Morgan Branch. A few weeks before they ripened, I watched a squirrel descend the tree, its jaws sunk into a huge apple. It chewed a big hole in it and dropped it on the ground. The next day it chose fresh apples.

All gardens attract some competition for the gardener, but it is far easier to defend a garden in suburbs than in a forest. Let no one be romantic or nostalgic for the pioneer families and their gardens. On the frontier the garden was often the difference between life and death, especially for children. For most of the twentieth century poor rural southerners depended on gardens to avoid malnutrition. Pioneers and rural people defended the fruit of their labors with traps and guns. Hunters, subdivisions, highways, and shopping malls did not cause the disappearance of wildlife in eastern North America. They took their share, but the people who lived in the country and depended on it for their livelihoods did most of the killing. They used chemical pesticides for the same reason they shot squirrels in an apple tree. They no more objected to killing a deer or squirrel or coon than most city people object to killing a rabid dog.

After a few summers of hard lessons I undertook my own defense. I built a six-foot-high wire fence around my garden. I bought a Havahart live trap and carried off dozens of coons and squirrels. I cleaned and oiled my .22 rifle. I thought defending the food supply did not count as the hunting banned by my covenants. Fences, netting, and guns got the warm-blooded invaders under control. Violence was the only way to deal with insect invaders, too. I had learned from my organic truck farm that the wonders of planting insect-repellent vegetables next to the insect attracters is either fiction or limited to people who have learned to emanate the right vibrations, those people who claim that talking to their plants makes them grow. (I suppose if you talk to them closely enough, the carbon dioxide you exhale might have an effect.) Only two kinds of violence kills bugs: pesticides or fingers. Every year I crush between my fingers or underfoot thousands of Japanese beetles, horn worms, cabbage loopers, and blister beetles. I still suspect that bugs eat as much of my garden as the woodchucks ate of Thoreau's. Whether Thoreau really passed off his tolerance for woodchucks as neighborly sharing, I don't know. I bear the sharing but I don't grin.

When I cleared and turned over my garden space by the Branch, I announced my ecological Declaration of Independence, although at the time I could still convince myself I was only entering into co-dependence or collaboration with nature. Gardening, like all dominion, like all conquest, is a system of government and manipulation. At best, it is benign tyranny. It is certainly not democracy. Independence is always a question of who has power over whom, whether that power triumphs in a territory as large as a corporate farm or as small as a single room. If we can carry out our lives without worrying about hostile forces, it is because we are convinced we have the power to defend ourselves.

Almost everything in nature conspires against a garden. Nature is against rows and regular patterns. Nature is against weeding. Nature is against the wholesale execution of beetles, borers, and caterpillars. Nature is against turning over the soil every year. Above all, nature is against growing the unnaturally large fruits and vegetables that appeal to the human eye and appetite. We are not even good at dispersing seeds; they pass through our digestive systems and instead of spreading them at random around the landscape, we flush them into the sewer.

I did not realize until I planted a garden in a forest how much a garden or orchard destroys natural order, defies chance, and exists like an alien landing zone. City environmentalists who campaign for the preservation of farmlands always amuse me. Few ways of treating the land diminish natural diversity more than farming. Diminishing and pushing aside natural diversity is the very heart and soul of farming. In almost all cases the farms that urban environmentalists want to save are places that follow this formula:

1. Take a large area of land with productive soil and clear off all plants and animals and lay the soil bare. Do this at least once a year.
2. Plant large areas with only one genetically manipulated plant that could never survive on its own in a natural setting.
3. Kill off any living thing, plant or animal, that seeks to feed on that plant or compete for its nutrients.
4. Spray large amounts of chemical fertilizers and pesticides over the land.

Now if any developer were to come before a city or county commission and say that he had a project and he intended to do those things, he would be considered an environmental Satan.

Agriculture and gardening can be gentler than the traditional farm, but not by much. Gardening is an aggression followed by the hope of a standoff followed by continual trickery and small acts of recruitment among alien forces (recruit the ladybug to eat the aphids, the bluebird to hunt caterpillars, or the bee to pollinate flowers).

We can pretend a garden grows in harmony and cooperation, but in reality it is as close to pure domination as any shopping center or supermarket. It has to be. Whether we create a garden for pleasure or for food, our gardens are the ultimate fulfillment of those famous words in Genesis: "Man shall have dominion." With the never-ending contest we must wage against nature to have things our way, every successful garden is a Victory Garden.

–chapter 22–

Territorial Disputes and Negotiations

Animals will take over whatever property suits them, including my house. I undertake experiments in cohabitation.

June 6, 1976. *Sylvan woke up this morning and I asked her if she dreamt of the seashell as big as a house that I suggested she dream about. "No, I dreamed of something more fantastic," she said. "I dreamed that all the birds in the world were in this house. They were flying around and sitting on our shoulders. We had such good bread that they all wanted to live here."*

Wild animals not only ignored the property rights I had in my garden, but some staked claim on all or part of my house. Perhaps this was fair and even neighborly because they did not insist that the human owner move out. They were quite willing to be guests, and very independent ones at that. They were also guests who would not be toilet trained, de-flead or de-loused. Occasionally they were dangerous. Life at Morgan Branch quickly became an unending series of negotiations about who lives where. Because I have never acquired that talent advertised on New Age bulletin boards and in course catalogs about talking with animals, my negotiations were not in words but in action and reaction.

The first animals had moved in before I did. I had started framing the house in spring. As soon as my friends from Heartwood Builders had moved on to their next job, I came to Morgan Branch one day and saw a pile of leaves and twigs in a corner of the framing. The nest was not finished, so I took it down. A few days later when I went to retrieve a tomato juice can full of nails, I stuck my hand into a finished nest with eggs. The eggs survived. In a few minutes the builder returned, a Carolina wren.

The Carolina wren is that canary-sized brown bird with the sharply upright tail that twitches constantly when the bird is angry or nervous. The operatic translation of the wren's song as *Figaro, Figaro, Figaro* probably originated with an educated American bird-watcher, one of the common breed of bird-watcher who prefers not to see any coarse or vulgar behavior in an animal possessing the coveted gifts of both song and flight. When Sylvan first heard a Carolina wren sing, she also translated it into a word, one fitting to her generation: *video, video, video.*

One of my bird books describes the wren's song as "very loud triplets." Another as "cheerily, cheerily, cheerily." What a bird says is not as important as how it says it. A woodland bird usually has a short clear song or call, and birds living in deserts, seashores, fields, and prairies have longer calls. In a dense forest, sound does not carry far; it ricochets and echoes. A long song with many similar notes running together sounds garbled and the singer cannot easily be located. Because the wren's song is generally heard when the bird is concerned about territory, enemies, or sex, why has no one in our liberated age suggested a more appropriate translation? "Cheerily" might do for sex, but not for warning enemies or proclaiming territory.

The wren is a fearless bird, maybe because it is also very quick. It will attack and pursue a much larger enemy even beyond death. One day in the middle of a severe freeze, a neighbor down the road brought me a small red-tailed hawk that he had found frozen to death in a tree. He said he thought that because I was interested in animals, I might like to see this. I carefully skinned the hawk and examined its stomach. Empty. It had run out of fuel for flight and for keeping warm. I rubbed the limp skin with boric acid and hung it upside down under the roof of my woodshed outside the front door. Later that afternoon, I heard a racket of birds outside: Four wrens were hopping all over the wood under and around that hawk skin as if it were alive.

The wrens were easy enough to keep out of the house and I enjoyed having them around. They are so self-sufficient that they seldom show up on or under the feeder. Over the years, they have regularly inhabited a hard hat, nail boxes, the top of a gas tank, and shelves in the workshop. They are reasonable guests because they are quiet at night, which is more than I can say for whippoorwills. The common name is not as descriptive as the Latin name: *Caprimulgus vociferous*, which translates as loud-mouthed goat-milker. I suppose this nocturnal bird was blamed when a goatherd found a dry goat in the morning. *Vociferous* I understand. At two or three any summer morning, a whippoorwill might station itself outside the open bedroom window and in loud voice repeat over and over a rapid *whippoor-will, whippoorwill, whippoorwill, whippoorwill.*

Just as we project our emotions and preferences into our stuffed animals, we project them into wild animals. At best this is an act of loneliness; at worst it is blind narcissism. For a few thousand years, projection was the best humans could do by way of understanding. Throughout the primitive world, assigning human motives and feelings to animal behavior provided a sense of order. No wonder primitive religions have nine measures of fear to every one measure of joy—they are warning us about the darker side of human nature. Maybe the identification of human motives in animals also created that reverential love of nature that modern humans like to read into primitive behavior.

Fear and a closeness to nature go hand in hand, as they do for so many people who have come to live in my house while I'm away. Humans have loved nature in proportion to the distance we have been able to place between us and the object of our affections. Nature has greatly disappointed modern humanity by failing to return our love. Our solace is stuffed animals, house pets, and a futile search for animal language and intellect. To create a human alternative to minds separated from nature by science and monotheism, we have reinvented primitive people much as we have turned grizzlies into Teddy bears.

I admit we have lost something beautiful by knowing that birds do not "sing" and the Carolina wren does not say *Figaro*. Sylvan and I sometimes played the recorder with the hope of coaxing a response from birds. In the spring of 1976, Sarah treated herself to a vacation in Europe and Sylvan stayed with me. Although she was not ready to read music, she learned to play the recorder by imitating my finger positions. Sometimes she would blow into her recorder to make it sound like a bird. She was no more naïve than professional composers of the seventeenth century who wrote songs with the intention of teaching them to captive larks and finches. I'm among the humans who still enjoy "Bird Fancier's Delight," but not one bird has ever imitated the songs.

Wordsworth said that "science murders to dissect." He was speaking of our understanding of the natural world. It dissects, of course. The discoveries made by scalpel and reason have indeed turned myth and poetry into cultural fossils. Yet to the charge of murdering truth, or understanding, or even wonder, science can only be found not guilty.

The best literature stands on its own, a flower of its time and place, a wonder of human song and story. Science, by showing us the world's creatures as more than variations on a human theme has shown us that we are small creatures in an unimaginably awesome universe. Now that worms and birds and elephants cannot be explained in human terms and we are free to dissect their behavior and their bodies, any simple question leads to wonder. Why, for instance, does the wren speak in triplets instead of couplets or quadruplets? Somewhere in evolution lies an answer. Why is such a small bird so aggressive and obvious? A battery of scientists could spend entire careers on these two questions. I found myself at Morgan Branch surrounded by millions of unexplained miracles and little to distract me. I found that Sylvan was as interested in the wren's defense of its territory as she was in trying to make it answer her recorder.

I had no hope of finding many answers, but every time I discovered a new question my world grew wider and more interesting. Primitive people live with an almost fixed and unexpanding mythology; they do not ask questions that open doors. I told Sylvan the answers I knew that she could understand about the forest around us, but I was even more pleased when we could think about a question together.

Every unanswered question suggests how much wider the world is than we ever thought. Einstein said, "We can only see the universe by the impressions of our senses reflecting indirectly the things of reality." As my world grew wider, I felt myself grow smaller by comparison. How small could I get? Maybe like the Cheshire Cat in *Alice in Wonderland* I would one day fade away to nothing more than a grin. Not a bad way to go.

The pleasures of observing wildlife led me to propose compromises with those who wanted to move in with me. In the good old days of rural medieval Europe, most peasants lived in the same building as their horses, sheep, pigs, and goats, at least in winter. The animals provided a source of heat that compensated in part for the noise and smell. When technology made building barns and cutting firewood or heating with coal or oil universally affordable, our ancestors decided to live more like royalty, with separate quarters for livestock. The goal of a modern house is to be an exclusive home to the human family and animals that are either caged or permanent guests—dogs, cats, birds, fish, gerbils, hamsters, or white mice. You can tell the wanted animals because we always give them a name. Others are evicted, swatted, stomped, poisoned, trapped, burned, or gassed to death. The uninvited animal lives in a human's lair at greater peril than a human might camp in any jungle. In my house, animals forced on me events that led me to try to compromise so that I would be comfortable with guests who invited themselves.

As part of my energy-saving construction plan I had designed vents at the edge of the ceiling above the south wall of the house. I hoped that during the summer hot air would rise and leave by these vents, drawing cool air in from the shaded north side. Where the vents opened inside the house I placed screening to keep out the insects. For winter, I covered the vents with attractive wooden panels. In the summer I could swing the panels by their hinges down against the walls.

Around Christmas time, I began to hear squeaking noises inside the vents above Sylvan's room and above the adjacent part of the living space. I suspected squirrels. I opened the vent panels. On top of the screening I could see only leaves and tufts of pink fiberglass insulation that had almost certainly been stolen out of the roof. I closed the vent panels and went to investigate the problem from outside. I leaned a long extension ladder against that side of the house; the vents were some eighteen feet above the ground because this was the downhill side of the house. When I stood on a rung near the top of the ladder, my face was level with the vent over the living area. I could see pink fiberglass insulation and leaves inside. I tapped on the wall. Nothing. I poked a stick slowly into the leaves and fiberglass. Something stirred inside and suddenly it ran out, stepped on my head, and jumped. I turned around. A gray-and-brown flying squirrel the size of a chipmunk had spread his forelegs and hind legs, stretching the long flaps of skin between wrist and ankles. He glided straight for a hickory tree, pulled up neatly before crashing, and disappeared into a hole in the trunk. I waited a minute and inserted the stick again, but very gently. A second squirrel came to the edge of the wall and stared out at me. I stared back. Here was an animal with the best attributes to appeal to the sympathy of a human. With its large eyes, soft fur, round nose, and big ears, it fit solidly among the first magnitude of creatures that human beings consider cute. It had also mastered the greatest of mammalian athletic feats—it could fly. After a minute, it did just that, and disappeared into the same hickory tree as its mate.

Humans have always envied animals that fly. Of our two flying mammals, it is easier to envy flying squirrels than bats. Although bats are real fliers and flying squirrels merely gliders, bats have been burdened with legends of vampires. On close inspection, bats are soft and furry, but people don't warm up to them the way they do to any kind of squirrel. Flying squirrels glide with a lot less effort than bats fly. The flap of skin between the squirrel's front leg wrists and back leg ankles bows upward as it falls. The air rushing over the curved surface creates the same kind of lift that allows an airplane to fly. Launched from a 50-foot tree limb, it can glide 150 feet. It moves through the forest by gliding and climbing, gliding and climbing.

The Latin name of the eastern flying squirrel that ran over my head is *Glaucomys volans*. *Volans*, of course, means flying. *Glauk* is from Greek and Latin words related to seeing and from *oma*, a suffix attached to medical words for various tumors and swellings (glaucoma, melanoma, hematoma, carcinoma, etc.). The eye of the flying squirrel, like eyes of many nocturnal mammals, is large and slightly domed. So it is that some unromantic classifier or taxonomist gave this appealing rodent the Latin name for an unfortunate eye disease.

After looking that second squirrel in the eye and watching it repeat the fine glide of the first, I decided they could do no harm if they stayed in the vents until spring. I had taken a certain part of their space in the woods and I was willing to share a house that had removed some of their food supply if not a den tree. Theodore Roosevelt had even shared the White House with a pet flying squirrel. (His efforts to preserve the American West's bears also began the craze for Teddy bears.)

The flying squirrels and I began our cohabitation with a friendly treaty. Treaties with animals, of course, remain forever unratified on the nonhuman side, and only our endless good will convinces us they are ever understood. Goodwill is another character trait that has evolved only in humans. If you have to live with real flying squirrels, you soon find out they have abilities and habits as unfortunate as their Latin name.

I must have had a pair of flying squirrels in both vents—over Sylvan's room and over the living area. Flying squirrels pair for only one reason; having accomplished his purpose, the male leaves before the babies are born. A period of relative silence ensued above the vent panels toward the end of January. In late February, noise and shuffling and scratching and crunching began again. How many babies lived up there I didn't know, but most litters number from two to six. The noises got louder. One evening in April I looked at the vent in the living room and noticed that the white wall had a long dark streak of something black. Because squirrels don't drink coffee or tea, the stain had to come from inside one or more squirrels. I cleaned out the vents and stapled screening across the outside this time.

One night in November I heard scratching and squeaking in the vent over the living room. I decided I should act before the female had a brood. I put the ladder in place and climbed up to the vent. The squirrels had pried one end of the screening loose and squeezed in. A flying squirrel can squeeze through a one-inch hole if it is determined enough. I stapled the screen back in place presumably with the squirrels inside. I then made a small hole in the screening and against it I fixed a small box into which I hoped they would exit during the night. In the morning I had two flying squirrels.

When I had fixed a heavy wire screen over the holes, I took the box up to the loft and out onto the roof. Sylvan stood at the window to watch. Instead of flying gliders as my father had done when I was a kid, I thought we would fly gliding squirrels. My squirrel box had a small hole in the top that was covered by a small sliding piece of plywood. I slid this open and tapped on the box. The first squirrel appeared at the opening, paused, and launched itself into the air. It glided beyond the roof and down the hill toward the creek, banking slightly among the trunks and steering with its tail. Just as it seemed about to crash into the trunk of a poplar, its tail went up, forward momentum stopped, and it was head up on the trunk. In an instinctual maneuver to outwit a following predator such as a hawk or owl, it immediately disappeared around the other side of the tree. The second squirrel followed the same flight path to the same tree. My only regret was that I might never again see a squirrel flying in daylight. By way of a peace offering, I cut into the wall of the house just below the eaves and installed a box almost exactly the size of the vents I had closed. On the outside face I closed it with a board and drilled a hole ideal for a flying squirrel. The back of the box was a piece of glass, and behind that on the inside wall of the house was a hinged panel that I could open to watch the tenants. One moved in and promptly moved out.

Was it that same winter or the next winter that I heard squirrels again, but this time in the ceiling above my bedroom? They would not live in the box I had built for them, but they had found a way into the attic space behind the loft. I am a good sleeper and I tolerated them for a couple of weeks, but even a good sleeper cannot ignore the kind of rioting and partying they carried on in the insulation. Besides, when I had looked into the low storage space above the ceiling where I stored old manuscripts, pictures, letters, and a few other things, the insulation was riddled with burrows, and the planks that I had set down to rest boxes on were peppered thickly with squirrel droppings. A package of old notebooks I had kept as a kid had a big dry brown stain on them.

The squirrels also found a way into the house. I would not have known this except that I had filled a small clay bowl with pecans and set it on a shelf in the eating area. One day I noticed the bowl was only two-thirds full. Maybe someone had eaten a few. Then I noticed it was half full. At about the same time I found in a pair of seldom-used hiking boots a stash of pecans.

I carefully examined places along the eaves where the squirrels might get into the attic and closed them with wood trim or screening. They chewed their way back in through one piece of screening. When I fixed that, they found another entry. They did, but I didn't.

One evening I was sitting in the living area with a friend when one appeared. It was clearly lost. My friend had never seen a flying squirrel, and she was delighted with how "cute" it was. I managed to catch it under a box, then turned the box over so that she could have a closer look. She reached in to pet it. The squirrel immediately reached up toward her and clamped its sharp teeth with the power of hickory-nut-cutting jaws onto the end of her index finger. She screamed and pulled her hand out of the box shouting, "It's biting me, get it off, get it off, get it off." I grabbed its neck and rather than choke it to death, I it let go. I threw it out into the night and it sailed off among the trees.

One winter night about three in the morning when their bickering woke me up from a much-needed sleep, I lost my patience. I draped a bathrobe over my shoulders, grabbed a good flashlight and my .22 rifle, and I opened the door to the attic. The attic space at its highest is just over three and a half feet, but except for a few boxes it is a shooting gallery more than thirty feet long. I pulled up a box and sat on it in the dark, flashlight and gun ready. I would not shoot down through the ceiling, of course, but I had no qualms about a few small .22 caliber holes in the siding or in the rafters. There I sat buck naked under the cloak of my bathrobe, rifle in hand, under the roof of my attic, ready to face the innocent violators of my naïve treaty. I had thought of putting a couple of big rat traps up there, but a bullet would be kinder.

They began to move. I heard feet scratching over the boards. I turned the flashlight on and found a squirrel just as it moved behind a box of papers. It reappeared on the other side going away from me toward the east wall where I would soon be able to get a shot. I kept the flashlight in my left hand and raised the light rifle in my right. No, I couldn't shoot there because he was above the kitchen where wires for the lights went through the joists and into the ceiling. Then it was behind another box. Then on the eaves and I was about to fire when it disappeared. I came to my senses. A lot of my dreams made more sense than sitting naked in a cold attic hoping to freeze a squirrel in a flashlight beam and shoot it at 3 A.M. I went back to bed and to those more reasonable dreams.

I worked on the squirrel problem for three years before I accepted that life would be a continuing series of negotiations. Survival is always a dynamic process, and never a permanent success.

chapter 23

Housing Discrimination

I find myself chosen by animals I would not choose for tenants, and I come to understand why animals have more to gain from living with me than vice versa.

The kinship between humankind and animals also has its saint, St. Francis, who preached to the fishes. Statues of St. Francis often have wild animals confidently resting at his feet or on his shoulders. I would also like to talk to animals, and for a while I worked hard at it. That was during those years before I decided I might gain some undefinable but great prize by learning to talk to girls. I tried to talk to a variety of animals, and I was sure I would learn the language. I read wildlife books by Ernest Thompson Seton, who claimed to have translated the languages of coyotes' howls and crows' calls. I listened hard to the various cries of seagulls for some kind of Morse code that went with a certain action—circling, diving, attacking, or eating garbage. Any afternoon or weekend when I went to the beach to dig bait, fish, or hide out on the wooded bluffs above the harbor, a small pack of neighborhood dogs followed me. Brownie, the Doberman, was too nervous. The next-door neighbor's brown-and-white boxer-shaped mongrel named Butch was too lazy. I had the greatest hope of talking to a big flop-eared dog named Dumbo because he was big, very attentive, and had sad and intelligent eyes. He listened very patiently but said nothing. I failed as a dog whisperer. I gave up any serious hope that I could talk to dogs or that they would talk to me when I was nine or ten.

In the last ten years or so, I have noticed that fully grown people have become filled with not only hope but the belief that they don't just talk to animals but converse with them. The bulletin board in the semi-organic and highly specialized Pittsboro General Store café has an advertisement for a course in which students learn to communicate with their pets. This new adult pursuit may have started when scientists began recording the plaintiff sounds of whales and folk singer Judy Collins sang along with them. Whales are not furry, and relative to their size, their eyes are small, but they long ago recovered from the image of brutishness laid on them by old whaling books and pictures. They do have huge faces, sing beautifully, take good care of their young, socialize with each other, and allow human beings not only to sing along but to swim along, too.

The compromise position to conversing with animals is creating a friendship. This used to be called taming animals, but that too strongly suggests a ruler and subject, an order often created through force. Most people who crave the companionship of animals prefer something like the bond of *The Yearling* where boy and fawn form a mutual attachment and respect.

I tried to do it with squirrels, the poor person's porpoise and the lazy person's deer. Getting to know a squirrel, I thought, would be a good experience for Sylvan, and besides, when I first came to Morgan Branch, I was lonely. I had not done so well with human relationships, but maybe I could do better with animal friends. A gray squirrel offered itself.

Sylvan and I often ate our meals sitting on the boards of the small deck at one corner of the house. From this platform we could reach out and touch a big hickory, a white oak, and a twisted black gum whose small crown of red fall leaves has decorated every autumn. The bird feeder hung over this deck and the squirrel made daily raids on it. I started putting sunflower seeds and peanuts at the edge of the deck by the trees the squirrel climbed. As long as we made no sudden or big moves, he grew as comfortable around us as a city squirrel. Then nearer, and even nearer. Over the next few weeks, I moved my hand closer and still closer to the peanuts. The squirrel would take peanuts only a few inches from my fingers, then an inch. We were making a friend, and Sylvan was learning the stillness and self-control needed to be close to wild animals. A sound or a smell does not signal the most immediate and the final danger to most animals. That last warning is a motion, a quick motion. Sylvan learned how slowly and smoothly she had to move in the presence of this squirrel.

One afternoon, I put a peanut in the palm of my hand and lay my hand on the deck. The squirrel approached. It edged closer, sniffed, studied Sylvan, studied me, and edged up to my fingertips, turning this way and that on its front legs, its back legs bunched under it ready to spring away; this was not exactly a close encounter of the third kind, but it might be contact with another being. The squirrel put his front paws on my fingers and sniffed. Then he did something entirely unexpected: He plunged his head at my index finger and bit down hard. I jerked my hand from under him and he leaped for the hickory tree. I had a few things to say to that squirrel, but he had not understood weeks of generosity and patience. He had communicated.

The lesson I learned took a while to sink in, but that unprovoked bite made me understand that taming—no, I mean making friends with—a wild animal is to deny yourself the opportunity of understanding its wildness. Taming brings the animal a good part of the way to becoming a toy.

I could not satisfy the flying squirrels with the wall boxes I offered them, but I did not give up on the idea of sharing the house this way; my hospitality would also be the lazy man's way to observe nature. Biologists and photographers spend days or months stalking and waiting for wildlife. Just to photograph the inside of a squirrel or woodpecker's nest they must climb trees, don camouflage, build blinds, or drill holes into trees. I decided that my house would be my tree. Who says a tree has to be round and grow branches? For most animals' purposes a tree is anything that rises into the air and has platforms, forks, and hollows and an exterior rough enough to climb.

Animals do not necessarily prefer wild places to civilization. Civilization has been a great boon to many wild animals; they adapt so well that they often seem like pets. Take the pigeon. The common pigeon once lived in a small part of the world where high ledges near sources of grain supported the species. Greek and Egyptian architecture provided the pigeon with ideal roosts on the tops of pillars and in the corners of triangular gables. Abandoned buildings also attract pigeons. Pigeons couldn't get to the world's greatest breadbasket, the American Midwest, however, until President Kennedy's administration began building the interstate highway system in earnest. The big metal I-beams under bridges and overpasses provide ideal roosts for pigeons. These same bridges all across America make fine habitat for swallows, too, who now return to Interstates 40 and 95 as readily as they do to Capistrano.

Animals are not purists or health nuts. They don't mind chemically treated lumber, paint, or even the fiberglass insulation that makes me sneeze and itch. Most don't mind rotten food. Mice love the artificial foam in pillows. The flying squirrels in my attic eaves find Owens-Corning fiberglass mixed with cedar bark and leaves a very warm and soft nest.

In my next cohabitation venture, I decided to imitate success.

The Smithsonian Institution has in the wall of one building a beehive made of Plexiglas. I had three beehives by my garden, and I saw no reason not to have one in the wall of the house. Bees often move into walls and eaves of houses of their own accord, especially in old country houses where the walls are not stuffed with insulation. My living-room wall provided a better place for bees than my hives. The one housing characteristic most important to bees is not the outside materials like the wood of a hive or the plaited straw of the preindustrial skep, but a hollow space neither too large nor too small. The optimum parameters are fairly obvious, at least from a bee's point of view, and explain why they like the walls of houses. The hollow should be at least 10 feet off the ground (above the height of most animals and the understory of the forest). A south-facing hollow allows the bees to warm up fast on chilly mornings. Inside, the space should be at least six inches in the narrowest dimension, and a minimum of 1 cubic foot of building space. Bees build their double-sided brood combs and honeycombs over an inch thick and hang them half an inch apart.

I modeled my own box after a commercially made brood chamber, a little more than a foot high, eighteen inches from front to back. The width was narrower at fourteen and a half inches because that is exactly the distance between the vertical studs in the wall. I cut a hole in the wall and slipped the box in. One morning in spring, I looked out of the window and saw bees flying in and out of the box. In a hollow tree, or maybe in one of my own bee hives, a queen and her workers had been too successful. They had run out of space for new comb. Maybe a new queen had been born. The old queen had left with thousands of workers. Perhaps for a night or two or even three she had survived inside a large cone of bees hanging from a limb in the forest, waiting for scouts to find a safe hollow place to start a new settlement. Not only did they find a good location, but I had hung in the box several frames with thin sheets of beeswax so they could make a quick start on their brood cells.

I made another observation box in the wall above the head of Sylvan's bed. I built a four-inch-high box with a round opening the size of a silver dollar. I meant this to be wren housing, and that first year a wren moved in. We watched it filling the box with twigs and leaves. After a week or two, the wren left the box, one of several nests wrens often build and never use. In a world where nature rewards efficiency and for an animal whose metabolism requires constant attention to food, I do not understand why the wren seems to waste time on unused nests. Wrens' nests are simple and messy piles of leaves and sticks. I suppose that, if my home had been the kind of packing crate Thoreau proposed as better than most houses, I also could have tried out and abandoned a few.

This particular nest has seldom sat empty. Occasionally a wren has used it, but more often a gray squirrel. Squirrels cannot squeeze through a hole made for a wren, but evolution has taught them that large cavities often lie behind small holes, and an hour or two of chewing at the entrance gets them in.

I have also found out that if you build a box, animals don't always come. High on the wall above Sylvan's east window I attached a bat box. The bats had never tried to move into the house, but they did good work and there were plenty of them. I owed them an effort at safe and ideal housing where they could hang during the day and throughout long cold spells. Besides the benefits to my garden, the bats controlled the mosquito population. One brown bat can eat six hundred mosquitoes an hour. I have sat by Morgan Branch at dusk and watched them racing up and down the valley. Sylvan and I had a favorite bat-watching spot alongside the drive and a strip of land I had cleared for garden vegetables and fruit trees. Bats flew back and forth above this clearing and made sudden dives at anything that moved through the air. We used to tease them into showing their stuff in front of us by tossing pebbles into the air. When a bat's echo locator found the pebble, horizontal flight gave way to a sudden descent. I would have stopped this practice had even one pebble not crashed to the ground. Bats scoop their prey to their mouths with their wings, so in the dusk and the fast action I have never discerned whether they detected our scam with wing or from closer sonar work, but every pebble returned to earth.

A bat box looks like a tall, wide, and thin bird house open at the bottom. Inside the box one or more rough slabs of board hang an inch and a half apart. The bats can hang sleeping on these boards during the day. My design followed instructions from Bat Conservation International. I had the ideal location—about twenty feet off the ground, within sight of water where insects breed, and facing southeast.

The only inhabitants who have ever moved in are successive colonies of brown wasps. The box hangs waiting year after year, there if the bats need it. That's about the most we can do for any wild animal without seducing it from its wildness.

The same has been true for a large box with a six-inch opening I placed under my bathroom window. I built it for a barn owl. I have come home at night to see a small screech owl sitting on a windowsill, and I have surprised a barred owl the size of a turkey feeding in my driveway, but no owl has taken up residence in the box.

I continue to offer experimental living spaces to wild animals, but as we say in the real estate rental business, the vacancy rates are high. Besides the regular tenancy of flying squirrels in the attic, I have had occasional surprise visits or short-term residencies.

Fall always brings a few brown woods mice into the pantry. Like most homeowners, I have no idea how they get in. Unfortunately for them, the only effective way to send them out is via the traditional death-dealing mousetrap. Mice would be as welcome as any pet in the house except that they cannot be readily housebroken like a cat or dog, and I don't welcome their droppings and urine stains. In my workshop they have favored the shallow draw of an old metal cabinet where I keep my best wood chisels, though they never nest there. What pleasure they find there I don't know, but I do know that they have left my tools corroding with their effluent. For nesting, they prefer the draw where I keep the scrapers and steel wool.

I don't owe the woods mice any special comforts. Their species has survived in the forests for thousands of years. When a wild animal comes into the house, it is chooses the benefits captive animals enjoy, but the wild ones never expect to give up their freedom. Better to be held captive and cared for, however. Almost any wild animal in captivity and fed well lives 100 to 500 percent longer than in the wild. Wild animals moving in uninvited may escape the fox or owl, but they do not reckon with the human animal, who kills as much for sanitary and aesthetic reasons as for food. I don't blame any animal for trying to find the greatest comfort, easiest food supply, and most secure shelter available, even if all three belong to me. Human beings have done exactly the same in settling wild lands. In our favor I should note that we are the one species that also puts out feeders and houses for others out of pure pleasure in their company and genuine desire to know their lives. If there is ever a Judgment Day in which the lives of all species are judged, let this outreach count in our favor.

In almost all cases I am patient and philosophical about my visitors, even if I must shoot them or trap them. The exceptions, and blessedly rare, are snakes. Emily Dickinson put snakes in the same position:

> Several of Nature's People
> I know, and they know me—
> I feel for them a transport
> Of cordiality—
> But never met this Fellow
> Attended, or alone
> Without a tighter breathing
> And Zero at the Bone—

Snakes have that special place among animals for all humans. Tim McLaurin, the carnival snake handler turned novelist, once told me, "Everybody has an almost involuntary response to snakes. I've handled them since I was six years old, and still today I can be walking along and look down and see a snake at my feet and I'll jump even though five seconds later I'm not at all afraid of it."

On the back of my bedroom door, I have six pegs where I hang clothes. One morning, I got up rubbing my eyes and was about to take a pair of pants from a peg when I noticed a belt hanging on the next peg. My eyes were still blurry and I was not wearing my glasses; when I grabbed the belt, it whipped out of my hand and disappeared under the door. In that instant the small harmless black snake changed from a belt to a snake in my mind, I felt "zero at the bone."

Black snakes like to climb when they are hunting or when they want to shed a skin, but this was the only one I ever met inside the house. They can go wherever mice go, but for their own reasons they have never come hunting in the pantry or anywhere else inside. The rarity of their appearances around the house is the reason I saw the form on the peg as a belt. I made a similar misinterpretation one afternoon when I carried a box of light fixtures down to the workshop. When I pushed open the door, a heavy rope fell on my neck. I have lots of rope around, but instantly I knew that none of it had been hanging over the door. I dropped the box and shook off a six-foot black snake who didn't want to be on my shoulders anyway. The door had been slightly ajar and he had been half on the door and half on the door frame when I walked through.

When we meet without surprise, I am pleased to see a black snake. They are beautiful animals and their diet includes the mice that might sneak into the house. Our one poisonous snake, the copperhead, never gets large enough to do much damage to birds or mammals, and it doesn't climb, but people who know of it revile it more than they do the black snake. I have gone a whole year without seeing a copperhead, but I have also found them under the house. In my work as an appraiser, I have often had to inspect houses; in the South, that means crawling under houses that have a space between floor and ground, often no more than a foot and a half high. To this day I wonder why I have never met a copperhead face to face, both of us lying on our stomachs, the snake having a distinct advantage in maneuverability. It might have been flashlight against fangs.

Under my own house, in that dirt-floored storage space above the workshop, I could at least stand up when I went in to rummage through boxes for plumbing parts. Once while I was looking, I heard water dripping rapidly—d d d d d d d d d d d. I checked the pipes overhead that run to the bath and kitchen. No leaks, but I could hear the water dripping on a coil of green hose. I looked at the coil where the sound of the dripping continued; a three-foot-long copperhead lay inside, his tail beating a warning on its vinyl coating. I don't kill copperheads outside the house, but in this case I had to whack him with a piece of iron pipe.

Set aside the danger and the copperhead is one of our most beautiful animals. Its skin is a rosy copper color with broad brown bands, its head the color of a bright penny. I have seen these same colors paired in African dashikis and Indonesian batiks. The copperhead is one of the few snakes that bears live young, and for a week or two the last inch of tail of these newborns is tipped with a flaming chartreuse. The only time I have ever been bitten was by one of these babies, which slithered out of a low stone wall where a friend sat; it came out between her sandals and paralyzed her with fear.

I wanted a photograph of the young copperhead, so I reached down to pin it behind the head. I miscalculated how thin it was. It slithered forward between my fingers, whipped around, and bit me in the thumb. Most snake bites are about as painless as a hypodermic, at least until the venom begins to work. My neighbor wanted me to rush to the doctor. For two reasons I didn't. First, contrary to popular belief, a young snake is no more poisonous than an old snake. The danger of a bite depends on how deep and where the bite is and on how much venom the snake injects. If it has just finished hunting, it may be out of venom (copperheads have inflicted dry bites on people). The copperhead's venom works on muscles, not nerves, so help is not as urgent as it is with the bite of a cobra. Nevertheless, I have had friends who have been seriously ill after a big dose of copperhead venom. The venom digests protein, which means muscle this case, and a bad bite can mean removing a hunk of partially digested foot or hand. The little snake that bit me had very little venom. I pinned him with a stick and scooped him into a jar. My thumb felt as if several bees had gone at it, but no worse. It swelled a little, but in a day or two it was back to normal. I chilled the snake in the fridge to slow him down, then shot several good pictures. I released him some distance from the house.

Local folklore says that if you have black snakes, you will not have copperheads because the black snakes will kill them. I know no one who has ever seen this happen and I have often seen the two snakes on the same day within a few yards of each other. I once took apart a pile of cedar boards I had set out to dry with small spacers between each layer. I found a black snake in one layer and two layers down, a large copperhead. Seeing a copperhead during the day, however, is unusual; in the cooling days of fall, however, they are out looking for a winter den in a rock pile or tree stump. Their nocturnal nature is the main reason for their salvation in the South; it is also the reason copperhead bites are relatively common. Most people suffer bites at night; my friend in Durham took her dog out for a walk one evening and was bitten in the arch of the foot as she brushed by some ground cover she had planted along her walk.

The copperhead among all snakes has adapted well to living near people. In 1904, an Ohio herpetologist predicted that civilization would quickly exterminate the copperhead. He was right about northern areas; the last copperhead was seen in New York City in 1936. Dr. Henry Fitch of Kansas says, "Indeed, the species has actually been favored by some of the changes brought about by man and its populations have increased in certain areas. Secretiveness, nocturnality, cryptic coloration, and a fairly wide choice of prey species are factors that have favored survival under altered conditions and in association with medium to dense populations of man." Also important, he said, was the copperhead's relatively small territory, which allows it to survive in the shrubbery and flower beds of subdivisions where traffic is light. Civilization has also helped the copperhead overcome another physical limitation.

This snake is particularly sensitive to temperature changes. When it gets too hot or too cool, it must find a place to thermoregulate. Houses with crawl spaces and garages offer a variety of temperature zones. A friend once found a copperhead contentedly curled up on top of his hot water heater. Lying around a water heater is a much safer and more reliable way for a cold-blooded creature to maintain body temperature than chasing sunlight, hugging warm stones, or lying on the pavement. All the most favorable factors in nature and the human environment meet in the Sun Belt states. What happens to the copperheads is one more way in which nature poses the question of how adaptable humans can be.

In the woods I have often come upon snakes killing or eating their prey. I have regretted their toll on local birds and chipmunks, but I have also regretted seeing a hawk carrying away a snake. I had not lived at Morgan Branch long when I recognized that I had a choice—either establish myself as owner and protector of nature, or accept its bloody way of allotting life and death. I can also be glad that the genius of my own species, at least in my own country, has made me generally immune to such random violence. I have traveled widely in cities and countries where the human animal is infamous for killing its own kind, but even residents of such places expect a life twice as long as any prehistoric hunter's. We have extended our lives by the same devices we have extended the lives of captive animals: We are our own captors. Dozens of magazines regularly publish articles on how to regain our place in nature. New Age summer camps and winter resorts offer to put people in touch again with their wild spirits. None of the prescriptions I have read yet recommends we leave the captivity of civilization.

For better or worse—and I think it is for the better—we have no choice but to live in the cages and mansions of our habitat called civilization. We are changed forever, and no fantasy of communing with dolphins or dancing with wolves will make us wild again. I am grateful for that. The wild is not gentle. Wild humans who come to mind are Geoffrey Dahmer, Charles Manson, Adolph Hitler, and Pol Pot.

The wild human, like the wild animal, lives a life preoccupied with the possibility of danger, and those who have the minds of predators respond with great violence and alertness to danger; they read in their fellow citizens the same wildness they know in themselves. A wild deer or wolf is alert. In a wild human animal, the gifts of imagination and foresight transform alertness into paranoia. The paranoia of Stalin and Mao murdered millions whose corpses fed nothing but despair.

On a late spring afternoon of heavy rain and thundershowers, I ate supper on the porch. I kept hearing bees buzzing, and one occasionally flew by. This was a lot of activity for the little group in the wall hive. I looked around the corner across the south wall of the house where I had built the hive and saw a small cloud of bees buzzing at the entry. The honey flow must have been dwindling in the woods, and some other hive had come to steal what little nectar my bees had stored in their new comb. From inside the house I looked through the observation glass. Inside, bees were buzzing insanely and fighting in furious knots of twos, threes, and fours. All over the comb, bees had their heads into the storage cells, sucking out the honey. Bees climbed on top of one another, biting furiously. This activity went on for two or three days until my bees were dead or gone and every cell they had made empty. The pillage was as savage as a Viking raid or a Mongol invasion.

Animals have good reason for preferring to live with us rather than in nature. I will continue to accommodate some of them. If my efforts have been only partly successful, at least I do not live like friends in the city, whose wildlife is cockroaches, flies, spiders, rats, mice, and silverfish. I admit to discrimination, and I admit my motives for it are impure. I do not grant any animal an inalienable right to housing. I undertook to compromise not because a squirrel or bird or bee has any more right to live here than I do, but because I am the animal who cares about other animals. I am also the only animal who is curious about others for the sake of knowledge.

Finally, I do this because I am lonely. Loneliness is an ancient feeling and maybe it has biological roots. A newly hatched duck or chicken imprints on and forever follows the first animal it sees when it hatches. Dogs befriend cats, and they are man's best friend not because they love human animals but because they are pack animals. Take away the pack and dogs bond with other animals, especially if you feed them. A few years ago, a moose became a media celebrity when it entered territory in upstate New York where no moose had lived for a century; it attached itself to a farmer's cow and refused to be driven off.

Having animals as companions is always a fail-safe position. Human companions are notorious for their insensitivity, their tendency to argue and talk back, and their conflicting habits. If animals understand speech at all, they understand nothing above the level of baby talk, and baby talk is more akin to cooing and purring and barking than conversation. Nevertheless, most humans talk to animals as readily as they talk to each other. When she was in her eighties, my mother started collecting stuffed animals and talked to them. She had lived alone since she was seventy and she enjoyed talking to her stuffed animals more than to the television or to herself. I have talked to birds, squirrels, and deer, or rather I have talked at them. If they bother to look at all, I can see in their eyes they are puzzled by the unfamiliar noise.

Years ago before multiculturalism came to include respect for animal minds as well as human intellect, the phrase "dumb animal" was common. Sometimes it meant voiceless, sometimes stupid. I have no doubt of my superior intelligence, but I nevertheless enjoy the company of animals, and I shall continue exercising my intelligence to decrease the vacancy rates in the accommodations I offer them.

chapter 24

Fall from Grace

*I set out to do a good deed: save a citizen's house
from a dead tree and bring back to the forest and a
fine home the bees inside the tree. The results are
that I yield to temptation and begin to bring modern
comforts to my simple house.*

In 1976, the two-hundredth anniversary of American independence, I had settled in to my own independence by Morgan Creek. Sarah and Sylvan had settled in at the old farmhouse. Sylvan told one of her friends proudly, "I have two houses." Sarah had a full-time position dealing with employment issues at the university and had let young pines and gums take over the plum groves, apple trees, and raspberry patches. During the winter, Sylvan and I with the help of a friend had finished a concrete floor in the workshop beneath the house. We had moved a pile of lumber from under Sylvan's bed and along the walls of her room to the shop. She now had her own space. For a door, I mounted a pair of honey red pine bifolds that had been given to us from the house Sarah had grown up in. Sarah's father had died a few months after Sylvan's birth, and I was pleased that every day of her stay with me she would now go in and out of her own space through doors built by her grandfather.

I was living a simple life that at least some of my friends in the environmental movement considered a good example. When they gave me the Conservation Council's New River Award, the document said, "For living a frugal and exemplary life that teaches by example." My example by that time included a simple house heated by wood and sunlight, water drawn from Morgan Branch, a two-seater composting outhouse, a small wood-heated sauna by Morgan Branch, home-grown vegetables, and three productive beehives. The bees forced me into the first of several compromises with the simple life.

Honeybees are no more American wildlife than Japanese honeysuckle, kudzu, or the German cockroach. They were brought to America as a domesticated animal to pollinate orchards and produce honey, the only kind of sweetener northern people knew how to produce three hundred years ago. In the many old-growth forests, storms, birds, and age had hollowed myriad limbs and trunks. The bees spread quickly. By the time loggers had cut most of the old growth, the houses and barns built with the lumber provided the spaces bees needed if a willing beekeeper didn't. I had become one of the most willing beekeepers: Whether bees were wild or not, I had great respect for their abilities and their organization, and a great love of honey. When I heard of someone exterminating a bee colony that had invaded a home or garage, I heard sacrilege.

Sylvan had also become a beekeeper. When it comes to creating the ties that bind (called bonding now that a world of glues has replaced a world of ropes), play is good, working together is better, and facing danger side by side is the best. Keeping bees is less dangerous than falling off a playground swing, but bees are less predictable than a swing. Dangerous aliens are scarier than dangerous mechanisms. In the summer of 1975, I had two or three active hives, and I invited Sylvan to stand by as I inspected one. I made sure she was out of the immediate danger zone should the bees turn crazy, and I dressed her in a couple of layers of shirts, two pairs of pants, and a hat. I tucked her hair under the hat and her pants into her socks—just in case.

The bees were tame and I felt confident enough to invite her to come close and look at a frame of honey. Whenever we walked by a hive that summer or fall, we often stopped and found a place to hunker and watch the work. I taught Sylvan how to determine the flight path and stay out of the traffic. We watched the workers coming in with their legs thick with yellow pollen. One day in early summer, we watched the workers driving out the excess drones, the male bees whose sole function and hope in life is to pollinate the queen when she flies on her one maiden flight. When the hive becomes too crowded with honey and brood cells, the workers bully the fat drones out of the hive. I have never been a militant feminist, but I was glad for Sylvan to know at least one world in which females rule.

The next summer, when the hives had finished a good spring honey flow from the poplars and hollies, Sylvan wanted her own beekeeping outfit so that she could help collect the honey. I have seen a lot of beekeeping catalogues, but I have never seen one with coveralls, gloves, hat, and veil for a five-year-old. We improvised from her toughest jeans and shirts, an adjustable pith helmet, tough women's gardening gloves, rubber rain boots, and a full-sized veil whose draw strings wrapped around her chest and waist a few times. We took apart the largest hive, carefully blowing smoke down into the combs. The day was calm and sunny, just right for collecting honeycomb. We were quickly surrounded by bees, and they crawled on our clothes and over our veils, but they were not angry. Sylvan served as my assistant, holding the smoker, blowing a little here and there. She handed me the pry bar to loosen the frames that the bees glued to the hive bodies with propolis, and she acquired the light touch needed to brush away bees clinging to the honeycomb.

We harvested sixty pounds of honey from the one hive and Sylvan became a confirmed beekeeper. When a neighbor called and asked if I could get bees out of the eaves of his house, Sylvan donned her costume and went up the ladder to help me set a capture hive on the roof.

In late October, a friend who knew I kept and loved bees and also owned a chainsaw called to ask if I could help her neighbor. The neighbor was afraid that a large dead oak behind her house in a subdivision might fall on the roof. High in the tree, where it forked into two main stems, a swarm of bees had taken up residence. If I could cut down the tree, I could take away the bees. Saving an innocent hive of bees from the exterminator is a less intrusive act than saving a vulture or titmouse doomed by nature. The tree was already dead, and dead trees do not make good neighbors even if they make good housing for a large number of wild animals—bats, squirrels, flying squirrels, raccoons, possums, woodpeckers, owls, and, of course, bees.

I do not climb mountains, but I like to climb trees. I have little fear of being fifty feet up a poplar tree swaying in the wind, but I never want to be roped to any piece of rock. The issue is not stability versus motion. Trees fall much more often than rocks break from mountains. The issue is technology. I prefer to rely on my own feet and arms and the branches of trees rather than on ropes and pitons. I don't have a good sense of when a piton is going to slip loose from a rock. I do have a good sense of when a limb is going to break. Dead trees, however, are another matter and therein lies the story.

The late October day when I went to take down the tree began bright and clear. I went out to my own hives about seven and watched as the sun on the front of the hives drew out the first workers. They flew off toward the sun, glistening like little gold aviators. At the end of October, bees do not have much work, but they still gather pollen from wild asters. The pollen and stored honey sustains them during the winter and nourishes the new workers they will need in the spring.

A couple of hours later, I showed up at the threatened house with my twenty-foot ladder, my chain saw, and a box to put the bees in. I had my bee gloves, my pith helmet, and the wire veil with cloth flaps that fit over the helmet and tied around my waist. Instead of the sting-proof coveralls many beekeepers use, I put on a white hospital smock I had bought in a secondhand store. Many beekeepers work their hives on an ordinary day without gloves or a mask, or even a smoker to calm the bees; on a windless and warm day, bees have too much work to do to worry when a keeper looks into the hive and gently examines the combs. When you are about to chainsaw a hive out of a tree, you had better be prepared for fury. Once a hive is aroused, 30,000 to 50,000 worker bees are willing to give their lives for the chance to leave one stinger in the enemy. In my first days as a bee-keeper, I learned that the high shrill noise of a disturbed hive is quite different from the low hum of confident work.

The tree was a red oak at least four feet in diameter. The trunk rose a good twenty feet, curving gently over the driveway before it divided into two small trunks. One leaned over the bedroom where the owners slept; the other rose almost vertically. When the builder had graded for the house and the drive, he had condemned the tree. The roots of red oaks seldom run more than a foot below the surface. Just above the fork, in the straighter of the two secondary trunks, I saw a hole the size of my fist. A steady flow of bees arced up out of the hole into the warming air, heading for the asters, goldenrod, and maybe what milkweed was left.

I leaned the ladder against the tree. From the top rung, I hauled myself into the crotch. I was wearing my smock and hat; the veil and gloves were stuffed into the pockets. Over my shoulder I carried a small bow saw and a coil of rope tied to the handle of the chain saw below. For a moment, I stood beside the hole in the upright secondary and watched the bees come and go. The woman who owned the house came out onto her back deck with her baby on her hip. "I'm afraid they'll sting you," she said. "Why don't you come down and we'll get an exterminator and a tree man."

I considered myself a tree man, at least a good amateur, but I didn't say so. "I'm a bee man," I joked. I hauled the chain saw into the tree and hung it securely on the stub of an old limb. I climbed out onto the limb that arched over the bedroom. I was almost over the bedroom when I noticed white streaks of fungus in crevices of the bark. From here on the wood was seriously decayed. I reached ahead of me as far as I could and tied the rope securely to the limb. I backed up about four feet and tied the rope to a solid part of the limb; with the bow saw I began cutting between the two knots. Cutting ahead of you across a limb that you're are sitting on is hard work, but I used the bow saw to avoid disturbing the bees until I was ready for them.

After fifteen minutes, the limb over the bedroom sagged. I stopped, then took a few more light strokes with the saw. The limb slowly arced downward, brushed the roof of the house, then cracked free. The rope pulled it up short and I lowered it gently to the driveway.

"That's enough," the woman said. "I don't want to see you fall."

"You won't," I assured her. I cut off another 3-foot section of the limb the same way I had cut the first section. I backed up toward the crotch of the tree where the bees were; I stood with my feet just below their hive entrance, my back against the vertical trunk, and I rested in the mild October sun. In the crown of a tree, I felt like a passenger on the Earth's spinning surface. Trees are like the horses on a great merry-go-round, but animals are their riders. Climbing trees does not require the courage or talents of a mountain climber, but mountain climbers go up and down in groups, and usually climb the same peaks over and over. I sometimes joke with myself in the top of a tree: Once again you have risen above your station in life. All climbers are active malcontents. I emphasize active. The inactive malcontents are the followers of Melville's Ishmael, people who stare at the water—mental divers, sinkers. I have sunk often enough and prefer climbing.

I have often looked at the limbs of a tree and thought, I am the only human being who has ever been here. I closed my eyes and listened to the light hum of the bees inside the tree. For them I did not yet exist. The only puzzle was that I could not tell if the brood and honeycombs were above the entrance, below, or both. I studied the trunk for a while and decided that most of the comb had to be below the entrance where the trunk was thicker and more likely hollow. I pulled the bee veil over my hat and stretched its skirt around my shoulders and chest. I checked to see that my jeans were tucked into the tops of my socks. I pulled on the gloves with the rubber hands and canvas gauntlets almost to my elbows. I looked up the trunk toward the sky. The right cut and this part of the tree would fall away from me, out into the drive, parallel to the house.

I braced myself with my back to the curved trunk and pulled the starter cord to the chain saw. I crouched a little, made sure my footing was good, and started to cut sideways into the vertical trunk a few inches above the hive entry. Within seconds I was aware of bees flying wildly around me, crawling on my smock, on my gloves, and some on the wire veil in front of my eyes. The chain was pulling out a steady stream of wood chips, which mixed with the bees. Suddenly, I smelled beeswax and honey.

I didn't see any value in stopping. The bees wouldn't settle down for a good half hour. I eased the saw harder into the tree. Bits and pieces of yellow wax flew out, and bees and white larvae. Honey ran onto the chain and mixed with the chain oil. I felt sorry for the bees and apologized silently. I eased my finger off the gas but left the chain in the tree, the motor running. The trunk had not yet begun to lean. I revved the saw and eased it into the wood again. I heard a loud crack and looked up. The weight of twenty or thirty feet of crown above the hive had sent a crack down through the hive toward the crotch and the trunk was coming my way. I looked up and saw an avalanche of wood rushing toward me. I stretched one foot down for the ladder but couldn't find it.

Maybe seconds later, maybe a minute, I knew I was on the ground. I could hear the chain saw running, but all I could see was red, bright blood red. My first thought was that I had cut off my head (logic is not the first faculty that returns with consciousness). I reached a hand toward my head and found it still there. My hat was gone but not the veil, and its wire screen was curtained with blood pouring out of my head. I pulled it off and the world was extremely bright, almost covered with snow. I felt something moving in my hair. Bees. My arm moved very slowly but I found them and lifted them out. I reached over and switched off the saw. The day was suddenly silent.

I got up on my knees, then slowly to my feet, but my back hurt badly. Fortunately, the trunk that had fallen was beside me, and I sat on it. At that moment, the woman came out onto her deck and started shouting, "Are you all right?"

I nodded yes and raised a hand.

"You're sitting on the tree. You're sitting on the tree," she said. I have never understood the importance of that alarm. The world suddenly became as bright white as lightning and I had just enough sense to lie down before I lost consciousness again. I woke up to the siren of the emergency squad. They strapped me onto a wooden board by the shoulders, hips, knees, and ankles.

In the course of an hour, my home had changed from a simple house in the woods to a high-tech home in Memorial Hospital where a machine monitored my heart and lungs, a precisely measured bag of nutrients fed me through a tube in my arm, and my bed raised and lowered with a motor. I could not raise myself. I could not roll over. The X-rays showed that I had crushed my fourth lumbar vertebra. The nerves that worked my stomach were not working my stomach. The nerves that worked my legs were not working my legs. Otherwise I was lucky. I had a mild concussion and twelve stitches in my head, stretched ligaments in my right shoulder, but nothing broken.

After three days, my stomach was working well again. After four days, I could ease out of bed and walk slowly to the toilet. I could not bend over. I could turn my head but not my shoulders. I could not lift anything heavier than a big book. I knew that if I did not recover, I would be as useless and unfit to live in the woods as a wingless bird. No. I could live in the woods, but not a simple life. I would no longer be able to cut trees and split wood, turn over the garden with a shovel or spade, climb on the roof to clean the chimney, carry water from Morgan Branch. The list of things I could not do with my own strength and hand tools was very long.

When I was a kid, I used to read Reader's Digest articles on how the world might end in a solar explosion, a collision with a comet, or a slow freeze as the sun's energy dissipated. These scenarios made me sad and angry. They still seem a great disappointment of all human hope, but they exhausted my capacity to worry about things I could not change or predict. So now I would make the best effort I could to return to a simple life in the forest, but lying in that hospital room I also realized that most civilized people live their entire lives happily supported by our best technology, our best labor saving devices, and our best power-enhancing tools. I would work on recovery and every day do whatever I could.

I had my first chance to do something in the world beyond the hospital even before I was discharged. My friends Wade and Marina Barber were working for the Carter-Mondale presidential ticket, and the doctor gave Marina permission to pick me up and drive me to the voting booth in Pittsboro. The nurse helped strap me into an elaborate metal back brace and pull on pants and a shirt. Leaning on Marina, I shuffled my way to the elevator. The front seat of her Volvo folded back like a bed. She delivered me to the voting booth and returned me to the hospital. A new duty nurse came to my room immediately.

"You are not supposed to be walking," she said. No one had told me not to walk. "At least the exercises are doing you some good," she said.

"What exercises?" I asked.

"Didn't Physical Therapy give you exercises to do?"

No again. After the pain killers and the intravenous food, the hospital had done nothing for me except clean me, feed me, and check my reflexes. The back brace I had used to go to Pittsboro was all wrong, the doctor said. He gave me a hip-to-chest, lace-up canvas corset with steel uprights in it. Two days after the election, he discharged me.

A friend drove me home and put a mattress and blankets on the floor next to the wood heater. The most difficult part of life that followed was getting up and out the door and into the outhouse. I had to go down a couple of steps, cross the drive, and go up three steps. I called a plumber who worked with Heartwood Builders. He came and put a toilet in the bathroom. I was moving away from that part of the simple life that makes contact with nature necessary. Almost as soon as human animals moved into houses, they found ways to move their fire and cooking inside with them. Moving the plumbing inside, in any manner other than a chamber pot, took a few thousand more years. Once a house has indoor cooking and plumbing, the human inhabitants have made most contact with nature truly optional. Americans used to sit on their porches in the cool summer evenings, talk to the neighbors, or watch the world go by. Builders still put expensive porches on houses, but it's been many years since I've seen anyone sitting on a front porch or even noticed a porch with chairs on it—not if the house has air conditioning and television.

Frank Lloyd Wright led an entire school of architecture to focus on this making contact between homeowners and nature optional. Americans have always enjoyed views of nature, but modern architecture and technology became focused on staying in touch, without compromising comfort and safety. Homes were built with glass walls and large picture windows. Sliding glass doors opened onto patios and decks that were no longer simply called porches and aimed toward the street and sociable intercourse with neighbors, but toward whatever privacy and greenery the back yard afforded. The patios and decks became outdoor living spaces.

Until the twentieth century, most human housing was an escape from nature. Wright adopted a sensible and civilized compromise: He taught Americans how to use the house as a way of filtering nature, a way to indulge the senses without discomforting the body. My first big step in that direction embarrassed me because it came from weakness.

Thoreau limited his own experiment with voluntary poverty and simplicity to two years and two months, then returned to the comforts of living with Emerson and other wealthy friends. We should not be surprised that no one took adopted prescription of voluntary simplicity as a full time life style until late in the twentieth century. Most who have tried it lasted no longer than Thoreau at Walden before they began to add complexity to simplicity. All the owner-built homes in Saralyn soon added not one but two bathrooms, central heat and central air, decks and screened porches. Voluntary simplicity still has strong advocates in the environmental movement, but I am not surprised to see those same advocates living in large homes and driving sport utility vehicles. Almost all the people who live simple lives in today's world are living in involuntary simplicity.

Most of us who went back to the land did not want a life nearly as simple as Thoreau recommended or that the old-timers in *The Foxfire Book* lived. We wanted a life that was simpler but not simple. We wanted to declare our disgust with a world of nuclear weapons and complex moral issues like Vietnam. We wanted innocence.

Alternative culture even had its own psychiatrist to certify the madness of mainstream America: R. D. Laing insisted that what society called psychotic and irrational was in fact a rational reaction to life in a crazy world. He would have been the perfect psychiatric expert witness for the Unabomber trial.

Theodore Kaczynski's loathing of society led him to kill its leaders. My own alternative life led me to nearly killing myself. As I was recovering from my injuries, a friend asked me, "Did you ever think maybe you were trying to commit suicide?"

She was referring to my taking risks such as climbing trees with a chain saw and no safety equipment. I answered, "No, of course not." At least, "trying" was the wrong word. Yet, I realized what the life story of any wild animal should have taught me about my decision to live in the woods and about voluntary simplicity. I knew that a simple life, depending on one's own hands (paws, beak, hooves) and on the bounty of nature, was usually a short life. Had I fallen from a tree in my own forest, my act might not have been suicide, but it would have been suicidal. I wanted to go on keeping bees with Sylvan and watching the seasons come and go at Morgan Branch. Wild animals live longer in captivity, and I was ready to become captive to the basic modern conveniences.

-chapter 25-

Squeaky Says I'm Dirty

A man with a gun comes visiting, but only to deliver a warning that I have a death threat from friends in California. I must do more for the environment, they say.

The tree and the simple life were not the only things I fell out of that autumn. I also began to fall out of the environmental movement, though a few more years would pass before I would understand that. One balmy day with a few dry leaves rattling their way down to the ground, my friend Elizabeth at Heartwood Realty's office in Chapel Hill called. "Wallace, there's a man here who says he has to talk to you."

"Who is he?"

"He says he's from the FBI."

I asked her to look at his credentials.

"He's from the FBI."

He wouldn't tell her what he wanted to talk to me about.

"He says he can talk only to you."

I told her he would have to come out to Saralyn if he wanted to talk to me because I was waiting for a truckload of gravel to show up. The day was also much too nice to drive out of the woods and into Chapel Hill. I began to list all the possible reasons the FBI might want to talk to me privately. I had friends who smoked pot, and a few neighbors grew it. I knew people who dropped acid, raised hallucinogenic mushrooms, or snorted coke. I had lots of friends who had been antiwar radicals. I frequently wrote for an alternative newspaper, but mostly about land-use issues, gardening, and wild food. I could not think of a crime in my own life.

On this most beautiful day the troubles of my species were coming to visit. I had moved to Morgan Creek and built my own house so that I would not be at the mercy of my own species. Although I was active in environmental organizations, fighting nuclear power plants and dams and industrial pollution, my life was also relief from the constant gloom of the movement. The scientists Paul and Ann Ehrlich were talking about the population bomb, predicting its explosion would bring doom by 1980. Astronomer Carl Sagan was predicting global cooling. (In the 1970s, cooling held sway among the climate forecasters.) Ralph Nader promised we were being poisoned by our own water supplies. Everyone knew that greed had all but exhausted world oil supplies. The Arab oil embargo in 1973 had closed American gas stations for the first time in memory, and at least one family left Saralyn rather than be marooned in the woods for lack of fuel.

All this doom and the way it was preached was not much different from the dire punishments predicted by church preachers from Cotton Mather to Jerry Falwell.

Morgan Branch was a good place to hide from both kinds of preachers and to atone for my sins of all kinds. The beauty of the forest moved me to confession and aspirations of a pure soul more powerfully than gothic architecture, stained-glass windows, and organ music could ever do. I believed the proximity to animals and plants would do more for me than the proximity to humans. Human sin has a long reach, however, and the only time it has found me here in the forest, it arrived in the name of environmentalism.

A few minutes after Elizabeth's call interrupted my afternoon, I heard the gravel truck slowly roaring down the narrow tracks alongside Seven Spring Branch toward my house. Harry Henderson owned the forest-green truck with its black bed, and he kept it as immaculately clean and unscratched as a chauffeured Cadillac. When he reached my drive, he shifted to a crawl, avoiding overhanging branches as best he could. Harry was tall, his skin varnished to his bones, one eye socket empty from a sawmill accident. He listened to Christian country music on his radio. In every sense he was a good Christian, which was why he brought his truck into the woods to deliver my gravel and didn't complain. When he had dumped the load on the red mud in front of the house, we stood outside talking.

A yellow convertible came up the drive and stopped where Harry's truck blocked the way. A man looking like Warren Beatty playing Clyde Barrow got out and came toward us. He had left his jacket in the car, and across the front of his pin-striped shirt and under his tie was the diagonal support of his pistol belt. Harry looked at the pistol in the belt, at his business-like face, and said, "Just a minute, I'll get out of your way."

The FBI agent backed up his car, let Harry pass, and emerged again without his pistol. I invited him in but I did not ask him to take off his shoes as I required of other guests walking on my heart pine floors. I had only one real chair in the house, the chair from my writing desk, and I gave it to him. I sat on a cushion at the low table where I ate.

"Do you know the name Squeaky Fromm?" he asked me.

"The woman who shot at President Ford?"

That was the woman. She was also connected with the Manson family, the group of drifters who had butchered actress Sharon Tate and her friends in a ritualistic killing. While they were working on the case, FBI agents had found a box of letters to environmentalists across the country that Fromm and her people had written but not mailed. (Fromm was now in prison for the attempted assassination of President Ford.) Here the FBI agent put on one of the nicest of bedside manners I have seen in or out of a hospital: "One of the letters was addressed to you, and that's why I'm here."

He explained that the federal judge in this case had ordered the FBI to contact all the addressees of these letters.

"Do you have the letter?" I asked. I wanted to see a letter to me from a celebrity, even a notorious one, whose name will appear in the history books.

"No, but I am going to tell you what it says. All the letters say the same thing. It says that you are a leader in an environmental group, but that you have not been sincere in your efforts."

I laughed. I was no longer the president of the Conservation Council of North Carolina, and I thought I had worked pretty hard. I did not know that Fromm had any interest in saving the environment. "So what do they want me to do?" I asked him.

"They don't say that. But the reason the judge asked us to notify you is that the letter contains a death threat." The writers had said that people who failed to work hard enough to save the environment might themselves be killed. "We have never seen any of these people in the East," the agent said, "and we don't expect to see any of them." He considered the threat so much hot air.

I thanked him for coming out to tell me about the letter. He said I should not hesitate to call the FBI if I heard anything at all from these people. He drove out of the woods in his yellow convertible and left me standing on Harry's fresh gravel, listening to the gentle rattle of dry leaves bumping tree limbs and each other as they fell.

The truth was I had not saved much of nature except what I owned, and then I had destroyed a lot to earn the money to put in roads. If my covenants held, someone during the next hundred years, noting the fate of other wild areas in the Triangle, might give me credit for a net benefit to nature. On the political front, the Conservation Council of North Carolina had made a lot of noise about the Shearon Harris Nuclear Plant, and we had spent $25,000 on lawsuits, but the plant was built. We had also spent thousands opposing Jordan Lake, built by the Corps of Engineers. Our real accomplishments were very small, and the council could hardly take even half the credit for higher water standards and a little land added to state parks. We had also supported a few stupid programs like subsidies for synthetic fuels and not one had turned out to be a good substitute for gasoline. Shale oil development wasted huge sums, and to our embarrassment, millions were spent to subsidize the use of eastern North Carolina peat as an alternative to coal.

All right, Squeaky, I'm guilty.

I took the Fromm threat seriously, but not very seriously. My letter was one of dozens, maybe hundreds. A mass mailing with about as much personal attention as any mass mailing. The first Unabomber letter had not yet reached its target. Although Unabomber didn't reach as many people, his letters made real explosions.

The threat from Fromm was not the first or last time someone had threatened to kill me. A writer friend who had gone crazy had made the threat. So had a few thugs in a bar when I was in college, and a gang of Gypsies in a hops field in Herefordshire when I took a working vacation from my graduate work at Oxford. Humans too live at the mercy of their species. At least we expect some. I have never seen real mercy among animals—a good Samaritan or real forgiveness. Perhaps mercy among animals exists, but it is far outweighed by the merciless. If I fell out of a tree in this forest, the main interest any raccoon, possum, fox, or vulture might take in me would concern tenderness and taste: less mercy than a farmer shows an old cow. A pack of wolves eating a moose, a moose eating mosses, grasses feeding on soils—they all serve themselves without any accounting or setting aside more than a season's reserves.

Even as I stood outside my house enjoying the sun and the golden palette of late fall, I knew that each bird, squirrel, and deer was busy about its own salvation and that even in North Carolina winter would show no mercy to any of us. *Homo sapiens* is the only species to show mercy to others and its own. The judge in California did not have to notify me of my name in the mass mailing. The FBI agent did not have to be polite or reassuring. The jury could have condemned Fromm to death.

I did not know what Squeaky Fromm might have wanted me to do for nature. I wrote to the FBI and asked for my letter to be sent to me, or at least a copy of it, but nothing ever came. I think she was right. Her own wildness and Manson's was not unlike the wildness of nature—a place without law or mercy. Somewhere in the back of my head there was another event that questioned what we in the environmental movement should really be trying to save, or how well we understood what it was in Thoreau's wildness that might save civilization.

–chapter 26–

The Pleasures of
Getting Lost

*After several years of living on and exploring my
land and the land around me, I get lost.*

By the fall of 1977 my back had recovered well enough that I was again
taking long walks and climbing trees. Except for the occasional animal observation box in the wall or a new bookshelf, the house had everything I
needed and I decided to put more time into seeing the world around me.
The president of the Chapel Hill Audubon Society called to ask if I would
take a few members bird-watching. I have never dedicated my life or spare
time to any one pursuit, but I have always learned from people who do,
whether they are stargazers, stock pickers, or English train spotters. The
best birders can imagine an entire bird from a few notes out of a dark
thicket or treetop. For my part, I was forever walking or sitting in the
woods and hearing a familiar call to which I could never attach an image.
Twelve birders came out on a cold, gray morning in fall. I said I would take
them northwest to an area where pines and hardwoods grew and the land
had a small creek as well as dry hilltops.

We walked slowly, spotting a bird here and there, examining the gray-
white pellet of an owl, the white splash of a vulture or turkey, the glistening fresh beads of deer droppings. After heading slowly northwest for
twenty minutes, I saw something that disturbed me: I saw the roof of a

house where no house should be. It was my house. I had lived in these woods for ten years communing with nature, studying landforms and individual trees, but I had guided the bird-watchers in a circle.

My only excuse is that I should have taken a compass. My internal compass had been trained on sunlight in the daytime. If you know the time roughly and can spot even the general location of the sun in a mist or at sunrise and sunset, you always know where north, south, east, and west are and which way you are moving. At night my internal compass fixes on the moon and stars and the shapes of the land, which are more generalized and less blurred by details in the dark. When I was a Boy Scout in New York we learned to find directions by the moss on the north side of trees. Here in the southern piedmont in our dark mature forests, the base of a tree is shaded on all sides and the moss grows north or south, or all around.

Guiding the Audubon birders was not the first time I lost myself. If they had not been present, I would have been glad of being lost, especially on my own land. On that day, I returned to the house for a compass. This time we moved steadily northwest, and as we crossed the broad flat hilltop north of my house, I saw where I had gone wrong. In the gray morning and light fog, I had begun to turn in a circle on that flat land. I know a lot of the trees and the occasional stone outcrop on that hilltop by their forms or scars, but that morning I had missed them. No matter where human beings are, they travel by fixed points. Usually, these points are so familiar that we don't think about them. A New Yorker knows Broadway and the Chrysler Building. We give directions by landmarks—go to the church, turn right, go past a house with a white fence, turn right at the park. I won't say, "Seen one tree, you've seen them all," but the markers in human-made landscapes are much easier to learn than the markers in a forest. The great value of the compass to me on that day with Audubon, or to Magellan or Columbus, was that it uses only one landmark, that magnetic mass of lodestone in the Canadian arctic.

The very first time friends got lost out here, the year before I began to build, I tried to give them guides almost as fixed as magnetic north. One of my former students suggested we get together a few people and have a picnic in the woods. The old trace of wagon road that would become my drive was obscured with brush, but we more or less followed it in and over Morgan Branch and on up to the top of the same hill where I misguided the birders. Where the hill falls sharply toward Morgan Branch next to an outcrop of white quartz, we cleared the leaves and built a small fire, ate, talked, and sang a few songs on into the darkness. We were eight—a couple with a child Sylvan's age, Sylvan, Sarah and me, and my student and a young woman he was going out with. I was not in a campfire mood. I left early and gave everyone instructions on how to find the way out. When we had walked in on a bright afternoon, no one had thought of a flashlight. Fortunately, the moon had risen in the east above the trees. My instructions to them were to keep the hillside on their right and the moon on their left and keep walking straight until they came to the Saralyn road half a mile south.

An hour later, I was already lost in sleep, and they were about to get lost in the woods. Sarah, Sylvan, and the couple with the other child gathered their things and began to walk. Because the hillside was steep, they walked on the top of the hill. They forgot whether the moon was supposed to be on the right or left, but they knew the hilltop should be on the right. By that time, however, they had wandered slightly over the hill into another valley. They stopped. They got the hill over their right shoulders and began a long march north instead of south. The November evening turned cold. They began to hear rushing water and they came out of the woods where the wide expanse of the Haw River stopped them. They found a dip in the ground large enough for everyone to lie in and covered themselves with leaves. My student and his friend started in the right direction, but almost instantly they confused themselves with their own doubts. He had served in the Army in Alaska and decided the most prudent course was to stay put and wait for light. That was Sylvan's first night in these woods.

As soon as I had begun taking Sylvan into the woods, she started naming things. Seven Spring Branch is one example. The outcrop of quartz rock where we picnicked is another. It stood at the head of a broad cleft of forest descending to Morgan Branch. Because we had gathered several bushels of brown milk mushrooms (*Lactarius corrugis*) there, she named it "Lactarius Gully." She didn't need to put up signs because the things she named were there. In American subdivisions we put up signs—White Tail Road, Red Oak Drive, Turkey Run, Sycamore Hill—because the things they name are not there. If the red oak does stand on Oak Street or the sycamore on Sycamore Lane, new residents can tell one tree from the other. If I'm biased against this practice, it's a bias I've had since I was Sylvan's age. My Uncle Harold used his GI loan to buy a new house in the first Levittown, a house like the thousands of other little houses in America's first mass-produced community. Even in second grade, I thought his address was absurd—105 Barnyard Lane.

I have never named any place in the forest, although I might have at Sylvan's age. Kids like names. It's a way of mapping the world. They know without numbers how far or how long from home to any name. Sarah and I had named our farm Heartwood, but I had not named the house or any place at Morgan Branch. I had also ignored my birthdays and nixed any suggestion from Sarah or anyone else that we have a party or even guests for cake. I had never had a birthday party when I was a kid. I didn't like counting everything, and it was too late to start. I didn't want to be numbered, and I didn't want my world to be full of place names. Names were too defining. They suggested a limit to where one place ends and another begins. Maybe I was a man who insisted on going blindfolded through the world. Being lost in the woods, however, was my way of trying to find something. The more I walked in the woods, the more I had to work at getting lost, but I could always do it by selecting the right circumstances.

Night is the easiest time to get lost. Put on a blindfold and you can get lost in a house you have lived in for decades. A cloudy and moonless night here can be as black as a blindfold. Of course, a few photons of light are bouncing around the forest even on the darkest night. Many nocturnal animals can see them, and these animals are never lost at night. I started to go out to get lost at night in part to appreciate the world these animals live in. I developed a ritual of walking into the woods and leaning against a tree or sitting on the ground. In a few minutes, I would begin to hear the action. Raccoons, possums, snakes, deer, owls, bats, flying squirrels, whippoorwills—they are all out there, not to mention hordes of insects, spiders, and other crawlers and borrowers.

I can still get lost at night, but near home I have come to know the land by its feel underfoot. Am I going up or down hill, how steep, for how long, through what kind of undergrowth, and how smooth is the ground? In the first few years I lived in the woods, I could lose myself even in the daytime. I would wait for a cloudy day to walk off my own land into a neighbor's land. I was blessed to have around me several large empty tracts, almost 2,200 acres in all. I don't know exactly what I enjoyed most about getting lost. I did it when I was unhappy and when I was happy. I always found something I didn't expect to find. I always came home with a souvenir: an unusual rock, mushrooms, a plant, a skeleton, turtle shells, a piece of wood that made a fine form or even mocked a face. I never carried a compass.

When you don't have a compass, you pay more attention to observing the land around you, or you ought to. You learn to see the distinctions between different kinds of trees and different kinds of white oaks and red oaks. You begin to see the infinite variety of forms trees take. You notice a poplar or beech whose roots snake along the ground for fifteen or twenty feet in their effort to find a hold or nutrients. You see that the rocks on the ground change color and texture. In a creek you see small and distinct pools or outcrops of solid clay in its banks. Each of these discoveries is part of a story, but few of these stories can be told accurately from beginning to end. Where did the clay come from? Did the pottery fragments in my garden come from this clay? What weather disintegrated the rock that made the blue clay? What was the landscape like when these fine particles were washed into this place beside the creek? Where will this clay be in a thousand years?

I could ask a list of questions equally long about each tree and animal. As soon as I began having trouble getting lost on the land, I realized I was in danger of going blind. The famous hymn, Amazing Grace, has the line, "I once was lost, but now I'm found." Truth is we are always lost. I feel sorry for both the fundamentalist and the atheist who are sure they know where they are. Theirs is a life similar to living in a sterile room with no windows or doors. Their perception is as simple as an animal's. Deer are easy prey to a hunter in a tree because deer never look up. Raccoons pursued climb a tree to escape the dogs and become an easy target for a gun. Animals do not expect the unexpected.

We never find anything unless we are first lost. Columbus was lost. DeSoto got lost. Bering was lost. Lewis and Clark were lost. Life cannot be a discovery unless we are lost. Many great stories revolve around a hero who gets lost at sea, in the desert, or in the forests. The lost hero is an allegory for everyone who has ventured into the unknown and made an unexpected discovery. Odysseus was lost in an island-dotted sea. Christ wandered in the desert. Robinson Crusoe found a new life on a strange island. The Mayflower was lost as she aimed for Virginia. Einstein said that he felt he was following the tracks of a great beast across the universe.

Scientists often get lost just before a discovery. With our great telescopes we have begun to make a map to the farthest reaches of the universe, but even in this purely physical space we are still lost. Inside a single living cell we are even more lost. We know roughly where we are, the way I knew roughly where I was when I took the birders onto the hill. I know scientists who have spent an entire lifetime on just a few structures inside one cell of one animal. Shinya Inouye at the Woods Hole Marine Biological Laboratory has spent an entire lifetime inventing and improving microscopic devices that enable us to better see our surroundings. But the more we see, the more questions we ask.

Whenever I turn to science to explain something I have found in the forest, I leave with a little learning and a lot of questions. I can never read *Nature*, *Science*, or any serious research magazine without the sense that we are all lost. Each discovery says, "I think this is the right direction." If scientists were solving problems once and for all, every year we would have fewer and fewer scientific journals. Some people become profoundly irritated when lost. Like my friend Bart who came to house-sit, they grab the best defensive weapon they can find and retreat to a corner of life. The unwavering atheist or fundamentalist decides on a few answers and sticks to them.

We don't enter life afraid of being lost. Children are entirely lost when they enter squalling into this world. Like Sylvan buried under leaves with her mother and friends in the woods that November night, if children know their parents are good protectors in this wilderness, their lives are infused with wonder. One of the great sins of television and even of schools is convincing young children that they are always about to be lost in a hostile and dangerous world. These children do not acquire the self-confidence to enjoy being lost. They never stop putting labels on everything or conquer the fear of venturing into the unknown. They are afraid even to ask directions from strangers.

The greatest threat to the environment is not the day Rachel Carson feared when spring comes and "no bird sings." The greatest threat is that day when spring comes and there is no wonder.

chapter 27

Dead Neighbors Make Good Company

The longer I live in the woods, the more signs I see of people who have lived here before me. I set out to learn more about them and they in turn teach me more about these woods.

Several visitors who have come to stay at my house when I'm away have been frightened by the noises of a summer night or by silence in the winter dark. The psychiatrist Carl Jung suggested that only in deep, utter silence could a person hear or see ghosts. I have never believed in ghosts, but I had brilliant friends who did, and they swore they had seen them and talked to them in the deep stillness of the night. I was willing to try talking to ghosts.

I didn't expect conversation and got none. The closest I got was being able to conjure the ghost of summers past, and I would do that on a cold night by opening a bottle of blackberry wine. I had plenty and never opened one until it was at least a year old and well settled. Then I would pour myself a glass of the dark purple and sit on a floor cushion with only one light lit on the other side of the room, the wood heater throwing off good warmth. I would take a sip of that strong, tart wine and look through the glass at the light; all the warmth of summer filled me and it was better than lying under the sun on the beach.

On those quiet nights listening for ghosts, I wondered who they might be, who had lived on this land or even passed through this forest before I came. When I had time during the day, I went looking for them.

All human animals who have resided in North America have left their marks on the land. I could not find a trace of animals who had disappeared ten years earlier, but the marks and consequences of human habitation, and even mere passing, began to show themselves everywhere. Looking for them and expecting to find them was more productive than listening for ghosts. Most people don't see the signs because they are not looking for them: They might as well be looking at a page full of Inuit or Mongolian script and saying they see only random scratches and squiggles. So filmmakers shot *The Last of the Mohicans*, and maybe one in a thousand or ten thousand people knew that the primeval evergreen forest was really a growth of twenty- or twenty-five-year-old pines in North Carolina, the aftermath of old logging or farming. Those pine groves in this region are no more than the first layer of new life put over the land when people take their hopes and dreams to places where they expect and usually find less disappointment. If you don't know what to look for in a forest, you have seen one tree and you've seen them all.

Nature fooled even Thoreau. Thoreau traveled through many forests, read the best naturalists of his day, and catalogued plants. When he considered what was essential to a forest, he wrote, "What is a country without rabbits and partridges? They are among the most simple and indigenous animal products. . . . That must be a poor country indeed that does not support a hare." Partridges and hares are not frequent in old forests. They like meadows and edges. In the East meadows and edges are made by disturbances, usually human disturbances.

I propose that we call the search for marks of human impact on nature forensic ecology. It is different from archaeology. Archaeology finds things people have left in or on the land or the seas. Forensic ecology looks at the land and finds in its condition evidence of past human activity. Archaeology and history can guide our efforts in forensic ecology and vice versa.

Sylvan was seven and I had been at Saralyn three years when we started a methodical archaeological search for the past next to the garden. I laid out five-foot-square plots and we troweled down inch by inch, recovering blackened shards of pottery and an occasional stone tool and mapping their locations on paper. Across Morgan Branch and just downstream from the small grove of old growth beech trees, I found the forensic evidence of Indian land use.

This site is a small piece of flat land, Seven Spring Branch and Morgan Branch bordering two sides and hills blocking the sun from the south and west. Water oozes out of the groin where the two hills meet and seeps over a shallow bed of stones to Morgan Branch. Large trees and small make this area dark and damp year round. As soon as I wandered around this area, I noticed the roots of a poplar and a beech. In the center of the site was a distinct but shallow depression not much bigger than a big dining table and only a few inches deep, but it affected the trees around it strangely. It appeared to attract and repel them. The largest trees were two big beeches and a poplar whose gnarled bark and big bumps suggested that it had survived great abuse or a powerful disease, or that it was very old. It had not grown upward in a smooth column like most poplars. The beeches had a normal shape, but the roots of both the poplar and the beeches were intent on embracing but not entering the depression. Each tree had long-muscled roots that ran along the surface of the ground like huge wooden boa constrictors. The trees wanted to be near the depression but had to send their roots around it and back again. A root as thick as my leg ran from the poplar around the edge of the depression and disappeared under one of the beeches. Three feet from the poplar's trunk the root had engulfed the trunk of a three-inch-thick holly tree that had seeded itself here. The roots of the beeches also spread out on the ground, large and small, a strong gray network looking for nutrients and anchorage.

Nothing grew in the depression itself, not even a blade of grass or reeds. I suspected this had been a clay pit. A few years later, I borrowed an earth auger from Heartwood Realty. An earth auger is a simple instrument five feet long with a foot of hard steel tubing at the end tipped with two spoon-like blades that draw down into the earth when the user turns the T-bar handle. I sunk the auger into the center of the depression. It went down easily and at each foot I pulled it up and emptied the tube of black and partly decayed leaves and twigs. At three feet, I ran through the debris into clay. It was a beautiful blue-green clay almost identical to the volcanic tufa I had pried and hammered out of the earth for my foundations. I augured the sides of the depression. Under a few inches of leaves I began pulling up almost pure clay. I took some to the house, shaped it into small bowls and a crude head and threw them into the ashes of the wood heater, where a strong winter fire would be going all night. The next morning, I pulled out these objects. They had turned brown and red and very hard.

My evidence that Indians or maybe early settlers had mined clay beside Morgan Branch was circumstantial but strong. If someone hadn't mined the clay, where did the clay from the center of the depression go? If a tree had grown there and the hole in the center was its deep taproot, what made the broader depression? When a tree falls over, its torn roots usually bring with them a disk of earth and rocks. The bottom of the disk slides backward toward the center of the hole. For a few years, the root disk stands like a saucer edged into the ground. The roots decay and the earth and rocks collapse into a low ridge, like the earth heaped over a grave. Because the disk is usually tilted toward the trunk, its collapse fills the front of the depression, leaving a shallow trench behind it.

Such is the evidence I can see with my own eyes. If I were better read in anthropology and had the tools of a paleobotanist, my forensic ecology might reveal much more. By studying the pollen trapped in the clay as it was laid down, I might find how the coming of Indians had changed these forests. Scientists have found evidence that for thousands of years African tribes managed the great Serengetti plains by burning them to stimulate new forage. They also culled the herds for their preferred animals. The "wild" Serengetti that safari operators show visitors is largely a human creation.

For more than a thousand years around Morgan Branch Indians burned the forests to drive wildlife into ambushes or to improve visibility for the hunt. John Lawson tells of being short on food during his travels in South Carolina, "but finding the Woods newly burnt, and on fire in many Places, which gave us great Hopes that Indians were not far off." The fire hunt had succeeded. After an hour or two of walking, Lawson found a large group of Santee Indians, who gave them "barbecued Turkeys, Bear's Oil and Venison." The large meadows of the southern states amazed French botanist François Andre Michaux in the 1790s. He asked settlers and Indians about these places and became convinced that they "owe their birth to some great conflagration that had consumed the forests and that they are kept as meadows by the custom that is still practiced annually setting them on fire."

After three hundred years, less than the lifetime of some trees, the consequences of Indian technology must still be present on and around Morgan Branch as it is throughout America. With the right scientific tools, I would find that my land at Morgan Branch is part wild, part garden.

Meanwhile, I occasionally dug a bucket of clay and crafted a figure or a dish. In digging and working the clay, I could talk, maybe indirectly, with the ghosts of Indians who had dug this same clay. Well, I talked with the Indian women and children.

On hot summer days I could always find the chill of autumn or spring in the waters of Morgan Branch, and I started a hobby that has not only satisfied my thermoregulatory needs but that has taught me prehistory and history. I started walking Morgan Branch and other streams to look at fish, snakes, crayfish, salamanders, birds, frogs, and insects.

None of these animals, or the coons and owls that hunt them, built the neat stone wall I found on the west bank of Morgan Branch north of my land. The remains of the wall rose straight from the edge of the bank about four feet high and ran back into the hillside. The stones that had not fallen stood neatly fit together like a puzzle. On the east bank the land lay flat, an acre of flood plain with wild grasses growing under large trees. The east bank had no structure, but clearly someone had lined the bank with large stones to keep the water from cutting into it. Was this Indian, colonial, or later? Based on strong circumstantial evidence, I decided that it was Indian or early-European settler. When I took a metal detector to this site, I found absolutely nothing. Metal provided even the earliest traders and settlers with their great advantage over Indians and the wilderness, and wherever they worked or lived for more than a day or two, some metal remains behind. Whether the structure was Indian or settler, it might have had one of two purposes. It could have been the site of a fish trap or it could have been a low dam to flood the plantable flatlands.

Indians often caught fish in weirs made of interwoven branches and saplings with a single escape funnel leading the fish to their capture. Because anyone could stretch a weir more easily between high banks on other parts of the stream, my guess is that these stones mark the site of a small dam. A few boards or logs slipped between the stone structures could block the stream and divert water into the flat land and its crops. Whatever these stones and the rip rap on the other side were meant to do, they have successfully channeled the stream for more than two hundred years. Without the stone works, nature would have eventually eroded the flat land and washed its soils downstream into the Haw River and onto the coastal plains or into the shoals off Cape Fear.

Neither Indian settlers nor Europeans favored these lands in the hills beyond the Haw River. The lands created by river-borne sediments and erosion of river valleys have been the cradle of culture around the world. That's another way of saying that human beings know where the easy life is.

The first English to settle in these piedmont hills established plantations along the bigger rivers—the Neuse, the Haw, the Rocky, and the Deep. Those who followed had to choose lands with much smaller flood plains and more hills. On my trips to Pittsboro, I would go to the courthouse and talk to Lemuel Johnson, the wily old Democratic loyalist, a "yellow dog Democrat," who had identified the Carney Bynum place for me. He was invaluable to lawyers and businessmen trying to clear up a fuzzy boundary or disputed title. He helped me trace my lands and those around me, to find the names and histories of the people whose marks I had begun to see in the land. Beginning with my discovery of the Carney Bynum place, gradually I had began to understand where the people at Saralyn stood in this history and how we would leave our marks.

My title went back to the people who bought this second-best land. They had to deal with the notoriously corrupt and bureaucratic agents of England's Lord Granville, the last of the "lord's proprietors" who held rights to the northern piedmont. Most of them were speculators. Some may never have seen the land they bought. The names of the men who bought tracts of five to six hundred acres on this side of the river often appear in the records only once, on the grants from the Earl of Granville. They were speculators who sold their land through colonial versions of pinhookers like O.K. Pettigrew.

Some of the earliest real settlers were Daniel Drummond, George Dismukes, Thomas Brooks, and Mark, Joseph, and John Morgan. Their names have stayed on the land, and on the maps and deeds for the lands, which eventually became Saralyn. The creek across which I built the Saralyn road is Brooks Creek. I settled by Morgan Branch (in early deeds called Zacharia Morgan's Old Spring Branch). I later bought a tract adjoining mine whose western border was Drummond's Branch. By the late 1770s, the citizens of the world's newest country owned the Indians' former lands. The English had been no kinder to the Indians than the Tuscarora had been to the Oconeechee and the Sissehaw. On the land around Morgan Branch, which had seemed so untouched when I first moved here and which still seems pristine to many visitors, the marks of Indians, settlers, and their successors are everywhere.

The most obvious mark on my land is the wagon trace of Pace Mill Road, which I had cleared to make the drive from the Saralyn road to my house. When I settled into the house, one of my first long walks followed this road north. It continued to follow Morgan Branch, first on the west side, then when the bank became too steep, on the east. Two miles north, I came to a wide creek where it joined the Haw River. This was Dry Creek, though I have never seen it dry. A wagon could easily have crossed the rocky wide mouth of Dry Creek; a hundred yards beyond that it would have come to the main reason for this road being etched into the landscape. On both sides of the two-hundred-foot-wide river and at two places rising fifteen feet above its waters stood broad and thick piers of red brick. An iron bridge with wooden planks had once crossed the river on these piers. On the other side, buried in briar, honeysuckle, and poison ivy lay the burned timbers of Pace's Mill.

The first settlers on the western side of the Haw River farmed the high but flat lands north of Dry Creek. Their crops or their political influence must have been powerful enough to merit a bridge early in the history of the county. In 1828, the diary of Methodist preacher Thomas Mann from Mt. Pleasant Church on the east side of the river says, "This evening I walked over the Haw River to Isaac West's and stayed all night." For almost a century, settlers from the west side of the river brought their corn and wheat through the hills of Saralyn, finally following the wagon trace along Morgan Branch and across the river to James Pace's Mill. Year by year, horses and the iron-rimmed wagon wheels dug the old road deeper into the land.

If the bridge had survived, Pace Mill Road would not have grown thick with trees but would have been widened for automobiles and become a main route to Chapel Hill. Houses and churches and maybe a hamlet or two would have grown up by the road. Today the state Department of Transportation might have been thinking of four-laning the road. Nature intervened and economics redirected history.

In early May of 1924, an "act of God" removed the small farms and forests here from the sights of development. A common thunderstorm gave birth to a tornado that followed the Haw River southwest. The twister lifted the bridge from its brick piers and dropped it broken and twisted into the river. It also tossed a baby into a tree and killed it. Economics was also preparing the wild land I would come to sixty years later. Steam, the internal combustion engine, and electricity had doomed Pace's Mill. Water power was cheap, but sometimes the river almost dried up. At other times it rose into the mill's belts and pulleys. The new fuels allowed mills to be located anywhere, to operate more consistently and with more power. Gasoline-powered trucks could take grain to the new mills on the main roads, but they couldn't use Pace Mill Road or descend to the mill on the steep slopes of the eastern side of the river. Four miles downstream on a direct route from Pittsboro to Chapel Hill, a reinforced concrete bridge had replaced a covered bridge. Farmers on the west side of the river no longer had the influence or a logical argument for reconstructing the bridge to Pace's Mill site a second time. Morgan Branch was suddenly at least eight miles farther away from Chapel Hill and the growing tobacco city in Durham. Eight miles of dirt road meant a lot to farmers still dependent on horses and mules. The increasing popularity of cars and trucks forced another decision on these farmers, which they resolved in favor of the forest at Morgan Branch.

In the 1950s when the State of North Carolina decided to take over all county roads, it left out small roads like Pace Mill Road and hundreds of other dirt roads that served a few farms here and there in the countryside. For wagons and horses, low traffic had meant low maintenance. When the state took over, low traffic meant abandonment, especially for poor farmers, black and white. Without the bridge to the mill, Pace Mill Road served four or five backwoods farms.

When Michael and I bought Saralyn, eleven years had passed since anyone had driven in and out of its forest to a home, and that had been to the Carney Bynum place next to Saralyn. The more I wandered through the woods, the more I found they were strewn with castoffs and garbage like the rags and papers in the old Carney Bynum farmhouse. Within half a mile of my house, I found the remains of six chimneys and sometimes the stone piers that supported the corners of corncribs or small barns. I began to understand why the aerial photographs of the region showed so many stands of pine trees. Pines are the fastest colonizers of old fields, and they hold their territory against the hardwoods for as long as a century. Any farmer who had more than a family garden or who had a family horse or mule had to have almost two acres for each animal and the same for a cow. Farmers, not loggers, prepared the land for pines where oak and hickory once dominated. Not until the 1960s did landowners begin to cut hardwood land and replant in pines. When a hardwood forest is cut over, unless it is heavily burned, the thousands of miles of roots and root hairs quickly send up new growth. I have learned to identify oaks and poplars growing from stumps of trees cut more than a half century ago.

Pine stands are not the only memorial to abandoned fields and pastures. The rippled earth of row cropping still lies under forest duff, but the greatest marks are from erosion. Between the Pace Mill Road and Morgan Branch, the land was either too rocky and steep or too wet for farming, but on the slope rising up from the old wagon trace the land is furrowed. It is also deeply creased by erosion gullies. Mamie Oldham, who was born in 1904, told me that when she was a girl, her father took her up the wagon trace and it ran past pastures and croplands and an occasional small cabin. It was a bright sun-filled road. It was also a road overwashed by eroding mud when heavy rains caught the fields bare. In two of the largest gullies, I found rough stone terraces built to hold back the mud flows.

I have walked in the woods all over Chatham and neighboring Orange County, and wherever a hillside was farmed, I see the gullies made by erosion. Some are ten or fifteen feet deep. Scrape off the leaves or pine needles and underneath is not topsoil but bare red clay. Heavy grazing and cow paths invited erosion. Farmers with horses and mules frequently plowed up and down hills. Seldom more than six inches of real loam covers any piedmont hill and less than a couple of inches on a hillside. Leaves and loose topsoil absorb rain and slow the motion of water over the land, but once exposed, our thin topsoils wash away. When they are gone, the clay beneath absorbs very little. The water runs off fast and fast water makes channels and gullies. I imagined these lands when they were naked and eroding and I was embarrassed for the land the way I would be if I had to remember an old disgrace to my mother or grandmother.

The people who did this were not stupid. I once asked Mamie Oldham if this was the result of tobacco farming. "Oh, no," she said, "we couldn't grow tobacco in that red dirt. Made the bottom leaves red when it rained, you know." Cotton brought the people in these hills almost all the cash money they saw from farming. "That land along Morgan Branch was good cotton land," Mamie said, "cause it had rocks in it. We had to roll the rocks in between the rows so they'd make the soil warm. Many summers I tended that cotton. Go out in the morning, then back out in the evening." Nobody called it child labor, and nobody thought much about what was happening to the land. It was survival. Mamie says that when her parents got married, "they didn't even had a change of clothes to wear. He and mama worked like two dogs." A good farmer could get a bale of cotton from every acre, and sell it for $50. I listened to Mamie and I understood the struggle that had taken place along Morgan Branch had gone on for more than a century and was a battle as bitter as any fought with guns.

The forests that had begun to reclaim so many old southern farms grew to be the live mantle covering an immense tragedy. By the late 1930s, erosion had rendered useless almost 30 million acres of southern lands. Settlers had come south with farming traditions inherited from the deep wet soils of England and the absorbent glacial lands of the mid-Atlantic states. They had come inland from the flat sandy soils or rich black peat of the coastal plains. They were not prepared for the demands of thin topsoils and ancient clays.

The wisdom of educated agricultural advisors did not conquer the erosion ditches on the slopes draining into Morgan Branch. Replacing the walking plow with the tractor did that. In the South it did not happen soon enough. Small farmers could not afford tractors. When they had exhausted their lands, they did what aboriginal farmers still do: They moved elsewhere. The exodus started in the 1870s. In the ten years between 1930 and 1940, Southerners abandoned 414,000 farms. The destruction of small cotton fields was stopped by the internal combustion engine, the villain of modern environmentalists who are long on foresight and short on history.

In 1937, sociologist Gerald Johnson made a prediction. He said the moment a mechanical cotton picker becomes efficient, "the living of some millions of Southern farm workers will vanish. . . . Cotton planters will also be out of work. . . . It will come with dramatic suddenness." In 1941, International Harvester introduced the first mechanical cotton picker. Too late for this land. The soils were long gone on their way to the Haw River, into the Cape Fear River, and down into the ship-wrecking shoals at Cape Fear.

The small farmers didn't have much garbage, but what they did have they dumped near home. Near almost every falling down chimney underneath the leaves and an inch or two of duff lies an old dump. Everything is gone but glass, crockery, and rusting iron. In the interest of finding these dumps and maybe salvaging something of value, I decided to buy a metal detector I couldn't afford. My friend Michael liked the idea and from New York sent half the price. We agreed he would get half the treasure. He has gotten the zinc or tin top of an old snuffbox, and that is 100 percent of the treasure.

With my metal detector extending my senses, I discovered one of the great disappointments of my life here. The forest is full of nails, bolts, pieces of wagon wheels, busted logging saws, farm machinery, horseshoes, and old stoves. I could not go more than three or four feet along the trace of the mill road without the detector wailing it had found metal. I took the metal detector into Morgan Branch one afternoon. Maybe I would find a rock with metal ore, or even gold. The community of "Gold Hill" is only fifteen miles north. Just below the garden, the detector wailed when it swung near the bank of the creek. I scratched into the clay and pulled out four or five lengths of iron pipe. Next to the garden I had discovered the telltale oblong pit of a portable sawmill. The slabs and sawdust had long ago melted into my garden soils. The pipe may have carried water to a steam engine.

Despite the changes humans before me have made to the land and all their garbage lying around the forest, I can ignore it and visitors seldom notice it any more than the dust under the bed or the mortar stains on the rocks in the chimney. I can thank the acid soils and the yearly blanketing of leaves; I also thank our abundant rain, the fungi it nourishes, and the rust it encourages.

The more I walked around the ruins and poked through the garbage and found what was lost, the clearer it became that I had come to Chatham County to buy land and to build my house in a special time. The land had done a good job of healing and covering up. The business, education, and population boom of the nearby Research Triangle Park region had not yet begun to spill over into Chatham County. Abandoned land was everywhere selling for $100 to $300 an acre. The old timers had left the forest to grow back to beech, hickory, and oak. The leavers run the gamut of human strengths and weaknesses, but on one thing they had been nearly unanimous: You had to keep nature in its place. By and large, these old homesteaders had been glad to move. I have talked to them in Pittsboro, Durham, Chapel Hill, and New York. They felt like the mother of *New York Times* columnist Russell Baker, who told him over and over through his boyhood, "I'll never go back to those sticks."

The same exodus from the land was happening in New England. What the poet Robert Tristram Coffin wrote about New England could have been about the South: "The forests are growing; they are putting out the lights in more and more mountain farmhouses year by year . . . The wild is coming back. Year by year it gains on man and his works. It swallows up his cultivated acres, his house, his very grave." Coffin called it "the leading New England tragedy. Trees that should feed children feed wild things. Land that once fed the tame feeds the wild." In fact it was an environmentalist's wish, being fulfilled by that dreaded bugaboo, the market economy.

To newcomers at Saralyn and all over rural America the "sticks" were like the woods Thoreau found growing on an abandoned farm near Walden Pond. He wrote of the trees there as "groves standing like temples, or like fleets at sea, full-rigged, with wavy boughs and rippling with light, so soft and green and shady that the Druids would have forsaken their oaks to worship in them."

Even the prophetic Gerald Johnson could not have known the web of events that would lead to the growth of the university and the arrival of newcomers like me who would find hope where others who had expected less and possessed more courage found only despair. So it had been when a new back-to-the-land movement started in the late 1960s. People are still coming and will continue to come for as long as they can make a living elsewhere. They use the money made elsewhere to bring into the woods the comforts that could never be earned by working the land itself, no less living in the woods without clearing the trees and bringing forth something of value to the outside world.

Those of us who came to places like Saralyn ten or twenty years after the exodus were attracted not so much by wilderness (because it did not really exist) as by the peacefulness death had brought.

> You might say this was a spot
> Where tame and wild for once forgot
> Their old hate; the partridge feeds
> On fruit sprung of men's tended seeds
> And pecks the apples touched by frost.
> But these are trees that have been lost;
> Here one draws a careful breath,
> This loveliness is so like death.
>   —Coffin, from "The Woodland Orchard"

We seemed strange and even crazy to the people who had seen their parents abandon these lands or who had moved out themselves. I came to know them at country stores, political meetings, hardware stores, and farm stores. They told me about how the land had been when they were young.

Not one man or woman wished to be still living out there. Only an outsider like me or impractical people with no sense of dignity and class would
want to go back out there and scratch that soil again or live in the shadows
of that forest. Maybe people who liked living in the woods and turning tobacco barns into cabins wanted to hide their laziness, their promiscuity,
and their slovenliness. All that was behind the name they had given to
Saralyn, "Hippie Town."

About ten years ago in early fall I was walking across the land north of
my house where an old chimney had collapsed upon itself. I was looking
for mushrooms, but I found two pears lying on the ground and I wondered
who had dropped them. When I saw more, I looked for the tree. Two tall
and skinny pear trees rose up into the pines, losing their hope of the sunlight they had enjoyed thirty or forty years earlier when the pines were
young. They were good pears. Obviously these trees were resistant to the
fire blight fungus that turned the two trees in my orchard into black
corpses in two weeks.

I asked Mamie Oldham whether she knew the cabin and the people who
had lived there. Her mind traveled back eighty-five or ninety years. The
trip took a minute or two. "Yes. I remember my daddy took me up there
sometimes. We would stop at a log cabin. He bought pears from them people." When Lee Calhoun said he would graft a few whips from these trees
onto good rootstock for me, I cleared some land behind my writing room. I
expect that in the first or second year of the new millennium I will be eating pears growing on wood that grew on trees a hundred years earlier, in
that time when these hills were a battleground of survival and Mamie's
parents worked like two dogs.

chapter 28

Success, Failure,
and Their Marks

*A follower of Meher Baba, the Indian mystic who
didn't speak for thirty years, takes me on a mission
into the past, and I begin to see the future.*

On an August day in 1978 when the summer lay on us like a steaming
blanket, a friend drove into the clearing at my back door. He was happily
following the instructions for living written by the Indian mystic of silence, Meher Baba, who was reputed to have not said a word for thirty
years. Two things characterized the followers of Baba whom I knew: They
tried to love everybody and everything, and they talked incessantly about
Meher Baba. My friend expected his kindness to be reciprocated by nature
and humanity, perhaps multiplied like the bread cast on the waters. He had
arrived at my house to involve me in his most recent program of humani-
tarian aid.

He said that several fine but unlucky people had taken up residence in
an abandoned house a few miles away by dirt road and truck. They needed
advice, he said, on how to live in the woods, especially since one of them
had broken out in a terrible rash. I followed him out of Saralyn and along
dirt roads I knew well. I knew the house, too. It was the old Weldon Perry
house, a square and simple cottage sinking into the ground as rapidly as
gum trees were rising around it like a green modesty curtain. Several times

I had wandered into the place from the woods, and I had sat in its low-ceilinged rooms with their bare, cheap pine board walls, looking out through absent windows at the oncoming trees, growing up to and occasionally through the porch boards. One corner of the house had slipped off its pile of stones and was beginning to melt into the earth. Rust had turned the metal roof as brown as the weathered siding.

The raw nakedness of cheap lumber had been nailed together to make a house. This was the familiar work of people still struggling to create a safe island in the sea of chaos that followed slavery. Who now could dream of making a life in this dying house and turning it into a home, except someone whose hope was equally decayed?

The new residents were heating coffee over a small campfire dangerously close to the front porch. The pot hanging from a stick was a badly dented and rusted dime-store pot I had seen among the junk inside. They offered us coffee. I recognized them because I had seen them hitchhiking on the road to Chapel Hill. My friend introduced me. The short, slightly stooped man with the long gray beard and flowing gray and black hair went by Popeye. A tall gangly man with intense blue eyes was plain old Bill. I couldn't tell whether the woman with a full leg cast was swarthy or just dirty. Her brown hair was almost ropy. Their clothes hadn't been washed since they had found them in a thrift store. When I didn't see any signs of work that might have gotten them dirty, I assumed they had not washed themselves for a few days, either. To one side of the house they had deposited the empties of their bottles of cheap wine and whiskey on a pile of older trash cleaned out of the house. The three of them could have been thirty or forty-five. They smelled of stale booze. They were alcoholic hippies.

I took my coffee in a quart Mason jar. The woman, Edna, had the rash, and the only place she didn't have it was under the cast on her leg. She lifted her skirt to show me her legs and turned around to show me her back. She was broken out from her bare feet to her face. Her skin itched intensely. She was terrified the rash would spread into her cast. Popeye and Bill also had the rash on their arms and feet. I verified that it certainly looked like poison ivy.

"What does a poison ivy plant look like?" Edna asked.

I pointed to the porch. "You see those vines growing up the posts and across the floor boards and around the windows? That's poison ivy." The vines had covered the porch posts and were crawling along the porch roof, their ends hanging off into midair and looking for more upward support.

"But they're so pretty," Edna said.

I controlled the urge to laugh. I explained to them that three shiny leaves growing on each leaf stalk made those vines poison ivy beyond any doubt. They had pulled up new shoots where we sat having coffee. They had even picked some of the new sprouts to put in a vase.

Poison ivy is not entirely useless if you believe accounts from past centuries. Indians used it as a kind of chemical warfare. In northern New York, fur traders in the mid-1500s saw Indians bundle it and burn it so that the smoke would blow onto their attacking enemies. In the early 1800s, Harvard medical professor Jacob Bigelow noted that at least one doctor had used a poison ivy tea to treat consumption and dropsy. Professor Bigelow was more enlightened: "My own opinion is, that the plant under consideration is too uncertain and hazardous to be employed in medicine, or kept in apothecaries' shops." Several other herbal healers of that time claimed to have used poison ivy tea to treat paralysis and chronic palsy "on account of their stimulating action on the nervous system." As late as 1960, Chippewa literature from the upper Midwest describes how to boil, drain, and mash the roots of poison ivy to create a mush used for curing skin infections and wounds.

History records a variety of treatments but no cures. I told Edna, Bill, and Popeye about the two immediately available treatments I knew of. The first was to collect jewelweed, a wild soft-stemmed plant a little like a tall version of impatiens. The crushed wet stems are supposed to relieve poison ivy's itch. I also told them the juice of jewelweed is poisonous. This treatment couldn't be as dangerous as the treatment Dr. Thomas Horsfield recommended in the early 1800s: "It is to be treated with rest, low diet, evacuations, purging with neutral salts is peculiarly useful, blood letting has been found of service . . . acetate of lead . . . should be used in solution rather than in the ointment . . . a solution of corrosive sublimate can be externally applied to this disease . . . I have found the lead more beneficial of the two."

The second treatment I recommended has always brought me ecstatic pleasure though I am not sure it speeds a cure. I told Edna to set aside a pot of boiling water. When it had cooled just enough so that she could stand it on her skin she should soak a rag and hold it on the poison ivy rash. The hot water application may speed healing by opening the blisters and taking away some of the toxic oil. Even if it does nothing, the feeling is far better than relief: It is a feeling near to ecstasy. I could do nothing more for Edna, Bill, or Popeye, and I didn't want to see Edna in ecstasy, so I left.

A week later, Edna, Bill, and Popeye left the old Perry place and returned to street life or a crash pad in Chapel Hill, where student nature is kinder to the unfortunate than forest nature. Nature is not the place to go for sympathy or healing. Nomadic Asians who became America's first natives, and even European colonists (whose descendants also became native Americans) enjoyed a rural tradition in their culture that allowed most of them to survive and adapt in the American wilderness. Most back-to-the-land people in the twentieth century substituted money and urban lifelines for tradition. Edna, Bill, and Popeye had no money, no tradition, and no lifeline. Their rapid failure at harmony with nature was only the distillation of what happened to thousands of others who came, spent a few years, and moved back to city or suburb.

I used to think that time travel, especially backwards in time, would be a pleasant journey into mainly pleasant places. The more I read the landscape in my forest and the lands around it, the more I knew I would have had to go back two hundred years or more. By the accounts of travelers like Lawson, Byrd, and DeSoto, the forests at the dawn of the colonial era were magnificent, but these travelers too had arrived at a time when population was waning. Hernando de Soto's scribe, the Gentleman of Elvas, noted the surroundings of an Indian village in South Carolina: "Within a league, and hallfe a league about this town, were great towns dispeopled, and overgrown with grasse; which shewed that they had been long without inhabitants."

Indians had entered North America from the ice age land bridge between Russia and Alaska. Their centuries of life in cold climates had served as a cold screen. This eliminated many diseases found in temperate and warm climates before the nomadic Asians came into the continent. The nomadic Asians, however, had their own deadly diseases, including syphilis, but they were almost entirely defenseless against European diseases like typhus, plague, and smallpox. At the dawn of the 1500s, Spanish, English, and French ships and their crews had seeded European diseases along the coast of North America. English and French fishing crews in the North Atlantic had put ashore to clean and salt their catches. Their illnesses swept through several million of the Indians living near the coasts. Elvas reported that the Indians said a plague had wiped out great numbers of them only two years before the Spaniards visited. Mayan chronicles also report a plague in the early 1500s.

If my time machine had carried me back before Columbus's contact, I might have found the banks of the Haw River well settled and the forest near Morgan Branch crisscrossed by hunting parties and clay gatherers. For over a thousand years Indians had populated this part of the world as densely as their technology and warfare allowed.

Although the forest was probably more majestic than it is now, it was also more dangerous. Without larger units of government than clans and villages, without written records or courts to settle disputes, Indians were frequently at war over property rights. A conquering tribe did not cede a reservation to the defeated, much less the rights for hunting, fishing, and Bingo.

If possible, I would program my time machine for 10,000 years in the past. That would have been the end of the ice age but earlier than any human population here. It was a time of the evergreen cold-climate forests that populated the region before the warm-climate oak, hickory, chestnut, and beech took over as the climax trees.

It's easy to think that a person can be alone with untouched nature in these woods or in our official wilderness areas, but in fact it is almost impossible. Usually we are only visiting a room someone else has just vacated. When Lewis and Clark trekked across the Rockies, they were not in pristine wilderness. Indeed, they usually tried to follow well-established "roads" used by natives. Only by luck had I built my house looking across the creek to that small patch of forest where I have yet to see the human mark. However, I have come to see the patch as a rare little thing, like the square foot of a city park that accidentally escapes being stepped on.

In 1974, I had moved into what seemed a nearly primeval forest, but four years later I could be alone there only through a strong effort of imagination—and then only if I did not imagine ghosts. Maybe this was not a place a human being should be alone. Even a thousand years ago, this was no place for one person. It required at least a family. They are gone. The traders, farmers, and squatters who followed them are also gone, not by necessity, but by choice, to be out of the woods, away from the hard work, away from the loneliness.

Daily and continuous solitude and the time to melt into nature itself is for the person, like myself or Thoreau, who has arranged his life to make solitude affordable. My life in the woods was a modern luxury. The forest itself had survived to bury the dreams and abuses of former residents, as it will bury mine.

I knew that Bill, Popeye, and Edna would be the last people ever to live in the Perry house; indeed, they would be the last poor people to live on this land for a long time. That's what Saralyn meant. We had been the first of the new wave of settlers. We had not come as a band of Scots-Irish immigrants, African slaves, English Quakers, or German Moravians, but we were an identifiable band. Our homeland was mainly city and suburb. Our culture was mainly middle class. By religion we were varying degrees of Thoreauvians. Some thought of themselves as poor, or at least committed to a simple life, but they were already starting businesses and returning to school. National magazines were recognizing the Research Triangle cities—Raleigh, Durham, and Chapel Hill—as some of the best places to live. I knew the land would not stay covered with its forest. Someone would buy the old Perry place and a bulldozer would scrape away all history down to the red clay.

Maybe Saralyn could keep its trees. The covenants I had written made everyone promise to keep at least half the trees in any one home site. These trees, if they did last, would cover most of our marks. But a good eye can learn to see them anyway. My marks would lie under the leaves and among the rocks of the creek along with those of thousands who have lived in this forest before me—immigrants from Asia, Scotland, Ireland, and Africa. The acid clays dissolve all bones, but under the leaves the marks we make in success and failure lie like corpses beneath their sheets.

-chapter 29-

How Much Land
Does a Man Need?

*History turns a corner with the auction of land over
the hill from me. I decide to buy time instead of land.*

December 1978. The weekly Chatham Record brought one of those fine-print legal notices I did not want to read. It was the almost inevitable re-sult of an obituary I had read a year earlier. On December 12, 1977, Clarence Dean died. Clarence was the man who had brought the first load of gravel to spread on the newly cleared Pace Mill Road when I reopened it and made part of it my driveway. "We are neighbors," he had said. He was the last of generations whose lives had depended on the land a few hills over from mine. They had depended on it for food, for money, for firewood, for building materials, and for a place to live and raise families. Clarence, late in his life, depended on it only for peace and quiet on weekends. During the week he lived with a woman friend in town. Peace and quiet was the last thing the land gave the Dean family. Those of us who moved to the woods in the 1970s had come looking for that same peace and quiet.

On a sunny and crisp February day two months after Clarence died, I walked northwest through the woods to find his house. I walked off my land and onto some two hundred acres of Pilkington land. A tobacco farmer, speculating with money the government had paid him when it took his farm to create Jordan Lake, had recently bought this land. He quickly resold it to a Chinese-American scientist at the university who believed that land was the best investment his money could buy. From the Pilkington piece I walked through tall pines that had grown on the lands owned by the descendants of the black Burnettes and Perrys. The northwest boundary of these lands was Drummond's Branch, named after Daniel Drummond about the time William Hooper, a Pittsboro lawyer, was signing the Declaration of Independence. The woman who paid the taxes on the Burnette land had long ago moved to Chicago. She had never seen the land her grandfather had plowed his hopes into. Steep slopes with fine hardwood trees lock Drummond's Branch within a deep shade. Halfway down the slope stood the remains of an old chimney where a cabin had stood in the middle of its red clay fields or pastures.

I crossed Drummond's Branch on its rocks and walked up into Clarence Dean's land. The three-room house was built on flat land, and the pines that had taken over the fields had been cleared a few yards short of the house. Clarence had kept a small lawn of weeds and wild grasses mowed clean of pine seedlings, which otherwise would have quickly grown against the walls of the house.

The Dean house may have been what the 1909 deed calls the Lucian Pilkington Home Place. The one-story cottage sits close to the ground. Clarence had painted the old pine clapboards gray and replaced the pine shingles on the roof with galvanized metal; otherwise the house had not changed much since the nineteenth century, when it had been built. The roof drained directly onto the ground. On the west side, it extended 6 feet beyond the wall to cover a porch. On an evenly-spaced row of pegs on the porch wall, Clarence had hung a mirror, a couple of wash basins, a ladle, a cooking pot, a metal pitcher, and a towel. A simple pine table and a couple of chairs were the only furniture.

The door was open. The walls, floors, and ceilings of the six small rooms were bare pine boards, but they were the very best pine and cut from heartwood. They were a deep honey red and the grain was straight and close. The few pieces of wooden furniture—a table and chairs— were also made from good pine. They had that country craftsmanship and frankness of purpose that had begun to bring high prices at antique stores. The bed was a metal cot with a thin mattress and a wire-mesh support.

On the day I visited Clarence's house, it was frozen in time like a museum piece. This would not last long. I didn't know what would happen to the house, but if someone did not come to cannibalize the heart pine boards and rip them from the floors and walls and ceilings, it would be remodeled and modernized and expanded. The furniture would find its way to the antique market, to be sold as "primitive." Even Clarence's chipped enameled basins where he washed and shaved would be sold for someone's collection.

I was an intruder in the house, even though Clarence would never return. The small windows brought little light and the wood was dark. Clothes, blankets, table clothes, and dishes can brighten a dark room, but there were none. Even noise can brighten a dark room, but nothing moved. I ran my hand over the widest boards in the wall. The trees that had given up these boards had grown slowly in a crowded forest. No more than a quarter inch separated any two growth rings. A tree had grown for at least seventy-five years to make an eighteen-inch board. Clarence would have been nearly seventy the year I visited.

I sat on the edge of the porch in the sunlight and looked across the narrow strip of mowed grass and weeds to the wall of trees rising darkly from the fields. For more than a century, the Pilkingtons and then the Deans had kept the fields clear, holding the forest back from the soils it had made.

Clarence had let the forest come back. It had started to return when he was a young man, and by 1959 he had enough good pine that he and his wife, Zena, sold the timber to a local logger, who had brought a portable sawmill. The portable mills suited a time when technology and entrepreneurs had not yet developed a market for the large amount of slabs and sawdust created in making timber and boards. Their circular saws chewed a path through a log almost half an inch wide and added that sawdust to the slabs cut off to square the log and shuck the bark.

A small logger without bulldozers and big trucks didn't want to carry any more weight out of the woods than he had to. Fifty years after they left the woods, I have climbed up their slab and sawdust piles or hauled loads of it to put on my garden. Millions of tons of it, however, simply decayed where it had been deposited. A walker in the woods notices nothing more than dark spongy ground underfoot and maybe an odd rectangular hole in the ground five or ten feet long and a foot or more deep. This was the pit under the three-to-four-foot disk of the saw blade.

As I sat on the porch thinking about who had been there and who might come, I asked myself, *Who will be next to own the Forest of Dean, and what will they know or care about its trees?*

If I had not spent so much time in the past ten years writing for the occasional small reward from magazines and newspapers, I would have been ready to put all my savings into the Dean land. Maybe one day Sylvan would need a piece of land and a simple home. The lands I had walked over between my land and Clarence Dean's had already been bought away from the line of farm families who had cleared most of the forests, pastured horses and mules and cows, and exhausted the best soils with their desperate cropping. The people who had bought them never intended to live on the land. They were investing. The Pilkingtons and Deans had also invested. They had been resident investors, and they had cleared the big trees and by hoe, plow, cow, and horse had denied the trees a chance to return until their investments in farming had worn out the soils, maybe the owners too, and didn't pay anymore. The new owners didn't know exactly how or when their investments would pay off. They had a faith that land near the high growth of the Research Triangle would pay off. They had the money to buy it and wait. They did not have to do anything to the land, and they didn't. They didn't know what to do. Nature did. Nature always does something. Until humans make up their minds, they prefer something else.

I soon found out what would happen to Clarence's land. A year after his death, a notice appeared in the fine print legal advertisements of the county's weekly paper. Clarence's brothers and sister had appointed Pittsboro lawyer Jim Sledd as executor of Clarence's estate. At his death, Clarence's possessions amounted to little more than $5,000 in bank accounts, his life's savings, a ten-year-old Chevrolet, and his land and house. Seven heirs—brothers, sister, sister-in-law, a niece, and his woman friend—wanted their share of the estate. Only Clarence's woman friend lived in Chatham. Dividing a piece of land with no road frontage into seven pieces was impractical. Lawyer Sledd advertised the property for sale at his office.

From New York, Michael wrote that he would be willing to invest again in land that we could resell. He had risen in the academic ranks at the City University of New York to head a program for adults who had decided late in life that they should get a college education. The City of New York was paying him well, and he had money in the bank. I had nothing of my own, but I could borrow money, and three of the people who had invested in Saralyn were willing to invest again. Several people at Saralyn had heard about the sale, and they had urged me not to let the Dean place fall into "the wrong hands." I was not enthusiastic about becoming a land developer again.

The people who had come to Saralyn to live in harmony with nature had not always played harmonious notes. Their dogs had been roaming in packs and chasing deer. At least two families had cleared right to their borders to plant big gardens. Some had saved the cost of a septic tank by draining their kitchens and bathrooms into open ditches not far from streams. Several cat owners had ignored their pets' toll on wildlife, a toll much more serious than the damage clumsy dogs do. Another resident was given to playing hard rock music so loud that I sometimes heard it a mile away. I considered all of this, and I thought, *Better us than anyone else*.

I was one of four people who gathered in Sledd's office for the bidding, each of whom had a different reason for being there. Nance Newland, a big dough-faced man retired from tobacco farming and a country store when the government bought his property for Jordan Lake, had grown rich speculating in land; he bought from country people he had known his entire life and sold high to strangers and strange people like the Chinese-American scientist, Dr. Zhang, who had bought the land between Dean's and mine. Hank Edwards was a young forester who worked for a local wood yard. In his pocket he had his company's authorization to bid on the timber or on both the timber and the land. He knew the board feet of poplar, walnut, and pine on Dean's land. He considered the timber second rate but usable. Amos Caines lived on the Old Graham Road just west of Dean's land. He had played there when he was a kid, hunted every foot of it, and saw cotton and corn fields grow up in the branchy field pines. He had watched them cut down when Clarence sold them, and had watched them come back again. Caines was not there to bid so much as to see what value the rest of us would place on the land that seemed so ordinary and familiar to him.

The three of them were sure I intended to do another Saralyn-Hippie Town. They still saw us as a colony of hippies, but they had never made us feel unwelcome. The South was used to eccentricity and in return for tolerance asked only politeness.

Lawyer Sledd shook hands with all of us. He was smiling a little smugly. He believed we were serious buyers and he would soon close this estate sale for seven anxious heirs. We discussed the nice fall weather outside. This is a traditional preliminary to any land transaction and all other business negotiations. It is a little like a prayer, discussing and naming the events of the eternal cycle of seasons. Lawyer Sledd cleared his throat to shift into his official voice. He sat behind his desk and opened the estate folder. The land, Sledd said, would be sold in three different ways to determine which brought the highest bid.

Hank Edwards from the wood yard bid $28,900 for the timber rights. No one bid against him. On the land stripped of its timber, Edwards bid $150 an acre. I bid $200. Edwards wouldn't be able to cut on a few areas where the land was very steep or where the trees were still too small. I was not authorized to bid my investors' money on stripped land. I bid on an impulse. Logging would leave some forest and the rest would recover; the hardwood roots would send up shoots from the stumps. While this went on, the thickets would come alive with rabbits, quail, snakes, lizards, fox, and deer. Hawks would appear to hunt. I had a daydream that I might find an investor who would enjoy watching natural succession and after twenty or thirty years take his timber profits by a selective cut that kept the forest intact. Finally, any land here was worth $200 an acre. I had gambled no money I couldn't get back. Our combined bids for timber and for stripped land came to $63,900, a total of $365 an acre.

Nance Newland had sat by expressionless, unmoving, as if his dough face were too heavy to move. Except that his eyes were open, he could have been asleep. Even his eyes did not move. Behind them, whatever part of the brain does math was fondling each number. He had grown up barefooted, lifting water from a well, tying tobacco early in the morning and late in the evenings. Growing money had been his greatest success once he had some to grow. He did it by a formula whose simplicity amused him: buy low and sell high. It's the secret of wealth that Daddy Warbucks used to give Orphan Annie. Nance couldn't bid much higher and double his money, however. He knew that if he bought the property, he would have to buy a right of way to it if he wanted to divide it and resell it. Clarence Dean's old wagon road wouldn't do.

Lawyer Sledd asked for bids on the house. A buyer would have thirty days to move it. Gaines, who had been leaning back against the wall as if to separate himself from people he considered tricky speculators, said in a hopeless voice, "Fifty dollars."

I said, "One hundred dollars."

"One hundred-fifty dollars," he said reluctantly.

He had a better right to Clarence's house than I had. I nodded to him, but he didn't respond.

"One hundred and fifty dollars for the house," Sledd mumbled and jotted it down on his yellow pad. "Gentlemen, are you ready to bid on the entire property?"

We nodded. Nance Newland sat up in his chair.

Sledd looked at us for a moment and a grin crossed his face, slightly higher on one side than the other. "What am I bid on the entire real estate including the house and outbuildings?" he asked.

"Eighty thousand dollars," Nance Newland said loud and clear. His figure was supposed to be a showstopper.

No one knew how much my partners had authorized me to bid. Many people in Pittsboro assumed I had made a small fortune from land. Newland didn't care. He had his limit in mind and he would stop there with an iron will. He was an opportunist, not a competitor. Gaines and Edwards stayed on to watch the farmer battle the young mayor of Hippie Town.

Bidders usually inch upwards, but Newland had leaped to what he hoped would be the finish line. His bid surprised Sledd, who would get 5 percent of the sale. As if he were at a charity auction, Sledd said in his most grateful voice, "I have eighty thousand. Do I hear eighty-five thousand?" He looked slowly at the three of us who had not bid. Sledd stared at me. He did not want to knock the property down too quickly. Five percent of another $5,000 is $250. He also wanted to be fair to me. I had done several appraisals for his clients in condemnation cases. Those cases brought him tens of thousands in fees.

I believed Newland had made his one and only bid. He was tight with his money. He was not impulsive. He was a farmer who planted and harvested carefully. His bid was an unexpected favor to me. I had lived in the forest at Morgan Branch across the hills from Dean's land for almost five years. I had always been thankful that I had chosen my land a half mile north of the nearest neighbor. I was thankful I was not in the middle of Saralyn where the lights of one house already twinkled through the woods to another, where neighborhood dogs and cats wandered from one lot to another, where the community road was never out of earshot. I really didn't want to divide a big piece of land near mine, to bulldoze roads, burn trees, drop culverts in creeks.

Newland would probably sell the timber and make most of his money back. Then he would hold the land or sell it to someone else who would hold it. The wildlife would come back. The trees would grow. I was gambling that no one would be very interested in paying Newland's asking price for a piece of land full of briars and young pines and that no developer would want land without a good road in. If I bought it for Saralyn, we'd have to start dividing and reselling quickly. By not buying the land, I was buying time.

Lawyer Sledd was looking at me. I shook my head no. He hesitated, then said, "I have eighty thousand. It is going, going at eighty thousand, going once, going twice, going three times." He paused for a last look in my direction. I shook my head no again. "Gone to Nance Newland for eighty thousand dollars."

Newland stood up and dug into his pocket for his wallet. He did not look once at the rest of us. Sledd thanked us all for coming and bent forward across his desk to tell Newland how to make out the deposit check and where to sign the bid sheet.

As I drove back to Morgan Branch I thought, *If only I had big money, Rockefeller-type money, I could simply buy all these woods and let them grow in their own style. Sylvan could have a place if she wanted it. Land would be ready if Michael ever gave up his dream of reforming education in the South Bronx.* At Saralyn and on other lands whose owners I had advised, I had done what I thought next best. Almost 2,000 acres of forest now had covenants I had helped write, roads and homesteads I had helped lay out. I had also seen people consistently work their way around the covenants. My best ideals and my covenants were failing to save nature from my neighbors. Their animals hunted wildlife. They cut down buffer strips for their gardens. They erected machine shops and filled the woods with the noise of machines. They let their washing machines drain detergents into the woods. They started businesses that brought dozens of clients to practice Zen, seek massage therapy, or buy vegetables and fruit trees. They cleared forest to pasture horses. A musician or two gathered his band and drowned out the crickets and frogs with rock music.

I was beginning to see that we were not so different from Nance Newland despite education, marijuana, Zen Buddhism, sexual liberation, granny skirts and miniskirts, men with beards and pony tails, and reading Thoreau.

The great difference lay in the fact that one generation was leaving the land, the other coming to it. People who formed rural communes or homesteads and farms in the 1970s were not picking up where the Deans, Perrys, and Newlands had left off. They were not in the mold of Abraham Lincoln or Pa Ingalls. They came for the reason Teddy Roosevelt went to the Amazon or the wilderness of the Rockies—for a grand adventure. They were also like the sons of English gentry who accompanied Captain John Smith to Jamestown. Smith's settlers had expected riches from exotic plants. They had even loaded the rich black peat soils onto ships so that alchemists might turn it into gold. The back-to-the-land settlers of the 1970s expected to get rich in a different way, but they came with the same spirit of adventure. They were the sons and daughters of middle-class Americans who had more than the seventeenth-century English gentry could dream of. They expected their riches to come with very little work. When the land disappointed them, they did what others here had done.

Already I had seen people resell homesteads for big profits. Houses were getting bigger and hungrier in their consumption of fuel and materials. I thought Saralyn and places like it would soon come to resemble the little estate enclaves of Long Island's North Shore, Riverdale in the Bronx, the New Jersey hunt country, and Malibu. Given the rapid growth of the balmy piedmont, the big universities, and the international research palaces in the Research Triangle Park, maybe I had steered the forests toward the least destructive future.

I returned from the Dean sale free, for the time being, of the ambition to save nature from humankind. As I drove up the gravel road into Saralyn's 330 acres of woods in the midst of several thousand acres more, I knew that with my neighbors here I had escaped nothing. We owned and would dispose of our ownership just as Newland would and just as the Dean heirs had. Our little community of some thirty-five families was a satellite moving alongside our parent society. My neighbors were moving back and forth with increasing frequency; half of them were already commuters to white-collar jobs.

After the Dean sale, I knew that if I was to learn anything really useful to the environmental movement, I would have to understand my neighbors and why we are so much like the Carney Bynums, like Clarence Dean and his heirs, and like Nance Newland. Even those of us who emigrated from New York and California and who seem as strange as moon men to Clarence's friends and relatives, we are Clarence Dean's heirs, too, and Nance Newland's cousins.

–chapter 30–

Sylvan

A summer with a rapidly changing daughter explains
why I decided not to become a diplomat.

In the spring of 1979, Sarah decided to move with Sylvan to Ada, Ohio, where Sarah had an offer from Ohio Northern University to teach law. Although Sylvan would come to visit on vacations and in the summers, she would no longer be with me every week at Morgan Branch. I wondered whether she would forget how life was here. If she remembered, would she miss it? I wondered whether I would become like Emily Dickinson, who wrote the loneliest line a writer can imagine: "This is my letter to the world that never wrote to me." Every week I sent Sylvan a report or notes from my journal. Every week she wrote back.

For the first time since coming to Morgan Branch, I thought about leaving for good. I did not think far ahead. I simply took a small first step and filled out the application for a position with the U.S. Foreign Service. A month later I went to Washington for the written exam. That winter I went back to Washington for the oral exams and interviews. Each time I went to Washington I thought, *If they take me, I'll go.* Each time I came back to Morgan Branch, I wondered where else in the world I would really have as many of the things in life I loved.

Sylvan would not change from a girl to a young woman for another two years, but in the summer of 1980, when she was still ten, she was no longer a child. No great event occurred, but my journal is full of small events that recorded a difference. She rode her bicycle down a mile and a half of gravel roads to see friends, and when she came back up the last hill, I saw her take a nasty spill. She got up, dusted herself off and kept coming. When I decided to invite people for a picnic, she could not carry the concrete blocks for the benches, but she did insist on carrying the six- and eight-foot pieces of beams for the seats. With the first board, she ran a half-inch splinter into her hand, but as soon as I had yanked it out, she returned to carrying the beams.

When I had to work alone, writing or appraising, Sylvan would take up a project of her own in the shop or at the creek. For her grandmother's birthday she created a small terrarium that she hoped would maintain itself with a few drops of water every day. To fish in the creek, she sharpened a bent finishing nail and tied it to her line and pole and used beetles and worms for bait.

Sylvan's only intense rebellion was almost over. When she was born, I decided she should be bilingual like so many immigrant kids I had grown up with. Sylvan and I had spoken nothing but Spanish when we were together, but when she started school, she said she didn't like it. I didn't push her, but I didn't speak English to her. I searched hard for the most interesting bedtime books I could find. When I seemed to be losing the battle, I could always bring her back to the language with the songs we had learned. They were songs that fit our life at Morgan. Nature worked for art and art worked for nature. How else could it be when you sat on your porch looking into the forest in April and sang

> De colores, de colores se visten los campos en la primavera
> (With colors, with colors are seen the country in spring)
> De colores, de colores son los pajaritos que vienen de afuera
> (With colors, with colors are the small birds that come from afar)

Nineteen eighty was also the summer Sylvan's first pet died. On a hot afternoon in July we set out to make several stops on our way to supper with a friend in Durham thirty miles away. We took along Sylvan's guinea pig, Blackie, who had come with her for the summer. Sylvan had decided to mate Blackie, her first venture in managing livestock. Blackie stayed in the truck when we made three short stops, but when I came out of the post office in Chapel Hill, Sylvan had Blackie lying on a Frisbee limp and panting. She was about dead from the heat. Neither of us had known that guinea pigs tolerate a very small temperature range. We rushed her to our friend Diana's house, where she was to be mated, dunked her in a full sink of cold water, and then laid her on an ice pack. Diana called her vet and on his advice I gave the guinea pig a couple of droppers of salt water every half hour. A couple of hours later when we left for Durham, Blackie stayed under Diana's care, gaining strength and lifting her head.

During the evening Sylvan called several times but got no answer. In the morning she got through. She put down the phone and grabbed me and cried quietly against my chest for a while. At noon we went to Diana's, and Sylvan laid Blackie on a bed of clean shavings in a shoebox. When we got home she said yes, it was a good idea to bury Blackie at the base of the bird feeder among the herbs. She petted Blackie and laughed at how stiff and cold she was from being in the refrigerator at Diana's.

That evening as I was talking to her at bedtime, a terrific thunderstorm broke. Every second the sky flashed, and thunder exploded on every side of the house. Hail beat on the roof. We laughed at how loud we had to talk to hear ourselves over the Götterdamerung of Blackie.

During the summer, the State Department notified me that I had passed all the requirements, and they would now move to a security investigation. Sylvan had gone back to Ohio when the State Department's investigator came to visit in early September. Jerry Karp had already acquired a mantle of white hair in his late thirties and kept it as neatly fixed as his dark suit and tie. He sat on the chair at my writing desk. I sat on one of my cushions in my faded corduroys and bare feet. I felt a little like Theresa's hip and pony-tailed husband must have felt being interviewed by the banker for a loan. Jerry had a long questionnaire to fill out, but first read me my privileges and rights to confidentiality. I had already answered most of the questions—where I had lived, who I had worked for, when, how long, why I had left.

"You've been living in the country for almost fifteen years," he said, and waited for my reply. I saw his eyes moving around the house, the four logs holding up the ridge of the roof, a goat skin hanging from a peg on the cedar log, the rough poplar boards on the wall behind me, the childish turtle and fox and tree that Sylvan and I had carved into an oak panel covering the beam that held up the loft.

The answer was already on paper. "Yes, almost fifteen years." I affirmed what he had already noted by subtracting 1965 from 1980.

"How do you think you'll be able to make the adjustment to living in a big city?"

I wondered what he knew about living in the country. Was he really asking how in the hell I thought I could step out of a cabin in the forest and become a diplomat in an embassy or the halls of the State Department? "I'm pretty flexible," I told him. "I was born in a big city and grew up in a suburb."

"Why would you want to leave the country?" he asked. He was talking about leaving rural North Carolina, not the United States.

I didn't have a good answer. I said something about having satisfied myself about country life. I could have said, "To change the world," because I thought just maybe I would do something as a diplomat that I could not do in Chatham County. It would have been an honest answer. I had wanted to change the world since I was Sylvan's age. That was the time my mother and father had begun fighting and she had plunged into depression.

He took down a list of people I had worked with in the real estate business so that he could verify that part of my résumé.

"Is there anyone out here that knows you pretty well?" he asked.

I had the answer to that already in mind. I wrote down on a card for him, Creighton L. Calhoun, Lt. Col. U.S. Army, retired. The "L" was for Lee, who with his wife, Edith, would do more than vouch for my character. They had finished the nicest house at Saralyn, a large Japanese-style house with a real lawn; I was aiming for merit by association. A few weeks later, I sent in the results of a medical exam and a set of fingerprints taken by the Chatham County sheriff, who only vaguely understood why I needed them and said I had been the first person to volunteer for a set of fingerprints.

In November, I drove to Ohio to spend Thanksgiving with Sylvan and Sarah. When Sarah had said they were in "the middle of nowhere," she meant more than she knew. Ada was a town about the size of Pittsboro's fifteen hundred people. To the very edge of the town and the athletic fields of the campus nothing but cornfields met the eye. Instead of the constant surprises of wildlife at Morgan Branch, Sylvan had her two dogs, her black cat Noche, and a room plastered with posters of kittens, horses, and dogs, a gauze hammock overflowing with stuffed mice, shelves and corners of the rooms crowded with seals, green-eyed polar bears, and all colors of droop-eared dogs.

Sarah was not enthusiastic about the administration of the university, its conservative oversight of faculty members' political expression, or the receptiveness of her colleagues to her interests in women's issues. Sylvan, as usual, had settled in nicely, made good grades in school, and joked about the town's commercial reputation being made by its fame as the producer of professional-league footballs.

In January I sent the State Department the required 1,000-word autobiography, wondering whether it would be forever on record with the autobiographies of men and women who had changed at least a corner of the world. Mine began, "I have been a seasoned tourist, in the best sense of the phrase, since I was fifteen. It was that year when I first left the town of Sea Cliff, New York, and traveled on my own by bus to Akaska, South Dakota, where I joined the University of South Dakota archeological team excavating the Swan Creek earth lodge complex." The thesis was that for a kid from a blue-collar family, the journey to a university and white-collar work is a journey to foreign places. I did not say that life at Morgan Branch had also been life among aliens, or an alien among the natives.

The day after my birthday in April, the Staff Director of the Board of Examiners of the Foreign Service wrote that he had placed my name on the list of "those awaiting appointment in the Economic/Commercial functional track." I smiled. My degrees were for English literature and I had never taken a course in economics, but I was now accepted to go abroad in the world manipulating economics and commerce. A week later, I was invited to join the State Department in its career candidate's class in late June. I wanted another summer at Morgan Branch with Sylvan. I put them off until August. We had a fine summer full of gardening, gathering berries, cooking, beekeeping, mushrooms, hummingbirds, and shop projects. I put off the State Department training until the spring of 1982. When they notified me that I would have to update my security check and send in new fingerprints, I decided to call a halt. I wrote to the Board of Examiners, "At some other time, in another way, I hope to serve my country. Rather than put you to the trouble of seeing if my fingerprints have changed or my alma mater disowned me, with this letter I respectfully ask that you end my candidacy for the Foreign Service."

I cannot sort through and assign weights to the reasons for my withdrawal. At the political level, I had listened to Secretary of State Alexander Haig declare "I am the vicar of foreign policy," and it ignited my blue-collar resentment of people who give themselves titles, especially with foreign flavors. If I went abroad, I might end up buying paper clips and toilet paper for an embassy. If I stayed at Morgan Branch, I would see Sylvan become a young woman. Also, I still had not answered the State Department investigator's question, "Why would I want to leave?"

Two years later, Sylvan was in junior high in Michigan, where Sarah and her new husband had moved so that Sarah could get her Juris Doctor. Her husband, Bob, had become head of the urban studies program at Wayne State in Detroit. Sylvan sent me a copy of an essay she wrote about the terrarium she had made for my mother's birthday in the summer of 1981. She had gone out by herself to gather the plants in the woods.

"Everywhere I went," she wrote, "had some memory to it. I stopped along an old roadbed where beech saplings and Christmas ferns grow in the center. This was the roadbed I used to walk along so that I would not get lost when I was younger. I remembered feeling so triumphant when I made my way back to the house along this road with no one to show me the way." Where she dug a pipsissewa from a mossy bank she remembered, "On this bank could be found small trumpet-shaped black chanterelles, a prized mushroom. I had found this particular patch, and after my father had told me they were edible, to my great excitement, I would go out and pick them, and he would cook some for supper. I always felt I was contributing to the household when I brought back my basket full of mushrooms." She went on to Morgan Branch looking for moss:

> This was where I used to launch boats made of wood or leaves. It was also a good spot to hunt tiny crayfish. You reached down into the icy water that flitted by your hand just as the chickadees flew through the air, and gently lifted up a promising stone. With luck, a crayfish would be sitting there. I sat on the rock in this reminiscent mood, staring at the ancient exposed roots of the beech tree on the other side of the creek. I thought of other walks, other mushrooms, other games, and other gifts. One memory would lead to another neverendingly.

As long as I stayed at Morgan Branch it would remain part of our letters and weekend calls and Sylvan's vacations. Buenos Aires, Paris, or Mongolia could wait.

chapter 31

Economics

*Land, like any other possession, can be carelessly
lost. I find some and the discovery adds another dimension to how much land a man needs, or an environmental movement.*

When I had left lawyer Sledd's office after Nance Newland won the bid
for the Dean lands, I understood how my colleagues had talked themselves out of buying McCauley's Mountain with me. When Sledd had
given me every chance to top Newland's bid, I shook my head *No*, but I
was far from confident in my decision. Two minutes of thinking later, I
might have topped Newland. Like my academic colleagues, I had not really made a decision. I had wandered in thought until I had to accept
someone else's decision.

The auction had come when events at Saralyn and beyond raised serious
doubts about how well my covenants and my style of dividing and selling
land really protected anything. The question that had paralyzed me at the
Dean auction was one that had not troubled Thoreau. His principles gave
him a decisive answer. The question is, Who should own and control land?

The environmental movement, Saralyn, and my decision to live at Morgan Branch are all about controlling the use of land and everything on it,
above it, and below it. Here we part company with Thoreau. He did not
believe in owning land, and he despised government regulations. Thoreau
made one deal to buy a farm and was glad the seller backed out:

I never got my fingers burned by actual possession. The nearest that I came to actual possession was when I bought the Hollowell place . . . but before the owner gave me a deed of it, his wife—every man has such a wife—changed her mind and wished to keep it, and he offered me ten dollars to release him. . . . I let him keep the ten dollars and the farm too, . . . I found thus that I had been a rich man without any damage to my poverty.

Thoreau worried about the destruction of New England's forests and he blamed the European mentality. He probably would have agreed with Vice President Al Gore, who wrote that the way Americans treat nature shows our nation is a "dysfunctional family." Thoreau worried and complained, but his dislike for government power steered him away from proposing zoning, planning, or any other regulation. Instead, on local matters he drew from his interpretation of Eastern mystics and proposed that a mind free of material concerns could apprehend the beauty of nature almost anywhere. Freeing the mind required living the simple life he had led at Walden. On the larger scale, he had the luxury of living when most of America's lands stood empty and were still owned by government. Thoreau may have been the first American writer to set down the concept of our national park system:

The kings of England formerly had their forests to hold the king's game, for sport or food, sometimes destroying villages to create or extend them, and I think that they were impelled by a true instinct. Why should not we, who have renounced the king's authority, have our national preserves, where no village need be destroyed, in which the bear and panther, and some even of the hunter race, may still exist, and not be 'civilized off the face of the earth,'—not for idle sport or food, but for inspiration and our own true recreation?

Thoreau tried to buy the Hollowell farm for the same reason I bought my land at Morgan Branch and had thought about buying Dean's land.

The real attractions of the Hollowell farm, to me, were: its complete retirement, being, about two miles from the village, half a mile from the nearest neighbor, and separated from the highway by a broad field; . . . the gray color and ruinous state of the house and barn, and the dilapidated fences, which put such an interval between me and the last occupant; the hollow and lichen-covered apple trees, gnawed by rabbits, showing what kind of neighbors I should have.

Thoreau was also moved by a concern what would happen if he did not step in quickly:

> I was in haste to buy it, before the proprietor finished getting out some rocks, cutting down the hollow apple trees, and grubbing up some young birches which had sprung up in the pasture, or, in short, had made any more of his improvements. To enjoy these advantages I was ready to carry it on; like Atlas, to take the world on my shoulders—I never heard what compensation he received for that—and do all those things which had no other motive or excuse but that I might pay for it and be unmolested in my possession of it; for I knew all the while that it would yield the most abundant crop of the kind I wanted, if I could only afford to let it alone. But it turned out as I have said.

I knew I could not buy the Dean land and let it alone to yield the crop of trees, wild animals, and solitude I wanted. I knew I didn't want to populate it with more human beings. After the sale, I also knew how much I wanted more land.

I had twenty-four acres, the northern-most finger of land Michael and I had bought from O.K. Pettigrew. With my house at the northern end of that northern finger, I enjoyed being a half mile from the nearest house. Twenty-four acres sounds like a lot of land, but that depends what crop you expect from it. I expected the same crop Thoreau expected from the Hollowell farm. Only my southern border was far enough away to guarantee that my neighbors' daily life would not be seen or heard at Morgan Branch. My land was narrow. The east and west boundaries were no more than 320 feet from my house, the northern boundary not much farther.

I imagined a time that might be one, ten, or thirty years in the future, when the Research Triangle cities of Durham, Chapel Hill, and Raleigh would be spread along the major highways into Chatham County. Their growth would spin off satellite developments, golf courses, equestrian communities, and retirement centers. Someone had proposed an airfield subdivision near Pittsboro—park your plane at your front door. From the beginning of civilization, the growth of prosperous cities had consumed the countryside around them. The engine of growth just over my eastern horizon was not one city but three cities, and enclosed in their geometry like an economic breeder reactor, the Research Triangle Park, the world's largest planned research park. A visionary southern developer named Romeo Guest had conceived the idea that would replace Tobacco Road farms with scientific think tanks and laboratories. The park replaced often-illiterate farmers scratching Triassic basin clays with Ph.D.'s paid handsomely for scratching their heads. To the park's 35,000 workers, international corporations like Mitsubishi, IBM, Glaxo-Wellcome, and Northern Telecom added tens of thousands of workers outside the park.

As early as the late 1960s, designers and government planners had begun promising that development would not mean sprawl, noise, air pollution, and traffic congestion. The University of North Carolina at Chapel Hill has a world-famous school of city and regional planning. Voters elected its former chairman as mayor. A five-county planning office received millions to propose standards and plans for coordinating utilities and services and preserving open space. All the planners were like kids building sand castles with their backs to the rising tide. In the early 1980s when the Reagan tax cuts restarted the economy after 20 percent inflation and recession, I knew that a great beast was slouching in my direction.

I wanted to buy land on my borders for myself—anything I could afford and that someone would sell. I started with little hope. All the land to the east of mine, from Seven Spring Branch and Morgan Branch to the Haw River, had been bought in the 1950s by a math professor at the university. His daughter and her husband had inherited it. Nance Newland had bought the 192 acres to the west from Pilkington heirs and resold it quickly to Dr. Zhang. I thought my northern border joined a five-hundred-acre tract recently inherited by one of the Merritt family. Eben Merritt, the late patriarch, had invested profits from a gas station next to the university to wheel and deal in rural lands. He kept the most remote and cheapest to hunt on.

None of these neighbors was likely to sell me a few acres, but it would not hurt to map their borders with me so that I would know what to ask for. I also had a far-out hope—a mistake, an oversight, a piece of land dropped out of descriptions and surveys.

In the late 1800s, landowners in this area were recording, buying, and selling land in descriptions like this:

Beginning at a ditch on the Pittsboro Road leading from Williams tract, said Williams tract now owned by Alieutian Pilkington heirs thence east to a branch at the corner between Woodson Lea and Eubanks the old Manly tract, thence down the branch as the fence run in 1866 in a northerly direction to another corner between Woodson Lea and the said Eubanks, thence east a few poles, thence west down the branch to a large poplar, thence north across the plantation.

Descriptions like this were clear to the Leas, the Pilkingtons, and the Eubanks, who lived on and worked these lands and knew the wagon roads, branches, and trees. They would leave the lands to heirs and the heirs to their heirs. Wagon roads were abandoned and their names forgotten. Large poplars fell down. Small streams changed courses. Old plantations turned into forests. Families emigrated along with their memories. Who cared about precise measurements when the land was worn out, people were leaving, and an acre sold for the price of a square yard today? The old measurement "a pole" means sixteen and one-half feet, but when a surveyor finally comes along with a transit and measuring tape, how does he determine what "east a few poles" means? The informal measurements of the past came from cheap land, friendly neighbors, clear physical boundary markers, and a scarcity of surveyors.

When I started Saralyn, Chatham County had one resident surveyor, a man who was drinking himself blind and sloppy. Before he came along, a lot of Chatham land had been surveyed by a Chapel Hill surveyor in his eighties who often set stakes along a road and drew the map of the remainder by guesswork. The Raleigh surveyor who had surveyed the boundaries of Saralyn for its former owners warned me that he had made a farm survey and could not guarantee the boundaries.

I started with the tax maps. They offered no hope. I decided to see if they were accurate or pieced together from the vagueness of old deeds. The Register of Deeds' vault room in the old county courthouse was no larger than two modern walk-in closets. Deep steel shelves lined the walls from floor to ceiling. I began to slide the huge maroon volumes of deeds, plat maps, and mortgages off their steel shelves. I started with Saralyn's deed and traced it back to a Depression era foreclosure and before that to a variety of divisions and recombinations. My oddly long and narrow northern finger (or chimney) of land had been deeded by white Millikens to a black woman named Bettie Ennis in 1904. To my east, the math professor's land had a clear chain and clear boundaries. To the west, Dr. Zhang's land had been acquired from the heirs of the Paces. From their deeds and Saralyn, I drew a map on which our boundaries matched almost perfectly.

I found what I was looking for on my northern boundary. As I drew maps from old deeds, I corrected the tax map to reflect history. To the north and northeast, Merritt's land had been assembled first in the 1880s when Weldon Perry, a black man, began putting together smaller pieces that freed slaves had bought or received from whites. The land was divided again when he died. The heirs had long since scattered. A timber company bought several pieces from Weldon Perry's heirs and resold them to Eben Merritt. Two of Weldon Perry's heirs did not sell. The tax mapmaker had one tract of thirty-seven acres in its approximate location on Drummond's Branch, but had lost a fifteen-acre tract between my northern line and Merritt's.

In the tax office, the record showed that every year, Mrs. Flora Stenberg at a certain address in Chicago had dutifully paid the small tax bill for thirty-seven acres. When her father, Weldon Perry, farmed these lands, he had gone to Pace's Mill or Pittsboro on wagon roads already sinking their wide grooves deep into the clay soils. Before World War II, the roads had been abandoned.

I took my discovery to my friend Ed Holmes, a Pittsboro lawyer whose senior partner had practiced country law in Pittsboro since World War I. Ed knew some of Mrs. Stenberg's Perry family. We called her. She had not thought much about "that old land," and she didn't know anything about the smaller piece. Whatever she owned, she said, she would be glad to have a little money for it. I would have to borrow from the bank for the first time since my divorce, but the opportunity would never come again. We agreed on a price. A year after I had hesitated to buy Dean's land, I had added fifty-two acres to my land at Saralyn. I was in debt again, but the land had been cheap, and I could do more appraisals. Thoreau had met his needs by surveying land, and I paid for my land by appraising other people's property. The smaller tract made my land longer but no wider. The larger tract on Drummond's Branch lay off to the northwest across the branch from Dean's but was not attached to my old land or to its new extension.

My next good luck came from a trick played on Dr. Zhang by Nance Newland and his pinhooker. When Newland's pinhooker had shown the doctor the old Pilkington land west of me, he drove him in over the new Saralyn Road. This road, he had said, was laid out on the old roads and was the doctor's right of way. The doctor's deed described the boundaries of his property and at the end contained a single separate sentence, "This deed includes a right of way over adjacent lands." That final statement was not false because every landowner in North Carolina is assumed to have the right to go to and from an existing home, croplands, or timberlands. Newland, his pinhooker, and his lawyer cleverly avoided designating in writing whether the "adjacent lands" were east, west, north, or south. Even if the doctor could get a court to designate a route, he would have to build a road more than a mile long or pay Saralyn a fair price for the use of its road. He was landlocked.

By 1985, I had paid off the loan I took for Mrs. Stenberg's two tracts. I went to see Dr. Zhang. He was a middle-aged man with a heavy accent and no pretensions, though he and his wife were highly respected and highly paid for their work on the biochemistry of cancer. We talked on and off for several years until, for his own reasons, he agreed to sell me thirty-six acres along the entire length of my western boundary.

This time I didn't have to borrow money from the bank. The doctor still owed Nance Newland seven annual payments for this land at a good interest rate. I paid several thousand dollars in cash to the doctor and assumed his debt to Newland. Within a few years I had paid Newland. Once again, I owned my house and land and owed no one for it. Now I owned 112 acres.

Except on my east, no one could build a house that I could see or hear under normal circumstances. My neighbors to the east retired from lives of interpreting satellite imagery for the government and its defense contractors. They bought a house in a subdivision created from a large dairy farm half way to Chapel Hill. Their land was an investment in timber and the hobby of reclaiming the old barns and open lands around an old home site a mile from me.

Still, any day someone could make them an offer they could not refuse and turn their land into a golf course stretching from the Haw River to Morgan Branch. Any offer I could afford to make would be easily refused. The Merritts could do the same. I began suffering from the human animal's ability to think ahead. I had protected my house and its privacy quite well, but I had built the house here so that I could enjoy the forest. I was far from safe. Like a grizzly bear, the crop I expected from living in the wild required a large habitat.

Easy enough for Thoreau to write that "a man is rich in proportion to the number of things which he can afford to let alone." I could not afford to let alone the land around mine, and I could not afford to buy all of it. If my America had been growing as slowly as Thoreau's or even depopulating as these hills had been doing for over fifty years, I might also have adopted Thoreau's happy conclusion that it's possible to own the landscape without owning the land. He said of the Hollowell farm, "I have since annually carried off what it yielded without a wheelbarrow. With respect to landscapes, 'I am monarch of all I survey, My right there is none to dispute.'"

What I surveyed around me could easily spoil. I did not enjoy describing my desires by glib aphorisms, but I admitted it was true that I knew how much land a man needed—I needed only my land and all the land around it. This feeling was my continuing brotherhood with environmentalists, who generally have as much regard for landowners as for children with guns; their constant proposals to saddle owners with regulations and restrictions prove it. Because ownership is not an absolute state of being but a bundle of rights, they are forever removing sticks from this bundle and giving them to the government. In a very real way they want the government to have rights to all the land it presently owns or controls, as well as all the land around that. Here we rejoin Thoreau, "the bad neighborhood to be avoided is our own scurvy selves."

-chapter 32-

Vultures

Jane Goodall had her chimps and one spring, against my principle of nonintervention, I decide to have my vulture.

When I was a boy and wanted to know everything about dogs, I could recite dozens of breeds and what was expected of their ears or tails, their minds, and their behavior. Maybe because I came from a blue-collar family or had already been infected by that smarmy political talk that idolizes "working people," I particularly admired that group of dogs called "working dogs." Later I found the distinction between a Hungarian sheepdog as a worker and a beagle as a hunting dog and a Pekinese as a toy dog very artificial. The Pekinese was bred as a temple watchdog. The beagle works hard chasing rabbits and coons. Every dog was bred as a kind of working slave for humanity. (Their condition ranges from brutal to pampered, but if they exist for their owners' pleasures and purposes, they are slaves.) The work of a Chihuahua might seem easier than the work of a St. Bernard hunting avalanche victims in five feet of snow, but this is relative. In the South, where Chihuahua's were clutched to the bosoms of asthmatic ladies as a curative, the dog might well have wished it were hunting avalanche victims. Dogs, like all domesticated animals, are slaves—turned into property for purposes in which they have no choice.

As a child I dreamed of and plotted a future in which I would be friends with wild animals, but it never occurred to me that they would be leading my kind of life rather than vice versa. I believed in the ideal of Bomba the Jungle Boy, Mowgli, and Tarzan. Bomba, Mowgli, and Tarzan live in untroubled friendship with the animals. This is a child's version of the biblical promise of "dominion over the birds of the air and the beasts of the land." Somewhere between those books and my move to Morgan Branch, I lost all desire to tame a wild animal or to live with one untamed. Circumstances once coerced me into violating my principles.

In the spring of 1987, I found an old house site on top of a hill not far from the Haw River. The house had fallen into its cellar hole and rotted to nothing. At one edge of this basin stood a fine stone chimney with a thick spiral of bronze lightning rod still attached to it. When I approached, I heard a loud rustling in the brush and poison ivy vines beyond the chimney. A black vulture rose into the air, clumsily at first, then with confidence. (Vultures do best launching themselves from high perches or from open ground.) It flew into the top of a young walnut tree behind me, but most vultures would have flown farther. This one perched in the walnut and spread its wings to impress me with those broad black flags across the blue sky above. A superstitious person might have seen in the vulture the spirit of a tortured soul who had once lived in the house now represented only by its chimney. The vulture's display tactic may scare other animals, but for a human who knows birds, behavior like this sends a clear message—a nest with eggs or chicks is almost underfoot.

At that point you can either walk away respectfully or you can indulge your curiosity and look for the nest. Thirty feet beyond the chimney, a large red oak had been hollowed out and then killed by heart rot. When the tree had fallen, it had left three or four feet of stump sticking up from the ground. Inside the stump I found the nest. On a three-foot-wide cushion of rotted wood and compost created by decades of ant and termite labor, two eggs lay side by side. I felt them and the warmth of the mother's body still on them. When I was a kid, people used to say that a bird would not sit on an egg or take back a chick that a human has handled. Any chicken farmer knows differently, and it's easy enough to observe in the wild. Many birds readily adopt eggs placed in their nest. Some will try to hatch a stone. A week later I went back and the mother was sitting on the same eggs I had touched.

A week after that, she did not fly out of the stump when I approached. She stood up inside and made a long hissing as she looked out through a crack in the stump wall. I took one slow smooth step forward and waited, another step and waited. When I was ten feet away, she jumped up onto the edge of the stump, paused briefly, then flew into the walnut tree from where she had threatened me two weeks before. Inside the stump, two downy chicks stood motionless side by side, facing in opposite directions. They were twice the size of poultry chicks. Thick beige down covered them except for the bare black skin around their black eyes and their three thick white toes. Their black beaks were almost as large as their heads but safely blunt at this tender age.

Sylvan came to stay with me for the summer, the last summer I could think of her as a girl, maybe the last summer I would think of her as my student. The next year she would start college as a biology major. We visited the vulture's nest at least once a week. We watched the chicks begin to grow black flight feathers beneath their down. Their wings began to take shape, but only three of their four wings: One chick developed a crooked wing. Maybe it had been broken. It hung twisted at the chick's side, but it grew. The chicks' heads grew into their beaks; the beaks grew longer and blacker.

I briefly thought I might take the chick with the misshapen wing to a raptor center or a vet to see if the wing could be reset to grow normally. It did not have the good fortune to be a rare or endangered bird, or I would have decided in its favor. Vultures may be more plentiful than before the coming of civilization thanks to abundant road kills, hunting, chicken farms that often pile their dead outside before burning, and the occasional farm animal that dies in the field. I have seen more than a hundred black vultures roosting together in trees near the river, and black clouds of them circling Pittsboro, enjoying the city air currents rather than keeping a death watch, I assume. I left the lame chick in the stump to endure whatever fate handicapped vultures endure. I had come to know nature, not to change it.

Toward the end of the summer when the chicks' down had diminished to small tufts at the ends of the new jet black adult feathers, we found one of the two chicks outside the stump, dead. It had been dead a day or two. Yellow jackets were already feeding on its eyes. I turned it over and looked for a wound, but I saw nothing. Whatever had launched the fatal attack had seized the healthy bird instead of the weak one. That's not supposed to happen in nature. We found the chick with the twisted wing hiding in weeds and wild grapevines a few yards away. Its wing still hung at its side, the big flight feathers splayed like a carelessly held hand of cards. The mother was in a tree. We left them to their own defenses.

I came back at least once a week. Sometimes the mother did not appear at all. The chick grew into a full-sized black vulture (*Coragyps atratus*). Unlike other vultures and buzzards, the black vulture does not have a naked neck, and instead of the red head and neck of a turkey vulture or the red and yellow of a condor, its head is black. Like all vultures, the naked head saves a lot of cleaning when the birds plunge into a carcass to eat. The black vulture has a shiny jet black head with black eyes and a black beak. Its legs are naked and white, like the legs of its distant relatives the chickens; they are also thick and strong and tipped with long claws, which are the vulture's best tools. Unlike condors and turkey vultures, the black vulture, like eagles and hawks, depends on its eyesight. The surviving chick was a perfect bird except for the useless wing that would soon make it a dead bird.

When the weather turned cool in mid-October and the mother did not appear when I visited, I knew the bird would not survive. I had come to know it too well, although I had never tried to befriend it. Although I occasionally brought a chicken neck or a dead animal from the road, whenever I approached, it ran for cover.

I often found it standing in the hearth of the old chimney. It was living prudently, with its back to the best wall it could find. Because it was a doomed bird, I would have welcomed a sign of appreciation, a willingness to be dependent, an acknowledgment that it knew where future safety could be found. However much I regretted that it could not understand, I also admired its unbending wildness. I did have its life on film from mother and egg to dead sibling and adult survivor. How it had survived I did not know; I found no clues, no bones, no uneaten remains. The ground was rich with worms and grubs. Maybe it had dealt death to nests of mice or ground birds as surely as something had killed its sibling. A healthy vulture is strong enough to attack newborn lambs and calves. For a grounded vulture, the hunting season was now over. Frost would come soon and drive food underground. I decided to take the bird home.

Behind my old outhouse, I fenced in a good-sized yard for the vulture and I built a small lean-to where it could shelter from the rain or snow. I made sure it always had a chicken neck or a chicken that had fallen off one of the many trucks that traveled the county's roads from farm to processing plant. When I saw a road-killed squirrel, or even a raccoon that had not been entirely flattened and dried, I took it home. The vulture ate well, but never showed pleasure at my arrival; in fact, I could never come near the yard without its getting excited and hissing at me.

One cold late afternoon in the middle of November when we had been together a month, I came home and the vulture was gone. I saw no sign of a struggle. The fence had not been opened or raised from the ground. The vulture could not have jumped or flown over. I guessed that my good supply of food had doomed it. In the morning I had dropped two chicken necks in the pen. They must have attracted a fox or a raccoon or even a possum. With nowhere to hide and no good battle position like the fireplace of the old chimney, the vulture was easy game for a good predator, no better equipped to defend itself than a big rooster.

I wanted to believe that the vulture had learned to fly, but the twisted wing made that impossible. The only crippled animals that live a normal life span are those tended by humankind. As crippled and pampered captives, they often live two or three times longer than their wild and free peers. With good care, this vulture might have lived thirty years in kind captivity. In the wild, with both wings flapping, it would have been lucky to live five years. Taking care of the lame and the wounded, not to mention imagining for them a productive life—that is a human trait. In the wild, an adult animal weakened by accident or illness receives no charity from the pack, the flock, or the herd.

Wild animals have no golden rule, only an iron rule of survival the most practical way. Physical ability is the greatest protection. Past associations and achievements count for nothing. What they are at the present second may be the total of their ability and conditioned learning, but they do not know it. Every minute is the entirety of existence. I will allow possible exceptions for the large pinnepeds (sea mammals), for apes, and perhaps for elephants. Thinking ahead, imagining possibilities, is the curse and genius of the human species. On the time scale of evolution, it was only yesterday that human animals began to bury their dead. Only seconds ago we became willing to sacrifice self-interest to carry the burden and nurture the future of the handicapped. Civilization is a marvelous and delicate spacecraft in a wild cosmos.

I told Sylvan about the vulture when I made my regular Saturday call. She said it was unfortunate, but she accepted it as something almost expected. For me, the bird's disappearance was a failure. I had failed to make it accept its limitations and my good will. It had failed to accept me as a substitute for its parent. I had remained its enemy until a real enemy had found it. I had, of course, chosen how much time and energy I would invest in its care and safety. Sylvan was seventeen that year and beginning to plan a life for herself, what college to attend, what career to prepare for. She, too, was leaving her shelter.

-part three-

Changes

chapter 33

Clear-Cut

*An alarm call in the night speaks of forest
Armageddon. Events reveal how one person's
Armageddon is another's paradise.*

Every few years the phone rings and a person in distress says, "Wallace,
something awful is going to happen." The caller's neighbor or someone
close by has decided to cut timber. The distress in the caller's voice verges
on panic, as if the house had started to burn. The end is near. And it's true.
Another forest is about to disappear—almost overnight.

In 1992, a caller from a mile north of me said the Merritt family was
about to cut all its land, including the Dean land, which by then had
passed from Nance Newland to others and on to Merritt. While out walking, the caller had met a forester laying out a road and cruising the timber.
The timber cruise figures would tell the owner approximately how many
board feet of each kind of timber he has and how many cords of pulpwood
could be chipped for particle board or paper mills. This was the first time
land bordering mine would be cut.

I had walked through this land many times. The Merritts had accumu-
lated almost 700 acres in a mile-and-a-half-long band stretching from the
Haw River on the east to a public road on the west. It spanned my northern border, and embraced the thirty-seven acres I had bought along Drummonds Branch. On a high hilltop, I had often stopped at the chimney of an
old cabin. A large, scarred walnut tree stood next to the foundations, and

in the spring, old-fashioned yellow jonquils sprouted where someone had planted them a century ago. The English poet Wordsworth stopped in a forest like this and looked on the foundations of cottages. He imagined the life there and thought about his own life. The lives gone and the slower life of the rejuvenated forest made him think of "the still, sad music of humanity." I had several Tintern Abbeys in the forests near me, but this was my favorite. Soon, the loud, rap orchestration of humanity's chainsaws, skidders, and logging trucks would surround it.

Robert Frost looked at an ancient forest and said,

> The woods are lovely, dark and deep.
> But I have promises to keep,
> And miles to go before I sleep.
> And miles to go before I sleep.

If we go into a beautiful forest with no business to conduct, no wood to cut, nothing to collect, no science to conduct, nothing to fear—the forest puts the mind at rest. Reason takes a welcome nap. I reasoned with my caller and with myself.

Cutting timber in the piedmont hills usually means clear-cutting. Clear-cutting turns woods that stand "lovely, dark and deep" into an expanse of naked ground, deeply rutted by skidders, punctuated with bleeding stumps, and strewn with the limbs and laps that are impossible to walk among. The people who call me about timber cutting have seen this before and have good cause to believe that ecological Armageddon has arrived. Seeing in this case should not lead to believing. People react to a clear-cut in this region the way they react to blood from a scalp wound. Usually, however, the face covered with blood does not signal a broken skull or severed brains; but clear-cutting clouds the brains of reasonable people.

Clear-cutting does not, as the Bible says of Armageddon, put an end to all things forever. To provide some perspective, a clear-cut destroys less than a fire, the eruption of Mount Saint Helens, a tidal wave, or a glacier. A clear-cut does not destroy nature itself but the nature we love and have become accustomed to seeing. It destroys, temporarily, for less than a heartbeat of geological time, the plants we love most, the trees. It destroys

> A tree whose hungry mouth is prest
> Against the earth's sweet flowing breast

It destroys

> A tree that may in Summer wear
> A nest of robins in her hair;
> Upon whose bosom snow has lain;
> Who intimately lives with rain.

I use Joyce Kilmer's words because so many of the people I know who almost weep at the thought of a clear-cut forest also believe they are above the sentimentality of this famous poem. (The poem, incidentally, was written by a U.S. Army sergeant who had a desk job during World War I, but who volunteered to replace a dead soldier on the front line in France. He was killed and buried in a creek bed beside the soldier he replaced.) Most of us are terribly sentimental about trees. I have dozens of trees in my forest that I know as individuals, and I visit them like old friends. I have an album with their pictures, some as they grew up. They serve me instead of pets, but I don't give them names, and I don't feed them. I don't talk to them. They have become what they are without me—interesting shapes, enormous sizes, a mystery book of scars. I like their independence.

If someone were to clear-cut my forest, I would not only be sad but angry enough to shoot. Every day I look at the small patch of old growth across Morgan Branch in front of my house, and no matter how dark the mood I wake up in or that I carry into the day's dusk, that little grove is as welcome as love. I understand why my neighbors call in alarm. I understand why John Muir, founder of the Sierra Club and America's greatest hiker, could conclude his defense of old forests by writing, "God has cared for these trees, saved them from drought, disease, avalanches, and a thousand straining, leveling tempests and floods; but he cannot save them from fools."

The Merritt who owns the land north of me is no fool. He is a plastic surgeon, a hunter, a reasonable and civil man. Like me, he can choose what he will do with his forest. The timber was worth maybe half a million dollars. Let's say that much money put in his retirement account might earn 10 percent a year, or $50,000. If he lets the forest stand, he is paying $50,000 a year for two or three weekends of hunting. Or maybe he is paying it so that his trees can absorb carbon dioxide, which is supposed to cause global warming. Even my strongest environmentalist friends would not pay $50,000 a year for the right to bird-watch, or hike among the California redwoods or the spruce trees of Alaska's Kodiak Island, or to lock up a few tons of greenhouse gas.

Much of the surgeon's land was covered in pine trees that had taken over old fields and pastures. He could cut selectively and leave twelve or fifteen good seed trees for every acre. Among the hardwoods he could also cut selectively and leave an essential shade and enough trees to continue making the mast crops (nuts and seeds) that sustain deer, squirrels, and wild turkey. He could do it this way, but he would give up $100,000 or more. So he would still be paying $10,000 a year for a few weekends of hunting. My other argument, if I wanted to argue with him, would have been that by selective cutting, the land would have a much greater appeal to the real estate market. Why would I argue that? Did I want to encourage him to sell it for development? I was better off if he clear-cut it. Even if he replanted it in pine, it would be an impenetrable thicket of saplings, blackberries, and smilax thorns for at least ten years.

The caller from the north side of Merritt's land asked, "Is there any way we can stop him? Isn't there some law about raping a forest like this?"

"If he cuts too close to the stream or leaves debris in the stream, he can be fined," was my answer.

"Then it's too late."

"The only way to stop him would be to go to the timber sale and buy the rights to the timber," I suggested. "Or call the owner now and ask him to sell you the rights. Then you sell the timber in a selective cut."

"I don't want to cut any timber," the caller said. "He doesn't need the money. Why is he doing this?"

The caller had a nice house, two expensive cars, and more than ten acres of land. "All of us have things we don't need," I said.

"Couldn't we get the state or someone to buy it for a park?"

Now we had come down to a fundamental obstacle to saving land the way environmentalists want to do it—someone else has to pay to rescue a favored piece of land. Only the Nature Conservancy, scattered land trusts, and a few sporting groups such as Ducks Unlimited have raised money to save wildlife habitat. I told the caller that Merritt's land was a beautiful piece of land, but it was not of great interest to the State Parks people or the Nature Conservancy.

The caller paused. I waited. "This is an environmental disaster."

I said, "It's not a disaster but it's going to be ugly and years will pass before anyone can walk through that land again." As a consolation, I explained that a clear-cut would explode with small animals—rabbits, mice, voles, moles, songbirds. Within months, those animals would attract snakes, fox, bobcats, hawks, owls, and eagles. "There will actually be more animals there after it's cut than now," I concluded.

The caller heard me out, waited a few seconds, sighed a four-letter word, thanked me, and hung up.

A month later, the chain saws were roaring and whining from dawn until late afternoon. Without even leaving the house I could sometimes hear big trees crack and crash. That went on for two months or more. During the entire time I did not venture far enough north on my land to see what was happening. When it was all over and the world had been quiet for a week or two, I walked up the old road to where the chimney stood by the walnut tree: Both had been knocked down. From that hilltop, I looked across several hundred acres. A quarter mile below me, a few trees stood along Morgan Branch as it runs out of my property on north through Merritt's. Otherwise, on hundreds of acres I did not see more than a dozen trees standing. The unusable crowns of trees and flattened saplings thickly littered the land; stumps poked out of the ground everywhere and their crowns lay a few feet off. The place looked like a battlefield on which the bodies of the slain have been carried off but the feet and heads have been left.

When the loggers had finished cutting, they came in with a large bulldozer. It rolled back and forth across the debris and among the whips of trees that were not worth cutting. In front of the dozer, a sturdy bar bent forward anything standing, and below the bar, the broad, bright steel of a K&G blade sliced through all obstacles. To break the debris into pieces, the dozer towed behind it a big roller ridged with sharp metal fins. I knew that within a month they would try to burn the trash. Then they would reseed the land with pines. If the stumps of poplar, oak, and hickory were not burned, they would sprout quickly and reestablish their hold on the land. Planted pines would fill the land as fully as corn fills a cornfield.

First, men with drip torches, one part gasoline to three parts diesel fuel, walked through the clear-cut spreading drops of fire. Fires started, burned patches here and there, and then smoldered and died. They did the second burn by helicopter on a still summer day. From the chopper, they dropped pellets of potassium permanganate and water. When the pellets hit the ground, the potassium permanganate and water mixed and the reaction started fires. Fire crews with tractors plowed a ten-foot-wide fire lane around the entire property. When the fire burned out, the world was quiet again. This time, they had burned everything.

The loggers had cut right up to my property line, then plowed the fire lane along my border. By the end of the summer, the weeds were growing. Hundreds of thousands of ankle-high pine seedlings rose from the ground on slender scaly stems bearing a single tuft of delicate needles. One late afternoon in October, I watched a hawk swoop into the blackened debris and emerge with a small creature in its talons.

I saw something else, too: For the first time since I had moved to Morgan Branch, I could look out from the edge of my forest across hills and open land toward a distant horizon. I could see the forms of the land that before I had seen only as a draftsman's lines on a topographical map drawn from an aerial photograph. I remembered visiting the house of a wealthy environmental patron in the Berkshire hills of New England. He and his wife were immensely pleased with their modern house and especially the views. They had built on a hill. The view to the north looked out over green pastures and stone walls to distant mountains and their forests. What had made that lovely view? Nothing less than the clear-cutting of an ancient New England forest. When farmers felled those forests, they removed millions of stones from the forest floor where they lay sheltering a diversity of animals. The farmers built straight lines of stone walls that patterned the fields and pastures. Their good fences made good neighbors; the stone fences also made a new kind of habitat for rabbits and weasels and snakes. On the cleared land, domestic animals and mowing machines ended the life of any tree or bush or weed that struggled to rise from the earth.

That attractive landscape feeds the soul if the body is already well fed, but it did not do well at providing for farm families. The old farming families had left New England's lands as they had left North Carolina's. The wild had begun to return, but too late: People with money arrived from Boston, Hartford, New Haven, and New York. They bought the old farms with the beautiful views and paid to keep the pastures clear. They stopped the return of the wild. As I stood with my friends before the windows of their elegant house, we talked about the beauty of the view and of the fine fellowship we had enjoyed that weekend at a fall gathering of nature writers.

chapter 34

The Complexity of
the Simple Life

*I look across the clear-cut and wonder why I don't
like the view. I go back to my childhood, back a few
more generations to when the motor car helped save
Chatham County's forests.*

The clear-cut at Merritt's transformed me into a de facto Pygmy. The anthropologist Colin Turnbull describes what happened when he took a
Pygmy who had lived his entire life in an African rain forest out onto the
open grasslands. The Pygmy stared off across the plains at a distant herd of
buffalo and asked Turnbull what kind of insects they were. "When I told
Kenge that the insects were buffalo, he roared with laughter and told me
not to tell such stupid lies." The Pygmy, who knew the danger of forest buffalo, said that if those small dots were buffalo, he would not be standing
where they could see him. The "insects" were buffalo, but the Pygmy's ex-
pectations of the world had matured in a forest where nothing could be
seen at a distance. Rain forest birds, animals, and humans evolve or learn
to detect distant friends and enemies largely by sound.

Not as thoroughly as the Pygmy, but just as surely, I had become a captive of my environment: Seven months of the year in this forest I live under a canopy of leaves, below the level of the understory of dogwood,
maple, sourwood, and holly. Summer here is like living at the bottom of a

green ocean. Even in winter the trees are close, and the pine stands are dark. I know individual trees and rocks, but I have to find them; nothing stands out in sharp detail. The calls and cries of birds have short clear notes.

I could stand in the northern edge of my forest with seventy- and eighty-foot oaks and hickories dropping a deep shade around me, the sun blazing on Merritt's bare hills at the same time blinding me. I was like a man emerging from life in a cave: The brightness shined like another world, like a vast room that had suddenly appeared in the middle of the forest. I did not want to imagine what acts might take place there.

I could talk to myself about regrowth and watch the grace of hawks hunting over the stripped land. I could watch the sun rise over the horizon and set again as I could not do in the forest at Morgan Branch. I knew that among the young pines, the weeds, the blackberry canes, and the broom-straw a whole new society of animal life had begun almost as soon as the potassium fires went cold. Still, I was as uneasy about that land as the Pygmy about the buffalo on the plains.

I am not a Freudian, but I see the origin of my anxiety in childhood. All the evidence I have seen in many countries convinces me that no human ever fully recovers from the shocks and fears of childhood or outlives its ideals. I came to Morgan Branch in part because it fulfilled an old ideal. Although I was born in New York City and grew up in the suburbs of Long Island, my imagination lived in books and movies about forests—*The Jungle Book, Bomba the Jungle Boy, Bambi, Snow White, The Yearling, Robinson Crusoe,* and *The Swiss Family Robinson.* As early as I can remember, I hated the city, its gritty winter cold, and the neighborhood bullies. My brother and I dreamed of living on a jungle farm. I had found refuge from my parents' fighting and depression in those few patches of woods left in the old estates of Long Island's north shore and on the steep bluffs above the harbor. I saw the trees in these places cut down for houses. I saw the few vacant lots bulldozed and built on and turned into lawns. Little patches of woods that other kids and I had possessed with our lean-tos and tree houses were cleared for houses. I saw hundreds of acres of fields covered with the houses of Levittown.

Even on the remote tundra I sometimes have the fear that, just beyond the horizon of land and time, development is coming. The open space that makes me feel 100 percent welcome is the arctic coast in winter where the whiteness of land and sea become one. There the world is frozen and clean and I cannot imagine a time when it will belong to us or be home. The arctic in winter is a blank page in someone else's book.

For the environmentalist, the ideal result of human contact with nature is to write as little as possible on any page of nature's book. Tread lightly, we are told, and "leave nothing but footprints, take away nothing but memories." Live simply. No command is so difficult for the free human animal. In the center of any life of simplicity is a rejection of material possessions. This rejection condemns a trait that seems almost hard-wired into the human character. Religions recognized this millennia ago. Buddhist monks and Indian holy men throw themselves on the charity of their societies. "Chastity, poverty, and obedience" is the vow of every Catholic priest. Thoreau, with a convenient ignorance of history and biography, said, "With respect to luxuries and comforts, the wisest have ever lived a more simple and meagre life than the poor. The ancient philosophers, Chinese, Hindoo, Persian, and Greek, were a class than which none has been poorer in outward riches, none so rich in inward."

Thoreau said voluntary poverty was necessary to be "an impartial or wise observer of human life." That is like saying to be an impartial observer of banquets or supermarkets, you have to be hungry.

Since *Homo sapiens* acquired fire and became *Homo pyroformis*, humans have improved their material lot at the expense of the natural environment. If American Indian culture had bred environmental or child safety activists, they certainly would have objected to the constant grubbing of stones, to breaking them by the thousands and leaving the unnatural sharp shards and flakes all over the landscape—not to mention the use of eagle feathers, fire hunting, and fish poisoning.

Europeans and Africans who replaced Indians were not more crassly materialistic. They simply had greater power to destroy nature, the technology to process more raw materials to make goods, and thus more pollution and garbage to leave on the land. By the middle of the twentieth century the new Americans had used their freedom and resources to invent and acquire material possessions and comforts to give average citizens a life that would have been envied by the courts of Queen Elizabeth I and King George III.

None of us who moved into rural Chatham County and built our own "simple" homes ever started out living as simply as the people who cleared the first fields, farmed them, then left them free to grow into our forest. As soon as we drove the first nail into our homes, we were using technology they never had. Even the basic possessions of a twenty-five-year-old back-to-the-land dropout were of better quality and more numerous than anything in the eighteenth century or even most of the nineteenth. When the well-to-do Chatham residents of the early 1800s recorded their wills in the country registry, they listed their most expensive possessions; the list never takes more than a page and the possessions are usually simple. John Hatley left to the daughter of his friend Elizabeth Bynum "One bed and Furniture one dish, two Basons, four Plates, one Iron Pot two Trunks one Frying Pan, one Pair of fire Tongs, one Candle stick—One Jug, one Sinning [sic] wheel, one cotton wheel."

We had not only started with more, we had quickly started increasing our possessions and improving our houses. No one ever turned back. The tobacco barn that Kathleen and Ralph first lived in has become a sprawling two-and-a-half-story house with wall-to-wall carpets, offices, a dark room, upper and lower decks, an efficiency apartment, and central heat and air. Susan and her husband, Dave Smith, have expanded the three-room house that Susan built on nine stone piers to five or six rooms with a back deck and a flagstone patio in front next to an artificial frog pond fed by an electric pump. The foam dome was sold and torn down and replaced with a modern one-story rambling house and a hobby shop next to it. A two-room cabin sided with barn boarding and built by an electrician from Brooklyn was bought by a painter and has become a three-story baroque palace with a twenty-foot-high greenhouse, chimneys accompanied by gargoyles, and rooms with walls covered in murals.

Most people improved their possessions to have at least what they had walked away from in their middle-class homes. Most have more—better stoves, freezers, sport utility vehicles, a second car or truck, televisions, dishwashers, air conditioning, telephones, garages, and vacuum cleaners. I still heat mostly with wood, have one bathroom, unheated bedrooms, no dishwasher, and no clothes drier, and not everyone is content to leave me to my choices. A year ago the Farm Bureau Mutual Insurance Company canceled my fire insurance, saying my house was not accessible by firetruck. I feel I have been left behind. But I chose my luxury differently.

The expensive thing I acquired was land. I preferred what the land offers more than I preferred driving a new car or having a second bathroom. If I fell out of a tree again and landed on my head this time, what would I rather leave for Sylvan—a forest or an extra bathroom? Nevertheless, I had also shamelessly started improving my comforts only a few years after moving in. A crushed vertebra had been the excuse for a toilet. A couple of years later when I sold *Redbook* a fictionalized account of my fall out of the bee tree, I moved the kitchen wall out another five feet and bought a refrigerator with a freezer box so that I could cut down on canning and drying my food. A few years later, I enlarged my bedroom so that I could have a closet large enough for the clothes I was accumulating. In the mid-1980s, after a spate of appraisal work and a book on the American coastline, I moved the south wall toward the beech tree, adding a small writing room, a sunroom, and more space in Sylvan's bedroom. I replaced the little sleeping platform that she folded up against the wall to have more space with a double bed. Along the new south wall I added a deck. I put in air conditioning to keep my books and clothes from turning green with mildew in the forest's summer humidity.

I also built the separate building that was a studio and that became my writing room. This room is as close as I can come to having my thinking space inside a tree in the forest. I didn't move my work into this room only for the love of light. The windows and their broad view are always at my side so that I miss as little as possible of what is happening from the clouds to the creek, from the sun 35 million miles away to the bird feeder eight feet from my left shoulder.

The saddest room I ever worked in was on the fourth floor in one of the World Bank's buildings in Washington, D.C. I spent ten days there writing a report on the newly liberated entrepreneurs I had interviewed during a bank project in Eastern Europe immediately after the fall of Communism. The room had a large window that stretched from floor to ceiling and looked into an airshaft surrounded by other offices in the same building. I could not see the ground below or the sky above. Cloud or sun, the daylight at my window was always the same. When rain came, it fell straight down. I never saw a bird or a falling leaf. Day after day when I lifted my head to look "outside," I saw the same lifeless light, the same offices across the airshaft. I came to envy the secretaries who worked in cubicles with no windows to remind them of the outside. They decorated their walls with bright posters of their homelands, countries they had visited, and photographs of family and friends. When I was a student at Duke University, the library had an airshaft like this but much smaller. The only thing that ever moved in it as far as I know was the professor of German Romantic poetry who, dressed in his black cloak, plunged past the windows on his way to meet death.

Thoreau said that nature is all the company a human being needs: "I never found the companion that was so companionable as solitude. We are for the most part more lonely when we go abroad among men than when we stay in our chambers. A man thinking or working is always alone, let him be where he will." Half of everything Thoreau wrote was tongue-in-cheek, satire, the cynicism of a man always arguing with his friends and editors. As far as we know he never got far enough in his relations with other people to suffer the failure of an intimate romance. Thoreau, however, craved company, live and in books.

I have always had less live company at Morgan Branch than Thoreau had at Walden, and I will not embarrass myself by speculating whether I am less interesting or more disagreeable. I have lived at Morgan Branch ten times longer than Thoreau lived at Walden, but not because I am any less in need of companions. My access to both living and literary company is much greater than his.

Thoreau kept on his table a copy of Homer's *Iliad*, and wrote, "Books are the treasured wealth of the world and the fit inheritance of generations and nations. Books, the oldest and the best, stand naturally and rightfully on the shelves of every cottage." I built into my writing room over one hundred feet of bookshelves for useful and enjoyable company on demand. It was not enough. I used to travel every few weeks to millions of books in the great libraries of Duke University and the University of North Carolina, but when the 1990s arrived, I expanded the library at home by hundreds of thousands of books. They arrived on computer disks and on the two copper phone wires under the old Pace Mill Road that connects me to the Internet. So long as I do not give in to endless visiting all over the world on the World Wide Web and the Internet, I have solitude in the exact measure that I want or need it for my work. The computer has made it less necessary than ever for me to leave Morgan Branch.

After the clear-cut at Merritt's, I began to think more about the company I could not control—on lands beside me and even in the sky overhead where an ever-increasing number of flights were going to and from Raleigh-Durham International Airport, which had just added flights to London and Paris. Every year was also bringing more private pilots sightseeing over the country the way people go for Sunday drives along parkways. The aircrafts' rasping motors broke into my privacy as surely as if they were chainsaws or skiddoos.

When Sylvan left for Ohio in 1979, I applied for a post in the U.S. Foreign Service. Now, for the second time, I began to think about leaving permanently one day. It would not be to seek company somewhere else, but to find another place whose wildness was less threatened by neighbors and the growth of cities. The previous summer, I had passed through the world's least populated wilderness when I floated hundreds of miles down Russia's Kolyma River to the Arctic Ocean. I wondered whether one day politics and Russian law would allow me to have a cabin there, solar power, fuel cells, and a satellite connection to the Internet. Thoreau could not have imagined a man living in such a wilderness and possessing the riches of a vast library.

Those two thin strands of copper buried beneath the road to the vanished Pace's Mill and the path to my house bring books written thousands of years ago on parchment and bark; they were later copied to linen or paper, and they now travel from earth to space and back to earth and under my driveway and under Morgan Branch to appear at my command on the computer monitor before me. Even without this humble connection, I have on a single ounce of compact disk *The Iliad*, *The Odyssey*, *The Bible*, *The Koran*, *The Upanishads*, *Moby Dick*, *War and Peace*, and 1,470 more titles, enough to fill Thoreau's cabin solid from floor to ceiling and spill out toward Walden Pond.

Not only do I sit here surrounded by woods enjoying books on paper, books on disk, and books brought to my monitor from around the world, but I can enjoy them also read aloud to me from tape or CD by the author's own voice or by a fine actor. The great and trivial of the entire world come to my eyes. Thoreau could chide his intellectual contemporaries for being isolated from culture beyond America and Europe. He took great pride in having read a few books by Eastern mystics. Today, at any minute, I can not only read books written in Japan or India but I can download wisdom and beauty written in a dozen languages and my computer will translate them into English. I can also talk by Web phone with a citizen in the places where these books were written.

For any person whose luxury is not material goods but ideas and knowledge, the complexity of the Internet has made a simple life of voluntary poverty and constant communion with nature more possible than ever.

The computer has allowed us to redefine a simple life so that we can truly live it. I came to Morgan Branch thinking the simple life was the kind of life the Bynums, Burnettes, Oldhams, Pilkingtons, Morgans, Perrys, and hundreds of other families had lived here. That was a simple life. That was a life of involuntary poverty, and it was terribly hard on the people who lived it and the land it was lived on. When those families left their lands in pursuit of material things, the forest began to heal because the families no longer needed the soil, the streams, and the trees.

The pillage of distant wilderness is not why the eastern forests and the forests of Europe have begun to spread again. As bad as the oil spill of a tanker may be, the substitution of oil and gas for wood and coal to make electricity, heat homes, fire ceramics, and make glass has saved vastly more of the environment than all the tanker spills combined have despoiled. In our quest for material wealth, we are finding substitutes for trees and metals.

The old Chatham families ran out of their homes by the hundreds to see the first automobile pass through Pittsboro in 1907, a man on his way from Danville, Virginia to South Carolina. Two years later, Chatham citizens bought the first two cars to reside here. Within a decade, forests were reclaiming some of the land cleared to feed mules and horses.

Environmentalists might scoff at a late nineteenth-century advertisement from an English magazine, but Chatham's farm families would have recognized the truth in the humor of an early advertisement for the motor car that listed among its benefits:

—There is no manure to poison the air.
—It consumes only when working, and then in exact proportion to the work done.
—It will do more work than any two horses.
—No cruelty is inflicted by climbing a steep hill with a full load.

The old Chatham families were escaping from the nineteenth century. The material goods of their own century not only made their lives better but brought a great new green mantle to the lands on which they had struggled. Nature, who abhors a vacuum, filled their place with their competitors—wildlife. It is good for nature that the Chatham families could abandon that simple life. It was good for nature that those of us who came later could not and did not want that old simple life.

-chapter 35-

Cutting at
Morgan Branch

*I begin to think about the value of my own trees. I
make a decision that changes the forest and my life.*

Twice during my time here, the post office has surprised me in late spring
by delivering a check from the U.S. Government for a few hundred dollars.
Each time I discovered that the income tax declaration I had filed in April
had marked me as one of several million working Americans living so
deeply in poverty that the federal government helps us out of our suffering
with an "earned income credit." I have never considered myself poor. I
have never been hungry or without heat. I have always had a car or pickup.
Two or three years I joined the millions without health insurance, but only
because I calculated my risks and decided to spend the money on travel or
tools. Every year I had the few hundred dollars necessary to visit Latin
America, and three times I spent a shade over a thousand dollars to visit
arctic Russia.

My parents were poor enough when I was growing up, so I did not consider the government's designation a novelty or an honor. It reminded me
that I was getting older and that the deer and squirrels were not going to
pay for gas, electricity, or property taxes if I couldn't work and cut firewood. When I considered the clear-cutting at Merritt's and that they
might have received half a million dollars, I wondered what the difference

was between having trees or gold on your land. If I had a gold mine, would I mine it?

In February of 1993, I took several long slow walks through my land. I particularly wanted to look at pine and poplar. Pine and poplar are second-growth trees; they spring up in sunny areas that have been cleared. On old fields they are like the "volunteer" tomatoes that appear every spring in my garden from the seeds of tomatoes fallen the year before. I had at least thirty acres where pines and poplars had grown on old fields. Throughout the forest, pine and poplar had taken advantage of openings created when old trees died or were blown down. The value of the trees on my land could quadruple my retirement savings or pay for several years of writing. Maybe I could use the money to save other land next to mine from being clear-cut. Behind the best uses of the money, I always knew that I was turning beautiful trees into personal gain. I didn't have to do it. Or maybe I did.

I had lived almost twenty years at Morgan Branch without cutting a single large tree. I had come and lived as an observer, not a manager. I would leave a small mark or two on the land. I took some comfort in knowing that my changed role was not new. I was joining the ranks of people who had managed the landscape for thousands of years. I still felt a little like excusing myself by saying, "Well, everybody does it."

I called my friend and former Duke classmate Dan Gelbert, who had worked as an independent forester for over twenty years. I had edited the literary magazine, always in jeans and a denim jacket, riding one of the two motorcycles then on campus. Dan had come to Duke from Pennsylvania, played football, belonged to a hard-drinking fraternity, dated a beauty queen. We had few common interests and met only when he appeared in Chatham County to appraise and sell timber. Dan is results oriented: "You'll get the most money if you clear-cut the pines," he told me. He laughed because he knew I wouldn't do it.

He told me that I could get twice as much for my timber if I at least clear-cut the areas where the pine was thick. "The loggers are going to damage a lot of the other trees anyway," he told me. "That's just the nature of logging." It's true. Loggers cannot drive their machines around a crowded forest and skid thirty-foot logs out to a loading area without tearing patches of bark from a lot of other trees. I told him that if logging carefully cost more, I was willing to lose the money.

We agreed that Dan would send a forester out to help me mark the trees I wanted to sell. He knew a logger who would use a "feller-buncher" and who worked carefully, although he might pay a little less. The feller-buncher is a heavy tractor whose massive steel claw grabs a tree by the trunk about eight feet high, then advances a huge circular saw just above ground level and severs the tree from its roots. It can lay a large tree down in the direction that does the least damage to neighboring trees. A feller-buncher, with its firm embrace, its neat cut, and its gentle laying down, actually seems kind and tender compared to a man with a roaring chain saw or a couple of men with axes who whack away at a gaping wound. It is another example of big-time technology, of industrial power, of doing a kinder job than preindustrial loggers did with their axes and two-man pit saws.

For several days, I crisscrossed the forest and looked carefully at the trees, marking with a red slash each tree to be cut. I never marked two or more standing close together. Cutting them all would open a wide hole in the canopy. The sun would come in early and stay late. Invasive weeds, brambles, and opportunistic sun-loving trees that don't belong in a mature forest would seize their opportunity.

My pines were not very large. Either farming had sucked out the nutrients or the land did not have the right soil and water conditions to grow big pine. Some of the poplars rose like temple columns into the canopy, but I doubted any were more than a hundred years old. The largest on my land already suffered gaping wounds or rotted hollows or gnarled scar tissue on their trunks. A commercial forester would say take them down to allow new growth, but I left them in place for the shelter they might give wildlife or simply because their endurance earned them my respect and their character was worth more to me than the few dollars they might bring. The bees from my hives and wild bees might miss the sticky poplar flowers that make a strong dark honey, but I would leave plenty. I also knew that within a year or two, wet weather would bring out on the stumps the crowded white shelves of oyster mushrooms.

For several weeks, the feller-buncher roared around the woods. Poplars and pines crashed and were slid off to a log deck on my border with Dr. Zhang. From there, trucks hauled them out on a logging road through Zhang and an adjoining timber company. I did not have to watch load after load of big trees cut into limbless logs rolling down the Old Pace Mill road and past angry neighbors. I did inspect the cutting; the worst was in the tick pines on the thirty-seven acres by Drummonds Branch. When the trees were cut, a tractor rammed them crown first into a delimbing gate.

The gate is a low and sturdy rectangle of steel about four feet high and fifteen feet long with uprights every two feet. It looks like a bicycle rack for motorcycles. The trunk of the pine tree passes through the uprights and the brittle limbs snap off. It's brutal but faster, safer, and more fuel-efficient than a man with a chain saw.

When the logger had finished, I walked through the woods. Among the hardwoods I barely noticed more sun. The logs had been hauled to the deck limbs and all to avoid littering the woods with unusable crowns. Few live trees had been wounded in the process. The woods would heal fast enough, and I was $20,000 richer.

I did not smile all the way to the bank. I knew that by cutting timber, I had made a transformation much more profound than adding a toilet or air conditioning to my house. I wondered whether the next time Sylvan came she would be disappointed by the loss of the big poplars and the heavily thinned pines. She had a degree in biology then, and science appeared to have preserved her from a sentimental political correctness that pervaded Vassar. When she interned for the Nature Conservancy, she wrote a plan to harmonize water levels in a swampy coastal pine forest to suit both loggers and preservationists.

I hoped that the way I cut marked a difference between me and the many generations who had managed these lands for a thousand years or more before me. Managing land and natural resources is built into human behavior and is part of the most primitive cultures. What people of other times did not do was think about the marks their management would leave for the future far beyond their own lives and needs. Necessity forced on them a short economic horizon. Exploitation had to come before the enjoyment of beauty or the understanding of science.

It is no accident that only since the Industrial Revolution have entire nations decided to reshape the human tradition of managing and changing nature. We have just begun to test our new dream of changing nature for the better. I looked around at the poplar and pine stumps and walked in the shade of the trees that would not be cut. The pines were already being turned into plywood, floor joists, beams, and decking. The poplar also became plywood and some became furniture. I would never know where it would come to rest or who would use it. Thirty years or one hundred years after my cutting someone might pull down a house built with pine from Morgan Branch. In ten years, a chair or couch will be dropped off at a thrift store. In twenty years, it might be set on the curb as trash. Here by Morgan

Branch most of the trees would get older. Today's old poplars would fall and grow mushrooms; the same fungus, along with insects, would digest the trees' remains. Then possums and birds would tear into the softened wood after the bugs.

By changing from a resident observer to the manager of the forest, I was an environmentalist who had come in from the cold, or come out of the woods. Many environmentalists grieve along with *New Yorker* writer Bill McKibben, who wrote in his best-seller, *The End of Nature*, that our power to govern nature, like my power over the trees at Morgan Branch, had "deprived nature of its independence, and that is fatal to its meaning." I, too, have crossed his line from living in a "separate and wild province" to becoming its governor. My act has not deprived nature of its separate meaning; my act has affirmed its separate meaning. The people who came before me at Morgan Branch—they were the ones who could not separate themselves and discover that meaning. McKibben wishes that humans would "choose to remain God's creatures instead of making ourselves gods." Not making ourselves gods would mean failing the test of humanity. We would be doing nature a disservice as serious as extinction if we denied our own character. We have been given god-like powers, and the test is not whether we give them up, but how we use them.

chapter 36

Departure and Return

Halfway around the world I learn something about life at Morgan Branch, and friends in Kazakhstan rename the old Pace Mill Road.

A few weeks after the logger left the woods in the summer of 1993, I left Morgan Branch and stayed away for two years. I went to Almaty, Kazakhstan, a city of 1.5 million people half way around the world. The same week I had talked to Dan Gelbert about cutting my timber, I also answered a small ad in *The Economist* magazine. *The Economist* is an international news magazine aimed six or eight grade levels higher than *Time* and *Newsweek*. The front and back of each weekly issue contain notices of "appointments"; that is British for high-level jobs. I replied to a call from International City/County Management Association (ICMA) in Washington, D.C., for a housing and real estate expert to work in the former Soviet Union.

I had a small-to-medium amount of each qualification required to become the resident advisor to the government of Kazakhstan on the subjects of housing and land reform. ICMA was not likely to hear from anyone who had all the qualifications. Even to find someone who had all or most of them in large quantity and who was willing to live in the backwaters of the former Soviet Union for two years was fishing for an unlikely trophy. ICMA invited me to the first interview on the basis of my experience in land development, real estate brokerage and appraisal, housing construction, volunteer work for the county housing authority, and a few regional and state committees I had sat on. The county, regional, and state groups had not acted on anything I proposed, but no one asked and I didn't tell. Besides, an association of city and county managers would understand that the political people who hired them spurned a lot of sound advice.

A few weeks after my interview, the man who supervised ICMA's offices in Armenia and Kazakhstan called me. "To be honest," he said, "you don't really have the experience at high levels of government that we want." If I had been cynical and pessimistic, I might have said, "Yes, and I live in a homemade house in the middle of a forest, and as a developer I'm known as the creator of Hippie Town." He didn't give me time to say anything. He went on, "But you can write and I can tell you that we need someone out there who can communicate clearly and on a regular basis." He suggested that I rewrite my résumé, add anything that possibly had to do with housing and international experience, and take out some of the unrelated items. I took out that I was a member in the North American Mycological Association, that I wrote fiction for *Redbook* and *Mademoiselle,* and that I was a translator of German lyric poetry. I lengthened the list of my contacts with government officials and would-be entrepreneurs on my three trips to the Russian arctic. Some of those contacts with regional administrators happened because one of my Russian friends had heard that I had written an article for *The New York Times*. I found out later that he would call an official and say, "A reporter for *The New York Times* would like to write about Magadan." Because *The New York Times* had been too busy to find Magadan, no one questioned my status. The resulting contacts looked good on my résumé.

The deleted literary notes may not have disappeared entirely from the supervisor's mind. He, too, had graduated from college with a love of literature and an ambition to write, then found himself studying city planning and working for a developer. ICMA sent me to Kazakhstan to replace a man who had been the manager of a city of more than 1 million people. He was gracious and sophisticated and liked by his staff and neighbors, but the office in Almaty was a dismal place and under siege. ICMA's resident advisor could speak no more than five words of Russian, could not use a computer, had no one on staff who knew word processing, and had no bank account for a $2-million-a-year project. When I arrived, the city *nomenklatura* were turning off the office lights and phone.

Whatever my successes and failures in the next two years, ICMA raised my salary after a year, and when my contract ended in September 1995, they asked me to stay on. I weighed Kazakhstan and an interesting job against the quiet life by Morgan Branch. I had made life in a drab city tolerable by finding a duplex in a neighborhood of quiet streets thick with fruit trees and friendly people. Government bureaucracy sometimes depressed me, sometimes outraged me, but on the worst mornings I could step outside on my way to work and see towering over the city and its troubles a wall of white mountains 15,000 feet high, a power so massive and beautiful that human troubles seemed small. I also had good Russian and Kazakh friends. I had used vacations to travel to some of the wildest places left on earth—the Russian arctic, Mongolia, and the glaciers of the Tien Shan mountains on the Chinese border. Sylvan had come for a month, and we rode in my clumsy but sturdy Russian jeep around Lake Issykul in Kyrgyzstan, climbed and hiked in the high pastures and mountain forests, and visited the glaciers 16,000 feet up by Peak Victory and Peak Communism. I became fast friends with Kazakh shepherds on the Chinese border and went fishing, mushroom foraging, and camping with Russian friends at beautiful resorts once reserved for the Communist Party elite.

I did not leave because I grew tired of Central Asia or my work. I left because I felt I had abandoned Morgan Branch just when I had begun a different kind of life there. I returned to Chatham County because I wanted to write a report on my life at Morgan Branch, and I had to be there to write it. Two years of absence in a different part of the world had raised questions that I could answer only at Morgan Branch.

When my staff and friends in Kazakhstan saw a picture of my house under the big trees, they often asked, "Is that your dacha?" The greatest forests in the world stand in Russia, but almost no one lives in them. The Soviet system did allow, and even encouraged, Russians to have garden plots and dachas, those small huts and cottages beyond the cities where millions of citizens still grow almost 40 percent of the country's vegetables. In Soviet times, Communist rulers forbade modern electrical, heating, and plumbing installations in dachas as a way of discouraging people from moving out of the cities. Naturally, people looked at my small house in the forest and thought it was a dacha.

More surprising to them was that I owned 112 acres of land. Even today in most of the former Soviet Union, real ownership of more than an acre or two of rural land is forbidden. When I said that I had cut some timber from my land, I strained belief.

"You own the trees?" they asked. "But you must get permission when you want to cut them?"

When I said I could cut every tree and shrub to the ground if I liked, they said it was incredible. Some thought it was dangerous. The great forests of the former Soviet Union as well as all underground minerals, oil, and gas are owned by the government or by government-controlled firms. Freedom to do business was one thing, but to do business with something like land and timber—that was inviting corruption and exploitation. They did not yet fully realize that no other country in the world has spilled so much oil, spread so much radioactive waste, poisoned so much ground with toxic chemicals, dried up such great lakes, sold forests so corruptly, or allowed its rare animals to be extinguished so casually as the former Soviet Union.

I returned from the wreckage of people and nature in that part of the world proud to be a private landowner with a new sense of my responsibilities. Socialism is the greatest test of government, and freedom is the greatest test of human character, morality, and understanding. I returned with a deeper understanding of why environmentalists so often fear private ownership and freedom to manage nature. They have a dim view of the human animal, and they believe that a human animal, set free to choose how to use a piece of land and its resources, will not choose to become a steward. It was easy enough to promise myself that I would become the steward of nature at Morgan Branch, but not so easy to imagine how.

In October of 1995, the forest was as I had left it two years earlier, but my house was not. I had rented the house to a confused man (who said he had retired from AT&T in his early fifties) and his new wife, an easy-going woman in her early forties. She announced that her profession was social therapy, but she was at the moment a waitress. They clearly needed and wanted each other and I thought I had been lucky to find a couple who could start their lives again in my forest; I agreed that they could also bring their aging German shepherd. I had never had a pet at Morgan Branch, partly out of respect for the natural order of things, partly because I do not enjoy living with an animal cut off from its own kind and totally dependent on a human being. The couple had assured me that their shepherd was too old to chase wildlife and that it was completely housebroken and would harm nothing inside. I signed a lease, and they had moved in with great joy, looking forward to the seclusion, the wildlife, the garden, and the serenity around them as a soft nest for the new peace of their life together.

At least some of the wildlife found them more hospitable than I had been, the mice especially. I had warned them about mice and had left traps and poison. This good couple, after seeing one mouse stagger around, probably the result of poison bate, ceased setting bait or traps. Mice enjoyed my closets, left two years of turds in my bookshelves, chewed the backing off pictures I had stored in the attic, and made a nest in my computer printer. My gentle renters also did not want to contaminate anything with pesticides, so they allowed the moths to eat two old and treasured Navajo rugs and a few other woolens.

The gentle, aging shepherd had made no noticeable dent and instilled no fear in the squirrel, chipmunk, raccoon, or deer population, but it did have one psychosis that destroyed parts of the house: It was mortally terrified of thunder and lightning. In its many panics, it had charged through the screen door, eaten pieces of the bathroom door, chewed up a door frame, and engraved long scratch marks in my heart pine floor outside Sylvan's room, where the renters slept.

After my tenants had harvested the crops I left behind the first fall, the following two summers they planted nothing; they could not stand the chiggers and the occasional tick. Both are easily defeated with common insect repellents or powdered sulfur around the waist, ankles, neck, and arms, but my tenants were the kind of people who are too ready to be defeated themselves. Besides, they had no time, they said, for weeding.

By E-mail I convinced them to cover the ground with black plastic so that weeds and tree seedlings would not take over the soils I had so carefully built up. I reminded them a couple of times that the small pile of crisscrossed logs beside the house in the shade of the hazel-nut bush would give them good crops of shitake mushrooms in wet weather. Sylvan and I had inoculated these logs with the mushroom spawn two years earlier. A few pounds can be sliced from the logs in two minutes. The shitakes came and went for two years, twenty or thirty pounds unpicked. The tenants occasionally mentioned their tight financial straits and exorbitant demands being made by lawyers for the man's previous wife, but despite the hardship, they did not drag themselves down into accepting charity from nature. They preferred to buy their gourmet food from the health food stores in Chapel Hill. I received an occasional chatty E-mail letter running on for several paragraphs about how much they were enjoying the house and the forest and how life by Morgan Branch continued to inspire them to find land for themselves.

Maybe they were the kind of people who really come and go without leaving a mark on the land. (Marks on my house were another matter.) If they found their land, they would have no garden and disturb no animal. They would also discover very little about nature. Humankind has learned all that it knows of other species and the earth itself by doing what every other animal and plant does—fighting for space, comfort, warmth, shelter, resources, and survival. We have been too brutal at times, but we have learned a lot along the way, including how to use our powers moderately.

I moved back into the house in October while the weather was still warm and the trees still green. I pulled the black plastic off the garden. I began to cut and split the winter's firewood. I set traps in the pantry, the kitchen, the attic, and my writing room. Within a few days, I dropped a dozen or more corpses on the porch where they were scavenged each night by a foraging raccoon.

Saralyn had not changed much. Kathleen and Nicholas had begun to build a large house on a vacant ten-acre tract just beyond my closest neighbors. The county had required that our two community roads and each driveway have a name. Where the old Pace Mill Road leaves the Saralyn road, my neighbors had placed a suburban street sign, Quartz Hill Road, in reflecting silver letters on a forest green background mounted on a round aluminum post. Where the Pace Mill Road leaves their drive and heads north toward Morgan Branch, I set a pole in the ground; on it I fastened a thick metal sign with white letters on a blue background. While I was in Kazakhstan, the city of Almaty, like cities across Central Asia, began replacing Russian street names with local names. I rescued a sign from the street my office had been on. It said, *у. л. Да7ЛаЯ*, "Dacha Street."

chapter 37

Boundaries

As I get reacquainted with the forest, my neighbors force on me an unpleasant recognition about ownership and property.

I did not wait for the new year to beat the bounds of my land and renew my acquaintance. I started walking the creeks and hills as soon as I had settled in. The strong living roots of the poplars cut two years earlier were sending up new shoots, some as high as my head. All had tried to rise again, but the deer had chewed nine out of ten to defeat. Others had sent up a ring of shoots around the old stump. I began to carry clippers with me. At each stump the deer had not killed, I cut all but one or two shoots. This was not kind to the deer, who get more to eat if multiple shoots compete and grow slowly, but deer have their own interests in mind, and I was interested in trees, not brush. The shoots I singled out for survival would grow faster. They would become new trees with old roots. I wanted the forest to erase the offense of my logging as quickly as possible. The offense would not be completely erased, of course. Whenever a hardwood forest regenerates like this, you can see its history in trees that grow double and triple trunks almost from the ground and in trunks that leave the ground at a slight angle and then straighten up.

The poplar stumps had also fulfilled expectation that they would produce fine crops of oyster mushrooms. The mushrooms, of course, took hold best on the dying stumps the deer browsed. I could have saved some of these stumps with fencing or by wrapping still-living shoots or spreading some kind of deer repellent. Although I believe most of human history and life is a struggle against nature, we have also learned when cooperation pays. Deer don't eat oyster mushrooms, so I decided to be content with harvesting the crops the habits of deer promoted.

Before the end of October, I decided to walk up Morgan Branch to its sources. The stream gathers waters from three little valleys below a ridge that curves from Saralyn lands in the south through the land I bought from Dr. Zhang and on to Merritt's land on the north. On a hill on the south side of the southernmost fork, I climbed among large old trees. My eyes were on the ground looking for rocks, mushrooms, and stump holes. When I looked up, I saw a bright blue plastic ribbon tied at eye level around a red oak. Beyond it, heading west, more blue ribbons. And more ribbons heading south. Here a surveyor had marked a corner where two property lines met. I followed the ribbons west along what would probably be the line between my land and the land of my Saralyn neighbors to the south.

The ribbons were the final result of a long and complex series of land divisions caused by divorces for Susan and Jason and Kathleen and Ralph. But those blue ribbons weren't the only boundaries being marked in the year I returned from Kazakhstan. My neighbors to the east, along Seven Spring Branch and Morgan Branch's northward run, hired a forester to help them manage their timber and lease hunting rights. As if the water courses might disappear or migrate a great distance, the forester painted broad orange bands every fifty feet. He also tacked up signs facing my way saying "No Trespassing or Hunting Without Permission." The couple who own that land are friends who came to see me even when they were on short visits from Mississippi or Texas. Their forester, however, knew how to paint a bold line no one could dispute.

The marking of boundaries has always revealed something about a local economy and what people value. The higher they value something, the more they fear their neighbors' trespass. When the Indians and the Lord Proprietors of England had possessed these lands, boundaries were stated but seldom well marked. Rivers, streams, coastlines, hilltops, and ridges were good enough. The Earl of Granville's agents sold a hundred acres for fifty shillings. They described it simply as "640 acres on the south side of the Haw River on both sides of Brooks Creek." Colonial surveyors could calculate and mark a precise straight line, but for most boundaries they let nature round off the difference. "From the white oak on Brooks Creek to a stone pile by Salem road to a large rock in Alston's pasture" was sometimes good enough. Boundaries were not worth arguing to the last yard or even the last acre. No one farmed every acre and trees were abundant.

When land was cheap, other possessions were much more carefully protected and catalogued. When Abraham Pilkington bought 133 acres across Drummonds Branch from my land in 1844 for nineteen cents an acre, an ordinary table or chest cost more than several acres of land. The price of a young slave might be more than the price of 1,000 acres. As land became more expensive, surveyors and lawyers began recording boundaries by the four compass points and by chains (one hundred links or sixty-six feet) and poles or rods (sixteen and one-half feet). "Running East Seventeen poles to a Dogwood, thence North two hundred and ninety-six poles to a Black Gum."

In 1875, the aging owner of large tracts sold 220 acres that included part of my land for $2.70 an acre. That $2.70 represented three days' wages for a farmhand. The price of the same acre today is almost a hundred times a farmhand's wages. An American earning a median year's income would spend more than a month's earnings to buy that acre. As the price of each acre rose, precision measurement became more important and affordable. Landowners began to pound iron spikes deep into the earth and paint lines with bright colors. Deeds now say, "thence a new line with Saralyn South 73 degrees 56 minutes 5 seconds East 885.09 feet to a stake in Saralyn Inc.'s eastern line." Even communism couldn't wipe out the territorial imperative: Across the lane from the house I rented in Kazakhstan, two old couples lived in a tiny duplex. The two husbands had argued and sometimes fought about every inch of the land and house to the point that one of them built a wire mesh fence across the yard, up the side of the building, over the roof, and on to their neighbor's fence. They grew old, each in silence and peace on his property. The fence was the last word of the last argument they had.

Americans were not less jealous of their property in 1850, 1770, or the year 1000 than they are today, but they balanced need and cost in choosing the degree of precision they ordered. How much precision and what kind of marking depends on who and where we are. Marking boundaries and defending territory is a universal trait among warm-blooded animals. Anyone who has walked a dog has seen the investigation or marking of boundaries. Cats, elephants, wrens, and deer mark their boundaries. Cats spray, wrens screech. As soon as fall starts in these woods, the bucks establish who rules a given territory. Without a clear sense of area, they simply mark bushes and the ground everywhere. Starting in September, I cannot walk a hundred yards without seeing a young cedar or maple rubbed raw where a buck has left his musk on a sapling. As fall gets colder, the bucks begin to paw the ground and urinate by their rubs. The songs I hear from cardinals, wrens, phoebes, and tanagers through spring and summer are their way of shouting their presence and their boundaries. The marking of animal territories is also no less economic than human marking. It's about who controls the currency of the animal world—nuts, grubs, game, browse, water, and sex.

The precision of humans in marking our boundaries is a credit to civilization. When we do have boundary disputes, we seldom attack each other violently. Maybe I should have been happy to have all my boundaries so well marked at no expense to me, but I was not. With my land now clearly marked on every side by paint, ribbons, and the edge of the clear-cut, my neighbors had unintentionally drawn a line around my life, or at least around what mattered most. I owned more land than most people in America can ever hope to own, but the drawing of boundaries said definitively that it was too little. It is too little because the boundaries drawn can have only one purpose, to tell me where I may at any time be unwelcome or where I may one morning find someone engaged in a very unwelcome assault on the land.

I have a friend who lives sixteen miles west of me far off the public road in a similar forest. We both have the same recurring nightmare: We come home from a day's travel and we find bulldozers roaring through the woods in sight of the house. New houses are already standing in their clearings; the woods are no longer ours. The dozers are building a highway or housing development. Everything we love most about where we live has been instantly lost.

I have always been in favor of private property with easily found borders, and I am not entirely sorry that my neighbors have marked their boundaries and mine. I know of more reasons for limiting people's freedom to wild places than for encouraging it. Not long ago when a prolonged autumn dry spell lowered the waters of Jordan Lake and exposed thousands of acres of submerged land, I walked along the lake bed looking for arrowheads. Boaters, picnickers, fishermen, and hunters using the lake and its surrounding lands in the seventeen years since it had become public had created an endless garbage dump of bottles, pieces of motors, tires, drink cans, coolers, plastic, foils, and paper. The world's greatest environmental tragedies are largely on public lands or lands to which no one has a secure title or protection for a claim. A few hills east of Morgan Branch, the common waters of the Haw River carry an endless load of both industry and city sewage. I can draw my water from my own rock or from Morgan Branch, but Pittsboro must take Haw River water and more than half of it has already passed through a factory processing line, a kitchen sink, a car wash, or at least one pair of human kidneys

I could not complain about boundaries marked so plainly around me, but I could still wish the marks were not there. They reminded me that my nightmare could come true. My control and the power of my wishes ended at the marked lines. They did not change my ownership or its rights at all, but before they appeared, I did not know and didn't want to know exactly where my land started and stopped. Without marked boundaries, I could still get lost if I tried.

I had been fortunate so far that for thousands of acres and several miles around me, the owners of the largest tracts had done less with their land than I had with mine, except for Merritt's clear-cut and smaller ones a few hills away. Nevertheless, I feared the boundaries and I coveted my neighbors' lands. If I were rich in dollars, I would be always at the ready to buy whatever my neighbors might sell, and at almost any price. I should like to assure myself that all of us who live in the woods now, myself and every animal, could always ramble farther than we habitually dwell.

Tolstoy was wrong. In "How Much Land Does a Man Need?" he made fun of the desire to possess land by concluding that we need only enough for burial. It's clever at first glance, but would anyone say the same of a lion or a turtle? A Carolina wren needs an acre. A white-tailed deer in a hardwood forest needs four or five acres. That does not vary much from wren to wren, or from deer to deer. Maybe the need was once uniform for all *Homo erectus* or Neanderthals.

If we talk only about the basics that an animal has—food and shelter—the human is a most marvelous animal indeed, the only one that has continuously decreased the territory that will supply basic needs. Humans tamed other animals so that we would not have to go so far to find an animal to kill. Agriculture adapted wild plants to grow in greater and greater concentrations with larger and larger seeds and fruits. The great variety of foods consumed by a resident of New York City or Moscow are now supplied from one or two acres. The land around Morgan Branch was cleared of farms and people because farmers with technology and science were producing more food from less land with less labor. In 1800, producing a hundred bushels of wheat required 344 hours of work. Farmers produced the same wheat in 1960 for ten times less labor on half the land.

The same intelligence that constantly produced more food and shelter from less land is also the source of our craving for more than the body needs. How much land and where a civilized person needs it varies wildly (if you will forgive the irony of the language.) People born in a big city and satisfied with urban life are willing to share a single street with hundreds of other human animals and their pets. People who move from the city to the country often think five acres can satisfy them. I thought five acres would be the minimum to achieve the goals of Saralyn—to separate houses from each other with trees and brush and to give wildlife a passage out of sight of people and their pets. At the time, five acres seemed enough for every person to enjoy a separate Walden.

I was wrong.

I had begun with twenty-four acres and bought more until I had 112 acres. I wanted thousands. The hundreds of stories whose threads I can find on, under, or over my land don't end at my neighbors' lines. My curiosity knows that my land contains few whole stories, but many beginnings and middles, and a few ends. A deer wants only what it needs. I need what my curiosity demands to know.

I confess this is the true mind of the environmental preservationist—everything is connected to everything else (the so-called first law of populist ecology), so that everything must be preserved. Dave Foreman, who founded the militant Earth First! eco-saboteurs who chained themselves to trees, drove spikes into sawmill logs, and destroyed earth-moving equipment, has also been the most honest about preservation. Foreman left Earth First! and founded The Wildlands Project, proposing to put almost 50 percent of the United States back into roadless wilderness:

> Our vision is simple: We live for the day when Grizzlies in Chihuahua have an unbroken connection to Grizzlies in Alaska; when Gray Wolf populations are restored from Durango to Labrador; when vast unbroken forests and flowing plains again thrive and support pre-Colombian populations of plants and animals. . . . To function properly, nature needs vast landscapes without roads, dams, motorized vehicles, power lines, over-flights, or other artifacts of

civilization, where evolutionary and ecological processes can continue. Such wild lands are absolutely essential to protect biodiversity.

This is not going to happen in North America or at Morgan Branch without erasing the property lines and ownership rights. That can only be done with enormous amounts of money or by applying the political power of a government dictatorship.

I am fortunate to own the headwaters of Morgan Branch, but if I follow its relations, I must go north to Dry Creek and then east to Haw River, then southeast to the Cape Fear River and down that river 150 miles to the Atlantic Ocean. Like the distant relatives of a family, no one there at the mouth of the Cape Fear watches the water run into the ocean and knows that some of it I bathed in at Morgan Branch. The story of Morgan Branch still reaches that far and farther.

In September, the ruby-throated hummingbirds that are born here in the summer return with their parents to Central America. A month later, slate gray juncos arrive for the winter from Canada. By Christmas, red finches arrive. The boundaries that have been marked around my land are none of their concern. They would never know as much about my boundaries as I knew about theirs, and that was very little. The meaning of these mathematically precise human boundaries was between my neighbors and me. It was their kind of musk, their spray on the earth, their warning call, their rubbing. We are kinder to each other than most animals. With permission, I could cross their lines, and if my neighbors were out for a walk, they were welcome to cross mine. Nevertheless, when the lines suddenly became clear, I knew they were there for a purpose and I knew their meaning—what you do on your land is not our concern, and what we might do on ours is not your business.

I had become the resident of a prison. Or perhaps it was a mental ward. I had come to Morgan Branch for my own good. I had committed myself. I knew I was free to leave.

–chapter 38–

Winter

I settle again into the routines and surprises of life around Morgan Branch, but each season asks a large question about my life.

Toward the end of November, a day always comes when a stronger than usual breeze removes the very last leaves from the trees. They rain down for hours on end, and the next day is suddenly brighter. The day after this breeze, no matter the date, that day is the beginning of a piedmont winter. In town, no one pays much attention except for dressing in heavier clothes. They have less work in the yard, they switch the thermostat from cool to heat, and they continue in whatever habits they have settled. A few will turn their weekend thoughts from east to west, from beaches to mountains and ski slopes. For me, the year changes profoundly, and it starts with light. We know that light and human moods were linked millions of years ago when the brain stem was evolving. I have no doubt that the sudden brightening of my days adds as much to the newness of the views around me as the new leaf fall or the coming of winter birds and colors. The sun now travels lower across the southern sky, reaches under the eaves, fills more of the windows, and reaches into parts of the house it never touches in summer. And from any high spot I can see a distant horizon that hid beyond trees all summer. When that first day of winter comes, the green sea has been drained, and I with every life around me seem to exist on a dry seabed. The brightness emphasizes the nakedness of the forest.

The season of survival, even in this mild climate, has begun. Nature will produce no more food until March. The deer begin to range farther. They push at the fence around the garden because the collards and turnips are still green in there. They eat cedar and nibble twigs; their struggle to survive is more visible. In the arctic, almost every living thing hibernates and becomes invisible under snow and ice; here in the piedmont, the lower end of the food chain withers—plants die or go dormant, bugs disappear, and grubs go underground. The decorations are stripped away and the struggle goes on.

When I walked out of the quiet house on a morning in late November after the leaves had fallen, I stepped into noise and frenzy. Thousands of birds were moving through the tops of the highest oak and poplar and warring with each other on the branches of the dogwoods and rummaging like hurried burglars through the leaves on the ground. Most of them were robins, but with the binoculars I found a few warblers. I stood and watched for a few minutes. They were a pillaging horde. Every year brought a few hordes like this. Twice I had hosted small flocks of grackles and cowbirds. Evening grosbeaks had passed through several times. The robin hordes and their hangers-on came every year, and sometimes in waves separated by a week or two.

The robins and I have nothing to do with each other because they don't come to the feeders, so I left them pillaging the woods and sat down to write. Outside the kitchen window and the window of my writing room are medium-sized dogwood trees. That year they were loaded with red berries. The brilliant red berries in the bare woods brightened my dark moods in the same way the mountains above Almaty did when I worked there. The lifting effect of the mountains and all their power I can account for. But why should a tree of inedible berries be cheerful? Bright red dots in the house, on someone's skin, on water, or in a plate of food are not usually sources of joy. The most joyous holiday of the year, Christmas, like its Roman antecedent, Saturnalia, calls for decking the halls with boughs of holly and its red berries. A neuropsychologist may find the answer one day, but it has nothing to do with logic.

A few minutes after I began writing, I became aware of movement outside the window: The robins had come to the dogwood tree. I saw among them one cedar waxwing with the bright yellow racing stripe across the end of its tail. A few yards away at the edge of the woods, a flicker moved from tree to tree in the chaos, never staying long in one place. In fifteen minutes, the robins had stripped my dogwood of all its red berries.

Nature made this process good for both the robin and the dogwood. (It left human happiness out of the equation.) The berries are no use to the dogwood species if they hang on the tree all winter only to fall to the ground below; there, they could only be competition for the parent. Nature's compromise between bird and tree has put the seed of the tree inside a berry whose meat nourishes birds. The bright color makes it easy to see, and if the bird that eats the berry needs red feathers to improve its sex life, the berry's pigments make their contribution to spring mating. By afternoon, the birds had left Morgan Branch and were carrying the dogwood seeds to a thousand other places. A few would become trees, crossbreed with other trees, and the cause of genetic diversity would be served. It would be served better than my aesthetic cause: I had hoped to have the bright red dogwood berries outside my window all winter. Someone might think a middle-aged man sulking over a few berries is a wimp. The stripping of the berries from my window was like having new wallpaper torn off the walls of a den or office.

Like many nature lovers, beauty first stirs me and fixes my attention. (Perhaps I should say "like lovers.") That magnetic beauty may lead to deeper interest and awe of natural processes. Sylvan's interest in nature had begun with collecting and drawing strange and colorful objects and it had progressed to graduate school at Rutgers to study ecology. Most people stay with the beauty or the exotic and accept a little science if it is in the service of beauty. Name any environmental campaign and you will see that it only gathers a critical weight of supporters when it makes its subject visually beautiful, or at least alluring and exotic. The most effective attacks on environmental regulations, such as the Endangered Species Act, are made using protected minnows, spiders, or rats, not eagles or owls. We have baseball teams named for big, fierce, or cute animals—Bears, Cubs, Dolphins, Tigers, Orioles, even burly meat packers—but where are the Baltimore Bats, the Miami Mice, Atlanta Ants, or the Washington Worms?

The result of the beauty bias is that in 1990, mammals and birds were getting 74 percent of the money spent on endangered species, with the spotted owl, grizzly bear, panther, ocelot, jaguarundi, and bald eagle in the top ten. Animals without backbones and the world of plants got only 5 percent of the funds. The message to the smaller animals that make the world work is "Get a backbone." Where would the big cats, bears, and birds be without them?

I was irritated with the birds for taking the berries, and I was disappointed they would not cheer me the rest of the winter, but my feelings, like feelings about most endangered plants and animals, were really about me. I could be less self-centered and say I was sad for the berries and the dogwood, but that's not better than the kind of tears politicians shed for children or old people when what they want most is votes. Gerard Manley Hopkins, the Jesuit poet of the nineteenth century, put the question bluntly to a young girl who was sad about the falling of yellow leaves in autumn:

> Margaret, are you grieving
> Over Goldengrove unleaving?
> Leaves, like the things of man, you
> With your fresh thought care for, can you? . . .
>
> It is the blight man was born for,
> It is Margaret you mourn for.

Robins and waxwings work only for their own bellies and have no mind for beauty. When Margaret and I and other environmentalists grieve for beauty, we usually have little mind for nature and less for science. I lived at Morgan Branch first of all for its beauty. Science made that beauty more interesting, but I could study the science of the place even if it were surrounded by factories and the rush of superhighways. Chatham County's growth had changed so much while I was in Kazakhstan that I began to wonder how much longer Morgan Branch could be wild.

By the time Sylvan arrived for Christmas in 1995, I had begun to think about leaving for good. She had not been at Morgan Branch for two years, and we had a Russian family with us for the holidays. We poked about the woods as we always did. We picked mushrooms from the poplar stumps. Sylvan remarked on the new houses along the paved roads outside Saralyn. I told her how Pittsboro had extended its planning area all the way to the entrance of Saralyn, but I didn't tell her I had begun thinking about leaving or that these new houses were making that decision more possible and more attractive. The growth in this part of North Carolina had made my land valuable. I could sell it, and somewhere else in the world I could buy land with boundaries I would find after an hour's walk or a day's hike instead of a few minutes.

I carried my thoughts into winter, but I settled into the routines. I collected mushrooms. I cut and split wood. I cleared springs. I trimmed the new growth of stumps. All the time I kept returning to the proposition—why not sell and go somewhere else? Yet when friends came to visit, they often suggested the opposite: Why go somewhere else when I had Morgan Branch?

To them a beautiful forest like this had all the natural communion anyone could hope for. Michael came down with his second wife, the singer and song writer Cathie Ryan, and Michael asked if I would think about selling them part of my land. Most visitors came in the best weather. We would walk up or down Morgan Branch, pick mushrooms, watch birds, dig clay from the creek, and return to the house. Their experience was a spot in time, a snapshot. From my experience I drew a sense of momentum. Visitors compared Morgan Branch to where they lived. I saw it and this entire part of the county for what they were, and what they were becoming.

I had been to the rain forests, to the arctic tundra, to islands in the Sea of Okhotsk teeming with subarctic birds and flowers, to the steppes of Mongolia, and to the glaciers of the Celestial Mountains at the union of China, Kazakhstan, and Kyrgyzstan. Those places had become my measures of what wild and natural meant. Compared to the vastness of the tundra, the endless Siberian forests, or glaciers grinding the world's greatest mountains to dust, my wild place at Morgan Branch was a small and fragile place surrounded by blue ribbons and bright paint. I could not yet live in those wilder places, but I had begun to think about the many choices between here and there.

I was not the only one concerned about the changes in Chatham County. As I was packing up my books and papers in Kazakhstan, some of my friends had embarked on a new effort to save what they considered beautiful. It was an effort that might cast the mantle of government preservation over a band of land up and down the Haw River, including Morgan Branch. For the third time in local history, the county commissioners decided to adopt a land-use plan—guidelines for locating or prohibiting everything from factories to greenbelts.

The county had adopted its first plan in 1970, but its pleasant words were more open to interpretation than the Bible. The county commissioners by and large ignored their old land-use plan. They had permitted subdivisions almost anywhere they were proposed, and by running water lines along rural roads they tempted more development. As more and more rural landowners sold to developers and businesses, newcomers organized opposition groups.

Several canoe and kayak enthusiasts formed The Haw River Assembly to fight pollution in the river. A businessman recently arrived from New Hampshire formed the Chatham 2000 alliance to publicize the cause of land-use planning. Ad hoc groups galvanized to oppose a four-lane by-pass around the north side of Pittsboro and subdivisions of more than a thousand houses, one next to Saralyn and one up the river a couple of miles. Those two subdivisions were among the few defeats for developers. The repeated rallying cry in the fight against development was always "save the rural character" of the county. Conspicuously absent among the ranks of the activists fighting to preserve rural character were rural characters themselves. In fact, the activists were almost always squared off against rural characters who had made up the five-member board of commissioners from time immemorial.

As more and more white-collar people had moved into the county in the wake of the back-to-the-land people, battles for seats on the planning board and the board of commissioners had heated up. The commissioners put a few environmentalists on the planning board, then voted against their most important recommendations. The planning-board member who proposed the new land-use plan in 1995 was my neighbor Susan who had come to Chatham County as a goatherd. After I had returned to the county, I attended a few of the meetings that were supposed to produce the new land-use plan. A young and earnest facilitator from a regional planning commission led the meetings. They droned on month after month and filled multiple scratch boards. They would continue for several years.

The supporters of a new land-use plan argued that farms and woodlands and land along rivers and streams should be protected for the sake of wildlife, biodiversity, natural balance, the fight against global warming, preservation of the family farm, a local food supply, and the health of the human spirit.

Lynn Barrett, a feisty farm mother with a long history in this area, joined the debate when one of the newest commissioners posted a note to the county's electronic discussion group. The commissioner, the first ever to call himself an environmentalist, had won his seat handily with the enthusiastic support of a liberal coalition. He was a one-time journalist turned Realtor and preacher and given to hugging his constituents in the manner of modern congregations when they "pass the peace" among each other. He promised that a land-use plan would benefit all citizens; it would be the result of "our collective vision."

The farm mother shot back, "Count me out of anything with the word 'collective' in it, please. Why do you growth controllers feel so constrained to put your government fingers on everything around you? Most of you would not be here if the original residents of Chatham County had wanted to control what they had *then*, you know."

A woman who had retired from up north tried to be conciliatory. "I think the problem is we don't know who we are yet," she said.

A planning-board member and old-guard Democratic Party activist asked wryly, "Who is '*we*'?"

The commonsense and understood meaning of "original residents" meant people who were born here in the days before Saralyn and the wave of newcomers that followed. They didn't want to maintain their status quo because by and large it kept them in poverty and hardship. Most of us who had come later had come because we could afford to come, and we thought the county's poverty would protect us from the things we didn't like about America's richer communities. I was no different from anyone else in wanting to preserve what I had come for. We were guilty as charged by the farm wife who warned the commissioner, "Don't take away *my* liberties for your aesthetics, please."

This difference of opinion is a larger version of the birds and my berries. The birds and I both needed the berries for the same reason—because winter strips the woods. Their need was the need of all animals, hunger. My need for the berries and the attempts to preserve the "rural character" of Chatham were the special needs of the human animal. John Keats caught it in his "Ode on a Grecian Urn," the poem that contemplates the painted figures of happy Greeks about to eat grapes and make love, and of a musician playing a tune that can only be imagined:

> Fair youth, beneath the trees, thou canst not leave
> Thy song, nor ever can those trees be bare. . . .
>
> Forever wilt thou love, and she be fair!

Preserve this moment forever. That sentiment brought out the supporters of the new land-use plan. The vision fills environmental books and films and turns citizens into lobbyists. Keep this species or that species. Maintain these forests as they are for us. Forget that this forest has been this way for only an instant of geological time. It is our time that counts. Keep the red berries, at least through the winter until we desert them for the carnival of spring. I will not stop reading the brilliantly expressed lines of Keats, but I am glad I stopped believing his conclusion: Beauty is truth, truth beauty. No. Beauty is pleasure, but not truth.

If we are going to extend our survival on this planet, we must be sure not to equate truth and beauty. If the robins are going to survive, I must let them have the berries. If I am going to get through the winters of life that surely will be colder and darker than any at Morgan Branch or on the arctic shores, I will have to let go of the red berries and understand that my life will continue to change. I will continue moving on through success and failure, not like the people frozen in their beautiful lives on the Greek urn, but like the birds moving through my woods to avoid freezing in winter.

Developers are a lot more flexible than robins and they can do without a good deal of land and water that's worth preserving for its beauty or resources, but preservation has the power to kill as surely as my preferences could starve the birds. In fact, that winter I was reminded that even the birds might prefer development to the forest.

Winter in the piedmont is indecisive. The first skim of ice on a puddle or water bucket may appear in late October or not until after Thanksgiving. Nine out of ten years I can count on a week of weather so cold that ponds freeze over and I can skate for a day or two. Those two days may come in early January or late February. I know that in the same two months we will have at least one five-day period when the temperature rises to seventy or higher; the spring peepers suddenly sing hard and loud along Morgan Branch and the anole lizards come out and sun themselves along the edges of the south windows of my writing room. But most of the winter is bare, cold, and damp.

The indecisive winter brings only one fine event from my point of view, and January brought a winner. At least two or three times each winter an arctic-like mass of cold air moves down from the north and meets a warm and wet air mass moving up from the Gulf of Mexico. The warm wet air rides up over the heavier cold air. The rain falls too fast to freeze into sleet or snow, but it is ready. In the darkness, whatever warmth of sun and daylight has gathered in twigs and limbs and leaves radiates back into the night. As soon as the rain touches any cold object, it instantly turns to ice.

Sylvan and my guests had been gone only a week and 1996 was five days old when it happened again. Late in the day, ice began to cover the forest as a paper-thin layer. During the night it smoothed all angles and points of branch and twig and stone. Hollies no taller than I am took on a hundred pounds of ice. Pines and maples bore a ton and their trunks bent into deeper and deeper bows with every additional pound. I opened the door and went outside to listen. The rain fell softly, but the forest rang with shots like a battleground full of snipers shooting from one direction, then the next. The trees with the greatest number of twigs and small branches started shedding first. Then brittle maple trunks began cracking. The slender pines that had grown for ten or twenty years along the Saralyn road bent over the electric lines; some broke and left their crowns dangling on the wires. The lights went out before midnight.

I always get up at dawn after an ice storm. I walked out away from the house to watch the sun come through the ice-coated trees. The display cases at Tiffany's are meager compared to the morning after an ice storm at Morgan Branch. The light ricocheted through the trees, each twig and limb and branch broke it into millions of small suns. I walked along Morgan Branch and enjoyed the wealth of jewelry. I don't have it quite as often as someone might wear a diamond tiepin or necklace, but I have so much more, and I don't worry about theft.

When I returned from my walk in the ice, I made sure the bird feeders were full. During the entire winter no time is more dangerous for birds. More than ever they needed energy to burn against the damp and cold. Only in ice storms is every source of food available locked in ice. The birds came to the feeder in a frenzy. They kept each hole in the long plastic feeder constantly occupied. They beat at each other. Finches pecked at finches. Several times a day a bird would smash against the window and leave an oil smudge and a few downy feathers. Sometimes the bird fell stunned or dead to the porch. The wrens, smallest of them all, seemed to have their way by sheer bravado, speed, and maybe a sharp beak. The woods stayed iced over for a second day. The ice made the Pace Mill Road impossible, and I was running out of seed. If I couldn't or didn't go out soon, a lot of the birds would die. The sun rose a third day, filling the woods with diamonds but melting nothing. I began rationing the seed.

Like so many things in nature, what is a rare and beautiful event for one means slaughter for others.

The feeding frenzy made me remember many years earlier stopping by the home of a very old man in Chapel Hill during a deep snow. He asked me to fill his bird feeder and suet block. I did it and watched the birds gather. If the birds could have known that subdivisions were a few miles away, Pittsboro six, Chapel Hill sixteen, they could have eaten from thousands of feeders. I thought about this and watched the birds at my dwindling supply of seeds, and I remembered that when I was a kid we threw crumbs out for the birds. That's all most people did. In the 1970s, however, rising incomes, technology in farming, and suburban sprawl made well-stocked bird feeders common. Cardinals and mockingbirds, until then rarely sighted north of the Mason-Dixon line, began to show up in New York and New England. The birds at my feeder would not live long enough to see suburbs take over around Morgan Branch, but if the suburbs were to happen, my birds' descendants would welcome them. If wild animals could have a vote on the county planning board and commission, they would be as split in their judgments as the humans.

Not long after the ice storm, I welcomed a heavy snow. It fell through the night into its own silence. The bright morning was just as silent. When I looked out on the deep snow, I was immediately surprised to see that it had even managed to close its cover over the Morgan Branch in places, breaking its course into a serious of small black squiggles, hieroglyphs, or ideograms cut deep into the *tabula rasa*. Directly in front of the house was a familiar form, a question mark. I thought of Frost's couplet:

> God, if you'll forgive my little jokes on thee,
> I'll forgive your great big joke on me.

I am not superstitious. I have never been blessed with the kind of faith that enables me to distinguish accidents of nature from signs from God.

The thick black question mark in the snow was the kind of joke that said, "Aha, you didn't think you would be asked again." Maybe because I have spent so much time wondering what to say on blank white pages, an expanse of new snow sometimes lays before me like a question, especially if it comes in the middle of trouble. It asked of me the same question that every blank piece of paper has asked of me, "What is the answer?" I could have asked, "What is the question?" as Gertrude Stein was reputed to have asked on her deathbed. I knew there was not a specific question, at least not a question with a single answer. It was the same question I used to worry to death when I was an unhappy kid hiding out on the deserted beach in the wintertime, hoping I would hear some answer out of the noise of waves or in the random crying of gulls. The question, because it was a feeling, could take a number of forms if it needed words: What is this all about? Why do you exist? Where are you going?

The only time such questions have not troubled me is when I've been in love. At other times I have tried to quiet the questions by losing myself in work, in other peoples' problems, and by taking off the lead shoes and weak eyes of reason. When my first marriage ended, I went to a Zen *sesshin* with my neighbors Kathleen and Nicholas. I sat on the brick floor of a Convent in Princeton, New Jersey, for two solid weeks trying to hush up or set aside my reason and answer the Roshi's question, "What is the nature of the pine tree outside?" I don't have the power of concentration or the power of will to quiet all the voices inside of me long enough to hear one hand clapping. Snow falling on snow is the closest answer I can give to "What is the sound of one hand clapping?"

If a Creator exists, I have no doubt that his or her mind can be found through the study of nature. On a grand scale, this is no stranger than a person's knowing my skills, my hopes, my pleasures, and my character because he pays close attention to the house I have built and everything I have put in it and around it. Isn't something exactly like this the ultimate and unspoken hope of science—to read the message? Galileo, Newton, and Einstein said *yes*.

Three hundred years ago, John Bartram and his son William came through the Carolinas to study plants and animals and send specimens to their English patron, the wool merchant Peter Collinson, who lavished a good part of his fortune on their studies. These men believed in science, but they were also looking for the mind of God. Collinson made this observation in a letter to William Bartram: "There is no end to the wonders of Nature. The more I see, the more I covet to see; not to gratify a trifling curiosity but to raise my mind in contemplation on the unlimited power and wisdom of the Great Creator of all things."

That winter morning in Carolina when I looked at the question mark in the snow over Morgan Branch, I laughed. Nature was playing Zen master again. I knew the answer was out there, all around me, and I knew I wouldn't find it, and no one would find it in my lifetime. The answer could be found anywhere in the world—inside a single cell in my body, in a city, among tube worms at the ocean floor, or on the planet of another star. In 1992, two biologists surveying the county for unique plants, animals, geology, and landscapes had examined my land. They found nothing unusual, nothing that could not be found in many other places. Why worry about this forest at Morgan Branch?

I could go on living at Morgan Branch with or without answers. Because I had watched life come and go here for more than twenty years, I was getting a sense of the rhythm of the place. My study had not been methodical, but because I had been watching so long I had made what scientists call a longitudinal study. The waist-high cedar that I left growing at the corner of my house rises above the roof. Summer and winter birds make their night shelter in it. The walnut I planted by the first garden near Morgan Branch bears walnuts every year. During the drought of 1976, a huge red oak died on the hillside opposite the house across the Branch. Two years later, I heard it fall. When I saw the question mark in the snow, the tree had rotted away.

I could stay here and watch it another twenty years, maybe another forty years. I would learn more, but I knew that if I looked out and saw that question mark forty years later, I still would not have the answer. I decided to narrow the question. What should I do with this forest? That was a question I might be able to answer.

chapter 39

The Storm to End All Dreams

*Overnight, a hurricane transforms my forest and my
life. It writes "The End" to dreams and to this book.*

In the last week of August 1996, I returned to Morgan Branch from several
weeks on the shores of the Russian arctic. I had gone to Cape Schmidt to
take pictures for my friend Bob Gleason, who had spent the winter of 1929,
at twenty-two years old, frozen in on the trading schooner *Nanuk*. The native village that Bob had known, with a single Russian commissar and
small warehouse, no longer existed. When I arrived, Cape Schmidt was a
town of 2,000 people and a military base. The once-pristine shore was littered with fuel barrels, junked boats and airplanes, the carcasses of trucks,
and all the garbage that had once been necessary to the town but was now
too expensive to take out. The arctic boom ended with the Soviet bust. In
1996, the town had already lost a thousand people, and everyone else was
planning to leave. The same economic laws that had once restored the forest to Morgan Branch would soon restore wilderness to Cape Schmidt.

I had left summer in the piedmont glad for a breath of cold air. I looked
forward to being scrubbed clean by north winds. Thanks to a Russian friend,
I spent my time walking the stony beaches and watching the pack ice drift
by. I picked mushrooms from the tundra. I hiked in the hills and watched the
hawks soaring and screaming above the ridges. I stood waist deep fishing in

the powerful rush of ice-water rivers. I raked berries out of the tundra sponge with my fingers. On the tundra, I was the tallest living thing, twice as tall as the desperate clumps of juniper bushes. The August days up there still stretched from four in the morning until one at night. The day before I left Cape Schmidt, the first snows fell and summer had ended. The first morning back at Morgan Branch, I felt as if I had awoken from a long dream.

Summer's frenzy of growth and reproduction had slowed into a sultry rest. Birds that had filled the air with song from April to July called occasionally. Morgan Branch had dried to a trickle. The lettuce and peas in the garden had long ago given up. Tomatoes, their best performance finished, had wilted. The okra, an African vegetable, was growing skyward faster than the runner beans could climb their stalks. The heat spawned thunderstorms and heavy warm rains; the rains brought out mushrooms, but in the heat they writhed with fly maggots. The summer had come to a heavy, dark slumbering maturity.

Three thousand miles southeast off the Atlantic coast of Africa, a breeze began to gather strength from the air rising off warm ocean waters. The rising air formed a trough of low pressure. It moved over open water westward toward the Americas. As August turned into September, the low pressure trough twisted itself into a circling tropical storm, then approached the Caribbean at hurricane strength. Meteorologists named it Fran.

On September 7, the wind from Africa had crossed the Atlantic Ocean and the shallow waters off Cape Fear. Without the slightest pause to consider turning north up the coast as almost all storms do, Fran entered the mouth of the Cape Fear River. Like the settlers who had come from England three hundred years earlier, Fran followed the river's valley inland. She was following it northwest directly toward the forest where I was once again working—building a new pump house and writing about the history of the Russian arctic. The writing was my way of living in one landscape without losing the other.

Morgan Branch and everyone who has lived along it has been blessed and burdened with hills and valleys. In an old forest, the trees and the hills break winds. My house, below the rise of close hills on the north and south and a half mile to the east and west, has been immune to the winds of swift frontal storms that occasionally rush across flatter lands near Pittsboro or on the coastal plains that begin forty miles east. On a summer day when a storm has rushed across Pittsboro, my mother calls and asks if I'm okay.

The woods are wet, the trees have blown around, but at ground level I have noticed only a strong breeze.

In the twenty-six years since I first saw this land, nature has visited with ice storms, snowstorms, the blackest thunderstorms, and the winds of suddenly clashing cold and warm fronts. Now and then a tree has fallen, but when I talk to people from flatter areas, they always describe wind and destruction that resemble a storm quite different from the one that passed over Morgan Branch.

Hurricane Fran's winds arrived at Morgan Branch and I felt them. By dark, the winds were whipping the heavy tops of trees and blasting rain against the walls. The electricity flickered several times after dusk, then died decisively at about nine o'clock. The electricity goes out here several times a year—in ice storms, heavy snowstorms, and occasionally in a hard wind, but it seldom signals disaster. I had already run a few pots of water and set two tin wash basins under the eaves so that I could wash and cook without the pump. I had lived here several years without a well. I had candles and kerosene lamps. I went to bed knowing that by morning the storm would have passed and I would enjoy the brightly scrubbed sky that follows hurricanes. I was also sure that as usual the shelter of my valley would protect me from serious damage.

Once every twenty or thirty years hurricanes or their land-tattered winds have passed this way, and each season brings a few brief but powerful windstorms. Not much changes. The trees suffer more from ice storms and snow, but silent drizzle causes greater damage on nights when the temperature hovers at freezing. The forest survives.

For over a quarter of a century I had watched these trees. I thought of them as the dinosaurs of the plant world. If I looked at them with the tundra in mind, they amazed me—so many huge plants springing up out of the earth, rising so far, so much weight poised in the sky. Occasionally, sitting on my porch on the stillest of days, I had heard and seen a giant fall. Perhaps a worm or a fungus severed one last finger-thick root. Maybe in wet and soft soil the tree's grip pulled loose a critical anchor stone.

Several times on the night of September 7 I woke to the storm pounding rain against the roof and windows and rushing by in squalls that sounded like freight trains. Every year brings a few squalls in thunderstorms, but in an entire year we don't have as many as I was hearing that one night. Once or twice I heard a limb crack and maybe the rush of a tree falling, but it was hard to know in the general noise. Toward dawn, the noise softened and I made up for lost sleep.

I went out in bright sunlight at eight o'clock. I turned to look down the drive to the little building a hundred feet away that serves as my writing room. I couldn't see it. Two oaks had fallen between the house and the office. I made my way around the crowns and I saw the building, barely. Three oaks falling from the north side had hidden my room inside their thick crowns, the top branches now draped over the roof and hanging in front of the windows across the drive and into the two apple trees.

I had been particularly unlucky, I thought. Why did the few trees to come down do it on my writing room? Never mind. A few hours with a chain saw and I would have the driveway cleared. If this was my luck, others may have suffered worse, possibly much worse. Because mine was the most sheltered of the houses in this part of the county, I decided to walk out to the main road that served about thirty homes south of me, all surrounded by forest. I didn't walk the length of my driveway. I climbed.

Over a hundred large trees, mostly red and white oaks and hickory, had fallen across the old Pace Mill Road, sometimes three and four in a bunch. Sometimes one had fallen against another, which had fallen against a third until the combined weight brought them all down like dominoes. I have climbed many trees vertically, but few horizontally. Walking in the crown of a live tree is a rare visit. I could marvel at that even amid the destruction. Maybe I was in shock, at least vicarious shock. I was perfectly healthy, but the trees, including many I had admired for years, were the living dead. The wind's relentless buffeting of the trees' rain-heavy, leaf-thick crowns had pushed most of them down. It was like shoving a tall man carrying cement blocks on his shoulders. The counterclockwise hurricane winds had pushed from the north only, the force against the heavy crowns breaking the roots out of the soil soaked by earlier rains. The principal roots still grasped soil and rocks. The base of each tree was a discus of dirt and root rising five, ten, and fifteen feet from the ground. The felled trees still drew water and nutrients from their trunks and roots, but they would quickly exhaust those stores. They were mortally wounded and beyond all help. Not one could be saved.

I had looked up to the shade of their crowns in summer, admired their forms in winter. Finding whole trees lying before me and walking up a trunk into the once unreachable crown had the intimacy of suddenly being admitted into a series of inner sanctums blasted open. I climbed and walked, climbed and walked. The power lines also ran this way between the road and the branch, but their corridor was now clear, the wires torn down between every set of poles. I was feeling unluckier all the time, but amazement kept disappointment at bay.

My Saralyn neighbors had had much better luck. Trees had fallen across the main road, but in the two miles that our community maintains together, not as many trees had fallen as they had on my driveway. A few other people were out surveying the damage and shaking their heads. We were all safe and we laughed with relief. Later in the day, we cleared the common roads with half a dozen chain saws. Jason, Susan and her husband, Dave, and another neighbor helped cut on my driveway. We cut for three days. We cut the narrowest path possible to let in a vehicle. Kathleen and Nicholas came with their tractor to drag off the heaviest logs. When we were done, the driveway looked like a road cut through a series of closely spaced log stockades. The neighbors agreed no place in the community had been hit this hard.

Seven Spring Branch begins near Susan and Dave's and parallels my drive to Morgan Branch; Morgan Branch then absorbs it and runs due north down a U-shaped valley between rounded hills toward the Haw River. Hurricane winds turn counterclockwise. The eye of the storm passed east of us; our winds had come out of the north. For almost a mile before they came to my land, they blew across Merritt's clear-cut. Where Morgan Branch flows north through Merritt's, its valley is flatter than in my land. The wind, like a cresting wave, reached the corner of my land on Morgan Branch. Here it rushed against the suddenly higher hills and the forest. The hills funneled the wall of rushing air into the valley that Morgan Branch had been carving for at least 50,000 years.

The usual southwest winds had always blown across the valley. Beech trees with enormous crowns had locked their branches across the creek; from April to November, their thick shade kept the waters cold and clear, the banks thick with moss. Morgan Branch lived in solid possession of the world it had made. Here I often picked orange and black chanterelle mushrooms on the slopes. Barred owls found the valley so dusky that they hunted in midafternoon, soaring easily through the open forest. Kingfishers sometimes sat on a low limb and plucked fish from the clear water. Because the water was always cold, it held more oxygen than most southern waters and it supported more life—minnows, crayfish, migrating eels, water snakes, frogs.

Mercifully, the leaves on the fallen trees were still so thick that I could not see the fullness of destruction until they began to wither and drop a few weeks later. At first, I could see only the opening in the forest. I could see a jumble of limbs and leaves, but I could not see the actual bodies. I started cutting open my favorite walking path, the faint flat terrace of Pace Mill Road that follows Morgan Branch north. I cut for two hours and made a path only a few yards through a barrier of fallen beech, oak, and poplar. Twenty feet down the path lay another mass, and beyond that another, and then destruction as far as I could see.

Above the fallen trees where their canopy once formed a green roof, I saw open sky, a highway of sky two hundred yards wide. It looked as if a jumbo jet had flown up the valley a few yards above the ground. Or as if the Department of Transportation had come in during the night and knocked down trees for a superhighway corridor. Here was a piece of my re-curring nightmare—that I return home one day and find someone is clear-ing a road within sight of the house.

By the time the leaves withered and dropped, I had walked over the rest of the land. The hills were not as thoroughly devastated as the valley of Morgan Branch, but they were strewn with trees, and I labored harder to walk on this land than in a logger's fresh clear-cut. Everywhere the biggest trees had been pushed over. In their falling, they usually pulled down younger trees or snapped their trunks a few feet or a few yards above the ground. Some oaks and maples even a foot in diameter were supple enough to have arced beneath the weight and bowed their tops to earth. The big trees pinned the bowed tops of the arched trees to the ground. All over the forest these younger trees formed natural archways.

Again I had the sense of walking over live bodies. The big trees on the ground were normal trees, green, almost undamaged. They had fallen slowly, leaning against others, pushing over lower trees as they fell. The small, springy branches of the crowns hit the ground first and cushioned the crash. The trees lay there almost intact; they just happened to be hori-zontal. Their new position made no difference to the squirrels: They were busy as usual gathering acorns and hickory nuts. When you have been with trees for a few decades and you learn to see them, each one tells a story in the way it grows, in the reach of its roots, in the lean of its trunk; it tells a story in the scars on the bark, in the marks of animals, in the bias of branches, and in the full symmetry of a crown that has conquered all com-petition for light. The older the tree, the longer and more intricate the story. All these stories had ended. One night, one act of nature had ended them.

I wanted to set the trees upright the way you can raise up a few rows of corn knocked over by a thunderstorm. What I really wanted was to set nature back on the course it had followed steadily and quietly through hundreds of years until September 7. Standing them up again and connecting the severed roots would have required Dr. Doolittle of the Trees as well as a Paul Bunyan of restoration ecology. The most beautiful part of my forest, the old growth, was down, and in a few days it would be dead.

When I walked through the wreckage of my forest, I knew that when summer came again, Morgan Branch valley would explode in a jungle of briars, poison ivy, cat briar, blackberry, and spiky *eleagnes*. I find this kind of young landscape hard to like and impossible to love. I am a human and I want to walk through my landscapes, not break my way through vines and thorns laden with ticks. I am not a rabbit, a warbler, a mouse, a fox, or a hawk. They all thrive in cutover land, the places Georgia Pacific, Weyerhauser, Willamette, or my neighbors make when they take down every tree in sight and replant.

It occurred to me one day as I was thinking about all this, trying to make sense of it, that no logger I had ever seen had been so wantonly destructive as this act of nature. Every logger now left a fifty-foot buffer along permanent creek beds. Few would bother to cut an old beech or a really big red oak because chances are it has heart rot and hollow spots.

Nature had been no kinder to this forest than God was to Job. Like the arctic river tearing at my legs or deadly winter on the tundra, nature would have had no remorse at all, would have been quite without conscience, had her storm dropped a tree through my roof and crushed me in bed. Nature would as soon make tundra out of forest as ice out of water. She makes black holes out of brilliant stars. She would as soon make maggot meat out of a squishy little human being as offer him or her a fine view.

If anyone was looking out for me on the night of Fran when the big trees came thundering down around the house, it was not Gaia, not Mother Nature. It was a more traditional god, the one whose words command us to "be fruitful and multiply, fill the earth and subdue it; and have dominion over the fish of the sea and over the birds of the air and over every living thing that moves upon the earth." What nature had done to me and the forest around me made me wonder if such an event might move Vice President Al Gore rethink his recommendation that we try harder to commune with nature. He blames materialism for spoiling our communion. He has it backward. The material things that protect us from nature—say hiking boots, foam sleeping pads, binoculars, wet suits, thermal-pane windows, and fiberglass insulation—those are the things that allow us the widest communion with nature and recovery from insults like Hurricane Fran.

I looked around at the trees left in the forest. It was still a forest, although the storm had reduced its average age by more than half a century. Of the few large trees left, some were quite close to the house. A sixty-foot red oak and a seventy-foot poplar still stood behind the house. With an eye sharpened by recent betrayal, I noticed they were inclined toward the house (and not favorably).

My covenants prohibited disturbing a lot of nature, but fortunately I was not in the position of some environmental groups. When the Nature Conservancy received the gift of the forty-two-acre Cathedral Pines in Cornwall, Connecticut, they were happy to sign the condition agreeing to keep the land in a natural state. The white pines were two hundred years old and 150 feet tall. In 1989, a hurricane crossed Long Island, roared across Long Island Sound, and cut down the grove as if with a scythe. Its natural state was then a junk heap of lumber like the forest at Morgan Branch.

Something similar had happened to the sixty-acre virgin forest purchased by Rutgers University. Descriptions of the land in the 1700s tell of an old-growth oak and hickory forest where a wagon could drive between the trees. That natural forest, celebrated by *Life* and *Audubon* magazines, was not natural at all; it was the result of centuries of native burning of undergrowth and saplings. This "natural" forest fell victim to storms that blew down the old trees. Sun-loving vines and weed trees then invaded the clearings. Much of Rutgers' ancient forest is a New Jersey thicket. I decided I would reshape my forest and protect my buildings, too.

In November, I bought a big chain saw, a Stihl 041 with a twenty-one-inch bar. I cut the trees that threatened the house; the Stihl chewed through the huge trunks like butter. I began to work my way north and south on Pace Mill Road, cutting the trees back from the right-of-way, cutting limbs and trunks to firewood length, and splitting and stacking these into neat piles. At two of my favorite pools on Seven Spring Branch, I cut away a mess of wood. I cut trees off other trees so they could grow again. I plunged into blow-downs twenty feet high and destroyed them limb by limb. The voice of my Stihl 041 and the crash of limbs and the crack of splitting wood filled the forest, or what was left of it. The first thing to rise among the dead in this forest had to be me.

chapter 40

Revenge and Recovery

I am invaded by city trees. Nature's disregard for my preferences and its acceptance of the destruction tempts me to agree with the despair of a famous lawyer. I look the future in the eye and make a decision.

My first considered reaction to the storm's insult was violent, vengeful, and useful. I bought a "Monster Maul." The maul is a three-foot-long iron bar of steel with a twenty-pound triangle welded to its splitting end. I became a wood-splitting maniac. I cut fallen trees into two-foot sections, stood them up along the old Pace Mill Road, then attacked. I began making order out of chaos, pyramids of wood six feet high and twenty feet long. For two years after the storm, I swung that maul through thousands of sections of the trees whose shade I used to enjoy. I worked at it until my heart banged on my ribs and I gasped for breath. Sometimes I would be so tired that I lay down on the ground to rest. I would lie there watching the sky and listening to my heart and laugh at myself. I was still trying to change the world.

When Sarah and I had the farm, I used to collapse like this after plowing the thick clay. I had worked like this hacking, pounding, and prying the rock to prepare the hillside for the foundation of my house. Sarah had done well as a lawyer, then law professor, then associate dean of a law school, and once or twice every year she would go someplace where the sun was warm and there was not much to do but swim and eat and drink and see the local sights. My last trip to the beach had been the summer before the storm when I watched the icebergs moving along the rocky garbage-strewn shore of Cape Schmidt.

> Two roads diverged in a wood, and I—
> I took the one less traveled by,
> And that has made all the difference.

The piles of split wood sat along the Pace Mill Road, between trees in the woods, and rose to the rafters of the woodshed outside the front door. The crack of splitting wood, the growing order of the piles, the prospect of free heat—all this was satisfying, but in the larger picture it was sound and fury signifying nothing. The trees that had fallen could heat my house for a hundred years, but three years after the storm they would be too rotten for firewood. I might clean a beauty strip along Pace Mill Road, but most of the trees would lie where they had fallen—rotting, giving up their carbon stores to the air as they decayed, adding to the greenhouse gases that are supposed to be building toward planetary disaster.

A few months after the storm, I called Doug Robbins, a logger I knew. "Wallace," he said, "to tell you the truth more hardwood came down in that storm than this region would have cut in seven years. Nobody wants it."

"Wouldn't it be worthwhile to cut it and store it till demand returns?"

"Maybe, but who's got the time? We're all busy."

"That's a lot of wonderful wood that is going to lie on the ground and rot."

"Yep."

How wasteful of nature, I thought. No market economy run by human beings would ever have cut more trees than it could sell profitably. In the hundred-mile swathe the storm cut across North Carolina, over 8.7 billion board feet of timber had been felled in one night. With winter rains and snows soaking the land, I called Doug Robbins again. "This wet weather slowing you down any?" I asked him. If I remembered correctly, he had a daughter in college.

"Well, it's kept me out of the woods now and then," he allowed.

"My land is pretty well drained and you could probably work on it most days without getting bogged down."

"Maybe I could," he said. "It's got some hills in it I don't like. But maybe I could. Let me think about it."

Doug found a mill willing to take the logs to cut them into railroad ties. Railroads use $1.5 billion worth of ties every year, and they use any wood that will hold preservatives. The logger and a helper worked on and off through the winter and early spring. They could not get to the fallen trees on the steeper slopes or on the soft land along Morgan Branch, but they took eighty or more loads from the easier sites. At the mill, sawyers sliced the round sides off the logs and sectioned them into uniform ties. The ties went to a treatment plant, got locked into steel pressure cookers as big as railroad tank cars, and preservatives replaced their sap. They came out like sections of embalmed bodies.

At this moment, travelers on an Amtrak train to Miami, New York, Chicago, or New Orleans are passing over those scattered bolts of trees that stood for fifty, one hundred, even two hundred years on the hills around Morgan Branch. In twenty or thirty years, maintenance crews will pull out the old ties from under the steel rails and throw them aside. Maybe they will be burned in a superheated, nonpolluting incinerator. Their ash will be made into block. Their carbon will return to the air. In the best of all possible worlds, the incinerator might produce electricity from my trees, and who knows if some of that electricity might power a reading light or the electronic book in which this chapter is written. That may be the end of wooden railroad ties. Already technology is replacing wooden ties with concrete and recycled plastic, the way the car and tractor replaced mules and horses and garages replaced acres of pastures.

The loggers finished their work in midspring. From the house, I looked across Morgan Branch valley into the forest whose nakedness was only beginning to show the first haze of green leaves. Corpses of trees still lay everywhere as if nothing had been cut and hauled away. When I walked in the woods, I could follow the tracks of Doug's skidder and loader and see that he had taken only the best and biggest. I counted 175 rings in the stump of a beech where Pace Mill Road was still only a blurred wagon trail. The tree had started to grow forty years after Zachariah Morgan's name became attached to this branch. Sylvan and I had picked black chanterelles in the moss around this tree year after year. This is the place she wrote about in her eighth-grade essay, the mushroom patch she had discovered. She had earned her first $100 selling the mushrooms to a French restaurant. A riot of broken branches buried the moss. The tree's falling with its roots intact had left a crater in the ground that now lay behind the stump like a soldier's foxhole.

Sometimes cutting a log free from its root disk freed the stump. Then the disk and the weight of earth pulled the roots back to the ground and set the stump upright. Where the loggers had cut the trunk five or ten feet up from the roots to avoid rot or scars, these stumps now stood in the forest as if a giant of a logger had cut them. Where the skidder had worked hard to pull logs across soft, wet earth, its big tires had dug ruts in the land eighteen inches wide and a foot deep; in these ruts, spring rain waters gathered. The skidder in its brute work also could not avoid banging its cargo against trees along its route so that most of them had been barked here and there. They would heal, but the scars would stay with them for life. After all the years of trying to leave only the lightest and kindest marks on this land, I would now leave marks visitors could find a hundred years later.

Everywhere I went, nothing I saw made me happy. When the first warm days of summer came, I looked at Morgan Branch flowing naked in the sunlight for the first time in centuries, or even millennia. Under the clear flowing water, the black stones were growing thick wigs of fine green algae. Sunlight worked its changes on the hills, too. When the storm had pushed down the biggest trees with the biggest crowns, it opened huge holes in the forest canopy. Light poured in. Seeds blew in. By July, grasses and weeds leaped out of the warm earth and grew chest high. In several openings, I saw city trees, those opportunists that migrated from Asia and now grow in New York City's sidewalk cracks, along railroad tracks, and around the edges of abandoned lots. They are innocent trees, brought to America by botanists in the 1700s, but I associate them with decay and garbage.

Royal paulownia seedlings started with dark green leaves as broad as table napkins. I have seen them grow out of the moss and sandy mortar in an old chimney; their small seeds travel easily on the winds. Ailanthus (or "tree of heaven") with its alternating spear-point leaves plays the joke of looking like walnut but growing a hundred times faster. I first saw it growing along the Long Island railroad tracks in the coal dust and trash and gravel. Ailanthus produces as many as 350,000 winged seeds a year. A single seed on moist ground develops a tap root within three months. As the tree grows, its bark and leaves produce a toxin that spreads in the soil and stunts or kills native species. This tree fell into my woods from heaven, but I welcomed it no more than the spray attack of a flying crop duster. My forest had been raped and now it was pregnant with alien beings. I felt like someone living in a dangerous city, my quarters pillaged, with taunting messages from the violator showing up unexpectedly from time to time.

I agreed with America's most famous lawyer, Clarence Darrow, who had defended the teaching of evolution in the Scopes trial of 1925. He also defended labor activists accused of bombing and murder, and the university students Leopold and Loeb, two rich intellectuals who killed a Chicago boy for thrills. Darrow was an atheist who had this to say about the natural world: "The truth is, Nature is a slaughter house. There are some pleasant sensations, some pleasures, . . . and scattered along the path is trouble and misery, and in the end, tragedy. It is all a nightmare, if you think. The animals have the advantage of us—they do not think, they simply live."

Hurricane Fran had come and gone, and the animals at Morgan Branch continued simply living. The trees continued simply to live and a few simply to die. Some were doing both. Many of the fallen trees still had a few roots left in the ground to draw water and food, and they put out new leaves. Along their horizontal trunks new shoots shot straight up toward the sun. One or two or more of these shoots might sink roots from the bottom of the trunk into the ground and survive. Years later, they would stand as a line of trees betraying their origin. Hope and courage had nothing to do with their effort to live and survive. Almost all of them were doomed, but they did not despair. They would fight with all their resources to the end, as surely as the three hundred Spartans fought thousands of Persians at the Hot Gates of Thermopylae. The trees were obeying the laws that evolution had programmed their species to obey. Hope, courage, and despair are peculiar to Spartans and others in the human species.

A forty-foot-high, eight-inch-thick white oak next to the west side of my house had arched its crown to the ground under the passing weight of a falling poplar but had not been pinned. Its strained fibers were able to raise the crown only fifteen feet, its trunk making an arc the width of my house. The forest was full of such *Arcs de Defaite*. The oak's crown was budding again in its permanent bow, growing sideways. Eventually, it would send up a vertical shoot near the beginning of the arch, and fifty years from now the present crown would be a thick side branch on a much larger trunk. The oak would be a perfectly readable cipher for an experienced forester. The mounds of the dead and the strange forms of many of the survivors would retain the story of this storm, the direction and force of the winds, the age of the fallen trees. The story would be as readable to someone who knew its alphabet as Herodotus's history of Thermopylae.

All this destruction, yet I was the only angry creature in the forest. I was the only one at Morgan Branch who cared. My neighbors to the south, Susan and Dave and their seven-year-old daughter, Lily, were also stunned. Susan told me later, "After the storm, this just wasn't the same place I came here to live in. It will never be the same in my lifetime." Dave, who has always played with popular local bands and written songs, had his say in music:

> You should a seen it move like a wreckin' ball,
> Lackin' all feature and form.

Lily, who knew every one of her father's songs, said her favorite lines were these:

> Feel a change in my regard,
> Picking up sticks in what was my yard.

Two months after the storm, when the green in the leaves was giving way to yellow and brown and red, Lily found that one of her favorite spots, on a hilltop behind their house, was covered with the trunks and limbs of trees. When the leaves were falling fast, she said, "I used to go there with my dad, and my dad and I would lie on our backs and put our hands out and catch the leaves coming down."

We share so much with all other forms of life that we can see our reflection even in the structures of single-celled animals, but the one thing we possess alone is our ability to think—to remember the past and to imagine the future. No wonder Darrow, an atheist who worked year after year with the crimes and mistakes of men and women, thought life was a nightmare. In his world, nothing in nature and no god cared for us, and we did not care enough about each other. "The poet may say that God is in heaven and all is well with the world," Darrow lamented, "but the poet is 'seeing things,' that's all; he is mistaken." Nature, including a good part of human nature, tends to build slaughterhouses rather than theater houses and houses of Congress.

As I watched the animals around me go about living as if nothing had happened, I learned something from the wildlife. One morning, as I approached the great tangle of beech and oak that lay across Morgan Branch just below Seven Spring Branch, a doe and her fawn sprang out of hiding. They had found a welcome cool shelter in the devastation.

A few days later, lower down the branch, I sat on a stump to look under fallen trees into a dark pool of water. I watched a short, pencil-thin water snake trying to swallow a minnow, a yellow-finned dace. The other minnows swam about searching for their own food. From under the bank below my stump slid a two-foot-long water snake. It rifled toward the smaller snake; the small one dropped its fish and shot off. The big snake swallowed the minnow.

Another evening in early summer, I climbed a tree next to the branch and waited for dusk. In a holly across the branch, I saw a small bird, a male yellowthroat. Then its mate. The female was carrying something in her beak. They flew from one tree to another, and finally the female dropped down into the brush and weeds on the far side of the fallen tree. Yellowthroats are ground nesters, and this pair had built their nest in the shelter of the horizontal tree stump and its disk of roots and earth. As darkness came on, I heard an owl in my neighbor's woods. This year it would have a much harder time picking off the yellowthroats.

The way animals ignored or used disaster amused me. Amusement and anger do not keep good company. I began to study and take pictures of the strange ways that trees had fallen on one another and what they had revealed when their roots tore huge disks of skin out of the forest floor. I have always had one photo album devoted to the forms of disaster and death. Philosophers in the Renaissance kept a skull, a *momento mori*, or reminder of mortality on their desks. I keep my reminders in albums.

Every animal had its life to live and accepted Morgan Branch and the forest around it the way they were, for better or worse. Slowly their attitude became mine. The storm took a lot of smaller trees as big ones fell on them. It washed eight hundred dollars worth of gravel from my drive. The trees that had fallen on my writing room meant that I had to rip off and replace half the roof, cement the chimney again, and replace several rafters. None of these things mattered much. The big trees did matter. I began to realize that almost all my shock and anger had to do with big trees. Not only were the trees down but, except to manufacture a few cross ties, nobody wanted them.

I imagined that I might take a portable sawmill out there and turn the big trees into beautiful wide boards and noble beams, but the few portable mills already had a world of business. Even if I could have obtained one, I would have needed a tractor to haul the logs in to the mill. When I had the boards, I would have needed a barn or shed in which to stack and dry them. To save anything much, I would have had to devote a year of my life to transforming wreckage into utility. I was condemned to watch them lying there for fifteen or twenty years, slowly turning to mush. The forest likes this mush, of course. Decay builds the soils. Organic matter is especially good for the clays that have lost their thin top soils to hard scrabble backwoods farming.

Environmentalism has too often encouraged us to be heroic fools. I am no different here at Morgan Branch. The forest I wanted to save was not the forest nature put here. The forest I wanted would be a forest shaped by three or four thousand years of Indian burning and two hundred years of farming and logging. The forests the first nomadic Indian hunters found here were not the forests nature nourished here 10,000 years ago when the ice age began to warm. The evergreen forests of the ice age were not the tropical forests of the Triassic era. Nature never had an environmental preference for Morgan Branch. I did. Nature took away my old-growth forest and planted exotic, toxic Asian trees. Nature would eventually restore something like my forest, but not in my lifetime. Not in Sylvan's lifetime. I could settle for what was left or I could try to find another old forest. Darrow was right about something: "Nature, after all, is strongest. It is life. Man wants life without paying the penalty for it. But, Nature has provided the way life shall come and the penalty that must be paid." Darrow, the great atheist, sounds almost Biblical—God made death, the Bible says, as the penalty for the sin of Adam and Eve. Nowhere is nature a Garden of Eden. Whenever consciousness dawned in the human brain, our ancestors found themselves in a wilderness. They set about conquering its dangers. They began to reshape it with Eden as their model. They knew, in those days before romantic illusions, that if nature was ever to be a friend to humankind, they would have to command it to be so. We did not come from Eden, but we intend to go there.

chapter 41

The Next
Morgan Branch

They say of money, "You can't take it with you."
Morgan Branch proves to be more portable.

I would have been content to accept the acts of nature and to watch the forest by Morgan Branch start a new life had I thought I would not be disturbed in my watching. The storm had been only one change among many changes. The people who moved to Saralyn in the early 1970s had begun a new era in the history of the land that is Chatham County—the first sprouts of an alien invasion of Chatham County. We were as alien and invasive as the ailanthus and pauwlonia trees that have come to Morgan Branch. We were the latest of several transforming invasions that included the coming of Indians, the arrival of European commerce, the establishment of agriculture, the replacement of horses and mules with the internal combustion engine, the collapse of agriculture as the economic engine of society, and now the embrace of Chatham's rural land for suburbs, industry, and modern homestead retreats.

The people who had grown up on farms had watched the trickle of hippies become a stream of newcomers, and now a political and social force. The Reeves, a family of dairy farmers, had donated the money for the county's first library building, but retired diplomats and executives and engineers became the most constant visitors and the movers of the annual fund-raising events. Many of them live in Fearrington Village, an eight-hundred-acre planned community of apartments, townhouses, condominiums, single family homes, and a luxury inn built on the dairy farm passed down in the Fearrington family for almost two centuries. Fearrington Village is too expensive for most people born in the county. The farm's Holsteins have been replaced in five acres of open space by designer cattle, or "belties," with their broad white middles framed by black heads and haunches. The hay barn hosts literary readings, wine tastings, and fund-raisers for hospice or family violence programs.

Mamie Oldham, who rode in a wagon up the Pace Mill Road to buy pears and whose father killed hogs with Carney Bynum, lives in the new nursing care facility next to Pittsboro's new post office. One son who raised chickens began selling the manure to gardeners, then composting it. His son has planted a nursery of trees and shrubs where the chicken houses were and started Poultry Villa, a landscaping service for the new suburbs. Another of Mamie's grandsons has recreated Dr. Pilkington's nineteenth-century pharmacy on the main street and has a thriving business selling old-fashioned malts, shakes, and sandwiches.

McCrimmon's Drugstore, where Baxter Riggsbee used to call me the Mayor of Hippie Town and invite me to have coffee with farmers, car salesmen, and lawyers, has closed and become an antique shop. The county's hot issues are now debated on an Internet mail list. Last fall, several members thought it was time we had a good art movie theater in town. A few months ago the following posting appeared: "Have you thought about a bagel shop in Pittsboro? We need something like this. A Brueggers with a Starbucks coffee and a wine shop all in one—would this not be fabulous? Chatters could come by and have coffee and continue discussions face-to-face." Another writer told everyone how much she loved the diner-health-food store. It's called The Pittsboro General Store, but is narrowly specialized on organic foods: "What a great place already. I love earthy stores and this definitely is one. A perfect location for wine tastings and accompaniments."

The Pittsboro General Store is a good store, but I never thought of it as being "earthy." Chatham used to be very earthy without wine tastings and bagel shops. I eat lunch at the General Store when I'm in Pittsboro. It has replaced McCrimmon's as the conversation corner, or rather one of two. People who have had offices and businesses in Pittsboro for a long time and most of the people who fix anything—a car, toilet, refrigerator, telephone, or power pole—eat in The Scoreboard, where they can have hamburgers, barbecue, slaw, and hushpuppies. Conversation has bifurcated like the county. In the General Store, the discussions are more varied. The nonsense is more whimsical. Half of the clients are women. The cook lives at Saralyn where he named his driveway Ho Chi Minh Trail in honor of the Vietnamese communist leader who sacrificed hundreds of thousands of his subjects in order to avoid the capitalism that makes the General Store possible.

The General Store is a "green" eatery, but it is not an earthy place or a general storage of anything—another example of inventing what doesn't exist. McCrimmon's Drugstore didn't call itself "Ye Olde Apothecary." Today we have subdivisions named Log Barn Acres that have no log barn, and Wolf's Pond that has no wolves. Names actually described the county when maps and deeds first recorded Bear Creek, Panther Branch, Tick Creek, and Stinking Creek. Our age indulges in this peculiar habit of dressing our places and businesses in names the way kids dress for Halloween.

As the Internet postings about restaurants, wine tastings, parks, and protecting the environment grew thicker, I posted a reply. I noted that the people wishing for these things were also often speaking against new roads, subdivisions, and industries. I asked if they were aware that the cafes, movies, parks, recreation programs, theaters, and fine restaurants would encourage more people to move to Chatham County and more visitors to pour in. No one replied. They went on wishing for and working for a county that would be like other well-developed enclaves of upper-middle-class America.

The growth of the county and the traffic that passes through on its way to service the population of the Research Triangle area that has now topped 1 million has caused the state to build a four-lane by-pass north of Pittsboro. The major north-south highway that was a dirt road when Mamie Oldham rode to school on the fender of the mill owner's one-seat car is being widened into a four-lane boulevard to Chapel Hill.

The mill village on the Haw River at Bynum, once forty-six two- and three-room cottages without indoor plumbing, was bought out by a county with a federal block grant and renovated. Some of the old mill hands stayed on. About half sold their newly renovated and underpinned houses to young faculty members and white-collar workers and artists. Harris and Farrell's General Store, where Sylvan and I bought ice-cream cones and were handed the mail out of a brass box, sells crafts, and the old men seldom sit on the bench outside under the awning. Clyde Jones, one of the natives who used to work at the mill for minimum wage, has become a famous folk artist. He uses his chain saw, odd pieces of wood, bright paint, and scavenged trash to create fanciful sculpture that has found its way into a few museums. A couple of years ago, a long white limousine pulled up by his cottage: Mikhail Baryshnikov had come to buy a piece for his collection. The county itself is becoming something of a museum or a zoo.

Just as the farmers once sold to the timber companies or people rich enough to buy and let the trees grow, the timber owners are now selling to developers. On my western border Dr. Zhang sold his timber to a logger who came in and cut every tree, hauling the big logs out for lumber and feeding the smaller trees into a giant chipper, then burning the stumps, weeds, and surviving brush and saplings. On the west my neighbors have marked almost every oak, beech, and hickory over twelve inches for cutting, respectfully leaving a 100-foot buffer along Seven Spring Branch and Morgan Branch. Neither they nor I will be alive to see the next crop of old trees, if the land stays idle long enough for the forest to mature again.

When I first started Saralyn, Realtors told me that no one would want to live so far away from Chapel Hill. Now people from Chapel Hill as well as Raleigh are moving to subdivisions on clear-cut land five and ten miles farther out than Saralyn.

At Saralyn, Kathleen and Nicholas finished and sold the house they built on speculation, priced at a quarter of a million dollars. The price is normal for houses near thriving cities, and that price sounds the red alert warning of imminent change. This is the first house at Saralyn built with no one in particular in mind. Over the past twenty-five years, all the Saralyn houses had been built by people who intended to live in them, or the owners had watched over the building. The new house could as easily be in the wooded neighborhoods of Chapel Hill as in the forest of Chatham County. When I come or go on the Pace Mill road at night, the lights of this house blaze through the forest like the windows of a big ship anchored in a small cove. Saralyn in 2000 is less a collection of small Waldens than a suburb with exceptionally large lots.

Twenty of the original thirty-four families who lived at Saralyn left, most of them for towns and cities, back to their cultural home ground. A year after the storm, Susan began talking to Dave and Lily about leaving. She realized she didn't know most of her neighbors any more. She didn't meet people when she walked down the road with Lily. Maybe it was her fault, she thought. She had gone down the road to introduce herself to a young couple who had been renting a nearby house for several months. "Maybe you've seen me out on the road, or maybe you have walked by our house," Susan told the young woman. She explained it was only a quarter mile north. "Oh, no," the woman said, "I hardly ever go out of the house. I'm deathly afraid of snakes."

Morgan Branch is surrounded but not under siege. Lily has a flock of chickens, and she takes her eggs to a few Saralyn people who buy them. She can even follow the traces of old roads through the woods, as Sylvan did at her age. I can live out here and never cut another tree or sell a foot of land. I can still take off my clothes and lie down in the cold waters of Morgan Branch. Still not a single window on my house has a shade or curtain because no one is close enough to look in. I am as secure as any American in my property rights, but I cannot keep out all of the trespassers civilization brings. Very quickly now civilization adds its intrusions between me and what is wild here.

Two years ago, in the early fall, I took a friend to the side of Morgan Branch at dusk to see what might happen as darkness came on. We went up two separate trees on opposite sides of the branch and waited. A human at night has to observe with ears instead of eyes. We each had a good flashlight ready to see whatever might come with an interesting noise. As we sat in the gathering darkness, I heard steps in the woods and stirrings in the water beneath me. And every few minutes all but the boldest sounds were drowned out by the high steady drone of a plane flying in or out of Raleigh-Durham International Airport forty miles east.

When the humidity goes up and the forest is bare, I can hear machinery working on the Pittsboro by-pass several miles south—the revving of diesel engines, the warning beepers on the earthmovers and trucks and dozers as they back up. I understand the warning, but I cannot move Morgan Branch.

A couple of days before Christmas 1998, the darkest day of the year whose daylight hours were darkened by a slate-gray sky, I came out of my shop where I was turning a dogwood mallet on the lathe. I stopped to look at the sky. I have noticed before that the sky to the east holds a glow long after night has extinguished the western glow of the setting sun. Raleigh is forty-five miles east, but Cary, its suburb-city, has been gobbling land in this direction. Its water and sewer lines tunnel through old tobacco lands in this direction. Houses and apartments follow, and shopping centers. The lights of Cary's streets and commerce shine into the sky. In my lifetime, I will never see this part of the night sky again from Morgan Branch.

The trees and the animals here don't care about these things. They go on with their wild lives. The slate-gray juncos that come every year from Canada welcome the invasive grasses that winter turns to mazes of stiff brown full of seeds. When I walk through the grasses, the juncos fly out like gray explosions. As the suburbs take over land, the birds will have more and more places to hide. Both the juncos and the red finches, who also come for the winter, will have more feeders to visit. The ruby-throated hummingbirds will undoubtedly find more flowers and sugar-water feeders in a suburb than in this old forest. The woods mice will enjoy safer havens despite traps and bait. The deer have already found the suburbs a great boon because they provide more winter browsing than the forest.

In the summer of 1998, I walked north up Morgan Branch to where it flowed out of my land into the clear-cut, and I saw the beginning of development. The young trees along the branch were being cut down along with trees on my property. A beaver had cut them for a dam across the branch. It had cut the last of Merritt's walnuts, a thirty-foot-high gum tree, and two equal-sized poplars. The water flooding onto the land beside the creek had killed two fifty-foot poplars and turned the land into marsh covered with tough grasses. Last year, the beaver began on my land, cutting young beech and dogwood. That summer when Sylvan came to watch the house and work on her data about invasive trees in the Everglades, she sent me an E-mail in Kazakhstan. Just below the house, a beaver had cut a redbud tree by the branch. In December, the beaver was cutting beech and dogwood again. I decided that if it touched the walnut tree I had planted by Morgan Branch, it would be a dead beaver. After the storm, I was in no mood to favor beavers over trees. Either beavers would manage this place or I would, and I decided that I had more right.

If I or the next owner protects this forest and gives it a nudge here and there, a little pruning, a little thinning, it will recover nicely from Hurricane Fran, and everything that lives in it will adapt. The forest can recover from many storms. That effort is nothing compared to the long recovery from cotton and crop farming. At best during the next twenty or thirty years, my land and Saralyn will remain highly sought after for estatelets, an island of large lots in a suburban sea. As the demand increases, the bidding will go up. The winners will tear down old houses and enlarge the present ones. They will cut more trees. They will pasture horses. They will spread out weedless green lawns that look like Astroturf. More artists will come and build studios, and their clients will increase the traffic on the community roads. In time, they will find the old covenants too restrictive and decide to get rid of them so they can divide their lands. They will not be able to resist the temptation to profit from the great demand for lots of two or three acres and offers of $75,000 or $100,000 per lot.

This does not have to happen. It is choice. Few people have been comfortable staying at my house in the forest by Morgan Branch, and some have run away. Few people want to live in a real forest, even with the company of a spouse or family. People like to have neighbors, a community. They might talk about rights for animals and plants, but they insist upon segregation and control. No snakes, no roaches, thank you. Trees are okay, but unless thinned and cleared of understory and brush, they make our world too dark and they block the view. Even wildflowers we like to arrange in gardens. Even the cultured Japanese, whom my environmentalist friends praise highly for their respect of nature, harbor a deep disdain for the unpredictability and disobedience of nature. Nowhere does human dominion show more than in a Japanese garden. Such a garden is the ideal toward which most humans, environmentalists included, gravitate—a beautiful dominion.

They will change Morgan Branch forever. But then it has always been changing forever. It's possible that what I have learned here and written as best I can in this report is the only part of Morgan Branch and this forest that might survive in the way I found them. To ensure that survival, my publisher caused someone to cut a few trees and then stained their pulp with my thoughts.

Whatever happens, none of the changes matter in the least to nature. We cry and shout and lobby about the changes that happen at Morgan Branch and all the large and small Waldens of the world, but it is not for nature that we do all this breast-beating and make all this noise. We can do it only for ourselves or for God. Who else could care? For a while I thought about leaving my land on Morgan Branch to the county for a park, but here I have again learned from Thoreau's mistake.

Thoreau was convinced that wildness would save civilization, or at least his neighbors. So three years before his death, he wrote in his journal for 1859 his hope that if Walden Pond and its woods were turned into a park, it might help civilize his neighbors of whom he had spoken so cynically: "I think that each town should have a park . . . a common possession forever, for instruction and recreation. All Walden wood might have been preserved for our park forever, with Walden [Pond] in its midst."

By 1866, an excursion park had been built on one shore of the pond and soon it was joined by concessions, swings, bathhouses, boats, an athletic track, dance halls, and restaurants. Since the 1930s, half a million visitors a year have been tramping around the lake, most of them coming for a swim or a picnic. The state of Massachusetts has declared Walden a "reserve" and is trying to reestablish the site's solitude by allowing no more than 1,000 visitors a day. Seventeen visitors for every acre of pond seems to be the Massachusetts definition of solitude.

As I was thinking about Walden, my discussion with Thoreau, and the fate of places like Walden and Morgan Branch, I reread an article by novelist Suzanne Berne that a friend had sent me from *The New York Times*. What caught my attention was not her description of the condition of the state park but a question in her closing. Her husband had grudgingly agreed to go to Walden with her and their two infants, but when they arrived, he decided to stay in the car with the kids. She wondered, "Would Walden have been written if Thoreau had been a family man? For an answer, a single robin sang out from a pine branch overhead."

I didn't need to listen to a robin for my own answer.

The same week I pulled the article from my files, I had an E-mail from Sylvan asking whether I would come to Rutgers for her thesis defense. I arrived a day early, a cold, wet New Jersey afternoon. Sylvan took me from the train to the hotel where Sarah and her husband, Bob, and their son, Joe, had just checked in. The five of us sat in a foaming hot jacuzzi. We talked about people we knew and about where Sylvan might find a job. Her fourteen-year old brother had a lot of questions about Baja California, where Sylvan would take him sea kayaking in April. The next morning, Sylvan gave a public slide show and presentation of her thesis. With a clear and fluent narrative, and slides appearing in perfect unison, she explained how she had set up her investigation in Florida and Australia, how she had analyzed the reams of data, and how and why Australian malaleuca trees had become a danger to the native species of the Florida Everglades and to its water table.

Sarah, Bob, Joe, and I waited in Sylvan's office for an hour and a half while she went through the formal part of her defense with her thesis committee. By noon, she had become Dr. Sylvan Ramsey Kaufman, Ph.D. Ecology. I thought about the irony of her name and her winning her degree with a thesis on forests. It was like an ichthyologist named Fish or an ornithologist named Finch or an economist named Cash. When she was born, Sarah and I had no name for a boy and only one for a girl, Sylvan.

When I flew home the next day, I had the satisfied feeling that something in my life was finally complete. I had left a few marks on Morgan Branch, some good, some not so good. Morgan Branch had laid a good hand on Sylvan.

For her birthday and graduation present, I had made a book for her called *Notes for the Biography of a Citizen and Scientist.* From my old journals, albums, letters, and her drawings and school papers, I had created on the computer an illustrated story of her first ten years, the years few of us remember very well in our own lives. When I was gathering that material from files and boxes, I found a handmade birthday card she had sent me. It had no date but I guessed she had written it when she was ten or twelve. The card was a sheet of purple craft paper folded in half. The only word on the cover was "Papa," written among several objects pasted on— a looped band of lace, a disk filled with fine ovals of colored lines, a tuft of brown and white feathers, and three small pictures cut from a magazine, mice dancing, a stalk of wild flowers, and two red mushrooms. Inside, she wrote in black ink these lines in Spanish:

> To the person who likes to dance and sing, walk and listen.
> You like to discover interesting and beautiful things.
> You like to listen to animals and birds and things full of happiness.
> Things intricate with fine and brilliant colors, these you like.
> Feathers of quail to hear
> Mushrooms and flowers to discover when walking
> Mice dancing and singing
> An intricate design of many brilliant colors
> And
> Lace beautiful and fine.

I could hear echoes of familiar phrases from our favorite Spanish songs. "Many colors" echoed the words "muchos colores" in the song whose verses end with "And so those great loves of many colors, that's what I like." We had sung those songs hundreds of times. Even when Sylvan was in college and graduate school, occasionally we had sung those songs or played them on the flute or the recorder.

We will do it again sometime—sit down and sing "De Colores," sing about "the colors that are seen in the spring, the colors of the small birds that come from afar." And when we sing the song that begins "*Gracias A La Vida, que me ha dado tanto*" (*Thanks to Life, that has given me so much*), we may be in Montana or Florida or Siberia, and the forest I sit in at this moment may have disappeared, but we will be at Morgan Branch.